extraordinary meals from ordinary ingredients

919 Fabulously Fast and Frugal Recipes

EACH WITH A SECRET INGREDIENT!

David Joachim

Recipe Editor

Reader's Digest

The Reader's Digest Association, Inc.
Pleasantville, New York • Montreal

Project Staff

BOOK EDITOR ❊ Neil Wertheimer

RECIPE EDITOR ❊ David Joachim

RECIPE CONTRIBUTOR ❊ David Bonom

DESIGNERS ❊ Elizabeth Tunnicliffe

COVER DESIGNER ❊ George McKeon

COVER PHOTOGRAPH ❊ Elizabeth Watt

ILLUSTRATOR ❊ Chuck Rekow

COPY EDITOR/PROOFREADER ❊
Lisa D. Andruscavage

INDEXER ❊ Cohen Carruth Indexes

Reader's Digest Home & Health Books

PRESIDENT, HOME & GARDEN AND
HEALTH & WELLNESS ❊ Alyce Alston

EDITOR IN CHIEF ❊ Neil Wertheimer

CREATIVE DIRECTOR ❊ Michele Laseau

EXECUTIVE MANAGING EDITOR ❊
Donna Ruvituso

ASSOCIATE DIRECTOR NORTH AMERICA
PREPRESS ❊ Douglas A. Croll

MANUFACTURING MANAGER ❊
John L. Cassidy

MARKETING DIRECTOR ❊ Dawn Nelson

The Reader's Digest Association, Inc.

PRESIDENT AND CHIEF EXECUTIVE
OFFICER ❊ Mary Berner

PRESIDENT, CONSUMER MARKETING ❊
Dawn Zier

Library of Congress Cataloging-in-Publication Data
Joachim, David.

Extraordinary meals from ordinary ingredients : more than 900
fabulously fast and frugal recipes, each with a secret ingredient! /
David Joachim, recipe editor.

      p. cm.
Includes index.
ISBN 978-0-7621-0763-6 (hardcover)
ISBN 978-0-7621-0934-0 (paperback)

1. Cookery   I. Title.
TX714.J56 2007
641.5--dc22

                              2007024390

Address any comments about *Extraordinary Meals from
Ordinary Ingredients* to:

The Reader's Digest Association, Inc.
Editor in Chief, Books
Reader's Digest Road
Pleasantville, NY 10570-7000

For more Reader's Digest products and information,
visit our website at www.rd.com (in the United States)

Printed in the United States of America

1 3 5 7 9 10 8 6 4 2 (hardcover)

1 3 5 7 9 10 8 6 4 2 (paperback)

contents

Extraordinary uses for Everyday Pantry Items

FOOD THEY WILL ALWAYS
{ Remember }

Just about everyone has a memory of a dish they've tried that tastes better than all the rest. Perhaps your Grandma's pumpkin pie has a unique flavor that makes it soar above every other pumpkin pie you've ever had. Or maybe Aunt Rosa's long-simmered tomato sauce has a savory spark that no other tomato sauce can match. Perhaps your Uncle Bob's beef stew has a rich consistency that outclasses all other stews in a single spoonful.

What's the secret to these dishes?

The answer, in most cases, is simple: a small amount of some secret ingredient, something easy to overlook, something only a seasoned cook would know to add. That special something in Grandma's pumpkin pie? It's probably not in the filling. Look in the crust. Finely ground nuts like pecans or walnuts mixed right into the pie dough create a crunchy, nutty-tasting crust that perfectly complements the sweet and creamy pumpkin filling.

How about that special flavor in Aunt Rosa's fabulous tomato sauce? A single mashed anchovy fillet is likely what gives the sauce all the savory spunk it needs.

And what's the velvety texture in Uncle Bob's beef stew? Most likely, it comes from plain old unflavored gelatin. Sprinkling a little gelatin into a soup, stew, or sauce creates a rich, mouth-filling consistency that's hard to duplicate any other way. It's an old chef's secret for giving thin sauces a little extra oomph.

You can spend a lifetime in the kitchen trying to identify those secret ingredients that transform good cooking into the best cooking. Or you can dive into the pages of *Extraordinary Meals from Ordinary Ingredients*, where we reveal the success secrets behind hundreds of fabulous recipes. We searched far and wide, tested exhaustively in our kitchens, and tapped into countless years of cooking experience to pinpoint those special add-ins that make any given recipe outshine all the others. In the end, we found 919 ways to use common kitchen

ingredients to transform everyday dishes. And they are all right here.

Pantry Staples Gone Crazy!

Most cooking secrets have been born out of sheer ingenuity. They are crafty solutions to everyday cooking problems discovered by everyday cooks. For instance, let's say the holidays have rolled around and you discover that you've run out of milk just as you are about to make your special Christmas Day waffles. And, of course, all the stores are closed on Christmas Day! What will you do? Why, use that jug of eggnog you stocked up on. Milk is the primary ingredient in eggnog, after all. Plus, the thickness of eggnog makes rich-textured waffles, and the spices in eggnog will gently flavor the waffles, making them taste even better. Voilà! Eggnog waffles—a new standard holiday breakfast dish.

The secrets to incredible-tasting recipes are often that simple. And the majority of secret ingredients can be found right in your own pantry. Take tea bags, for instance. Here are little packets of flavor sitting right in the cupboards of the average home. Yet tea bags rarely see anything beyond a teacup. Why not use bags of mint tea to infuse fresh aroma into rice? Add some to the boiling water and you have instant mint-flavored rice—with no flecks of mint! Everyone will marvel at the flavor and wonder where it came from. Add a little lemon juice to it and you've created a refreshing lemon-mint rice that makes a fabulous accompaniment to lamb chops or a chicken dish.

Do you keep Earl Grey tea at home? The defining flavor of Earl Grey comes from bergamot, a sour orange with an incredibly aromatic peel. Anytime you want to infuse a little orange flavor into a dish, simply drop an Earl Grey tea bag into the cooking liquid and presto!—instant orange flavor. Tea bags can easily flavor a sauce or stew for chicken, the poaching liquid for salmon or other fish, or even mulled wine and hot cider.

Here are the surprising secrets behind some other remarkable meals:

❋ How do you make scrambled eggs so soft, so silky that you'll want to savor them with a spoon? The key is blending a little cream cheese into the beaten eggs.

❋ How do you get an extra-crunchy topping on apple crisp? Use Grape-Nuts cereal instead of oats. When baked with butter, brown sugar, and cinnamon, Grape-Nuts deliver a delicious crunch and satisfying chew.

❋ What's the secret behind a pillowy-soft texture in homemade focaccia bread? Add mashed potatoes to the dough. The starch in the potatoes lends a smooth consistency to the interior crumb of the bread that yeast alone cannot produce. Try it today in Rosemary Focaccia (page 34).

❋ How do you create a delightfully sweet, ultra-crunchy breading on fried chicken? Use cornflakes instead of plain bread-crumbs.

❋ What's the secret behind a rich-tasting, well-balanced pork stew? Look no further than a can of cola. See the fabulous results in Asian-Style Pork Stew on page 84.

❋ How do you give vegetarian chili a little more pizzazz? Stir in some semi-sweet chocolate until it melts and blends with the other ingredients. Chocolate has an edge and sweetness that balances out the spiciness of the chili, as you will discover with Vegetarian Chili on page 80. It also adds a touch of fat for richness.

❋ What can you do with leftover cooked spaghetti other than reheat it for lunch? Turn it into a Sicilian Omelet (page 18) by mixing the cooked spaghetti right into the egg mixture. The spaghetti fills out the meal with a little starch and makes it more substantial and satisfying. It may sound odd to add pasta to eggs, but Italians have been doing it for centuries.

❋ What's the secret to a light, cracklingly crisp batter on fried fish? Stout beer. The carbonation of beer aerates the batter and the dark, malty flavor enhances the mild taste of the fish.

Beer. Cola. Cornflakes. Cream cheese. These are not exotic, hard-to-find ingredients. But they can be used in surprisingly creative ways to make your meals seem more exotic and far more delicious!

Cooking Made Easy

Some pantry staples can help you save time in the kitchen. These are often mixes or sauces that spare you hours of chopping, mixing, and cooking. For instance, spaghetti sauce isn't just for spaghetti—it can become an instant sauce for baked fish. Bake fish fillets right in the sauce to keep them from drying out and to infuse them with flavor. Spaghetti sauce can also give you a jump-start as a base for making a soup or creating a braising liquid for meat.

Canned pumpkin is another time-saver that most people have on hand, especially at Thanksgiving. But why limit the pumpkin to pies? You can use canned pumpkin to get a head start on making pumpkin soup, saving you the effort of peeling, cooking, and pureeing fresh pumpkin. Plus, canned pumpkin is made with a super-creamy breed of pumpkin that's unavailable to consumers, so you'll actually get better results than if you made it yourself. And why not open a can of pumpkin to whip up sumptuous Pumpkin Spice Waffles (page 13)? Kids will love it at Halloween! Or make pumpkin the key flavor in a fancy dish like Pumpkin-Nut Ravioli with Sage-Brown Butter (page 208). This recipe uses store-bought wonton wrappers for the pasta to reduce hassle. Your guests will think you slaved for hours making fresh pasta, when in reality, the recipe takes only 20 minutes of prep time.

Other common kitchen ingredients make it easy to update old favorites to today's lighter, healthier standards. Have some applesauce on hand? Use it to replace one-fourth of the butter in your favorite cakes and tea breads. The pectin in applesauce adds moisture and tenderness, creating low-calorie baked goods with delicious texture. The same can be said for mashed banana. And canned evaporated milk. Just like cream, evaporated milk creates thick, rich texture in baked goods, quiches, and creamy soups—but without all the fat and calories.

And that's just the start. Salsa, coffee, peanut butter, jam, potato chips, even pickles can be used in clever ways to make your meals sing with taste and delight.

Extraordinary Meals from Ordinary Ingredients is packed with recipes, tips, and innovations for every caliber of cook—from kitchen newcomers to seasoned professionals.

Much of the book is taken up by our favorite secret-ingredient recipes for everything from appetizers to desserts. We know that most people just need to get dinner on the table, so we've devoted entire chapters to main dishes for poultry; beef, pork, and lamb; seafood; and pasta. Some recipes are for quick-and-easy weeknight cooking, while others are perfect for special occasions and holidays.

The recipes also include fun notes like "That's Ingenious!" offering remarkable hints and tips for prepping or cooking the dish faster, easier, or better. "Personalize It!" notes allow you to substitute your favorite ingredients with confidence. And "One More Notch!" offers ideas for adding even more flavor or visual appeal to the dish.

Extraordinary Meals from Ordinary Ingredients is not just another ordinary cookbook. It will help you discover your own "secret" ingredients, too. That's why we've included a truly unique A-to-Z section packed with more than 550 recipes and tips for using your favorite kitchen staples in wonderful new ways. The best part is that you don't have to run out to the store for special ingredients. Your arsenal of secret weapons—your keys to outstanding snacks, beverages, breakfasts, lunches, dinners, or sweet desserts—are already sitting right there on your shelves.

Dive into these recipes today! And we're certain that in no time, many of your dishes will be the ones that your family and friends will long remember as the very best they have ever had.

—*David Joachim*

{ extraordinary recipes }

What makes a recipe go from "OK" to "Wow!"? Often, just one secret ingredient! Here are more than 340 recipes—each fresh, easy, and delicious, and each featuring a clever extra ingredient to take the flavor to the best possible level. From breakfasts to snacks, light weekday meals to rich holiday entrées, you are sure to find an enormous number of recipes you'll be eager to try.

extraordinary breakfasts

HEARTY MORNING PANCAKES

SECRET INGREDIENT:
sausage

Most people limit their add-ins for flapjacks to blueberries. These amazing pancakes contain apple and sausage. They're perfect for cool fall mornings.

Prep Time: 10 min   **Cook Time:** 15 min   **Serves** 2

1/2 pound bulk pork sausage

1 egg

2/3 cup milk

2 tablespoons vegetable oil

1 cup pancake mix

1/2 teaspoon ground cinnamon

1/2 cup peeled, shredded apple

1. In a medium nonstick skillet, cook the sausage over medium heat until no longer pink, breaking up the meat with a wooden spoon. Drain and set aside.

2. Preheat the oven to 200°F.

3. In a medium bowl, beat the egg, milk, and oil. Stir in pancake mix and cinnamon until just moistened. Fold in the apple and sausage.

4. Pour batter by 1/4 cupfuls onto a lightly greased hot griddle and cook until the top of each pancake has tiny bubbles, about 3 minutes. Turn the pancakes and cook until the bottoms are golden brown, 1 1/2 minutes longer. Transfer to a plate and keep warm in the oven. Repeat with the remaining batter.

One More Notch! To take the flavor of these pancakes over the top, use pumpkin pie spice in place of the cinnamon. This commercial spice mix usually includes the flavors of cinnamon, ginger, nutmeg, and allspice.

LIGHT AND FLUFFY LEMON PANCAKES

SECRET INGREDIENT:
ricotta cheese

Pancakes are typically a combination of flour, eggs, and milk. This one has ricotta cheese and whipped egg whites to give the pancakes an airy, light texture. Lemon juice and lemon peel lend refreshingly bright flavor.
See photograph on page 162.

Prep Time: 20 min   **Cook Time:** 15 min   **Serves** 4

4 large eggs, separated

4 tablespoons sugar, divided

1 cup part-skim ricotta cheese

3 tablespoons unsalted butter, melted

1 tablespoon fresh lemon juice

2 teaspoons grated lemon peel

1/2 cup all-purpose flour

2 to 3 teaspoons canola oil

1 cup vanilla low-fat yogurt

1. Beat the egg whites in a medium bowl with an electric mixer on high speed until soft peaks begin to form. Beat in 2 tablespoons of the sugar until the egg whites hold stiff peaks, being sure not to overbeat them.

2. In a large bowl, whisk together the egg yolks, the remaining 2 tablespoons sugar, ricotta cheese, butter, lemon juice, and lemon peel. Gently fold in the flour until just combined. Fold the beaten egg whites into the ricotta mixture in three additions until just incorporated.

3. Preheat the oven to 200°F.

4. Lightly oil a large nonstick skillet or griddle with 1 teaspoon of the oil and heat over medium heat. When the skillet is hot, add the batter in 1/4 cupfuls and cook until lightly browned and puffed, 2 1/2 to 3 minutes. Turn the pancakes and cook until the bottoms are golden brown, 1 to 2 minutes longer. Transfer to a plate and keep warm in the oven. Repeat with remaining batter and oil.

5. Serve the pancakes topped with 1/4 cup of yogurt; bananas and pecans are optional.

Personalize It!

If you want to vary this recipe, you can leave out the lemon and substitute in equal amounts of orange juice and orange peel. For a more tropical flavor, try lime but cut the juice back to 2 teaspoons.

OLD-TIME PANCAKES

SECRET INGREDIENT:
malt powder

Lazy Sunday mornings were made for home-made pancakes. But what's the secret to that sweet aroma of pancake house pancakes? It's malt powder. Look for some in your grocery store near the dry milk or cocoa mix. A few tablespoons added to your favorite recipe gives the pancakes an old-time country farmhouse flavor that you can't find in packaged mixes.

Prep Time: 10 min   **Cook Time:** 15 min   **Serves** 4

1 1/2 cups all-purpose flour

3 tablespoons malt powder

2 teaspoons baking powder

1 1/2 cups buttermilk

1 teaspoon vanilla extract

2 eggs, separated

2 tablespoons sugar

2 tablespoons unsalted butter, divided

1/2 cup maple syrup

1. Combine the flour, malt powder, and baking powder in a large bowl.

2. Combine the buttermilk, vanilla, and egg yolks in a medium bowl and mix well.

3. Preheat the oven to 200°F.

4. In a small bowl, with a wire whisk, beat the egg whites until soft peaks begin to form. Continue whisking while adding the sugar in a slow, steady stream, beating until the whites hold stiff peaks.

5. Stir the buttermilk mixture into the flour mixture until combined. Stir one-quarter of the egg whites into the flour mixture until combined. Gently fold in the remaining whites.

6. Melt 1 teaspoon of the butter in a large nonstick griddle over medium heat. Add four scant 1/4 cupfuls of batter and cook until the top of each pancake has tiny bubbles, about 3 minutes. Turn the pancakes and cook until the bottoms are golden brown, 1 1/2 minutes longer. Transfer to a plate and keep warm in the oven. Repeat with 3 more teaspoons of the butter and remaining batter.

7. Serve the pancakes topped with the remaining butter and the maple syrup.

Personalize It!

If you like fruit in your pancakes, try stirring in 3/4 cup fresh or frozen raspberries to the batter. Or, top your pancakes with fresh fruit preserves rather than maple syrup.

BREAKFASTS

COUNTRY CRUNCH PANCAKES

SECRET INGREDIENT:

oats

Too many pancakes taste weak and flabby. A little whole-wheat flour makes a heartier-tasting pancake. But the real surprise here is a crunchy-crisp topping made with oats, almonds, brown sugar, and cinnamon.

Prep Time: 10 min **Cook Time:** 20 min **Serves** 4

PANCAKES

2 cups all-purpose flour

1/3 cup whole-wheat flour

1/3 cup quick-cooking oats

2 tablespoons sugar

2 teaspoons baking powder

1 teaspoon baking soda

1 teaspoon salt

1 teaspoon ground cinnamon

2 1/4 cups buttermilk

2 eggs, lightly beaten

2 tablespoons vegetable oil

1 cup fresh or frozen blueberries (optional)

TOPPING

1/2 cup quick-cooking oats

1/4 cup chopped slivered almonds

1/4 cup firmly packed brown sugar

1 teaspoon ground cinnamon

1. For pancakes, in a large bowl, combine the all-purpose flour, whole-wheat flour, oats, sugar, baking powder, baking soda, salt, and cinnamon.

2. Combine the buttermilk, eggs, and oil in a medium bowl and stir into the dry ingredients until just blended. Fold in the blueberries, if using.

3. Preheat the oven to 200°F.

4. For topping, combine the oats, almonds, brown sugar, and cinnamon in a small bowl. Sprinkle about 1 teaspoon for each pancake onto a lightly greased hot griddle. Pour batter by 1/4 cupfuls over the topping. Immediately sprinkle with another teaspoonful of topping and cook until the top of each pancake has tiny bubbles, about 3 minutes. Turn the pancakes and cook until the bottoms are golden brown, 1 1/2 minutes longer. Transfer to a plate and keep warm in the oven. Repeat with the remaining batter.

that's **ingenious**

> If you don't have buttermilk, make a quick substitute. Mix together 2 cups whole milk and 1/4 cup lemon juice. Let sit for 5 minutes until the milk is thickened.

PUMPKIN SPICE WAFFLES

SECRET INGREDIENT:

canned pumpkin pie filling

Waffles are always a treat for breakfast, and even more so in the fall when it's pumpkin season. The trick to these special waffles is canned pumpkin pie filling, which comes perfectly pre-spiced and pre-sweetened. *See photograph on page 163.*

Prep Time: 10 min **Cook Time:** 15 min **Serves** 4

2 1/2 cups all-purpose flour

2 teaspoons baking powder

1 teaspoon baking soda

3 large eggs

1 1/2 cups buttermilk

1 cup canned pumpkin pie filling

6 tablespoons unsalted butter, melted

1/3 cup firmly packed brown sugar

1/2 cup maple syrup

1. Preheat the oven to 200°F.

2. In a large bowl, whisk together the flour, baking powder, and baking soda.

3. In a medium bowl, whisk together the eggs, buttermilk, pumpkin pie filling, butter, and brown sugar. Stir the egg mixture into the flour mixture until well-combined.

4. Heat a waffle iron, according to manufacturer's directions. For a double waffle maker, spoon in 2/3 cup of the batter and spread quickly. Close the top and cook until the waffles are well-puffed and golden, 3 to 4 minutes, or according to manufacturer's directions.

5. Keep the waffles warm on a baking sheet in the oven. Repeat making waffles with remaining batter. Serve with maple syrup.

One More Notch! Combine the maple syrup and 1/4 cup coarsely chopped pecans in a small saucepan. Heat over low heat until warm and serve over the waffles.

STUFFED ENGLISH MUFFIN FRENCH TOAST

SECRET INGREDIENT:

raspberry jam

English muffins are mostly used for toasting or for egg sandwiches. But their great texture and flavor make them a natural for stuffed French toast. Raspberry jam swirled into cream cheese is used here both as a filling and a sauce, making this recipe a snap.

Prep Time: 15 min   **Cook Time:** 10 min   **Serves** 4

2 ounces cream cheese, softened

5 tablespoons red seedless raspberry jam, divided

4 English muffins

2 large eggs

3 tablespoons half-and-half

1/2 teaspoon vanilla extract

1 tablespoon unsalted butter

1. In a small bowl, whisk together the cream cheese and 1 tablespoon of the jam until well-combined. With the tip of a sharp knife, make a 1 1/2-inch horizontal slit in the side of each muffin to form a pocket. Fill each muffin with 1 slightly rounded tablespoon of the cream cheese mixture.

2. In a small bowl, whisk together the eggs, half-and-half, and vanilla. Prick the top and bottom of each muffin several times with a fork. Soak each muffin, one at a time, in the egg mixture for 1 minute, turning occasionally.

3. Heat the butter in a large nonstick skillet over medium heat. When melted and hot, add the muffins and cook until golden and the cheese filling is softened and hot, about 4 minutes per side.

4. Meanwhile, place the remaining 4 tablespoons of raspberry jam in a small microwavable bowl and microwave on high until melted and hot, 45 to 55 seconds.

5. To serve, place a French toast on each of four plates and spoon 1 tablespoon of the melted jam over each.

Personalize It!

If you don't like raspberry, simply substitute your favorite flavor jam or leave it out all together. Stuff the muffins with plain cream cheese and serve with warm maple syrup.

OVERNIGHT FRENCH TOAST

SECRET INGREDIENT:
rum extract

A smidge of rum extract gives this overnight breakfast treat exceptional flavor. Put it together the night before, then bake it in the morning and enjoy the aromas of vanilla, nutmeg, and toasted pecans wafting through your kitchen.

Prep Time: 10 min   **Cook Time:** 20 min   **Serves** 10

FRENCH TOAST

9 eggs

3 cups half-and-half

1/3 cup sugar

1 1/2 teaspoons rum extract

1 1/2 teaspoons vanilla extract

1/2 teaspoon ground nutmeg

24 to 30 slices (3/4-inch thick) French bread

SYRUP

1 1/2 cups firmly packed brown sugar

1/2 cup light corn syrup

1/2 cup water

1/2 cup chopped toasted pecans

2 tablespoons unsalted butter or margarine

1. For French toast, in a large bowl, lightly beat the eggs. Mix in the half-and-half, sugar, rum extract, vanilla, and nutmeg.

2. Place the bread in a single layer in two well-greased 10 x 15-inch baking pans. Pour the egg mixture over bread in each pan. Turn bread over to coat both sides. Cover and refrigerate overnight.

3. Preheat the oven to 400°F.

4. Bake, uncovered, until golden, 20 to 25 minutes.

5. Meanwhile, for syrup, bring the brown sugar, corn syrup, and water to a boil in a medium saucepan. Reduce the heat and simmer for 3 minutes.

6. Add the pecans and butter or margarine and simmer 2 minutes longer. Serve with the French toast.

One More Notch! To make this dish even richer, use challah or another eggy bread in place of the French bread.

HUEVOS RANCHEROS

SECRET INGREDIENT:
vinegar

The secret to perfectly poached eggs? Add vinegar to the poaching water. It helps to hold the egg whites together. For a fun weekend brunch, serve this Mexican-style dish of perfectly poached eggs and toppings on a warm flour tortilla. *See photograph on page 163.*

Prep Time: 10 min   **Cook Time:** 20 min   **Serves** 4

4 flour tortillas (10-inch)

SALSA

5 tomatoes, finely chopped

1 mild fresh red chile pepper, seeded and finely chopped (wear gloves when handling)

1 small red onion, finely chopped

1 small garlic clove, finely chopped

2 tablespoons finely chopped fresh cilantro

1 tablespoon olive oil

2 to 3 teaspoons lime juice

Salt and freshly ground black pepper

EGGS

1 teaspoon vinegar

4 eggs

Salt and freshly ground black pepper

2 ounces coarsely grated cheddar cheese

6 tablespoons sour cream

4 scallions, chopped

Chopped fresh cilantro

Lime wedges

1. Preheat the oven to 350°F. Stack and wrap the tortillas in foil and put them in the oven to warm for 10 minutes.

2. For salsa, place the tomatoes in a large bowl and stir in the chiles, onion, garlic, and cilantro. Add the oil and lime juice. Season with salt and pepper, to taste, then set aside.

3. Meanwhile, for eggs, half-fill a large nonstick skillet with water. Heat until simmering, but do not boil. Add the vinegar. Break the eggs into a cup one at a time, then slide each into the water and poach for 3 minutes. Toward the end of cooking, spoon the water over the yolks. When cooked, remove the eggs with a slotted spoon and drain on a paper towel–lined plate.

4. Place the warmed tortillas on plates. Spoon on a little salsa, then put the eggs on top and season with salt and pepper, to taste. Let everyone help themselves to the rest of the salsa, the grated cheese, sour cream, and scallions, plus chopped cilantro for sprinkling over the top and lime wedges for squeezing.

One More Notch! To make this a more substantial breakfast, serve the eggs with homemade refried beans. Sauté 1 minced garlic clove and 1/2 teaspoon ground cumin in 1 tablespoon olive oil for 1 minute. Drain and stir in 1 can (14 ounces) pinto beans and 1/2 cup water. Cover and simmer until the beans are soft enough to mash, about 5 minutes. Roughly mash them with a fork, then cook, uncovered, for 3 minutes. If the mixture is too runny, cook for a few more minutes then season lightly with salt.

POACHED EGGS IN A BLANKET

SECRET INGREDIENT:
smoked salmon

For a new twist on poached eggs, this dish wraps the eggs in slices of smoked salmon. Set atop a toasted English muffin with sliced tomato, onion, and avocado, this may be the breakfast "sandwich" you always go for.

Prep Time: 10 min   **Cook Time:** 10 min   **Serves** 2

SAUCE
1/4 cup sour cream
1 1/2 teaspoons drained chopped capers
1 teaspoon grated fresh lemon zest

EGGS
2 tablespoons distilled vinegar
4 large eggs
2 English muffins, split
4 thin red onion slices
4 tomato slices, 1/4-inch thick
1/2 Haas avocado, peeled, pitted, and cut into 8 slices
4 slices (about 4 ounces) smoked salmon

1. For sauce, combine the sour cream, capers, and lemon zest in a small bowl.

2. Meanwhile, for eggs, half-fill a large nonstick skillet with water. Heat until simmering, but do not boil. Add the vinegar. Break the eggs into a cup one at a time, then slide each into the water and poach for 3 minutes. Toward the end of cooking, spoon the water over the yolks. When cooked, remove the eggs with a slotted spoon and drain on a paper towel–lined plate.

3. Meanwhile, toast the English muffins and set them, cut side up, on two serving plates. Top each half with 1 onion slice, 1 tomato slice, and 2 avocado slices.

4. Place an egg on top of a slice of salmon and fold the sides of the salmon over like a wrap. Set the salmon-wrapped egg on an English muffin half. Repeat with the remaining eggs and salmon.

5. Top each egg with one-quarter of the sauce. Serve immediately.

Personalize It!

Prefer bagels and cream cheese? Simply substitute your favorite bagels for the English muffins and cream cheese for the sour cream. Just be sure to soften the cream cheese for 15 minutes to make it easier to mix. Instead of topping the eggs with the sauce, spread it directly on the toasted bagels.

EASY EGGS BENEDICT

SECRET INGREDIENT:

horseradish sauce

In the morning fog, who has the wherewithal to make hollandaise sauce for eggs benedict? Instead, try this simple blend of mayonnaise, cream, herbs, and horseradish sauce for extra oomph. It's equally luxurious as hollandaise yet infinitely easier.

Prep Time: 20 min **Cook Time:** 10 min **Serves** 4

SAUCE

Few sprigs each of basil, chives, parsley, and thyme

1/2 cup whipping cream

1/2 cup mayonnaise

1 teaspoon horseradish sauce

EGGS

2 English muffins

4 thick slices ham, preferably carved off the bone

2 tablespoons distilled vinegar

4 large eggs

Salt and freshly ground black pepper

1. For sauce, chop the herbs, setting the parsley aside. Combine the rest of the herbs in a small saucepan with the cream, mayonnaise, and horseradish. Heat gently, but do not allow to boil. Remove from the heat, cover, and keep warm.

2. For eggs, halve the muffins and toast in a toaster. Put a slice of ham on each muffin, and leave on the top of the toaster (or under a heated broiler) to warm through.

3. Cook the eggs in an egg poacher, or half-fill a large nonstick skillet with water. Heat until simmering, but do not boil. Add the vinegar. Break the eggs into a cup one at a time, then slide each into the water and poach for 3 minutes. Toward the end of cooking, spoon the water over the yolks. When cooked, remove the eggs with a slotted spoon and drain on a paper towel–lined plate.

4. Put each muffin half on a plate and place a poached egg on top. Spoon over the sauce, add salt and pepper, to taste, and sprinkle with the parsley.

One More Notch! Get a richer taste from the ham by frying it gently in a little olive oil until heated through instead of warming on a toaster or under a broiler.

SUPER SILKY SCRAMBLED EGGS

SECRET INGREDIENT:
cream cheese

Once you try this dish, you may never want your eggs any other way. Cream cheese gives the eggs a delicate, smooth texture that drapes your palate in irresistible silkiness.

Prep Time: 5 min   **Cook Time:** 5 min   **Serves** 2

2 tablespoons unsalted butter

1/4 cup cream cheese

4 eggs, lightly beaten

1/4 teaspoon salt

Pinch of freshly ground black pepper

1. Melt the butter in a small nonstick skillet over medium heat. When the butter foam subsides, add the cream cheese and cook, stirring, until melted, about 45 seconds.

2. Stir in the eggs, salt, and pepper and cook, stirring, until the eggs are soft and set, about 1 1/2 minutes.

One More Notch! For added flavor and a nice contrast, stir in 2 teaspoons finely chopped fresh chives with the eggs.

SICILIAN OMELET

SECRET INGREDIENT:
spaghetti

The typical omelet contains predictable add-ins like ham, peppers, tomatoes, and onions. This version is special: Spaghetti takes the starring role, supported by eggs, bacon, cheese, and sun-dried tomatoes. It's great for breakfast and hearty enough to serve for dinner!

Prep Time: 10 min   **Cook Time:** 35 min   **Serves** 6

6 ounces spaghetti

8 slices bacon

8 large eggs, lightly beaten

3 ounces sharp provolone cheese, shredded

1/3 cup chopped oil-packed sun-dried tomatoes

1/3 cup grated Parmesan cheese

1/2 teaspoon salt

1/4 teaspoon freshly ground black pepper

1 1/2 cups prepared tomato sauce

1. Preheat the oven to 400°F. Bring a large pot of salted water to a boil over high heat. Cook the spaghetti according to the package directions. Drain the spaghetti in a colander and run under cold water to stop the cooking. Drain again.

2. Heat a large ovenproof nonstick skillet over medium heat and add the bacon slices. Cook the bacon, turning occasionally, until crisp, about 4 minutes per side. Transfer the bacon to a paper–towel lined plate to cool. Chop the bacon and reserve. Discard all but 2 tablespoons of the bacon fat in the skillet.

3. In a large bowl, combine the eggs, bacon, provolone, tomatoes, Parmesan, salt, and pepper, mixing well. Stir in the spaghetti.

4. Return the skillet to the stove and heat the bacon fat over medium-high heat until hot.

Add the egg mixture to the skillet and cook until the eggs begin to set, 2 to 3 minutes. Transfer the skillet to the oven and bake until completely set, 11 to 12 minutes. If desired, lightly brown the top of the omelet under the broiler.

5. Meanwhile, heat the tomato sauce in a small saucepan over medium heat until hot.

6. To serve, cut the omelet into six wedges and top each with 1/4 cup of the tomato sauce.

One More Notch! Pull out all the stops by sautéing some minced garlic and onion in olive oil and stirring it, along with some pitted chopped calamata olives, into the egg mixture.

SPINACH AND MUSHROOM FRITTATA

SECRET INGREDIENT:
cashews

Open-face omelets often taste creamy and comforting but lack interesting texture. Our version includes cashews for extra crunch. Ribbons of spinach and savory mushrooms fill out the flavors. *See photograph on page 163.*

Prep Time: 10 min   **Cook Time:** 20 min   **Serves** 4

1 package (6 ounces) young spinach leaves

Small bunch of fresh parsley

2 tablespoons olive oil

1 small onion, chopped

3/4 pound small button mushrooms, quartered

3/4 cup roasted cashews

5 large eggs

2 tablespoons cold water

Salt and freshly ground black pepper

3 ounces grated cheddar or Parmesan cheese

1. Preheat the broiler to high. Rinse and dry the spinach and parsley. Chop enough parsley to make 2 tablespoons; set aside.

2. Heat the oil in a large nonstick skillet. Fry the onion over medium heat until soft, stirring, 3 to 4 minutes.

3. Add the mushrooms to the onion, and sauté, stirring frequently, for 3 to 4 minutes longer.

4. Add the spinach and cook over medium-high heat, stirring frequently, until the leaves have wilted and the excess liquid has evaporated, 3 to 4 minutes. Stir in the cashews and reduce the heat to low.

5. Break the eggs into a small bowl, then add the water and the reserved parsley. Add salt and pepper, to taste, and beat together.

6. Pour the egg mixture into the spinach and cook until the egg is just set and golden underneath, 5 minutes, lifting the edges to let the uncooked egg run underneath.

7. Sprinkle with the cheese and put the frittata under the broiler until it is set and golden, 2 to 3 minutes.

that's **ingenious** !

A nonstick skillet with a metal or heat-proof handle works best since the pan goes under the broiler. But don't worry if your skillet doesn't have a heat-proof handle. In that case, simply wrap the handle in heavy-duty foil to protect it from the broiler.

SMOKED HADDOCK SOUFFLÉ

SECRET INGREDIENT:
mustard

Light, fluffy soufflés rarely fail to impress, yet they are surprisingly easy to make. This recipe uses the fish-poaching milk to make the soufflé base, and fresh herbs, chopped tomatoes, and grainy mustard are added for extra flavor. *See photograph on page 163.*

Prep Time: 20 min   **Cook Time:** 55 min   **Serves** 6

2/3 pound smoked haddock fillet

1 1/4 cups milk

1 teaspoon unsalted butter

1 tablespoon Parmesan cheese

1 tablespoon dry bread crumbs

3 tablespoons flour

3 eggs, separated

2 tomatoes, peeled, seeded, and diced

1 teaspoon coarse mustard

2 tablespoons finely chopped parsley

2 tablespoons finely snipped fresh chives

Salt and freshly ground black pepper

1 egg white

1. Place the haddock and milk in a medium saucepan and heat until simmering. Simmer gently until the fish just flakes when tested with a fork, about 8 minutes. Remove the pan from the heat and leave the fish to cool in the milk. When the fish is cool enough to handle, remove it, and flake the flesh, discarding the skin and any bones. Set the poaching milk aside to cool.

2. Preheat the oven, with a metal baking sheet inside, to 375°F. Lightly grease a 6-cup soufflé dish with the butter. Mix together the Parmesan and bread crumbs in a small bowl and sprinkle over the bottom and side of the dish, turning the dish to coat evenly. Shake out any excess crumb mixture and reserve.

3. Mix the flour with a little of the reserved, cooled poaching milk to make a smooth paste. Heat the remaining milk in a small saucepan until almost boiling, then pour into the flour mixture, stirring constantly. Return to the pan and bring to a boil, stirring to make a thick sauce.

4. Pour the sauce into a large bowl. Add the egg yolks, one by one, beating them thoroughly into the sauce. Stir in the haddock, tomatoes, mustard, parsley, chives, and salt and pepper, to taste.

5. In a small bowl, whisk the 4 egg whites until stiff enough to hold soft peaks. Fold 1/4 of the whites into the sauce mixture to lighten it, then gently fold in the remaining whites.

6. Spoon the mixture into the soufflé dish and sprinkle the top with the reserved Parmesan and bread crumb mixture. Set the dish on the hot baking sheet and bake until well-puffed and golden brown, about 35 minutes. Serve immediately.

Personalize It!

If you can't get or don't like smoked haddock, use your favorite smoked fish such as smoked salmon or smoked trout.

FARMER'S CASSEROLE

canned evaporated milk

This handy breakfast casserole can be assembled the night before. In fact, it's better that way because the flavors have time to blend. In the morning, just pop it in the oven. The secret to its richness is plain ol' evaporated milk.

Prep Time: 5 min   **Cook Time:** 55 min   **Serves** 6

3 cups frozen shredded hash browns

3/4 cup shredded Monterey Jack cheese

1 cup diced fully cooked ham

1/4 cup chopped green onions

4 eggs

1 can (12 ounces) evaporated milk

1/4 teaspoon freshly ground black pepper

1/8 teaspoon salt

1. Place the hash browns in an 8-inch square baking dish. Sprinkle with the cheese, ham, and onions.

2. Beat together the eggs, milk, pepper, and salt and pour over all. Cover and refrigerate for several hours or overnight. Remove from the refrigerator 30 minutes before baking.

3. Preheat the oven to 350°F.

4. Bake, uncovered, until a knife inserted near the center comes out clean, 55 to 60 minutes.

Personalize It!

Almost any cheese can be used. Choose your favorite: cheddar, fontina, Gruyère, and mozzarella all work well.

HAM 'N' CHEESE STRATA

cornflakes

Stratas are made with layers of egg-soaked bread, cheese, and your favorite high-flavor ingredients like bacon, sausage, sun-dried tomatoes, or other vegetables. Our version includes ham and a surprisingly crisp topping made with cornflakes.
See photograph on page 161.

Prep Time: 10 min   **Cook Time:** 50 min   **Serves** 8

12 slices white bread, crusts removed

1 pound fully cooked ham, diced

2 cups shredded cheddar cheese (about 8 ounces)

6 eggs

3 cups milk

2 teaspoons Worcestershire sauce

1 teaspoon ground mustard

1/2 teaspoon salt

1/4 teaspoon freshly ground black pepper

Dash of cayenne pepper

1/4 cup minced onion

1/4 cup minced seeded green bell pepper

1/4 cup unsalted butter or margarine, melted

1 cup crushed cornflakes

1. Grease a 9 x 13-inch baking dish, then arrange 6 bread slices in the bottom. Top with the ham and cheese. Cover with the remaining bread slices.

2. In a medium bowl, beat together the eggs, milk, Worcestershire sauce, mustard, salt, black pepper, and cayenne. Stir in the onion and green pepper and pour over all. Cover and refrigerate for several hours or overnight. Remove from the refrigerator 30 minutes before baking.

3. Preheat the oven to 350°F.

4. Pour the butter over the bread and sprinkle with the cornflakes. Bake, uncovered, until a knife inserted near the center comes out clean, 50 to 60 minutes. Let stand for 10 minutes before serving.

One More Notch! What could make ham and cheese taste even better? Spinach and mushrooms. Sauté some sliced mushrooms and baby spinach leaves until the spinach is wilted and the liquid in the pan is mostly evaporated, then layer these on top of the ham and cheese.

BRUNCH ENCHILADAS

SECRET INGREDIENT:
canned cream-style corn

Looking for an easy, savory dish to serve to company? This Southwestern breakfast casserole has an incredibly creamy texture from canned corn mixed with cheddar cheese and hard-cooked eggs. Corn tortillas give these enchiladas the perfect amount of chew.

Prep Time: 15 min   **Cook Time:** 20 min   **Serves** 8

8 corn tortillas

8 hard-cooked eggs, chopped

1 can (8 1/2 ounces) cream-style corn

2/3 cup shredded cheddar cheese

1 can (4 ounces) chopped green chile peppers, undrained

2 teaspoons taco seasoning mix

1/4 teaspoon salt

1 bottle (8 ounces) mild taco sauce

Sour cream (optional)

1. Preheat the oven to 350°F.

2. Heat a large nonstick skillet over medium-high heat. Add two tortillas to the skillet at a time along with a few drops of water. Cover and cook, turning once, until soft and pliable, 1 minute per side. Set aside and cover to keep warm.

3. Combine the eggs, corn, cheese, chiles, seasoning mix, and salt in a medium bowl. Spoon 1/2 cup of the mixture down the center of each tortilla and roll up tightly. Place the enchiladas, seam side down, in a greased 9 x 13-inch baking dish. Top with taco sauce.

4. Bake, uncovered, until heated through, about 15 minutes. Serve with sour cream, if using.

that's **ingenious**

Hard-cooked eggs aren't difficult to make, but they do take time. Fortunately, you can buy already-hard-cooked eggs in most grocery stores these days. Look for these timesavers next to the regular eggs in the dairy section.

BREAKFASTS

SUNDAY MORNING QUESADILLAS WITH AVOCADO AND TOMATOES

SECRET INGREDIENT:
smoked salmon

Quesadillas are a popular Mexican appetizer or dinner dish. In this version, we use classic brunch ingredients for a surprisingly fun, warm meal. It's no longer the same old bagels and lox!

Prep Time: 15 min	Cook Time: 10 min	Serves 2

1/2 cup peeled, pitted, and finely chopped Haas avocado

1/2 cup finely chopped tomato

2 teaspoons chopped cilantro

1/8 teaspoon salt

2 flour tortillas (8-inch)

1 1/2 ounces cream cheese, softened

2 large slices (about 2 ounces) smoked salmon

2 very thin red onion slices

2 teaspoons drained chopped capers

1. In a small bowl, combine the avocado, tomato, cilantro, and salt and mix well.

2. Spread each tortilla with the cream cheese. Lay 1 slice of the salmon on half of each tortilla. Separate the onion into rings and spread them over the salmon then sprinkle with the capers. Fold the tortilla over to form a half-moon.

3. Heat a large nonstick skillet over medium heat until hot. Add the quesadillas and cook until lightly browned and heated through, 3 to 4 minutes per side.

4. Transfer the quesadillas to two serving plates and top each with half of the avocado mixture.

SOUTHERN BREAKFAST SKILLET

SECRET INGREDIENT:
canned hominy

Hominy is nothing more than dried corn kernels with the hull and germ removed. But oh, the taste! It's a favorite flavor in the South and the featured ingredient in this quick breakfast scramble. Look for white or yellow hominy in the canned vegetable section.
See photograph on page 163.

Prep Time: 5 min	Cook Time: 15 min	Serves 2

1/4 pound bacon, diced

1/4 cup chopped onion

1 can (15 1/2 ounces) hominy, drained

4 eggs, beaten

1/8 teaspoon freshly ground black pepper

1. In a medium nonstick skillet, cook the bacon until almost crisp, then drain.

2. Add the onion and continue cooking until the bacon is crisp and the onion is tender, about 4 minutes.

3. Stir in the hominy, eggs, and pepper. Cook and stir until the eggs are completely set, about 5 minutes. Plate and serve.

One More Notch! Kick up the flavor of the eggs by sautéing 1/2 cup seeded, chopped red bell pepper with the onion and adding a dash of hot red-pepper sauce to the eggs.

that's ingenious

The quesadillas can be assembled several hours in advance. Wrap them in plastic and keep them in the refrigerator. This is great for a large brunch, where they can be assembled long before guests arrive and then cooked at the last minute. Even better is that they make great hors d'oeuvres when you cut each cooked quesadilla into 4 or 5 wedges.

TOMATO AND PECORINO CHEESE PUDDING

SECRET INGREDIENT:

sour cream

Many egg dishes are made with whole eggs and cream. The custard for this savory pudding is made with a combination of whole eggs, egg whites, and low-fat sour cream to make a delightfully lower-fat version. *See photograph on page 172.*

Prep Time: 10 min   **Cook Time:** 30 min   **Serves** 4

1 pound cherry tomatoes

4 tablespoons snipped fresh chives

1/3 cup coarsely grated Pecorino Romano cheese, divided

3 large eggs

3 egg whites

2 tablespoons flour

3 tablespoons low-fat sour cream

1 1/4 cups low-fat (1%) milk

Salt and freshly ground black pepper

1. Preheat the oven to 375°F. Lightly spray 4 shallow ovenproof dishes, each 5 to 6 inches in diameter.

2. Divide the cherry tomatoes among the dishes, spreading them out, and sprinkle with the chives and 4 tablespoons of the cheese.

3. In a medium bowl, whisk together the eggs and egg whites, then gradually whisk in the flour until smooth. Add the sour cream and gradually whisk in the milk to make a thin, smooth batter. Season with salt and pepper, to taste.

4. Pour the batter over the tomatoes, dividing it evenly among the dishes. Sprinkle with the remaining cheese and extra pepper, if desired.

5. Bake until set, puffed, and lightly golden, 30 to 35 minutes.

6. Remove the puddings from the oven and let cool for a few minutes before serving.

that's ingenious !

If you don't have individual baking dishes, bake one large pudding, using a lightly sprayed 9-inch round ovenproof dish that is about 2 inches deep. Increase the baking time to 35 to 40 minutes.

CHERRY-TOPPED HONEY-CREAM BREAKFAST POLENTA

SECRET INGREDIENT:

cream cheese

Polenta is normally served as a delicious side dish. But its ease of preparation makes it an ideal breakfast food, too. Honey adds a kiss of sweetness but the creaminess and tang comes from the addition of cream cheese.

Prep Time: 10 min   **Cook Time:** 15 min   **Serves** 4

1 1/2 cups frozen dark cherries

3 tablespoons sugar

2 cups milk

1/4 cup honey

1/2 teaspoon vanilla extract

1/2 cup yellow cornmeal

2 ounces cream cheese

1 tablespoon unsalted butter

1. In a small saucepan over medium heat, combine the cherries and sugar. Bring the mixture to a simmer, then reduce the heat

BREAKFASTS

to medium-low and cook until the cherries are tender, 6 to 7 minutes.

2. Meanwhile, combine the milk, honey, and vanilla in a medium saucepan over medium-high heat. Bring the mixture just to a boil, then whisk in the cornmeal in a slow, steady stream. Cook, stirring constantly, until the polenta is thick and creamy, about 5 minutes.

3. Remove from the heat and stir in the cream cheese and butter.

4. Divide the polenta among four bowls and top each with some of the cherry mixture. Serve immediately.

that's **ingenious**

Even though it is a snap to make this dish, it works well if made the night before. Cool the polenta to room temperature, then store in an airtight container in the refrigerator. In the morning, combine 1/2 cup of the prepared polenta and 1/3 cup milk in a small saucepan over medium heat. Cook, stirring, until the polenta is hot and creamy. Serve topped with some of the warmed cherry mixture, or microwave some of your favorite jam, honey, or even maple syrup instead.

CRUNCHY BREAKFAST PARFAIT

SECRET INGREDIENT:
granola

This simple twist on dessert makes a tasty and healthy breakfast. Store-bought granola stays wonderfully crisp when layered between plain yogurt and warm sautéed bananas.
See photograph on page 161.

Prep Time: 5 min	**Cook Time:** 5 min	**Serves** 1

1 teaspoon unsalted butter

1 small ripe banana, cut into 1/4-inch-thick slices

1 tablespoon light brown sugar

1 teaspoon dark rum (optional)

1/2 cup plain low-fat yogurt, divided

1/2 cup granola, divided

1. Heat the butter in a small nonstick skillet over medium-high heat. When it melts, add the banana slices and cook for 1 minute.

2. Add the brown sugar and cook, stirring occasionally, until the sugar melts and the bananas soften, 1 to 2 minutes. Off the heat, stir in the rum, if using, then return to the stove and cook until the rum evaporates, about 15 seconds. Remove from the heat and let stand 3 minutes.

3. Spoon 1/4 cup of the yogurt into the bottom of a tall parfait or wine glass. Top with 1/4 cup of the granola and half of the bananas. Repeat with the remaining ingredients.

One More Notch! Take this morning treat to the next level by drizzling each layer of granola with 1 teaspoon honey or maple syrup.

FRUITY OATMEAL SURPRISE GRANOLA

SECRET INGREDIENT:
dried cherries

Granola has long been thought of as a "health" food and overlooked for its great taste and versatility, like topping fruit crisps or baking into muffins. What stands out in this granola is the refreshing taste of dried cranberries and cherries instead of the ubiquitous raisin.

Prep Time: 10 min **Cook Time:** 45 min **Makes** 6 cups

4 cups old-fashioned oatmeal (rolled oats)

1 cup coarsely chopped walnuts

1 teaspoon ground cinnamon

1/8 teaspoon ground nutmeg

1/4 teaspoon salt

1/2 cup maple syrup

1/4 cup honey

1/4 cup canola oil

2 teaspoons vanilla extract

1 cup dried cranberries

1 cup dried cherries

1. Preheat the oven to 300°F. Coat a large baking sheet with cooking spray.

2. In a large bowl, combine the oatmeal, walnuts, cinnamon, nutmeg, and salt.

3. In a small bowl, whisk together the syrup, honey, oil, and vanilla.

4. Pour the syrup mixture over the oatmeal mixture and mix well to combine. Spread the oatmeal mixture evenly onto the baking sheet. Bake, stirring every 10 minutes, until the mixture is lightly golden and toasted, 45 to 55 minutes.

5. Remove from the oven and stir in the cranberries and cherries. Cool completely on the baking sheet. Store in an airtight container for up to 2 weeks.

One More Notch! To make a granola that stands out even more, try adding 1/4 cup sesame seeds, 1/4 cup slivered almonds, and 1/2 cup sweetened coconut flakes.

extraordinary
breads, rolls,
and muffins

NUTTY QUICK BREAD

SECRET INGREDIENT:
Grape-Nuts cereal

Grape-Nuts gives these fast-to-fix loaves their nutty flavor and chewy texture. The extra fiber is a nice health bonus, too.

Prep Time: 10 min   **Cook Time:** 30 min   **Makes** 2

2 cups buttermilk

1 cup Grape-Nuts Cereal

1 egg, lightly beaten

3 cups all-purpose flour

1 cup sugar

1 teaspoon baking powder

1 teaspoon baking soda

1/2 teaspoon salt

1. Preheat the oven to 375°F. Grease two 8 x 4-inch loaf pans.

2. In a large bowl, combine the buttermilk and cereal. Let stand for 10 minutes, then add the egg.

3. In a large bowl, combine the flour, sugar, baking powder, baking soda, and salt. Stir into the cereal mixture until just moistened.

4. Spoon the batter into the loaf pans. Bake until a toothpick inserted near the center comes out clean, 30 to 35 minutes.

5. Cool for 10 minutes before removing from the pans to wire racks.

One More Notch! For extra flavor and crunch, sprinkle some Grape-Nuts cereal on top of the loaves just before baking.

SOUTHERN NUT BREAD

SECRET INGREDIENT:
bananas

Pecans give this quick bread an earthy Southern flavor, but the sweetness and richness come from mashed bananas. If your bananas look almost ready for the trash bin, they're perfect for this recipe.
See photograph on page 165.

Prep Time: 10 min   **Cook Time:** 45 min   **Makes** 2

BREAD

1/2 cup butter-flavored shortening

1 1/2 cups sugar

2 eggs

2 ripe bananas, mashed (about 1 cup)

1 teaspoon vanilla extract

2 cups self-rising flour

1/2 cup buttermilk

3/4 cup chopped pecans

TOPPING

1/4 to 1/3 cup mashed ripe banana

1 1/4 cups confectioners' sugar

1 teaspoon lemon juice

Chopped pecans

1. Preheat the oven to 350°F. Grease two 8 x 4-inch loaf pans.

2. For bread, in a large bowl, cream the shortening and sugar.

3. Beat in the eggs, then blend in the bananas and vanilla. Add the flour alternately with the buttermilk. Fold in the pecans.

4. Pour into the loaf pans and bake until a toothpick inserted near the center comes out clean, 45 to 55 minutes. Cool in the pans for 10 minutes before removing to a wire rack; cool completely.

5. For topping, combine the bananas, confectioners' sugar, and lemon juice. Spread over the loaves. Sprinkle with the pecans.

that's **ingenious** !

Don't have self-rising flour? Replace it with all-purpose flour, 1 tablespoon baking powder, and 3/4 teaspoon salt.

ROSEMARY TEA BREAD

SECRET INGREDIENT:
orange juice

Herbed breads taste great, but pair the herbs with sweet ingredients and the combination is heavenly. Rosemary and orange are a perfect example. This aromatic bread goes great with chicken, a roast, or pasta with red sauce.

Prep Time: 30 min   **Cook Time:** 45 min   **Makes** 1

1 package (1/4 ounce) active dry yeast

3/4 cup warm water (110°-115°F)

3/4 cup orange juice

2 tablespoons honey

4 teaspoons vegetable oil, divided

1 tablespoon minced fresh rosemary or
    1 teaspoon dried rosemary, crushed

2 teaspoons salt

1 teaspoon grated orange peel

3 3/4 to 4 1/2 cups all-purpose flour

1. In a medium bowl, dissolve the yeast in the water. Add orange juice, honey, 1 tablespoon of the oil, rosemary, salt, orange peel, and 2 cups flour. Beat until smooth. Stir in enough of the remaining flour to form a soft dough.

2. Turn onto a floured board; knead until smooth and elastic, 6 to 8 minutes. Coat a large bowl with the remaining 1 teaspoon of

oil and add the dough, turning to coat. Cover the bowl and let rise in a warm place (85°F) free from drafts until the dough has doubled in bulk, about 1 hour.

3. Punch the dough down. Roll it into a 10 x 15-inch rectangle. Starting at the short end, roll up jelly-roll style. Pinch the edges to seal and shape into an oval. Place, seam side down, on a greased baking sheet. Cover and let rise until nearly doubled, about 30 minutes.

4. Preheat the oven to 375°F.

5. Bake until browned, about 45 minutes. Cool on a wire rack.

One More Notch! To give the bread a pretty topping, whisk an egg white and brush it over the loaf after 20 minutes of baking. Place small sprigs of fresh rosemary and whole or cracked peppercorns over the egg-white-brushed bread and bake until browned, about 25 minutes longer.

PEACHES-AND-CREAM QUICK BREAD

SECRET INGREDIENT:
olive oil

Fresh peaches and lush sour cream combine in this delicious tea bread. Extra-light olive oil lends another layer of richness that enhances the bread's texture without adding an olive flavor. *See photograph on page 165.*

Prep Time: 15 min   **Cook Time:** 1 hr 5 min   **Serves** 16

2 peaches

1 1/2 cups all-purpose flour

3/4 cup whole-wheat flour

1/4 cup toasted wheat germ

3/4 cup sugar

1 teaspoon baking soda

Salt

1/2 cup sour cream

2 large eggs

2 tablespoons extra-light olive oil

1 teaspoon almond extract

1. Preheat the oven to 350°F. Lightly spray a 9 x 5-inch loaf pan with nonstick cooking spray.

2. Blanch the peaches in a medium saucepan of boiling water for 20 seconds. Peel, pit, and finely chop them (you should have about 1 cup).

3. Combine the all-purpose flour, whole-wheat flour, wheat germ, sugar, baking soda, and salt, to taste, in a large bowl.

4. Combine the sour cream, eggs, oil, and almond extract in a small bowl. Make a well in the center of the dry ingredients and pour in the sour cream mixture. Stir until just combined. Fold in the peaches.

5. Spoon the batter into the pan, smoothing the top. Bake until a toothpick inserted in the center comes out clean, about 1 hour. Cool in the pan on a wire rack for 10 minutes, then turn out onto the rack to cool completely before slicing.

TRIPLE CHOCOLATE QUICK BREAD

SECRET INGREDIENT:
applesauce

These mini loaves make the perfect food gift, particularly when wrapped in colored foil and tied with ribbon. Applesauce blends perfectly with chocolate to keep these treats ultra-rich and moist. *See photograph on page 165.*

Prep Time: 15 min   **Cook Time:** 35 min   **Makes** 4

BREAD

1/2 cup unsalted butter or margarine, softened

2/3 cup firmly packed brown sugar

2 eggs

1 cup (6 ounces) miniature semi-sweet chocolate chips, melted

1 1/2 cups applesauce

2 teaspoons vanilla extract

2 1/2 cups all-purpose flour

1 teaspoon baking powder

1 teaspoon baking soda

1 teaspoon salt

1/2 cup miniature semi-sweet chocolate chips

GLAZE

1/2 cup miniature semi-sweet chocolate chips

1 tablespoon unsalted butter or margarine

2 to 3 tablespoons half-and-half

1/2 cup confectioners' sugar

1/4 teaspoon vanilla extract

Pinch of salt

1. Preheat the oven to 350°F. Grease four 5 1/2 x 3-inch mini loaf pans.

2. For bread, cream the butter or margarine and brown sugar in a large bowl. Add the eggs and chocolate and mix well. Add the applesauce and vanilla, then set aside.

3. In a medium bowl, combine the flour, baking powder, baking soda, and salt; add to the creamed mixture and mix well. Stir in the chocolate chips.

4. Spoon the batter into the loaf pans. Bake until a toothpick inserted near the center comes out clean, 35 to 40 minutes. Cool in the pans for 10 minutes before removing to wire racks to cool completely.

5. For glaze, melt the chocolate chips and butter or margarine in a saucepan; stir in half-and-half. Remove from the heat; stir in the sugar, vanilla, and salt. Drizzle over the warm bread.

One More Notch! To give this bread a mocha flavor, stir 1/2 cup finely ground espresso into the flour mixture.

GOLDEN AUTUMN BRAID

SECRET INGREDIENT:
butternut squash

Many tender breads get their pleasing texture from pureed vegetables. Here, butternut squash lends a soft texture and beautiful sunny color to the bread. Try it with hearty beef or pork stews.

Prep Time: 30 min	**Cook Time:** 20 min	**Makes** 1

BREAD

1 package (1/4 ounce) active dry yeast

2 tablespoons warm (110°-115°F) water

1 cup mashed cooked butternut squash

1/3 cup warm (110°-115°F) milk

1/4 cup unsalted butter or margarine, softened

1 egg

3 tablespoons brown sugar

1/4 teaspoon salt

3 to 3 1/2 cups all-purpose flour

1 teaspoon oil

GLAZE

1 egg, beaten

1 tablespoon water

1. For bread, in a small bowl, dissolve the yeast in the water.

2. In a large bowl, combine the squash, milk, butter or margarine, egg, brown sugar, and salt. Mix well.

3. Add the yeast mixture and 1 1/2 cups of the flour, then mix well. Add enough remaining flour to form a soft dough. Turn onto a floured surface; knead until smooth and elastic, 6 to 8 minutes. Coat a large bowl with the oil and add the dough, turning to coat. Cover the bowl and let rise in a warm place (85°F) free from drafts until the dough has doubled in bulk, about 1 hour.

4. Punch dough down. Divide into thirds; roll each third into an 18-inch rope. Braid the ropes together on a greased baking sheet. Pinch ends. Cover and let rise until nearly doubled, about 30 minutes.

5. Preheat the oven to 350°F.

6. For glaze, combine the egg and water in a cup and brush over the braid. Bake until golden brown, 20 to 25 minutes. Remove from the pan and cool on a wire rack.

Personalize It!
Replace the butternut squash with cooked mashed sweet potatoes. Or, for a quick switch, use canned pumpkin puree instead.

BRAIDED CRANBERRY BREAD

SECRET INGREDIENT:
eggnog

A beautifully braided sweet bread filled with cranberries and drizzled with glaze makes a welcome addition to any holiday. By using eggnog instead of milk, the bread's texture is particularly rich and yummy.
See photograph on page 165.

Prep Time: 35 min	**Cook Time:** 30 min	**Makes** 1

BREAD

3 to 3 1/2 cups all-purpose flour, divided

1/4 cup sugar

1/2 teaspoon salt

1 package (1/4 ounce) active dry yeast

1/2 teaspoon ground nutmeg

1 1/4 cups eggnog

1/4 cup unsalted butter or margarine

1/2 cup dried cranberries

1 teaspoon oil

GLAZE

1 cup confectioners' sugar

1 to 2 tablespoons eggnog

1/4 teaspoon vanilla extract

Dash of nutmeg

1. For bread, in a large bowl, combine 1 1/2 cups of the flour, the sugar, salt, yeast, and nutmeg; set aside.

2. In a medium saucepan, heat the eggnog and butter or margarine to 120° to 130°F; add to the flour mixture. Beat on low until moistened, then beat on medium for 3 minutes.

3. Stir in the cranberries and enough remaining flour to make a soft dough. Turn onto a floured surface; knead until smooth and elastic, 6 to 8 minutes. Coat a large bowl with the oil and add the dough, turning to coat. Cover the bowl and let rise in a warm place (85°F) free from drafts until the dough has doubled in bulk, about 1 hour.

4. Punch dough down and divide into thirds. Shape each third into a 16-inch rope. Braid the ropes on a greased baking sheet and seal the ends. Cover and let rise until nearly doubled, about 30 minutes.

5. Preheat the oven to 350°F. Bake until golden, 25 to 30 minutes. Immediately remove from the pan to a wire rack to cool completely.

6. For glaze, combine the confectioners' sugar, eggnog, and vanilla in a small bowl. Drizzle over the braid, then dust with nutmeg.

Personalize It!
If you prefer not to use eggnog, use whole milk or half-and-half instead. ❊

GRILLED CHEESE LOAF

SECRET INGREDIENT:
cream cheese

Here's something different to put on the grill or over a campfire—a loaf of bread! The cream cheese and mozzarella make this bread deliciously rich.

Prep Time: 10 min	**Cook Time:** 15 min	**Serves** 10

1 package (3 ounces) cream cheese, softened

2 tablespoons unsalted butter or margarine, softened

1 cup shredded mozzarella cheese (about 4 ounces)

1/4 cup chopped green onions

1/2 teaspoon garlic salt

1 loaf (about 1 pound) French bread, sliced

1. Preheat a grill to medium. In a small bowl, beat the cream cheese and butter or margarine. Add the cheese, onions, and garlic salt and mix well. Spread on both sides of each slice of bread.

2. Wrap the loaf in a large piece of heavy-duty foil (about 28 x 18 inches) and seal tightly. Grill, covered, for 8 to 10 minutes, turning once. Unwrap foil and grill for 5 minutes longer.

Personalize It!
Switch things up by using goat cheese instead of cream cheese and smoked Gouda in place of the mozzarella. You can also add grated Parmesan for a spark of flavor.

CHEESE DANISH

SECRET INGREDIENT:

apricot preserves

Put this easy breakfast bread together the night before. In the morning, all you do is roll it out and bake it. Using apricot preserves gives the Danish loads of flavor with little effort.

Prep Time: 20 min   **Cook Time:** 20 min   **Makes** 2

DANISH
1 package (1/4 ounce) active dry yeast

1/4 cup warm (110°-115°F) water

3 tablespoons sugar

1/2 cup (1 stick) unsalted butter or margarine, softened

2 eggs

1/2 cup sour cream

1/4 teaspoon salt

3 cups all-purpose flour, divided

1 teaspoon oil

FILLING
2 packages (8 ounces each) cream cheese, softened

1/2 cup sugar

2 egg yolks

2 teaspoons vanilla extract

1/4 cup apricot preserves

Confectioners' sugar

1. For Danish, in a large bowl, dissolve the yeast in the water. Add the sugar, butter or margarine, eggs, and sour cream. Gradually add the salt and 2 cups of the flour, beating until smooth. Stir in enough of the remaining flour until the dough is soft and sticky.

2. Coat a large bowl with the oil and add the dough, turning to coat. Cover and refrigerate overnight.

3. For filling, beat the cream cheese, sugar, egg yolks, and vanilla in a medium bowl until smooth.

4. Turn the dough onto a floured board and knead two or three times. Divide in half. Roll each half into a 10 x 16-inch oval and place on greased baking sheets.

5. Spread 1 1/4 cups filling over each oval to within 1 inch of the edges. Fold the longest side over the filling and pinch the edges to seal. Cover and let rise in a warm place (85°F) free from drafts until the dough has doubled in bulk, about 1 hour.

6. Preheat the oven to 375°F.

7. Bake until golden brown, 20 to 22 minutes. Cool on a wire rack. Spread the preserves on top and dust with confectioners' sugar. Store in the refrigerator.

Personalize It!
Use whatever flavor jam or jelly you like in this recipe. Swap the apricot preserves for raspberry jam, cherry preserves, or even guava jelly.

ROSEMARY FOCACCIA

SECRET INGREDIENT:
instant mashed potatoes

The secret to getting a moist, light texture in this popular Italian bread is to add mashed potatoes. However, there's no reason to peel, boil, and mash the spuds when instant mashed potatoes work just fine.
See photograph on page 187.

Prep Time: 20 min   **Cook Time:** 25 min   **Serves** 8

2/3 cup instant mashed potato flakes

1/4 cup warm (100°-110°F) water

1 package (1/4 ounce) active dry yeast

2 teaspoons sugar

3 tablespoons plus 1 teaspoon extra-virgin olive oil

3 cups all-purpose flour

2 teaspoons salt, divided

1 tablespoon chopped fresh rosemary

12 cherry tomatoes, halved

1. Prepare the mashed potatoes according to the package directions. Cool for 10 minutes.

2. Meanwhile, in a small bowl, whisk the water, yeast, sugar, and 2 tablespoons of the oil until the yeast is dissolved. Let the mixture stand until frothy, about 5 minutes.

3. In a large bowl, combine the flour and 1 1/2 teaspoons of the salt. Stir the mashed potatoes and yeast into the flour mixture. Stir until combined and a soft ragged dough begins to form.

4. Turn the dough out onto a lightly floured surface and knead until fairly smooth, 4 to 5 minutes. Coat a large bowl with 1 teaspoon of the oil and add the dough, turning to coat. Cover the bowl and let rise in a warm place (85°F) free from drafts until the dough has doubled in bulk, about 1 1/2 hours.

5. Preheat the oven to 425°F. Coat a 9 x 13-inch baking pan with the remaining 1 tablespoon of oil. With lightly floured hands, transfer the dough to the baking pan and press and stretch it to fit. Sprinkle the dough with the remaining 1/2 teaspoon salt and the rosemary. Arrange the tomatoes, cut side down, in equally spaced rows over the dough.

6. Bake until the bread is lightly golden, 20 to 25 minutes. Remove from the pan immediately and cool on a wire rack before slicing.

that's **ingenious**

If you want fresh focaccia for dinner but don't want to deal with kneading and rising, just prepare the dough in the morning or the night before and place it in the oiled bowl, cover it, and then put it in the coldest part of your refrigerator. The dough will still rise but at a much slower rate. It also allows more flavor to build up.

SAUSAGE CORNBREAD

SECRET INGREDIENT:
canned cream-style corn

Cornbread is a staple in the South. Adding sausage and cheddar cheese makes it a more filling side dish and the perfect accompaniment to soups and stews. The key to its tender crumb is canned creamed corn.

Prep Time: 10 min   **Cook Time:** 50 min   **Serves** 8

1 pound bulk pork sausage

1 large onion, chopped

1 1/2 cups self-rising cornmeal

1 can (14 3/4 ounces) cream-style corn

3/4 cup milk

2 eggs

1/4 cup vegetable oil

2 cups shredded sharp cheddar cheese (8 ounces)

1. In a large nonstick skillet, cook the sausage and onion until the meat is browned and the onion is tender; drain.

2. Preheat the oven to 425°F. Grease a 10-inch ovenproof iron skillet.

3. In a medium bowl, combine the cornmeal, corn, milk, eggs, and oil. Pour half the batter into the skillet. Sprinkle with the sausage mixture and cheese. Spread remaining cornmeal mixture on top.

4. Bake until a toothpick inserted in the center comes out clean, 40 to 45 minutes.

that's ingenious

If you don't have self-rising cornmeal, mix your own at home. Combine 1 1/3 cups cornmeal, 2 tablespoons baking powder, and 3/4 teaspoon salt.

SPICY SURPRISE BISCUITS

SECRET INGREDIENT:
Pepper Jack cheese

Nothing beats the smell of freshly baking biscuits—except maybe the smell of baking cheese biscuits! This recipe has been ratcheted up a few notches with the surprise addition of a little heat in the form of Pepper Jack cheese. *See photograph on page 192.*

Prep Time: 10 min   **Cook Time:** 12 min   **Makes** 8

1 1/2 cups all-purpose flour

1 teaspoon baking powder

1 teaspoon chili powder

1 teaspoon salt

1/4 teaspoon baking soda

6 tablespoons unsalted butter, chilled and cut into small pieces

4 ounces shredded Pepper Jack cheese (about 1 cup)

1/2 cup buttermilk

1 teaspoon unsalted butter, melted

1. Preheat the oven to 425°F.

2. In a medium bowl, whisk together the flour, baking powder, chili powder, salt, and baking soda. Using a pastry blender or two forks, cut the chilled butter into the flour mixture until it resembles coarse crumbs.

3. With a wooden spoon, stir in the cheese until well-distributed. Pour in the buttermilk and stir until just moistened. Quickly knead the dough in the bowl four to six times until the dough comes together and is fairly smooth.

4. On a lightly floured surface, pat or roll out the dough to a 1/2-inch thickness. Cut out 7 biscuits with a floured 2 1/2-inch round biscuit cutter. Re-roll the scraps and cut out 1 more biscuit.

5. Place the biscuits on an ungreased baking sheet. Brush the tops with the melted butter. Bake the biscuits until puffed and golden, 12 to 15 minutes. Remove from the baking sheet and serve hot, warm, or room temperature.

Personalize It!

If you don't like Pepper Jack cheese, try sharp cheddar, Colby, or a sharp aged provolone. You can even leave the cheese out all together and have plain buttermilk biscuits, or try stirring in cracked pepper, chopped herbs, or your favorite seasonings. ❄

OLD-FASHIONED GLAZED GINGERBREAD

SECRET INGREDIENT:

applesauce

Grated fresh ginger, chopped crystallized ginger, and ground ginger in the pumpkin pie spice give this tea bread a triple hit of ginger flavor. But applesauce is the real secret ingredient, adding moisture and tenderness. *See photograph on page 165.*

Prep Time: 30 min   **Cook Time:** 45 min   **Serves** 12

GINGERBREAD

1 1/3 cups all-purpose flour

1 1/2 teaspoons pumpkin pie spice

3/4 teaspoon baking soda

1/2 teaspoon salt

1/2 cup unsweetened applesauce

1/4 cup light molasses

1 large egg, lightly beaten

1/4 cup (1/2 stick) unsalted butter or margarine

1/2 cup firmly packed dark brown sugar

2 teaspoons grated peeled fresh ginger

3 tablespoons finely chopped crystallized ginger

GLAZE

3/4 cup sifted confectioners' sugar

1 tablespoon water

1. Preheat the oven to 350°F. Generously coat an 8-inch square cake pan with nonstick cooking spray. Place a cooling rack on waxed paper.

2. For gingerbread, whisk the flour, pumpkin pie spice, baking soda, and salt in a medium bowl.

3. Blend the applesauce, molasses, and egg in a small bowl.

4. Cream the butter or margarine and brown sugar in a medium bowl with an electric mixer on high until light, 3 to 4 minutes. Reduce speed to low and beat in the applesauce mixture. Stir in the flour mixture with a wooden spoon until just combined. Blend in fresh ginger.

5. Scrape the batter into the cake pan. Bake until a toothpick inserted in the center comes out with moist crumbs clinging, about 45 minutes. Cool in the pan on a wire rack for 10 minutes. Remove from the pan and set right side up on the rack. Cool completely.

6. Scatter crystallized ginger on top of the gingerbread.

7. For glaze, blend confectioners' sugar and water in a cup to make a spreadable glaze, adding more water, if necessary. Drizzle the glaze over the gingerbread with a fork, letting some glaze drizzle the down sides.

that's **ingenious** !

The easiest way to peel fresh ginger is to scrape off the peel with a spoon.

BLUEBERRY SWIRL COFFEECAKE

SECRET INGREDIENT:
lemon zest

This moist and tender cake is bursting with juicy berries. Brown sugar and cinnamon make it melt-in-your-mouth delicious. Lemon zest adds a bright burst of flavor that perfectly complements the berries. *See photograph on page 165.*

Prep Time: 15 min   **Cook Time:** 40 min   **Serves** 16

2 1/2 cups fresh or frozen blueberries, divided

1/3 cup firmly packed light brown sugar

1 teaspoon cinnamon

1/2 cup (1 stick) margarine

1 cup granulated sugar

1 large egg

1 large egg white

1 tablespoon grated lemon zest

2 1/2 cups self-rising flour

1 1/4 cups reduced-fat (2%) milk

1. Preheat the oven to 350°F. Grease and flour a 9 x 13-inch baking pan.

2. Toss 2 cups of the blueberries, the brown sugar, and cinnamon in small bowl until the berries are coated.

3. Cream the margarine and granulated sugar in a large bowl with an electric mixer at high speed until light and fluffy, about 4 minutes. Add egg and egg white and beat for 2 minutes. Beat in the lemon zest. Reduce speed to low. Add flour alternately with milk, one-third at a time, stopping mixer occasionally to scrape the sides of the bowl with a rubber spatula. Do not overbeat.

4. Spread half of the batter into the pan and sprinkle with the blueberry mixture. Spoon the remaining batter on top, spreading evenly. Swirl through batter several times with a knife, then top with the remaining blueberries.

5. Bake until a toothpick inserted in the center comes out with moist crumbs clinging, 40 to 45 minutes. Cool in the pan on a wire rack for 15 minutes. Serve warm or at room temperature.

Personalize It!
Replace the blueberries with fresh raspberries or sliced strawberries. You can use orange zest instead of lemon zest. In that case, add 2 tablespoons fresh orange juice to the batter to enhance the citrus flavor.

GOLDEN ROLLS

SECRET INGREDIENT:
carrots

Everybody wonders how these rolls get their subtly sweet flavor and gorgeous golden color. Look no further than the humble carrot.

Prep Time: 30 min **Cook Time:** 30 min **Makes** 4 doz

4 cups sliced carrots

2 eggs, beaten

1 cup warm (110°-115°F), divided

2 packages (1/4 ounce each) active dry yeast

3/4 cup plus 1 teaspoon vegetable oil

1/2 cup sugar

1 tablespoon molasses

2 teaspoons salt

5 1/2 to 6 cups all-purpose flour

1. Place the carrots in a large saucepan and cover with water; cook until tender. Drain and place in a blender or food processor.

2. Add the eggs and 1/2 cup of the water and puree until smooth.

3. In a large bowl, dissolve the yeast in the remaining 1/2 cup water. Add the carrot mixture. Stir in 3/4 cup of the oil, the sugar, molasses, salt, and 5 cups of the flour. Beat until smooth. Add enough remaining flour to form a soft dough. Turn onto a floured

board and knead until smooth and elastic, 6 to 8 minutes.

4. Coat a large bowl with the remaining teaspoon of oil and add the dough, turning to coat. Cover the bowl and let rise in a warm place (85°F) free from drafts until the dough has doubled in bulk, about 1 hour.

5. Punch dough down. Shape into 48 balls. Place 2 inches apart on greased baking sheets. Cover the pans and let rise in a warm place (85°F) free from drafts until the dough has almost doubled in bulk, about 1 hour.

6. Preheat the oven to 350°F.

7. Bake until browned, 18 to 20 minutes. Serve warm.

that's **ingenious**

If you prefer not to chop 4 cups of carrots, buy pre-sliced carrots in the refrigerated produce section of your grocery store.

HOLIDAY CINNAMON ROLLS

SECRET INGREDIENT:
cranberries

Christmas morning will be sweeter than ever when you serve these festive cinnamon rolls topped with a rich and creamy frosting. The surprise ingredient: fresh cranberries for a burst of jolly red flavor.

Prep Time: 25 min **Cook Time:** 50 min **Serves** 15

ROLLS

1 1/4 cups sugar, divided

1/2 cup water

2 cups cranberries

1 teaspoon grated orange peel

2 packages (1/4 ounce each) active dry yeast

1/2 cup warm (110°-115°F) water

1/2 cup (1 stick) unsalted butter or margarine, softened

1/2 cup milk

2 eggs

1 teaspoon salt

1 teaspoon ground cinnamon

1/2 teaspoon ground nutmeg

4 1/2 to 5 cups all-purpose flour

1 teaspoon oil

Melted unsalted butter or margarine

FROSTING

1 cup confectioners' sugar

1 1/2 ounces cream cheese, softened

1/4 cup (1/2 stick) unsalted butter or margarine, softened

1/2 teaspoon vanilla extract

1/2 teaspoon milk

1. For rolls, in a medium saucepan, bring 3/4 cup sugar and the water to a boil. Add the cranberries and return to a boil. Boil, uncovered, for 20 minutes, stirring occasionally. Stir in the orange peel, remove from heat, and let cool. Cover and chill.

2. In a small bowl, dissolve the yeast in the water. Add the butter or margarine, milk, eggs, salt, cinnamon, nutmeg, the remaining sugar and 3 cups of the flour. Beat until smooth. Add enough remaining flour to form a soft dough.

3. Turn onto a floured surface; knead until smooth and elastic, 6 to 8 minutes. Coat a large bowl with the oil and add the dough, turning to coat. Cover the bowl and let rise in a warm place (85°F) free from drafts until the dough has doubled in bulk, about 1 hour.

4. Punch dough down. Roll into a 10 x 15-inch rectangle and brush with butter. Spread the cranberry filling over the dough to within 1 inch of the edges. Roll up, jelly-roll style, starting at a long side.

5. Cut into 15 slices. Place in a greased 9 x 13-inch baking pan. Cover and let rise until doubled, about 30 minutes.

6. Preheat the oven to 375°F.

7. Bake until golden brown , 25 to 30 minutes. Cool in the pan for 5 minutes, then remove to a wire rack.

8. Meanwhile, for frosting, in a small bowl, beat together the confectioners' sugar, cream cheese, butter or margarine, vanilla, and milk until smooth. Spread over the warm rolls.

One More Notch! For a dash of Christmas color, scatter red and green colored sugar over the white frosting on the rolls.

CARAMEL PECAN ROLLS

SECRET INGREDIENT:

cornmeal

There's nothing quite like a sweet roll redolent with cinnamon aromas. To give this version an even more pleasing texture, we added a bit of cornmeal to the dough. It's what sets these sweet rolls apart from any other we've tasted.

Prep Time: 30 min **Cook Time:** 25 min **Makes** 24

ROLLS

2 cups milk

1/2 cup water

1/2 cup sugar

1/2 cup (1 stick) unsalted butter or margarine

1/3 cup cornmeal

2 teaspoons salt

3 to 3 1/2 cups all-purpose flour, divided

2 packages (1/4 ounce each) active dry yeast

2 eggs

1 teaspoon oil

TOPPING

2 cups firmly packed brown sugar

1/2 cup (1 stick) unsalted butter or margarine

1/2 cup milk

1/2 to 1 cup chopped pecans

FILLING

1/4 cup (1/2 stick) unsalted butter or margarine, softened

1/2 cup sugar

2 teaspoons ground cinnamon

1. For rolls, combine the milk, water, sugar, butter or margarine, cornmeal, and salt in a medium saucepan. Bring to a boil, stirring frequently. Set aside to cool to 120° to 130°F.

2. In a large bowl, combine 2 cups of the flour and the yeast. Add the cooled cornmeal mixture and beat on low speed until smooth. Add the eggs and 1 cup of flour; mix for 1 minute. Stir in enough remaining flour to form a soft dough.

3. Turn onto a floured board; knead until smooth and elastic, 6 to 8 minutes.

4. Coat a large bowl with the oil and add the dough, turning to coat. Cover the bowl and let rise in a warm place (85°F) free from drafts until the dough has doubled in bulk, about 1 hour.

5. For topping, combine the brown sugar, butter or margarine, and milk in a small saucepan. Bring to a boil, stirring occasionally. Pour into two greased 9 x 13-inch baking pans. Sprinkle with the pecans and set aside.

6. Punch dough down and divide in half. Roll each into a 12 x 15-inch rectangle.

7. For filling, spread the dough with butter or margarine. Combine the sugar and cinnamon in a cup and sprinkle over the butter. Roll up the dough from one long side; pinch seams and turn ends under. Cut

each roll into 12 slices. Place the slices in each baking pan. Cover the pans and let rise in a warm place (85°F) free from drafts until the dough has nearly doubled in bulk, about 30 minutes.

8. Preheat the oven to 375°F.

9. Bake until golden brown, 20 to 25 minutes. Let cool for 1 minute, then invert onto a serving platter.

One More Notch! To pump up the flavor, toast the pecans in a dry skillet until fragrant, about 5 minutes. Let cool then add to the topping.

GARLIC BREAD MUFFINS

SECRET INGREDIENT:
grated Parmesan cheese

Typical garlic bread consists of garlic powder and butter or olive oil on toasted Italian bread. This recipe takes it a step further by incorporating fresh garlic into a muffin with bursts of flavor from grated Parmesan cheese, dried basil, and oregano. *See photograph on page 168.*

Prep Time: 15 min	**Cook Time:** 25 min	**Makes** 12

7 tablespoons olive oil, divided

1 cup finely chopped onion

5 garlic cloves, minced

2 cups all-purpose flour

2 teaspoons baking powder

1 teaspoon dried oregano

1 teaspoon dried basil

1/2 teaspoon salt

1 cup milk

1 egg

1/3 cup plus 2 tablespoons grated
    Parmesan cheese

1. Preheat the oven to 350°F. Line 12 muffin cups with aluminum or paper liners.

2. Heat 1 tablespoon of the oil in a medium nonstick skillet over medium-high heat. Add the onion and cook, stirring often, until they start to soften, 3 to 4 minutes.

3. Add the garlic and cook until the onions just begin to brown, 3 to 4 minutes longer. Remove from the heat and cool for 5 minutes.

4. In a large bowl, whisk together the flour, baking powder, oregano, basil, and salt.

5. In a medium bowl, whisk together the remaining 6 tablespoons of the oil, the cooled onion mixture, milk, egg, and 1/3 cup of the Parmesan. Add the milk mixture into the flour mixture and mix well. Spoon the batter into the muffin cups.

6. Sprinkle the remaining 2 tablespoons of the cheese evenly over the muffin batter.

7. Bake until a toothpick inserted into the center of a muffin comes out with a few moist crumbs, 16 to 17 minutes. If desired, broil the muffins for 30 seconds to brown the cheese. Transfer the muffins to a wire rack. Cool for 10 minutes before serving.

One More Notch! Really kick it up by adding 1/8 to 1/4 teaspoon crushed red-pepper flakes to the batter.

SOUTHWESTERN SAVORY MUFFINS

SECRET INGREDIENT:
bacon

Most muffins are sweet, but savory muffins are a revelation. With bacon, cheddar cheese, and chiles, these go perfectly with scrambled eggs—especially with a little salsa on the side!

Prep Time: 10 min   **Cook Time:** 20 min   **Makes** 14

10 bacon strips

2 cups all-purpose flour

1/4 cup sugar

1 tablespoon baking powder

3/4 cup milk

1 egg

1 1/2 cups shredded cheddar cheese
  (about 6 ounces)

1/4 cup diced canned green chiles

1. Preheat the oven to 400°F.

2. In a medium nonstick skillet, cook the bacon until crisp; reserve 1/3 cup of the drippings. Crumble the bacon and set aside.

3. In a large bowl, combine the flour, sugar, and baking powder. In a small bowl, beat the milk, egg, and reserved bacon drippings. Stir into the dry ingredients until just moistened. Fold in the cheese, chiles, and bacon. Fill greased or paper-lined muffin cups three-quarters full.

4. Bake until golden brown, 15 to 20 minutes. Serve warm.

that's **ingenious**

> To get two ingredients for the price of one, replace the cheddar and diced green chiles with Pepper Jack cheese.

SMOKY CORN MUFFINS

SECRET INGREDIENT:
ground chipotle chile pepper

It's hard to resist a warm corn muffin. Ground chipotle chile pepper, made from dried, smoked jalapeño peppers, gives these tasty muffins a touch of smoke and a hint of spice that helps to separate them from the rest. *See photograph on page 178.*

Prep Time: 10 min   **Cook Time:** 25 min   **Makes** 12

1 cup all-purpose flour

1 cup yellow cornmeal

6 tablespoons sugar

2 teaspoons baking powder

1 teaspoon salt

1/2 teaspoon ground chipotle chile pepper

2/3 cup milk

1/2 cup (1 stick) unsalted butter, melted

1 large egg

1. Preheat the oven to 375°F. Line 12 muffin cups with aluminum or paper liners.

2. In a medium bowl, whisk together the flour, cornmeal, sugar, baking powder, salt, and chile pepper.

3. In a small bowl, whisk together the milk, butter, and egg. Add the milk mixture to the flour mixture and mix well. Spoon the batter into the muffin cups.

4. Bake until golden and a toothpick inserted into the center of a muffin comes out with a few moist crumbs, 16 to 18 minutes. Transfer the muffins to a wire rack immediately and cool for 10 minutes before serving.

One More Notch! Give these south-of-the-border muffins even more of a Mexican flair by stirring 1/2 teaspoon ground cumin and 1/2 teaspoon dried oregano into the flour mixture.

LEMON POUND CAKE MUFFINS

SECRET INGREDIENT:
tea leaves

Tea bags are bundles of flavor in your cupboard. Here, tea imparts a distinctive flavor to muffins while giving them a unique look in the form of tea specks in the pale yellow crumb. *See photograph on page 164.*

Prep Time: 15 min   **Cook Time:** 15 min   **Makes** 12

MUFFINS

1/2 cup (1 stick) unsalted butter, softened

1 cup sugar

3 eggs, at room temperature

1 teaspoon lemon extract

2 teaspoons grated lemon peel

2 cups cake flour

2 English breakfast or Earl Grey tea bags, cut open

1 teaspoon baking soda

1/4 teaspoon salt

1/4 cup milk

GLAZE

1 cup confectioners' sugar

4 1/2 teaspoons lemon juice

1. Preheat the oven to 375°F. Line 12 muffin cups with aluminum or paper liners.

2. For muffins, combine the butter and sugar in a medium bowl and beat with an electric mixer on high speed until light and fluffy. Beat in the eggs one at a time, stopping to scrape down the sides of the bowl in between additions. Beat in the lemon extract and lemon peel.

3. In a large bowl, combine the flour, tea from the bags, baking soda, and salt; mix well. Decrease the speed to low and beat in the flour mixture alternately with the milk in two additions, until just moistened. Spoon the batter into the muffin cups.

4. Bake until a toothpick inserted into the center of a muffin comes out with a few moist crumbs, 15 to 17 minutes. Cool the muffins in the pan on a wire rack for 10 minutes. Remove the muffins from the pan and cool on the wire rack 5 minutes longer.

5. Meanwhile, for glaze, in a small bowl, stir together the confectioners' sugar and lemon juice. With a spoon, drizzle the glaze over the muffins, and let stand at least 5 minutes to allow the glaze to set before serving.

One More Notch! Add another layer of flavor by substituting orange juice for the lemon juice in the glaze, and add in 1/2 teaspoon grated orange peel.

ENLIGHTENED BLUEBERRY MUFFINS

SECRET INGREDIENT:
banana

The addition of mashed ripe banana gives these popular treats a hint of tropical flavor and a wonderfully moist texture. The banana also helps reduce the amount of oil usually used to make muffins, which is a nice health bonus. *See photograph on page 164.*

Prep Time: 15 min   **Cook Time:** 18 min   **Makes** 12

3/4 cup evaporated skim milk

3 tablespoons canola oil

1 large very ripe banana, mashed (about 2/3 cup)

1 large egg

1/2 cup plus 1 tablespoon sugar

1 teaspoon grated lemon peel

2 cups all-purpose flour

2 teaspoons baking powder

1/4 teaspoon salt

1 cup frozen blueberries

1. Preheat the oven to 400°F. Line 12 muffin cups with aluminum or paper liners.

2. In a medium bowl, whisk together the milk, oil, banana, egg, 1/2 cup of the sugar, and the lemon peel.

3. In a large bowl, whisk together the flour, baking powder, and salt. Add the milk mixture to the flour mixture and mix well. Fold in the blueberries. Spoon the batter into the muffin cups. Sprinkle the remaining 1 tablespoon sugar evenly over the muffin batter.

4. Bake until golden and a toothpick inserted into the center of a muffin comes out with a few moist crumbs, 18 to 20 minutes. Transfer the muffins to a wire rack immediately. Cool for 10 minutes before serving.

One More Notch! Like a little crunch to your muffins? Fold in 1/2 cup toasted chopped walnuts with the blueberries. For a little more flavor, you can also add 1 teaspoon chopped fresh thyme to the flour mixture.

CINNAMON STREUSEL-TOPPED MUFFINS

SECRET INGREDIENT:

applesauce

Everyone has a favorite apple muffin recipe, but this one is a lot less work. Applesauce lends both great taste and texture, and there is no peeling, coring, dicing, or shredding. *See photograph on page 164.*

Prep Time: 15 min   **Cook Time:** 16 min   **Makes** 12

MUFFINS

3/4 cup sweetened cinnamon applesauce

1 large egg

1/2 cup milk

3 tablespoons unsalted butter, melted

2 cups all-purpose flour

1/2 cup firmly packed light brown sugar

2 teaspoons baking powder

1/4 teaspoon salt

1/8 teaspoon ground nutmeg

STREUSEL

1/3 cup all-purpose flour

1/3 cup firmly packed light brown sugar

3 tablespoons unsalted butter, cut into small pieces

1. Preheat the oven to 400°F. Line 12 muffin cups with aluminum or paper liners.

2. For muffins, in a medium bowl, whisk together the applesauce, egg, milk, and butter.

3. In a large bowl, whisk together the flour, brown sugar, baking powder, salt, and nutmeg. Add the milk mixture into the flour mixture and mix well. Spoon the batter into the muffin cups.

4. For streusel, in a small bowl, combine the flour, brown sugar, and butter. Press the mixture together with your fingers until it holds together in clumps when pinched between your fingertips. Sprinkle the streusel over the muffin batter.

5. Bake until golden and a toothpick inserted into the center of a muffin comes out with a few moist crumbs, 16 to 18 minutes. Transfer the muffins to a wire rack immediately. Cool for 10 minutes before serving.

One More Notch! For a touch more apple flavor, substitute 1/4 cup apple cider for 1/4 cup of the milk.

CHOCOLATE CHERRY MUFFINS

SECRET INGREDIENT:
coffee

Coffee and chocolate are two bold flavors born to be married as one. Here, both brewed coffee and ground coffee amplify the rich aromas of the chocolate.

Prep Time: 15 min   **Cook Time:** 20 min   **Makes** 12

MUFFINS

2 cups all-purpose flour

1 cup firmly packed brown sugar

1/4 cup cocoa powder

2 tablespoons ground coffee

2 1/2 teaspoons baking powder

1/4 teaspoon salt

3/4 cup milk

1/2 cup canola oil

2 large eggs

1 teaspoon vanilla extract

3/4 cup semi-sweet chocolate chips

1/2 cup dried cherries

GLAZE

1 cup confectioners' sugar

1 tablespoon plus 2 teaspoons brewed coffee

1. Preheat the oven to 375°F. Line 12 muffin cups with aluminum or paper liners.

2. For muffins, in a medium bowl, whisk together the flour, brown sugar, cocoa powder, coffee, baking powder, and salt.

3. In a large bowl, whisk together the milk, oil, eggs, and vanilla. Add the milk mixture to the flour mixture and mix well. Fold in the chocolate chips and cherries. Spoon the batter into the muffin cups.

4. Bake until a toothpick inserted into the center of a muffin comes out with a few moist crumbs, 20 to 22 minutes. Transfer the muffins to a wire rack and cool for 10 minutes.

5. For glaze, combine the confectioners' sugar and coffee in a small bowl. Transfer the mixture into a small zip-close bag with the tip of one corner snipped off. Squeeze the glaze over the muffins while making a quick back-and-forth motion. Let stand for 10 minutes to allow the glaze to set before serving.

Personalize It!

If you would like a little more cherry flavor and less coffee flavor, make the glaze with milk instead of coffee, and stir in 1/4 teaspoon almond extract.

extraordinary
appetizers
and snacks

BEEF, SCALLION, AND ASPARAGUS ROLL-UPS

SECRET INGREDIENT:
teriyaki sauce

Fresh, light Asian flavors taste incredible paired with the bold flavor of beef. To keep this elegant appetizer simple to prepare, we use prepared teriyaki sauce. Chopped fresh cilantro and toasted sesame seeds add intoxicating aromas and crunch.

Prep Time: 15 min   **Cook Time:** 20 min   **Serves** 4

8 asparagus stalks, trimmed and cut into 3-inch lengths

8 thin slices (1/4 pound) sirloin steak

4 scallions, trimmed and cut into 3-inch lengths

2 teaspoons vegetable oil

3 tablespoons bottled teriyaki sauce

1 tablespoon toasted sesame seeds

1 tablespoon chopped cilantro

1. Bring a small saucepan of water to a boil. Blanch the asparagus in the water for 1 minute, then drain. Meanwhile, pound the steak slices to 1/8-inch thickness.

2. Place 2 pieces of asparagus and 1 piece of scallion near one end of a beef strip. Roll the beef around the vegetables. Repeat to form 8 bundles.

3. In a large nonstick skillet over medium-high heat, heat the oil. Add the beef rolls. Brown for 2 minutes, turning frequently. Add teriyaki sauce, lower the heat to medium, and simmer for 3 minutes.

4. Transfer the rolls to a serving platter. Sprinkle with the sesame seeds and cilantro.

Personalize It!
If you prefer, make this appetizer with sliced duck breast or pork loin. ❄

LAMB BURGERS WITH FRUIT RELISH

SECRET INGREDIENT:
carrot

Tired of plain old beef burgers? Ground lamb mixed with onions and grated carrots tastes anything but ordinary. An orange-raspberry relish stands in for ketchup and brightens the flavors even further. Serve with a green or mixed salad. *See photograph on page 167.*

Prep Time: 20 min   **Cook Time:** 10 min   **Serves** 4

BURGERS

1 pound lean ground lamb

1 carrot, peeled and grated

1 small onion, finely chopped

1/2 cup fresh whole-wheat bread crumbs

Pinch of freshly grated nutmeg

2 teaspoons fresh thyme leaves or 1 teaspoon dried thyme

Salt and freshly ground black pepper

1 large egg, beaten

2 teaspoons olive oil

4 whole-wheat English muffins

Shredded lettuce

RELISH

1 orange

1/2 cup fresh or thawed frozen raspberries

2 teaspoons sugar

1. Preheat a grill or oven broiler.

2. For burgers, put the lamb into a large bowl. Add the carrot, onion, bread crumbs, nutmeg, and thyme, and season with salt and pepper, to taste. Mix well.

3. Add the egg and use your hands to mix the ingredients together thoroughly.

4. Divide the mixture into 4 patties. Brush both sides of the burgers with oil, then put them in the grill pan. Cook for 4 to 5 minutes on each side, depending on thickness.

5. For relish, cut the peel and pith from the orange with a sharp knife, and, holding it over a medium bowl to catch the juice, cut between the membrane to release the segments. Roughly chop the segments and add them to the juice.

6. Add the raspberries and sugar, lightly crushing the fruit with a fork to mix it together.

7. Split the English muffins and toast lightly. Put a lamb burger on each muffin, then add some lettuce and a generous spoonful of relish. Serve with the remaining relish.

Personalize It!
Don't like lamb? Use ground turkey instead. Replace the nutmeg and thyme with the zest of 1 lemon and 1/4 cup chopped parsley; omit the bread crumbs. Use arugula instead of lettuce.

CHICKEN DUMPLINGS WITH SESAME DIPPING SAUCE

SECRET INGREDIENT:
canned water chestnuts

These tasty Asian-style packets are boiled, not fried, to keep them low-fat and low-calorie. Water chestnuts give the aromatic chicken filling some extra crunch.

Prep Time: 30 min   **Cook Time:** 15 min   **Serves** 12

DUMPLINGS
1/2 pound ground chicken

1/4 cup thinly sliced scallions

1/4 cup minced canned water chestnuts

1/4 cup chopped cilantro

4 teaspoons reduced-sodium soy sauce

1/2 teaspoon ground ginger

1/4 teaspoon freshly ground black pepper

24 wonton wrappers (3-inch square)

DIPPING SAUCE
1/4 cup low-sodium soy sauce

1 tablespoon sesame oil

2 teaspoons rice vinegar

1/2 teaspoon sugar

1/4 cup thinly sliced scallions

1. For dumplings, in a medium bowl, combine the chicken, scallions, water chestnuts, cilantro, soy sauce, ginger, and pepper. Mix well.

2. Work with several wonton wrappers at a time and keep the remainder loosely covered with a dampened cloth. To fill the wontons, place a generous teaspoonful of filling on the bottom half of each wrapper. With wet fingers or a pastry brush, moisten two edges of the wonton. Fold the two moistened sides over the filling to form a triangle and press to seal. Repeat with the remaining wonton wrappers and filling.

3. For dipping sauce, in a small bowl, whisk together the soy sauce, oil, vinegar, sugar, and scallions. Set aside.

4. Bring a large pot of water to a boil. Add the dumplings and cook until they float to the surface and the chicken is cooked through (filling will be firm to the touch), about 4 minutes. Drain. Serve with the dipping sauce.

Personalize It!
For vegetarian dumplings, replace the chicken with a mixture of shredded carrots, finely diced red peppers, and sautéed spinach leaves.

SHRIMP DUMPLINGS

turkey

Dumplings, neatly wrapped and stuffed until plump, make an ideal appetizer. Shrimp and mushrooms get a little extra body from ground turkey in this stuffing. Ginger-spiked, honey-sweetened soy sauce makes the perfect dip.

Prep Time: 20 min   **Cook Time:** 20 min   **Makes** 24

DUMPLINGS

4 large dried mushrooms, such as shiitake

3 scallions, cut into pieces

1/2 garlic clove

8 ounces shrimp, peeled and deveined

6 ounces ground turkey

2 teaspoons soy sauce

1 teaspoon dark sesame oil

3 dashes of hot red-pepper sauce

6 egg roll wrappers (6-inch square), each cut into 4 squares

DIPPING SAUCE

2 tablespoons soy sauce

2 teaspoons rice-wine vinegar

1/2 teaspoon honey

1/2 teaspoon dark sesame oil

1/2 teaspoon minced fresh ginger or 1/8 teaspoon ground ginger

1. Coat a steamer basket with nonstick cooking spray and set aside. In a small saucepan, soak the mushrooms in boiling water to cover for 15 minutes, then drain. Remove and discard the stems; cut the caps into quarters.

2. In a food processor, combine the mushroom caps, scallions, and garlic and whirl until coarsely chopped. Add the shrimp and whirl until finely chopped. Transfer to a medium bowl and stir in the turkey, soy sauce, oil, and red-pepper sauce.

3. Place 1 tablespoon of the shrimp mixture in the center of each egg roll wrapper square. Dampen the edges with water, then fold up the sides around the filling, pleating the edges. Place in the steamer basket, leaving 1/2 inch of space between the dumplings for the steam to circulate. Set over boiling water, cover, and steam for 15 minutes.

4. For the dipping sauce, in a small bowl, whisk together the soy sauce, vinegar, honey, oil, and ginger. Serve the dumplings hot with the dipping sauce.

Personalize It!

For a different flavor, use ground pork in place of the ground turkey. You can also drop a pinch of chopped scallions into the dipping sauce if you like. ❄

SWEET-AND-SOUR CHICKEN WINGS

maple syrup

Sweet and sour flavors typically come from sugar and vinegar, but this recipe gets a little more oomph from maple syrup. Grilling the wings adds a hint of smoke as well.

Prep Time: 20 min   **Cook Time:** 10 min   **Serves** 4

2 to 3 pounds whole chicken wings

1 cup maple syrup

2/3 cup chili sauce

1/2 cup finely chopped onion

2 tablespoons Dijon mustard

2 teaspoons Worcestershire sauce

1/4 to 1/2 teaspoon crushed red-pepper flakes

1. Cut the chicken wings into three sections, discarding the wing tips.

2. In a large zip-close plastic bag or shallow glass container, combine the syrup, chili sauce, onion, mustard, Worcestershire sauce, and red-pepper flakes. Reserve 1 cup for basting and refrigerate. Add the chicken to the remaining marinade and turn to coat. Seal the bag or cover container. Refrigerate for 4 hours, turning occasionally.

3. Drain and discard the marinade. Grill the chicken, covered, over medium heat for 12 to 16 minutes, turning occasionally. Brush with the reserved marinade. Grill, uncovered, for 8 to 10 minutes, or until the juices run clear, basting and turning several times.

Personalize It!

If you prefer, bake the wings in a 375°F oven for 30 to 40 minutes, or until the juices run clear, basting and turning several times. ❄

CHICKEN LIVERS WITH GRAPES

SECRET INGREDIENT:
juniper berries

Chicken livers and grapes make a fabulous combination. But when you pair them with juniper—the characteristic flavor of gin—the combo jumps to a whole new level. Look for juniper berries in the spice aisle of health food stores and well-stocked supermarkets.

Prep Time: 10 min   **Cook Time:** 10 min   **Serves** 4

1 tablespoon olive oil

1 pound fresh chicken livers, cut into bite-size pieces

1 shallot, finely chopped

1 garlic clove, crushed

10 juniper berries, lightly crushed

2 tablespoons fresh thyme

Freshly ground black pepper

2 tablespoons dry sherry

6 ounces small, seedless, green and red grapes

Salt

2 large, thick slices white country-style bread

2 tablespoons chopped flat-leaved parsley

1. Heat the oil in a large, heavy skillet. When the pan is very hot, add the chicken livers and toss quickly to sear the surfaces. Cook over high heat, stirring, for 2 minutes.

2. Add the shallot, garlic, juniper berries, thyme, and pepper, to taste, to the pan, then lower the heat and continue cooking for another 3 to 4 minutes, stirring to prevent burning.

3. Add the sherry and grapes to the pan and add salt, to taste. Cook the chicken livers for another minute, then turn off the heat, cover, and keep warm.

4. Toast the bread and cut each slice into four triangles. Spoon the chicken livers onto individual serving plates, sprinkle with the chopped parsley and serve accompanied with the toast.

One More Notch! To turn this appetizer into a fast pasta sauce, add 3/4 cup light whipping cream or buttermilk with the sherry.

HEAVENLY DEVILED EGGS

SECRET INGREDIENT:

sour cream

A low-cholesterol deviled egg? Yes, indeed! Filled with a delicious blend of egg yolks, vegetables, and spices, these are lighter than traditional deviled eggs (thanks to nonfat sour cream), yet have a richer flavor. *See photograph on page 172.*

Prep Time: 20 min   **Cook Time:** 15 min   **Serves** 10

12 large eggs

3/4 cup nonfat sour cream

2 scallions, finely chopped

1/3 cup finely chopped seeded green bell pepper

1/3 cup finely chopped seeded red bell pepper

2 teaspoons Dijon mustard

Salt

3 tablespoons finely chopped parsley

Paprika

1. In a large saucepan, add the eggs and enough cold water to cover them. Bring the water to a full boil. Remove from the heat, cover, and let stand for 15 minutes. Drain the eggs and rinse under cold water to cool them. Peel the eggs, then cut in half lengthwise and remove the yolks. Discard 8 yolks or reserve them for another use.

2. Arrange 20 egg white halves on a platter. In a medium bowl, chop the remaining 4 egg white halves very finely. Mash in the 4 yolks with a fork. Stir in the sour cream, scallions, peppers, mustard, and salt, to taste.

3. Pipe or spoon the egg mixture into the egg white halves. Sprinkle with parsley and dust with paprika.

One More Notch! Make these eggs spicy! Add 1/2 teaspoon chili powder or 1/4 teaspoon cayenne pepper to the egg mixture. Or substitute a seeded, deveined, very finely minced jalapeño pepper (wear gloves when handling) for the green bell pepper.

BRANDIED CHESTNUT AND MUSHROOM TERRINE

SECRET INGREDIENT:

orange juice

Here's an impressive dish for an autumn feast that takes very little effort to prepare. It is rich with the flavors of mushroom and chestnut, while orange juice gives it a welcome spark of freshness. *See photograph on page 182.*

Prep Time: 20 min   **Cook Time:** 55 min   **Serves** 8

1 tablespoon olive oil

2 to 4 garlic cloves, crushed

6 ounces mushrooms, sliced

1 1/2 cups (about 6 ounces) thinly sliced red onions

6 tablespoons grape brandy

8 vacuum-packed or canned unsweetened, whole chestnuts

1 egg, beaten

4 ounces fresh bread crumbs

14 ounces canned unsweetened chestnut puree

Grated zest plus juice of 1 orange

1 tablespoon chopped fresh parsley

1 tablespoon fresh thyme

Salt and freshly ground black pepper

Chopped fresh basil

Mixed salad leaves

1. Preheat the oven to 350°F. Lightly grease an 8 x 4-inch loaf pan.

2. Heat the oil in a large saucepan over medium heat and gently sauté the garlic, mushrooms, and onions until they are tender and lightly browned, stirring frequently, 7 to 8 minutes.

3. Add the brandy to the pan and allow it to simmer until reduced, 1 to 2 minutes, then remove the pan from the heat and let the mixture cool for about 3 minutes.

4. Break the chestnuts into pieces and stir them into the mushroom mixture with the egg, bread crumbs, chestnut puree, orange zest and juice, parsley, thyme, and salt and pepper, to taste, using a wooden spoon to break up the chestnut puree.

5. When the mixture is thoroughly combined, spoon it into the loaf pan, smooth the top, and bake it until the top is browned, about 45 minutes.

6. Remove the terrine from the oven and let it cool in the pan, then turn out onto a plate and cut it into neat slices. Sprinkle with a little basil and serve it with the salad leaves.

that's ingenious

Look for canned chestnut puree in supermarkets in the fall. But if you can't find it, make your own at home. Soak 1 2/3 cups vacuum-packed or canned unsweetened whole peeled chestnuts in a small saucepan and add milk or water to cover. Simmer over low heat until very tender, about 1 hour. Add more milk or water as necessary to keep the chestnuts covered. Puree in a blender until smooth.

FISH TERRINE

SECRET INGREDIENT:
buttermilk

Make this terrine to start an alfresco summer dinner. A puree of buttermilk and cooked potato gives it rich texture and down-to-earth flavor that perfectly complements the lightness of the fish.

Prep Time: 20 min　**Cook Time:** 40 min　**Serves** 6

1 all-purpose potato, peeled and cubed

3 garlic cloves

5 large scallions, trimmed

1 small carrot, peeled and cut into matchstick strips

1 1/4 pounds scrod fillets, cut into chunks

1 large egg

1 large egg white

3/4 teaspoon salt

1/8 teaspoon cayenne pepper

3/4 cup buttermilk

1 small seeded roasted red bell pepper, cut into strips

Lemon quarters

1. In a large saucepan of lightly salted boiling water, cook the potato and garlic for 8 minutes. Place a colander over the pan, lay the scallions and carrots in the colander, cover, and steam until the vegetables are tender and the potato is cooked through, about 5 minutes. Drain well.

2. Preheat the oven to 375°F.

3. Line an 8 x 4-inch loaf pan with plastic wrap, extending it up and over the long sides so that it overhangs 3 inches on each side. Set aside.

4. In a food processor, puree the fish, until it is smooth, scraping down the sides occasionally. Add the potato and garlic mixture and puree until no lumps remain. Add the egg,

egg white, salt, cayenne, and buttermilk and whirl until well-combined.

5. Spread 1 cup of the fish mixture in the prepared pan. Lay the carrot strips in 4 rows down the length of the pan. Spread another cup of the mixture over the carrots and lay the scallions down the length of the pan. Spread another cup of the mixture over the scallions and lay the pepper strips down the length of the pan in 4 rows. Spread the last cup of the mixture over the pepper strips and smooth the top. Fold the plastic wrap over the fish, then cover with foil.

6. Set the pan in a larger pan and pour enough hot water in the larger pan to come halfway up the sides of the loaf pan. Bake until set, about 1 hour 10 minutes. Remove the loaf pan from the water and let cool to room temperature. Remove the foil and peel the plastic wrap off the top of the terrine. Invert onto a serving platter and discard any liquid. Remove the plastic wrap. Chill. Slice and serve cold with lemon quarters.

Personalize It!

If scrod isn't your favorite fish or it isn't fresh at the market, use haddock, orange roughy, or tilapia instead. ✳

PAN-SEARED SHRIMP COCKTAIL WITH PINEAPPLE RELISH

SECRET INGREDIENT:
hibiscus herb tea

Fruit salsas and relishes make a terrific accompaniment to shrimp. Here, a unique syrup made with hibiscus tea infuses the shrimp with a subtle floral aroma and gives it a stunning scarlet color.

Prep Time: 15 min	Cook Time: 20 min	Serves 4

3 hibiscus or rosehip and hibiscus tea bags

1 1/2 cups boiling water

1 1/2 cups very finely chopped fresh pineapple cubes

1/2 Gala apple, peeled and very finely chopped

1/3 cup sugar

2 tablespoons finely chopped shallots

1/2 teaspoon plus 1/8 teaspoon salt

32 extra-large peeled and deveined shrimp

3 tablespoons olive oil

1. Place the tea bags in a 2-cup liquid measure and add the water. Let steep 10 minutes.

2. Meanwhile, combine the pineapple and apple in a wire mesh sieve and strain for 10 minutes.

3. Remove the tea bags and pour the tea into a small saucepan. Stir in the sugar and bring to a boil, stirring until the sugar dissolves. Continue boiling until the mixture becomes a syrup, 12 to 15 minutes. Remove from the heat and let cool for 5 minutes.

4. Combine the pineapple mixture, shallots, 1/8 teaspoon of the salt and the syrup in a medium bowl. Mix well.

5. Sprinkle the shrimp with the remaining 1/2 teaspoon salt. Heat 1 1/2 tablespoons of the oil in a large nonstick skillet over medium-high heat. Add half of the shrimp and cook, turning once, until cooked through, about 2 minutes per side. Transfer to a plate and repeat with the remaining oil and shrimp.

6. To serve, spoon 1/4 cup of the relish into each of four martini glasses. Hang 8 shrimp on the rim of each and serve.

One More Notch! To really spark the flavor, try tossing the shrimp with 1 to 2 teaspoons of a jerk seasoning rub. The added heat works well with the sweet fruit relish.

GINGERED CRAB PHYLLO DUMPLINGS

SECRET INGREDIENT:
canned water chestnuts

Canned water chestnuts usually turn up in stir-fries and salads. Here, they lend fantastic crunch to phyllo-wrapped pastries. You can prepare and refrigerate these up to 8 hours before serving; just add a few minutes to the cooking time. *See photograph on page 167.*

Prep Time: 30 min   **Cook Time:** 15 min   **Makes** 18

1 can (7 ounces) white crabmeat

1 can (4 ounces) water chestnuts, drained and coarsely chopped

1 1/2 cups frozen corn, thawed

4 scallions, chopped

1 tablespoon finely chopped fresh ginger

1 fresh red chile pepper, seeded, deveined, and finely chopped (wear gloves when handling)

2 tablespoons Chinese cooking wine or dry sherry

Salt and freshly ground black pepper

2 tablespoons canola oil

1 tablespoon toasted sesame oil

6 sheets phyllo pastry (20 x 12 inches)

1 tablespoon sesame seeds

Bottled chili sauce, preferably Thai-style

Scallions

1. Preheat the oven to 400°F.

2. Combine the crabmeat, water chestnuts, corn, chopped scallions, ginger, chile pepper, and wine or sherry in a large bowl. Season lightly with salt and pepper. Mix the canola and sesame oils in a cup.

3. Stack and roll up the sheets of phyllo pastry loosely, starting from a short side. Using a sharp knife, cut the roll crosswise into 3 equal pieces. Unravel a roll, remove 1 of the strips, and set the rest aside, covered with plastic wrap.

4. Lay the strip of phyllo flat on the work surface, with a short end nearest to you, and brush with a little of the oil mixture. Place a heaping teaspoon of the crab mixture near the bottom, toward the right-hand corner of the short end, and fold the pastry diagonally over it. Continue folding diagonally, over and over, until you reach the end of the strip, making a neat triangular parcel. Place on a baking sheet, seam side down.

5. Repeat with remaining strips of phyllo, uncovering them only when needed, until all of the crab mixture is used.

6. Lightly brush the tops of the dumplings with any remaining oil mixture and sprinkle with the sesame seeds. Bake until crisp and golden, 12 to 13 minutes.

7. Transfer the dumplings to a wire rack and cool slightly. Meanwhile, shred the tops of the scallions to form "brushes." Serve the dumplings warm, on a tray along with the scallion brushes and a little dish of chili sauce for dipping.

Personalize It!

For shrimp phyllo dumplings, use cooked, peeled, deveined, and chopped shrimp in place of the crabmeat. ❊

BAKED SPINACH-STUFFED CLAMS

SECRET INGREDIENT:
half-and-half

Don't save these stuffed clams for a special occasion. They require only 15 minutes of work but make a striking presentation topped with crisp bread crumbs and filled with a delicious spinach mixture.

Prep Time: 15 min   **Cook Time:** 25 min   **Serves** 4

12 cherrystone or other hardshell clams

4 teaspoons unsalted butter, melted, divided

1/4 cup finely chopped onion

2 garlic cloves, minced

4 teaspoons flour

2/3 cup half-and-half

1/8 teaspoon cayenne pepper

Salt

1/3 cup frozen chopped spinach, well-drained

1/3 cup fresh bread crumbs

4 teaspoons grated Parmesan cheese

1. Place the clams in a large skillet with 1/2 inch of water. Bring to a boil, cover, and cook just until the clams open, about 4 minutes. (Start checking after 2 minutes and remove clams as they open; discard any that do not open.) Transfer the clams to a large bowl. When they are cool enough to handle, remove the top shell halves and discard them. Place the bottom shell halves with clams attached on a baking sheet.

2. Preheat the oven to 450°F.

3. In a small saucepan, heat 2 teaspoons of the butter over low heat. Add the onion and garlic, and sauté until soft, about 5 minutes. Whisk in the flour and cook for 1 minute. Whisk in the half-and-half, cayenne, and salt, to taste, and cook until the mixture is lightly thickened, about 3 minutes. Stir in the spinach. Spoon the mixture over clams.

4. In a small bowl, toss together the bread crumbs and Parmesan. Top the clams with the bread crumb mixture and drizzle with the remaining 2 teaspoons of the butter. Bake just until clams are bubbly and hot, about 5 minutes.

Personalize It!

If you're watching calories, use fat-free half-and-half and use olive oil instead of butter. ❊

POTATO AND ZUCCHINI TORTILLA

SECRET INGREDIENT:
bacon

Spain's most famous *tapa,* or snack, is made from the simplest of ingredients—eggs, onions, and potatoes—cooked like a flat omelet and served warm or cold. All kinds of extra ingredients can be added. Bacon and zucchini give ours a just-right balance of sweet and savory tastes.

Prep Time: 15 min   **Cook Time:** 15 min   **Serves** 8

1 1/2 pounds new potatoes, peeled and cut into 1/2-inch cubes

2 tablespoons olive oil

1 red onion, finely chopped

1 zucchini, diced

2 slices uncooked bacon, chopped

6 eggs

1 tablespoon cold water

2 tablespoons chopped fresh parsley

Freshly ground black pepper

1. Place the potatoes in a saucepan and add enough water to cover. Bring to a boil, then lower the heat slightly and cook for 3 minutes. Drain completely.

2. Heat the oil in a heavy 10-inch nonstick skillet. Add the potatoes, onion, zucchini, and bacon, and cook over medium heat until the potatoes are tender and lightly golden, about 10 minutes, turning and stirring occasionally.

3. Preheat the broiler to high. In a small bowl, beat the eggs with the water. Add the parsley and pepper, to taste. Pour the egg mixture over the vegetables in the skillet and cook until the egg has set, 3 to 4 minutes, lifting the edges to allow the uncooked egg mixture to run onto the pan.

4. When there is just a little uncooked egg on the top, place the pan under the broiler and cook for 2 minutes to set the top. Slide the egg out onto a plate or board and allow to cool for 2 to 3 minutes. Cut into small wedges and serve warm, or leave to cool completely before cutting and serving.

NACHOS GRANDE

SECRET INGREDIENT:

diced fresh pineapple

Put out a plate of nachos and they'll disappear in no time. Here's a plate of nachos that's anything but ordinary. Fresh pineapple complements the creamy avocado and creates a spicy-sweet flavor to contrast the jalapeño peppers. *See photograph on page 166.*

| **Prep Time:** 10 min | **Cook Time:** 10 min | **Serves** 6 |

1 can (16 ounces) refried beans

1 bag (10 ounces) restaurant-style tortilla chips

1/4 cup drained sliced pickled jalapeño peppers

3 cups shredded Monterey Jack cheese

1 1/2 cups diced fresh pineapple

1 Haas avocado, peeled, pitted, and diced into 1/4-inch pieces

1/2 cup sour cream

1. Preheat the oven to 425°F. Coat a large baking sheet with cooking spray.

2. Heat the beans according to package directions.

3. Arrange the tortilla chips on the baking sheet and top with the warmed beans, jalapeños, cheese, and pineapple. Bake until the cheese melts, 4 to 5 minutes. Remove from the oven and slide the mixture onto a large serving platter. Top with the avocado and sour cream. Serve immediately.

Personalize It!

Instead of refried beans, try substituting 1 1/2 cups of your favorite chili (drain to remove excess moisture). Try mango instead of the pineapple.

EASY JALAPEÑO POPPERS

SECRET INGREDIENT:

bacon

Most jalapeño poppers are battered and deep-fried. Our version skips all that. Instead, we wrap the chiles in bacon for extra flavor and bake them until the bacon is crisp. These poppers are so easy—and so good—they can be habit-forming! *See photograph on page 167.*

| **Prep Time:** 10 min | **Cook Time:** 25 min | **Makes** 20 |

10 jalapeño peppers, seeded, deveined, and halved lengthwise (wear gloves when handling)

4 ounces cream cheese, softened

10 uncooked bacon strips, cut in half

1. Preheat the oven to 350°F.

2. Stuff each jalapeño half with about 2 teaspoons of cream cheese. Wrap with bacon and secure with a toothpick.

3. Place on a broiler rack that has been coated with nonstick cooking spray. Bake until the bacon is crisp, 20 to 25 minutes. Remove the toothpicks and serve immediately.

One More Notch! Mix some chopped fresh cilantro and lime zest into the cream cheese before stuffing the peppers.

BARBECUED NUTBALLS

SECRET INGREDIENT:
Worcestershire sauce

Worcestershire sauce is the secret ingredient of many of the best barbecue sauces. Here, it is used in both the sauce and the cheeseballs for lots of smoky flavor. This is the perfect pass-around appetizer for parties.

Prep Time: 15 min   **Cook Time:** 1 hr   **Makes** 5 1/2 doz

NUTBALLS

2 cups crushed butter-flavored crackers, such as Ritz

1 cup finely shredded cheddar cheese (about 4 ounces)

1 cup ground pecans

1/2 cup finely chopped onion

2 tablespoons wheat germ

6 eggs

1 tablespoon Worcestershire sauce

1 1/2 teaspoons dark brown sugar

SAUCE

1/4 cup water

1 cup ketchup

2 tablespoons dark brown sugar

2 tablespoons molasses

2 tablespoons Worcestershire sauce

1 tablespoon finely chopped onion

1 teaspoon salt

1/4 teaspoon freshly ground black pepper

1. Preheat the oven to 350°F.

2. For nutballs, in a large bowl, combine the crackers, cheese, pecans, onion, and wheat germ.

3. In a small bowl, whisk the eggs, Worcestershire sauce, and brown sugar. Add to the cracker mixture. Shape into 1-inch balls. Place in a greased 9 x 13-inch baking dish.

4. For sauce, in a medium bowl, combine the water, ketchup, brown sugar, molasses, Worcestershire sauce, onion, salt, and pepper. Pour over the nutballs. Cover and bake for 1 hour (do not stir). Serve warm with toothpicks.

that's **ingenious**

To save time, use 1 1/2 cups of your favorite bottled barbecue sauce in place of the sauce given here. If your barbecue sauce doesn't already include Worcestershire sauce, stir in a tablespoon or two for extra flavor.

PROSCIUTTO-WRAPPED DATES

SECRET INGREDIENT:
hot Italian sausage

Prosciutto-wrapped dates are a classic party appetizer in Italy. They are easy to make, and many versions are stuffed with almonds. We kick up the flavor by stuffing the dates with hot Italian sausage and a little cream cheese. Yum!

Prep Time: 20 min   **Cook Time:** 15 min   **Serves** 8

4 ounces hot Italian sausage, casing removed, if necessary

2 tablespoons cream cheese, softened

32 pitted dates

8 thin slices (about 1/4 pound) prosciutto, each cut into 4 lengthwise strips

1. Preheat the oven to 425°F. Coat a baking sheet with cooking spray.

2. Heat a small nonstick skillet over medium-high heat. Crumble the sausage into the pan and cook, breaking into smaller pieces with a wooden spoon, until browned, 3 to 4 minutes. Transfer to a medium bowl and cool 5 minutes. Stir in the cream cheese.

3. Meanwhile, use a small knife to cut a lengthwise slit in each date so that each will open like a book. Slightly overfill each date with some of the sausage mixture. Roll each date in 1 strip of prosciutto and set on the prepared baking sheet. Repeat to form 32 rolls.

4. Bake until hot and the prosciutto just barely begins to crisp, about 5 minutes. Serve immediately.

BACON-CHEDDAR TOASTS

SECRET INGREDIENT:
almonds

These American-style bruschetta (savory toasts) feature a creamy rich topping made with cheddar cheese, bacon, and mayonnaise. Almonds add crunch and nutty flavor. Serve as a snack or alongside a soup or light entrée. *See photograph on page 167.*

Prep Time: 10 min **Cook Time:** 10 min **Makes** 4 doz

1 cup mayonnaise

2 teaspoons Worcestershire sauce

1 cup shredded sharp cheddar cheese (about 4 ounces)

1 onion, chopped

3/4 cup slivered almonds, chopped

6 bacon strips, cooked and crumbled

1 loaf (about 1 pound) French bread

1. Preheat the oven to 400°F. In a medium bowl, combine the mayonnaise and

Worcestershire sauce. Stir in the cheese, onion, almonds, and bacon.

2. Cut the bread into 1/2-inch slices, then spread with the cheese mixture. Cut the slices in half and place on a greased baking sheet. Bake until bubbly, 8 to 10 minutes.

that's **ingenious**

> Keep these snacks in the freezer for unexpected company or snack attacks. Freeze the toasts directly on the baking sheet until solid, about 1 hour. Transfer them to an airtight container and freeze for up to 2 months. To serve, place the frozen appetizers on a greased baking sheet and bake until bubbly, 10 to 12 minutes.

GRILLED CHEESE WITH BACON

SECRET INGREDIENT:
apple

Here's a nice change of pace from traditional grilled cheese sandwiches. The bacon complements the cheese, of course, and sliced apple ties together the savory flavors with a touch of sweetness.

Prep Time: 10 min **Cook Time:** 5 min **Serves** 6

6 thick slices sourdough, white, or French bread

2 tablespoons mayonnaise

6 slices (about 6 ounces) cheddar cheese

1 tart apple, peeled, cored and cut crosswise into 6 rings

1 tablespoon brown sugar

12 bacon strips, cooked and drained

1. Under a broiler, toast one side of each slice of bread. Spread the untoasted side with mayonnaise. Top with the cheese and an apple ring, then sprinkle with brown sugar.

2. Crisscross 2 strips of bacon over each. Broil 6 inches from the heat until the cheese melts, 2 to 3 minutes.

that's **ingenious**

To save a little cooking time, use pre-cooked, ready-to-eat bacon, which is available near the regular bacon in most grocery stores.

FALAFEL PITAS

SECRET INGREDIENT:

carrot

Falafel, traditional Middle Eastern bean patties, are usually deep-fried. Our version, delicately spiced and crunchy with grated carrot, is baked for a lower-fat result, but is just as delicious. *See photograph on page 167.*

Prep Time: 15 min   **Cook Time:** 20 min   **Serves** 4

PITAS

1 can (15 ounces) chickpeas, drained and rinsed

1 teaspoon olive oil

1/2 teaspoon ground cumin

Pinch of cayenne pepper

Pinch of turmeric

1 garlic clove, crushed

1 tablespoon fresh lemon juice

1 carrot, finely grated

1 tablespoon chopped fresh cilantro

Salt and freshly ground black pepper

4 large pita breads

1 heart of romaine lettuce, shredded

2 plum tomatoes, thinly sliced

DIPPING SAUCE

1/2 cup plain low-fat yogurt

2 tablespoons chopped fresh mint

Salt and freshly ground black pepper

1. Preheat the oven to 400°F. Line a baking sheet with parchment paper.

2. For pitas, put the chickpeas in a medium bowl with the oil and use a potato masher to mash them until smooth. Mix in the cumin, cayenne, turmeric, garlic, lemon juice, carrot, cilantro, and salt and pepper, to taste. Alternatively, mix the chickpeas, oil, cumin, cayenne, turmeric, garlic, lemon juice, and salt and pepper, to taste, in a food processor. Transfer the mixture to a large bowl, then stir in the carrot and cilantro.

3. Shape the mixture into 16 flat, round patties, each about 1 1/4 inches across, and place them on the baking sheet. Bake until crisp and lightly browned, 15 to 20 minutes, turning them over halfway through the cooking time.

4. About 3 minutes before the falafel have finished cooking, put the pita breads in the oven to warm. Then split the breads in half widthwise and gently open out each half to make a pocket.

5. Half-fill the pita bread pockets with the lettuce and tomatoes, then divide the falafel among them.

6. For the dipping sauce, in a small bowl, mix together the yogurt and mint, season with salt and pepper, to taste, and drizzle over the falafel. Serve hot.

that's **ingenious**

Need a great veggie appetizer for the party? Serve the falafel patties without the pita bread. Use toothpicks for dipping in the yogurt-mint sauce.

BLACK BEAN AND AVOCADO QUESADILLAS

SECRET INGREDIENT:
feta cheese

Black beans and avocado are a natural in quesadillas. The secret to sparking up the flavor here is feta cheese. Serve these as an afternoon snack or cut into small wedges on an appetizer tray.

Prep Time: 15 min **Cook Time:** 10 min **Serves** 4

1 can (15 ounces) black beans, drained and rinsed

3/4 teaspoon ground cumin

1/2 teaspoon chili powder

1 tablespoon lime juice

1/2 Haas avocado, peeled, pitted, and diced

1/3 cup diced red onion

1 can (8 1/2 ounces) yellow corn kernels, drained

1/2 cup shredded Monterey Jack cheese

8 flour tortillas (8-inch)

4 ounces crumbled feta cheese

1. Preheat the oven to 200°F.

2. Combine the beans, cumin, chili powder, and lime juice in the bowl of a food processor. Pulse the mixture to form a chunky puree. Transfer to a medium bowl and stir in the avocado, onion, corn, and Monterey Jack cheese.

3. Spread 4 tortillas with one-quarter of the bean mixture. Sprinkle each with 1 ounce of the feta cheese, then place a second tortilla on top of each pressing down to flatten slightly.

4. Heat a large nonstick skillet over medium heat. Place a quesadilla in the skillet and cook until golden, 2 to 3 minutes per side. Transfer to a cutting board and cut each into 4 wedges. Keep warm on a baking sheet in the oven and repeat with the remaining 3 quesadillas.

One More Notch! Give this easy appetizer a shot of heat by adding some sliced pickled jalapeño peppers. For a more herby aroma, stir in 2 tablespoons chopped cilantro.

PACIFIC CHICKEN PIZZETTAS

SECRET INGREDIENT:
peanut butter

Could there be yet another variation on pizza? Absolutely! Here, tortillas are the flatbread, peanut sauce stands in for traditional tomato sauce, the cheese is Monterey Jack, and the topping is ginger-spiked sautéed chicken. It's a fun combination you won't soon forget!

Prep Time: 15 min **Cook Time:** 20 min **Serves** 2

1/2 cup rice vinegar

2 1/2 tablespoons light brown sugar

2 tablespoons peanut butter

1 tablespoon soy sauce

5 teaspoons canola oil, divided

1 1/2 teaspoons peeled grated fresh ginger

1 garlic clove, minced

1 tablespoon chopped fresh cilantro

8 ounces boneless, skinless chicken breast halves, cut crosswise into 1/4-inch-thick strips

2 flour tortillas (8-inch)

1 cup shredded Monterey Jack cheese

1. Preheat the oven to 425°F. Coat a baking sheet with cooking spray.

2. Combine the vinegar, brown sugar, peanut butter, and soy sauce in a small bowl. Heat 2 teaspoons of the oil in a medium saucepan over medium-high heat; add the ginger and garlic and cook until fragrant, about 15 seconds. Add the vinegar mixture and bring to a boil. Cook until the mixture is thick, 5 to 6 minutes. Remove from the heat and stir in the cilantro.

3. Heat the remaining 1 tablespoon oil in a large nonstick skillet over medium-high heat. Add the chicken and cook until lightly browned, about 1 1/2 minutes per side. Transfer to the saucepan with the vinegar mixture.

4. Place the tortillas on the baking sheet and bake until lightly toasted, about 5 minutes. Remove from the oven and sprinkle each with 1/2 cup of the cheese. Top each with half of the chicken mixture. Bake until hot and the tortillas are crisp, about 7 minutes. Cut into wedges and serve immediately.

One More Notch! To put the final touches to this dish, sprinkle the top with a couple tablespoons of chopped hot-spiced peanuts. Look for them in the snack aisle of your grocery store.

PARTY PINWHEELS THREE WAYS

SECRET INGREDIENT:
pickles

Actually, each of these pinwheels has a secret ingredient. Pickles add lively flavor to the ham wrap; olives add surprise to the turkey wrap; and barbecue sauce blended with cream cheese gives full flavor to the beef wrap. You can make these ahead and freeze them. Just thaw for 10 minutes before slicing and serving.

Prep Time: 20 min   **Cook Time:** 0 min   **Makes** 50

6 packages (8 ounces each) cream cheese, softened, divided

2 jars (5 3/4 ounces each) stuffed olives, drained and finely chopped

12 flour tortillas (10-inch), divided

1 package (6 ounces) thinly sliced cooked turkey

1 cup finely chopped dill pickles

2 tablespoons Dijon mustard

1 package (6 ounces) thinly sliced fully cooked ham

3/4 cup finely chopped celery

1/2 cup hickory-flavored barbecue sauce

1 package (6 ounces) thinly sliced cooked roast beef

1. In a medium bowl or food processor, beat 2 packages of cream cheese until smooth. Add the olives and mix well.

2. Spread about 3/4 cup each on 4 tortillas; top with 4 slices of turkey. Roll up tightly; wrap in plastic.

3. Beat 2 packages of cream cheese with the pickles and mustard. Spread about 3/4 cup each on 4 tortillas; top with 4 slices of ham. Roll up tightly; wrap in plastic.

4 Beat the remaining 2 packages of cream cheese with the celery and barbecue sauce. Spread about 3/4 cup each on the remaining 4 tortillas; top with 4 slices of beef. Roll up tightly; wrap in plastic.

5. Refrigerate the wraps at least 2 hours. Slice into 1/2-inch pieces and serve.

One More Notch! For more flavor and a colorful presentation, use a different flavored tortilla wrap for each type of pinwheel. Try spinach tortillas with the turkey wrap, regular wheat tortillas with the ham wrap, and sun-dried tomato tortillas with the roast beef wrap.

extraordinary
salads and
dressings

COBB SALAD WITH WARM BACON DRESSING

SECRET INGREDIENT:
maple syrup

Usually found atop a stack of pancakes, maple syrup works wonders in savory recipes as well. When mixed into a salad dressing, the syrup imparts a subtle sweetness and irresistible aromas than meld perfectly with crisped bacon. *See photograph on page 168.*

Prep Time: 10 min **Cook Time:** 10 min **Serves** 2

SALAD

5 thick slices bacon

4 cups chopped romaine lettuce

1 1/2 cups cubed cooked chicken or turkey

1 cup chopped tomato

1/2 cup chopped Haas avocado

2 hard-cooked eggs, chopped

1/4 cup crumbled blue cheese

DRESSING

2 tablespoons red-wine vinegar

1 tablespoon maple syrup

2 teaspoons Dijon mustard

1/2 teaspoon salt

1/4 teaspoon freshly ground black pepper

1 tablespoon extra-virgin olive oil

1. For salad, heat a medium nonstick skillet over medium-high heat and add the bacon. Cook, turning once, until crisp, 4 to 5 minutes per side. Transfer the bacon to a paper towel–lined plate to cool, then crumble. Reserve 3 tablespoons of the bacon fat and keep warm in the skillet.

2. In a large bowl, gently combine the lettuce, chicken or turkey, bacon, tomato, avocado, eggs, and blue cheese.

3. For dressing, in a small bowl, whisk together the vinegar, syrup, mustard, salt, and pepper. Slowly whisk in the oil, then Pour the mixture into the skillet and whisk it in with the reserved bacon fat. Heat over low heat until warm, about 1 minute.

4. To serve, pour the warm dressing over the salad and toss with salad spoons. Divide the salad between two plates.

Personalize It!

The great thing about cobb salad is that just about anything can go in it and it will still be delicious. If you don't have any chicken or turkey on hand, or if you prefer, add some chopped roast beef, pork tenderloin, or even a can of drained tuna!

ITALIAN CHEF SALAD

SECRET INGREDIENT:
pepperoni

A staple on most diner menus, the chef salads usually consists of torn iceberg lettuce, a few tomato wedges, cucumbers, and strips of deli sliced ham, turkey, and Swiss cheese. Our supercharged salad gets a flavor infusion from sliced pepperoni and creamy-smooth fresh mozzarella. Smoky roasted red peppers and puckery pepperoncini round out the plate.

Prep Time: 15 min **Cook Time:** 0 min **Serves** 4

DRESSING

2 tablespoons balsamic vinegar

1 teaspoon Dijon mustard

1 teaspoon salt

1/4 teaspoon freshly ground black pepper

1/3 cup extra-virgin olive oil

SALAD

6 cups mixed baby greens

1 ounce shaved Parmesan cheese

4 hard-cooked eggs, peeled and cut into 4 wedges each

2 ounces sliced pepperoni, cut into 1/4-inch wide strips

6 ounces cherry-size fresh mozzarella balls

SALADS AND DRESSINGS

1 bottled roasted red pepper, cut into strips

1 cup cherry tomatoes, halved

4 pepperoncini

1. For dressing, in a small bowl, whisk together the vinegar, mustard, salt, and pepper. Slowly whisk in the oil until well-incorporated.

2. For salad, in a large bowl, toss the greens and Parmesan with 3 tablespoons of the dressing.

3. Arrange the eggs, yolk side up, around the edge of the bowl. Arrange the pepperoni, mozzarella, red pepper, and tomatoes in triangles around the bowl, leaving a 2-inch diameter space in the center. Fill the center space with the pepperoncini. Spoon the remaining dressing over the top of the salad.

Personalize It!

If you prefer a heartier salad, try adding some sliced grilled chicken breast, roasted pork tenderloin, or grilled shrimp.

FIG AND PROSCIUTTO SALAD

SECRET INGREDIENT:
pineapple

This elegant salad takes the classic combination of pork and fruit to new heights. Minted salad leaves with sliced fennel and green beans are crowned with prosciutto, halved figs, and juicy pineapple. A balsamic vinaigrette balances the flavors.

Prep Time: 20 min   **Cook Time:** 2 min   **Serves** 4

SALAD

1 3/4 ounces thin green beans

3 1/2 ounces mixed salad leaves

2 tablespoons chopped fresh mint

1/4 bulb of fennel, cut into thin strips

2 shallots, finely chopped

2 ripe fresh figs, halved lengthwise

3 1/4 ounces prosciutto, cut into thin strips

1 large slice of pineapple (about 5 ounces), cut into small strips

DRESSING

2 tablespoons extra-virgin olive oil

1 tablespoon balsamic vinegar

Juice of 1/2 lemon

Salt and freshly ground black pepper

1. For salad, add the beans to a small saucepan of boiling water and cook for 2 minutes. Drain and refresh under cold running water. In a medium bowl, mix the green beans, salad leaves, mint, fennel, and shallots.

2. For dressing, whisk together the oil, vinegar, and lemon juice in a small bowl, and season with salt and pepper, to taste.

3. Toss the salad with the dressing. Arrange the salad on four plates or on a serving platter. Place the figs on the plates or the platter. Add a mound of shredded prosciutto and a mound of pineapple beside them.

One More Notch! To take this salad over the top, add tangerine segments and drizzle honey over the top. Italian chestnut honey is particularly good.

ARUGULA SALAD WITH GOAT CHEESE

SECRET INGREDIENT:
bacon

Look for small, young arugula leaves for this salad. They'll taste less pungent than more mature leaves. Either way, the melted rounds of soft goat cheese will tame the tanginess of the arugula as crisp cubes of smoked back bacon punch up the flavor. If you can't find back bacon, use Canadian bacon.

Prep Time: 5 min   **Cook Time:** 10 min   **Serves** 4

SALAD

1 tablespoon vegetable oil

1/2 pound smoked back bacon
   (rind removed), diced

2 small (4 ounces each), round, soft goat
   cheeses, halved horizontally

3 ounces arugula, trimmed,
   rinsed, and dried

DRESSING

1 garlic clove, crushed

1 teaspoon whole-grain mustard

2 teaspoons white-wine vinegar

2 tablespoons extra-virgin olive oil

Salt and freshly ground black pepper

1. Preheat the oven to 475°F. Line a baking sheet with parchment paper.

2. For salad, heat the oil in a large skillet and fry the bacon until crisp, 8 to 9 minutes, then drain it on a paper towel–lined plate.

3. Lay the cheese rounds on the baking sheet. Bake until they begin to melt and turn a toasty brown on top, about 5 minutes.

4. Meanwhile, for dressing, place the garlic in a small bowl, then whisk in the mustard, vinegar, and oil. Season with salt and pepper, to taste.

5. Put the arugula in a medium bowl with the bacon. Pour the dressing in and toss lightly, then arrange in an open circle on each plate.

6. Remove the cheese from the oven, place one round in the center of each salad, and serve immediately.

Personalize It!

If you don't like the peppery bite of arugula, try milder watercress, baby spinach leaves, or escarole. ✳

FRENCH BISTRO SALAD

SECRET INGREDIENT:
poached eggs

What makes a salad great is the dressing, and white-wine vinegar lends just the right acidity to this one. But this salad's real showstopper is the poached egg. When broken, the egg yolk spreads over the greens to balance the dressing's acidity with creamy richness.

Prep Time: 10 min   **Cook Time:** 12 min   **Serves** 4

SALAD

4 ounces slab bacon, cut into
   1/4-inch rectangles

1 large bunch chicory, trimmed and
   torn into bite-size pieces (about 8 cups)

3/4 cup plain or seasoned croutons

4 large eggs

DRESSING

1 tablespoon white-wine vinegar

3 tablespoons minced shallots

2 teaspoons Dijon mustard

1/2 teaspoon salt

2 tablespoons olive oil

1. For salad, heat a medium skillet over medium-high heat and add the bacon. Cook the bacon, stirring occasionally, until browned and crisp, 8 to 9 minutes.

2. Drain the bacon on a paper towel–lined plate and reserve 1 tablespoon of the fat.

3. For dressing, in a small bowl, whisk together the vinegar, shallots, mustard, and salt. Slowly whisk in the oil and the reserved bacon fat.

4. In a large bowl, toss the chicory with the bacon, dressing, and croutons and divide among four serving plates.

5. Half-fill a large nonstick skillet with water. Heat until simmering, but do not boil. Add the vinegar. Break the eggs into a cup one at a time, then slide each into the water and poach for 3 minutes. Toward the end of cooking, spoon the water over the yolks. When cooked, remove the eggs with a slotted spoon and drain on a paper towel–lined plate.

6. Slide an egg onto the top of each salad. If the yolks don't break, poke them gently to release their liquid. Serve immediately.

that's **ingenious**

If you don't want to poach the eggs at the last minute, they can be done several hours ahead and refrigerated in a small amount of cold water. Then just before serving, place them into a pan of simmering water for a minute to warm them up.

CURRIED EGG SALAD

SECRET INGREDIENT:
golden raisins

Egg salad is such a time-honored dish that nearly everyone claims that their mother's recipe is the best ever. This one jazzes up the salad with curry powder, chopped sweet gherkins, and golden raisins for extra chew, aroma, and sweet-tart flavor.

Prep Time: 10 min	**Cook Time:** 0 min	**Serves** 4

8 hard-cooked eggs, peeled, halved,
  and separated

1/2 cup mayonnaise

1/3 cup golden raisins

1/3 cup chopped sweet gherkins

1/3 cup chopped red onion

2 tablespoons chopped fresh cilantro

1 1/2 teaspoons curry powder

1/4 teaspoon salt

1/8 teaspoon freshly ground black pepper

1. In a large bowl, mash the yolks with a fork.

2. Chop the egg whites and add to the bowl, along with the mayonnaise, raisins, gherkins, onion, cilantro, curry powder, salt, and pepper. Mix well.

One More Notch! For a touch more flavor, stir in 2 teaspoons drained chopped capers and 2 teaspoons Dijon mustard.

BEET SALAD WITH CREAMY DILL DRESSING

SECRET INGREDIENT:
horseradish

If you've never had a fresh beet salad, here's a great introduction. Grated beets and chopped red onions are marinated in orange juice then tossed with a sour cream and dill dressing spiked with peppery horseradish.

Prep Time: 20 min	**Cook Time:** 0 min	**Serves** 4

SALAD

1 1/2 pounds raw beets, peeled

1 small red onion, finely chopped

1 tablespoon sunflower oil

2 tablespoons orange juice

2 teaspoons red-wine vinegar

Salt and freshly ground black pepper

5 1/2 ounces beet tops and other mixed baby greens

DRESSING

3 tablespoons sour cream

3 tablespoons plain yogurt

1 teaspoon grated fresh horseradish or 2 teaspoons prepared horseradish

2 tablespoons chopped fresh dill

1. For salad, grate the beets in a medium bowl, keeping all the juices (this can also be done in a food processor with a coarse grating disc). Add the onion and stir to mix.

2 Whisk together the oil, orange juice, and vinegar in a small bowl. Season with salt and pepper, to taste. Pour over the beet mixture and toss well. Cover and marinate at room temperature for 30 minutes or refrigerate overnight.

3. Put the salad leaves in a large serving bowl. Add the marinated beet mixture and toss together.

4. For dressing, in a small bowl, stir together the sour cream, yogurt, horseradish, and dill. Spoon the dressing onto the salad and serve immediately.

Personalize It!
If you don't like sunflower oil, use extra-virgin olive oil. Better yet, try walnut oil.

FETA-BARLEY SALAD WITH CITRUS DRESSING

SECRET INGREDIENT:
dried cranberries

Need to fill out a meat-based meal? Serve a grain salad on the side. Even more versatile than pasta salads, grain salads welcome a range of additions from vegetables and fruits to cheeses. Dried cranberries lend a sweet and colorful contrast to the briny tang of feta cheese in this Mediterranean version of barley salad. *See photograph on page 177.*

Prep Time: 15 min	**Cook Time:** 20 min	**Serves** 4

SALAD

1 cup quick-cooking barley

1 cup crumbled feta cheese

1 cup diced seeded cucumber

1 cup diced seeded green bell pepper

1/2 cup dried cranberries

1/3 cup finely chopped red onion

1/4 cup thinly sliced fresh basil

DRESSING

3 tablespoons fresh orange juice

1 tablespoon fresh lemon juice

Grated zest of 1 orange

3/4 teaspoon salt

1/4 teaspoon freshly ground black pepper

1/4 cup extra-virgin olive oil

1. For salad, cook the barley according to the package directions. Transfer to a medium bowl and cool for 5 minutes.

2. Stir in the cheese, cucumber, pepper, cranberries, and onion.

3. For dressing, in a large bowl, whisk together the orange juice, lemon juice, orange zest, salt, and pepper. Slowly whisk in the oil until combined.

4. Add the barley mixture and toss well. Stir in the basil and serve.

Personalize It!

To give this salad your own touch, switch up the dried fruit and herbs. Try raisins or cherries instead of cranberries and parsley instead of basil. ❄

BULGUR SALAD WITH TANGERINE-POMEGRANATE DRESSING

SECRET INGREDIENT:

sweet corn

Bulgur salads usually include lemon juice and tomatoes and taste rather one dimensional. Not this version. Flavor comes from tangerines, pomegranate molasses, dried cherries, peanuts, and sweet corn.

| **Prep Time:** 10 min | **Cook Time:** 30 min | **Serves** 4 |

SALAD

1 cup medium-grain bulgur

2 1/2 cups boiling water

1 1/2 cups sweet corn kernels

2/3 cup dried cherries

2/3 cup thinly sliced scallions

1/3 cup roasted peanuts, coarsely chopped

DRESSING

1 teaspoon grated tangerine or orange zest

1 cup fresh tangerine or orange juice

2 tablespoons tomato paste

2 tablespoons pomegranate molasses

2 tablespoons olive oil

3/4 teaspoon salt

1. For salad, in a large bowl, stir the bulgur into the water. Let stand for 30 minutes. Drain well.

2. For dressing, in a large bowl, whisk together the tangerine or orange zest, tangerine or orange juice, tomato paste, pomegranate molasses, oil, and salt.

3. Add the bulgur to the dressing and fluff with a fork. Add the corn, cherries, scallions, and peanuts, tossing to combine. Serve at room temperature or chilled.

that's ingenious !

Look for pomegranate molasses (a.k.a. pomegranate syrup) in Middle-Eastern grocery stores or the international section of well-stocked supermarkets. Or, make it at home by boiling 1 cup pomegranate juice until syrupy and reduced to 2 tablespoons, about 20 minutes.

HEARTY TABBOULEH

SECRET INGREDIENT:
canned chickpeas

Classic Middle-Eastern Tabbouleh is a salad made with bulgur wheat, parsley, tomatoes, and a lively lemon–olive oil dressing. We add chickpeas to make the salad more substantial and give it a slightly nutty flavor.

Prep Time: 10 min	**Cook Time:** 15 min	**Serves** 4

1 cup bulgur

1 1/4 cups boiling water

1/4 cup fresh lemon juice

1/4 cup chopped fresh parsley

2 tablespoons chopped fresh cilantro

1 garlic clove, minced

1 cup chopped seeded tomatoes

1 teaspoon grated fresh lemon zest

3 tablespoons extra-virgin olive oil

3/4 teaspoon salt

1/4 teaspoon freshly ground black pepper

1 can (15 ounces) chickpeas,
　　drained and rinsed

1. Place the bulgur in a medium bowl and pour the water over it. Let stand until all the water has been absorbed, 15 to 20 minutes.

2. Combine the lemon juice, parsley, cilantro, garlic, tomatoes, lemon zest, oil, salt, and pepper in a small bowl. Pour over the bulgur and toss well.

3. Stir in the chickpeas and serve.

One More Notch! For a little more flavor and aroma, stir in 2 tablespoons chopped fresh mint. The clean, bright taste of mint marries well with the lemon, parsley, and tomatoes.

MOROCCAN COUSCOUS SALAD

SECRET INGREDIENT:
cinnamon-spiced almonds

If you love grain salads, get to know couscous. It can be flavored in countless ways and cooks in just 5 minutes. Cinnamon-spiced almonds give this quick salad a North African flair.

Prep Time: 5 min	**Cook Time:** 10 min	**Serves** 6

1 1/4 cups water

1 teaspoon ground cumin

1 teaspoon salt

1 cup couscous

1/2 cup pitted dates, sliced crosswise

1 cup diced cucumber

1/2 cup cinnamon-spiced almonds

1/3 cup finely chopped red onion

1/3 cup pitted calamata olives

Juice and grated peel of 1 lemon

2 tablespoons extra-virgin olive oil

1. Combine the water, cumin, and salt in a medium saucepan and bring to a boil over medium-high heat.

2. Remove the pan from the heat, stir in the couscous, cover with a tight-fitting lid and let stand for 5 minutes. After 5 minutes, fluff the couscous with a fork and transfer to a large bowl.

3. Add the dates, cucumber, almonds, onion, olives, lemon juice, lemon peel, and oil to the couscous. Toss well to combine.

One More Notch! To kick the flavor up on this dish, substitute 1/2 cup orange juice for 1/2 cup of the water.

BARLEY, BLACK BEAN, AND AVOCADO SALAD

SECRET INGREDIENT:
carrot juice

We often think of barley as a soup ingredient, but it makes great salads, too. Think of it as a chewier, heartier rice salad. Cooking the barley in carrot juice instead of plain water adds sweetness and a golden glow that perfectly complements the black beans, avocado, and tomato. *See photograph on page 169.*

Prep Time: 10 min	Cook Time: 20 min	Serves 4

1 cup carrot juice

1/2 teaspoon dried thyme

1/8 teaspoon cayenne pepper

Salt

1/2 cup quick-cooking barley

3 tablespoons fresh lemon juice

1 tablespoon olive oil

1 can (19 ounces) black beans, rinsed and drained

1 cup fresh diced tomatoes

1/2 cup peeled, pitted, and diced avocado

1. Combine the carrot juice, thyme, cayenne, and salt, to taste, in a medium saucepan. Bring to a boil over medium heat, add barley, then reduce to a simmer. Cover and cook until the barley is tender, about 15 minutes.

2. Meanwhile, whisk together the lemon juice and oil in a large bowl. Transfer the barley and any remaining liquid to the bowl with the lemon juice mixture. Toss to coat.

3. Add the beans and tomatoes and toss to combine. Add the avocado and gently toss. Serve at room temperature or refrigerate for

up to 2 days. For best flavor, remove from the refrigerator 20 minutes before serving.

Personalize It!
You can make the salad with brown rice in place of the barley, if you like. Add 1/2 cup chicken broth to the carrot juice mixture and cook until tender, about 45 minutes. You can also use red kidney beans or pinto beans instead of black beans.

CARROT AND GINGER SALAD

SECRET INGREDIENT:
sour cream

Carrot salads often feature lively flavors, and this one is no exception. Grated fresh ginger and the zests of orange and lemon give it plenty of perk. But the secret to balance here is the equalizing flavor and creamy texture of sour cream. *See photograph on page 172.*

Prep Time: 10 min	Cook Time: 10 min	Serves 4

SALAD

1/2 cup raisins

3/4 cup boiling water

3/4 pound young carrots

Salt

1/2 teaspoon honey or sugar

1 3/4 ounces chopped almonds

DRESSING

1 piece (2 inches) fresh ginger, peeled

1/2 cup sour cream

Zest and juice of 1/2 lemon

Zest and juice of 1/2 orange

1. For salad, put the raisins in a small bowl, then cover them with the boiling water and set aside.

2. Peel and grate the carrots and add them to a serving bowl.

3. Drain the raisins and add them to the carrots.

4. For dressing, finely grate the ginger into a small bowl. Stir in the sour cream along with the lemon zest, lemon juice, orange zest, and orange juice.

5. Stir the dressing into the carrot and raisin mixture, then season with salt, to taste, and add the honey or sugar. Finally, stir in the almonds and serve.

Personalize It!

To switch up the flavor, swap the almonds for pecans, walnuts, or peanuts. You could also use plain yogurt instead of sour cream. ❄

SUMMERTIME SPINACH SALAD

SECRET INGREDIENT:
blueberries

The secret to a great vegetable salad is to add a little something sweet to balance the flavors. Blueberries do the trick here as a delightful counterpoint to the savory spinach and pungent blue cheese. *See photograph on page 169.*

Prep Time: 10 min   **Cook Time:** 0 min   **Serves** 6

DRESSING

1/2 cup vegetable oil

1/4 cup raspberry vinegar

2 teaspoons Dijon mustard

1 teaspoon sugar

1/2 teaspoon salt

SALAD

1 package (10 ounces) fresh spinach, torn

4 ounces crumbled blue cheese

1 cup fresh blueberries

1/2 cup chopped toasted pecans

1. For dressing, in a jar with a tight-fitting lid, combine the oil, vinegar, mustard, sugar, and salt. Shake well.

2. For salad, toss the spinach, blue cheese, blueberries, and pecans in a large salad bowl. Add the dressing and toss gently. Serve immediately.

Personalize It!

Raspberry vinegar enhances the touch of fruit in this salad, but you can use another vinegar, if you like. Try sherry vinegar, champagne vinegar, white balsamic vinegar, or red-wine vinegar. ❄

ROASTED SWEET POTATO SALAD WITH ORANGE DRESSING

SECRET INGREDIENT:
raisins

Sweet potatoes dance the line between sweet and savory, equally at home with honey as they are with black pepper. This salad pushes the limits of both flavors with honey, oranges, and chewy raisins on the sweet side, and arugula, onions, salt, and pepper on the savory side. It's a fantastic combination.
See photograph on page 174.

Prep Time: 25 min   **Cook Time:** 20 min   **Serves** 4

SALAD

1 pound sweet potatoes, peeled, quartered lengthwise, and cut into 1/2-inch-thick slices

1 tablespoons olive oil

1 bunch arugula, torn into pieces

1 navel orange, peeled and cut into sections

1/2 small red onion, thinly sliced crosswise

3 tablespoons raisins

DRESSING

2 tablespoons olive oil, divided

1 tablespoon fresh lemon juice

1 tablespoon fresh orange juice

1 teaspoon honey

1/4 teaspoon salt

1/4 teaspoon freshly ground black pepper

1. Preheat the oven to 400°F. Line a large baking pan with foil. Lightly coat with nonstick cooking spray.

2. For salad, toss the sweet potatoes in the baking pan with the oil. Spread in an even layer. Roast the potatoes until tender and lightly browned, about 20 minutes.

3. For dressing, in a small bowl, whisk together the oil, lemon juice, orange juice, honey, salt, and pepper. Taste the dressing and add more lemon juice, if desired.

4. In a large bowl, toss together the potatoes and the dressing. Add the arugula, orange sections, onion, and raisins. Toss to mix.

One More Notch! To push the savory-sweet interplay even further, add 1 chopped apple and 1 finely chopped celery stalk.

CHICKEN TARRAGON SALAD

SECRET INGREDIENT:
peaches

Here's a chicken salad with Southern style. Peaches and pecans give it juiciness and crunch behind the creamy backdrop of mayonnaise.

Prep Time: 10 min   **Cook Time:** 0 min   **Serves** 4

1/3 cup mayonnaise

2 tablespoons milk

1/2 teaspoon salt

1/4 teaspoon freshly ground black pepper

1 teaspoon chopped fresh tarragon or 1/4 teaspoon dried

2 1/2 cups cubed cooked chicken

1 cup seedless red grapes, halved

1 cup frozen tiny peas, thawed

2 large peaches, peeled, pitted, and chopped

1 cup toasted pecan halves

Lettuce leaves (optional)

1. In a large bowl, stir together the mayonnaise, milk, salt, pepper, and tarragon until smooth. Add the chicken and toss to coat.

2. Stir in the grapes, peas, peaches, and pecans. Line a serving bowl with lettuce, if using, then add the chicken mixture.

One More Notch! To enhance the Southern flair, use buttermilk instead of milk in the dressing, and top the salad with crispy bits of crumbled bacon.

ASIAN CHICKEN SALAD

SECRET INGREDIENT:
peanut butter

Peanut butter creates the base for an easy Asian-style salad dressing. Canned mandarin oranges offer bursts of bright citrus flavor and crispy Chinese noodles add contrasting texture. *See photograph on page 183.*

Prep Time: 15 min   **Cook Time:** 10 min   **Serves** 4

1 pound boneless, skinless chicken breast halves

2 tablespoons soy sauce, divided

3 tablespoons creamy peanut butter

1 1/2 tablespoons lime juice

1 1/2 tablespoons sugar

1 1/2 tablespoons peanut oil

8 cups mixed baby greens

1 1/2 cups crispy Chinese noodles, divided

1 cup sliced seeded cucumber

1 can (11 ounces) mandarin orange segments, drained

1/2 cup shredded carrots

1. Heat a lightly oiled grill pan over medium-high heat.

2. Brush the chicken with 1 tablespoon of the soy sauce and grill until cooked through, about 5 minutes per side. Transfer to a

cutting board and let cool for 5 minutes. Thinly slice the chicken crosswise.

3. In a small bowl, whisk together the remaining 1 tablespoon soy sauce, peanut butter, lime juice, sugar, and oil.

4. In a large bowl, toss the greens, 1 cup of the noodles, cucumber, oranges, carrots, and 3 tablespoons of the dressing.

5. Divide among 4 plates. Top each salad with the sliced chicken and sprinkle with the remaining 1/2 cup noodles. Drizzle the remaining dressing evenly over the salad plates.

One More Notch! For a nuttier salad, sprinkle each salad with 1 tablespoon chopped honey-roasted peanuts or cashews.

WARM SESAME-CHICKEN SALAD

SECRET INGREDIENT:
cornflakes

This chicken salad is anything but ordinary. Chicory, frisée, and green cabbage tossed with a white wine–tarragon vinaigrette make a lively bed for strips of breaded chicken coated in crisp cornflakes and aromatic sesame seeds. A little chili powder in the coating adds a bit of kick. *See photograph on page 161.*

Prep Time: 15 min   **Cook Time:** 15 min   **Serves** 4

SALAD

1/2 cup fresh white bread crumbs

1 cup cornflakes, lightly crushed

4 teaspoons sesame seeds

1 teaspoon hot chili powder

2 eggs

1 pound skinless, boneless chicken breasts, cut into short strips

1/4 head green cabbage

1/2 head frisée (curly endive)

2 heads chicory

Sesame seeds

DRESSING

1 teaspoon chopped parsley

1 teaspoon chopped fresh oregano

1 tablespoon chopped fresh tarragon

1 tablespoon white-wine vinegar

1/4 cup olive oil

1 teaspoon honey

Salt and freshly ground black pepper

1. Preheat the oven to 400°F.

2. For salad, put the bread crumbs, cornflakes, sesame seeds, and chili powder in a large zip-close plastic bag and shake to mix well. Break the eggs into a shallow dish and beat together lightly.

3. Dip the chicken strips, one at a time, in the egg, then drop into the plastic bag. When a few pieces of chicken are in the bag, shake to coat evenly. Transfer to two nonstick baking trays, spreading out the pieces in a single layer.

4. Bake the chicken strips, until the juices run clear when pierced with a knife, 15 to 20 minutes, turning the pieces over halfway through the baking time.

5. Meanwhile, finely shred the cabbage and place in a large bowl. Pull the frisée and chicory leaves apart and tear any large ones into smaller pieces. Add to the bowl.

6. For dressing, in a small jar with a tight-fitting lid, shake together the parsley, oregano, tarragon, vinegar, oil, and honey. Season with salt and pepper, to taste. Pour the dressing over the salad and toss well.

7. Divide the salad among four plates and pile the cooked chicken pieces on top.

Sprinkle with a few more sesame seeds, then serve.

One More Notch! Give the dressing even more flavor by mixing in 1/2 teaspoon minced fresh garlic and 1/2 teaspoon minced fresh ginger.

SWEET-AND-SOUR DUCK SALAD

SECRET INGREDIENT:
apricot jam

Jams and jellies have dozens of uses beyond bread. Why not use apricot jam to flavor and thicken salad dressing? When seared duck breast is in the salad, apricot jam makes perfect sense. Watercress, grapes, and pumpkin seeds round out the flavors in this main-dish flavor explosion. *See photograph on page 169.*

Prep Time: 10 min   **Cook Time:** 30 min   **Serves** 4

SALAD

1 cup mixed basmati and wild rice

1 pound skinless, boneless duck breasts, excess fat removed

2 teaspoons olive oil

Salt and freshly ground black pepper

2 cups watercress, tough stalks discarded

1 cup seedless green grapes, halved

4 scallions, thinly sliced

3 celery stalks, thinly sliced

8 radicchio leaves or other red salad leaves

4 nectarines, thinly sliced

3 tablespoons toasted pumpkin seeds

DRESSING

1 teaspoon grated fresh ginger

1 small garlic clove, very finely chopped

1 tablespoon apricot jam

2 teaspoons raspberry vinegar or white-wine vinegar

2 tablespoons hazelnut oil

Salt

1. For salad, cook the rice according to the package instructions. Transfer to a large bowl and allow to cool.

2. Preheat a grill pan. Brush the duck breasts on both sides with oil. Season with salt and pepper, to taste. Place them on the grill pan and cook over medium-high heat for 3 to 5 minutes on each side for rare to medium-rare (cook longer if you prefer it medium or well-done). Allow the duck breasts to cool briefly, then cut into thin slices.

3. For dressing, put the ginger, garlic, jam, vinegar, and oil in a small bowl and stir to combine. Season with salt, to taste.

4. Chop half the watercress and add to the rice together with the grapes, scallions, and celery. Drizzle with half the dressing and mix gently.

5. Arrange the radicchio and remaining watercress leaves on four plates and divide the rice salad among them. Arrange the duck and nectarine slices on top, drizzle with the remaining dressing, and sprinkle with the pumpkin seeds.

Personalize It!

To switch things up, make grilled duck, sweet potato, and apple salad instead. Cook 1 1/2 pounds peeled, cubed sweet potatoes in enough boiling water to cover, until tender, 6 to 8 minutes. Drain well and cool slightly. For the dressing, stir 2 1/2 tablespoons mayonnaise, 2 1/2 tablespoons plain yogurt, and 1 tablespoon Dijon mustard in a small bowl. Core and chop 1 large apple and toss with 2 tablespoons lemon juice in a large bowl. Add 3 celery stalks and 4 scallions, all thinly sliced, and stir in the dressing. Fold in the sweet potatoes and the hot sliced duck. Serve warm on a bed of mixed salad leaves.

THAI-STYLE BEEF SALAD

SECRET INGREDIENT:
chili sauce

Bracing limes and lemongrass. Refreshing cucumber. Fragrant basil and coriander. What's not to love about Thai flavors? Pair them with spicy chili sauce and they make an outstanding main dish beef salad.

Prep Time: 20 min | **Cook Time:** 5 min | **Serves** 4

12 ounces crisp lettuce leaves, shredded

1 cucumber, peeled, seeded, and cubed

2 carrots, grated

1/4 pound fresh bean sprouts

1 stalk lemongrass

2 teaspoons vegetable oil

1 garlic clove, crushed

1 pound lean beef steak, thinly sliced

2 limes

Small bunch of fresh coriander, finely chopped

Small bunch of basil, finely chopped

2 tablespoons olive oil

1 tablespoon sweet chili sauce

1. Arrange the lettuce, cucumber, carrots, and bean sprouts on a large serving dish or on individual plates.

2. Remove the outer leaves from the lemongrass and chop enough of the inner stalk to give 1 teaspoon.

3. Heat the vegetable oil in a large nonstick skillet and gently cook the garlic and lemongrass until just golden brown, about 30 seconds.

4. Add the beef to the skillet and fry over high heat until just slightly pink, 1 to 2 minutes, stirring continuously to keep the slices separate. Then remove the meat from the pan and place it on top of the salad vegetables.

5. Squeeze 2 tablespoons of juice from the limes and add it to the pan with the coriander, basil, olive oil, and chili sauce. Cook, stirring, until heated through, about 1 minute, then pour over the salad and serve.

One More Notch! Send your senses into a tailspin—top the salad with chopped roasted peanuts and slivers of grated fresh coconut.

ITALIAN POTATO SALAD

SECRET INGREDIENT:
horseradish

Potato salads tend to be mild and creamy from mayonnaise or sharp and puckery from vinegar. This one achieves a bit of both with mayo, sour cream, Italian salad dressing, and a healthy shot of horseradish. Try it with steaks or burgers at your next cookout.

Prep Time: 10 min | **Cook Time:** 25 min | **Serves** 8

3 pounds potatoes

1/3 cup Italian salad dressing

4 hard-cooked eggs, chopped

3/4 cup chopped celery

1/3 cup chopped onion

1/4 cup chopped cucumber

1/4 cup chopped seeded green bell pepper

1/2 cup mayonnaise

1/4 cup sour cream

1 teaspoon prepared horseradish

Chopped fresh tomatoes

1. Place the potatoes in a large pot and cover with water. Bring to a boil and cook until tender, 25 to 30 minutes. Drain and cool.

2. Peel and cube the potatoes and place in a large bowl. Add the dressing and toss to coat. Cover and chill for 2 hours.

3. Add the eggs, celery, onion, cucumber, and pepper. Mix well.

4. In a small bowl, combine the mayonnaise, sour cream, and horseradish; mix well. Pour over the potato mixture and toss to coat. Chill for at least 1 hour. Top with the tomatoes.

that's **ingenious**

Boiling potatoes in their skins retains more moisture and flavor in the potato flesh. But if you need to shorten the cooking time, peel and chop the potatoes then cook for just 15 to 20 minutes.

CRAB AND GRAPEFRUIT SALAD

SECRET INGREDIENT:
mango chutney

Seafood and citrus make a good combination, but the combo becomes extraordinary when you pair crab with grapefruit. Mango chutney adds just the right amount of sweetness and spice.

Prep Time: 15 min	**Cook Time:** 0 min	**Serves** 4

4 grapefruits

2 tablespoons mayonnaise

1 tablespoon finely chopped mango chutney

2 teaspoons Dijon mustard

1 teaspoon sesame oil

1/4 teaspoon freshly ground black pepper

Salt

3/4 pound lump crabmeat, picked over to remove any cartilage

2 cups watercress, tough stems trimmed

1 Belgian endive, cut crosswise into 1/2-inch-wide strips

1 head Bibb lettuce, separated into leaves

1. Peel the grapefruits. Working over a large bowl, separate the grapefruit sections from the membranes, reserving any juice that collects in the bowl. Discard the membranes.

2. In a medium bowl, whisk together the mayonnaise, chutney, mustard, oil, pepper, 3 tablespoons of the reserved grapefruit juice, and salt, to taste.

3. Add the crabmeat, tossing to combine. Add the watercress, endive, and grapefruit sections, and toss. Serve the salad on a bed of Bibb lettuce.

Personalize It!

Look for refrigerated lump crabmeat for the best flavor. If you can't find it, use cooked shrimp, lobster, scallops, or good-size cubes of poached chicken breasts. You can also substitute oranges for the grapefruits, if you like.

APPLE AND DATE SALAD

SECRET INGREDIENT:
hazelnuts

If you ever need a little more crunch and rich-ness in a salad, add nuts. Hazelnuts fill the bill here, complementing sweet apples and dates, bitter chicory, and a creamy lemon dressing. *See photograph on page 169.*

Prep Time: 15 min **Cook Time:** 3 min **Serves** 4

SALAD

1/2 cup chopped hazelnuts

2 green-skinned apples, cored and roughly chopped

6 ounces dates, pitted and roughly chopped (about 1 cup)

1 small red bell pepper, seeded and chopped

2 celery stalks, sliced

1/2 cup halved seedless green grapes

2 heads red or white chicory

2 tablespoons chopped parsley (optional)

DRESSING

1/2 cup plain low-fat yogurt

1/4 cup nonfat mayonnaise

1 tablespoon lemon juice

1 teaspoon sugar

Salt and freshly ground black pepper

1. For salad, toast the hazelnuts in a small dry skillet over medium heat, stirring, until you can smell the nutty fragrance, about 3 minutes. Add the nuts to a small bowl and set aside.

2. For dressing, put the yogurt, mayonnaise, lemon juice, and sugar into a large bowl with salt and pepper, to taste, and mix well.

3. Add the apples to the bowl and stir until the pieces are well-coated with the dressing. Add the dates, red pepper, celery, and grapes. Stir to mix.

4. Separate the heads of chicory into leaves, trimming off the hard bases.

5. Slice the bottom half of the leaves and add to the salad. Pile the salad on a large plate or in a shallow serving dish and arrange the tops of the chicory leaves around the edge. Sprinkle with the toasted nuts and parsley, if using.

Personalize It!

Dress the salad with a vinaigrette instead. Whisk together 3 tablespoons olive oil, 1 tablespoon red-wine vinegar or lemon juice, 1/4 teaspoon Dijon mustard, 1/4 teaspoon sugar, and salt and freshly ground black pepper, to taste. You can also use 1/2 cup raisins in place of the dates. ❋

CRUNCHY NUT COLESLAW

SECRET INGREDIENT:
radishes

Everyone loves coleslaw. The combination of creamy and crunchy is simply irresistible. Our version gets a sweet touch from raisins and a bit more bite and crunch from sliced radishes. *See photograph on page 169.*

Prep Time: 15 min **Cook Time:** 0 min **Serves** 4

1/2 head green cabbage, finely shredded

1 large carrot, coarsely grated

2/3 cup raisins

4 scallions, finely chopped, with the white and green parts kept separate

1/2 cup mayonnaise

1/3 cup plain yogurt

Salt and freshly ground black pepper

6 radishes, sliced

1/3 cup unsalted roasted peanuts

3 tablespoons chopped parsley and/or snipped fresh chives (optional)

1. Mix together the cabbage, carrot, raisins, and white parts of the scallions in a large bowl.

2. In a small bowl, stir the mayonnaise and yogurt together and season with salt and pepper, to taste. Add to the cabbage mixture and toss to coat evenly.

3. Just before serving, stir in the radishes and peanuts, and sprinkle with the green parts of the scallions and the parsley and/or chives, if using.

One More Notch! Toss 1 cored and diced red-skinned apple with 2 tablespoons lemon juice, then stir into the coleslaw with 1 teaspoon caraway seeds. Garnish with 1 tablespoon toasted pumpkin seeds and 2 tablespoons sunflower seeds.

MINTED MELON SALAD

SECRET INGREDIENT:

cucumber

Here's the perfect summertime pick-me-up. A juicy and refreshing combination of melons, strawberries, pears, and starfruit drizzled with orange liqueur and topped with fresh mint. Extra crunch and a backdrop of savoriness come from a surprise ingredient: diced cucumber.

Prep Time: 25 min	**Cook Time:** 3 min	**Serves** 6

1 small cantaloupe (about 1 pound), washed, halved, and seeded

1 small honeydew melon (about 1 pound), washed, halved, and seeded

1 pint ripe strawberries, hulled and sliced (about 1 1/2 cups)

1 large pear, cut into 1/2-inch pieces

1/2 small cucumber, diced (about 1/2 cup)

2 starfruits, cut in 1/4-inch-thick slices

6 tablespoons Grand Marnier or brandy

2 tablespoons shredded fresh mint

1. Using a melon baller or a small spoon, scoop out balls of melon into a large bowl. With a tablespoon, scoop out any remaining melon into the bowl, leaving smooth shells.

2. Add the strawberries, pear, and cucumber to the bowl. Set aside 4 starfruit slices. Dice the remaining starfruit and add to the bowl.

3. Drizzle the Grand Marnier or brandy over the fruit, sprinkle with the mint, and toss gently to mix well. Cover with plastic wrap and let soak in the refrigerator for 20 minutes.

4. Pile the fruit mixture into the melon shells and decorate with the reserved slices of starfruit.

One More Notch! To make this a more substantial luncheon salad, toss 6 cups mesclun salad leaves, 2 cups watercress, 1/2 cup chopped scallions, 1/4 cup extra-virgin olive oil, and 2 tablespoons orange juice in a large bowl. Arrange on six salad plates and spoon the fruit salad on top. Add a scoop of cottage cheese, drizzle with the Grand Marnier or sherry, and sprinkle with the shredded fresh mint.

MEXICAN FRUIT SALAD

SECRET INGREDIENT:
flour tortillas

Fresh fruit salad is great to have on hand as a midday snack or to fill out a light lunch. The juicy crunch and subtle apple flavor of jicama provides a great contrast to the soft fruit in most fruit salads. Crispy flour tortillas dressed up with cinnamon-sugar make the perfect bed for this salad and give it a boost of sweetness.

Prep Time: 15 min **Cook Time:** 1 hr 30 min **Serves** 4

1/2 cup plus 2 tablespoons sugar

1/2 cup water

3 tablespoons chopped fresh cilantro

2 tablespoons fresh lime juice

1 teaspoon grated lime zest

3 cups honeydew melon cubes

3 cups pineapple cubes

2 cups cantaloupe cubes

1 1/2 cups diced jicama

1 cup mango cubes

1/4 teaspoon ground cinnamon

4 flour tortillas (8-inch)

2 tablespoons unsalted butter, melted

1. Combine 1/2 cup of the sugar and the water in a small saucepan over high heat. Bring to a boil and cook for 2 minutes.

2. Remove from the heat and stir in the cilantro and lime juice; let stand for 15 minutes.

3. Pour the mixture through a sieve into a large bowl and stir in the lime zest. Add the honeydew, pineapple, cantaloupe, jicama, and mango. Toss well and chill for 1 hour.

4. Meanwhile, preheat the oven to 400°F.

5. Combine the remaining 2 tablespoons of sugar and the cinnamon in a small bowl. Brush the tops of the tortillas with half of the butter. Sprinkle with half of the sugar mixture. Turn the tortillas over and repeat with the remaining butter and sugar mixture.

6. Place 2 tortillas on a large baking sheet and bake for 7 minutes. Turn the tortillas over and bake until crisp, 2 to 3 minutes longer. Repeat with the remaining tortillas.

7. To serve, place a tortilla on each of 4 plates and top with 2 cups of the fruit salad.

One More Notch! Heat-lovers can kick this dish up a bit by adding 1/4 to 1/2 teaspoon ground chipotle chile pepper. The smoke and heat perfectly complement the sweet citrusy salad.

SALADS AND DRESSINGS

extraordinary

soups and stews

MEATY THREE-BEAN CHILI

SECRET INGREDIENT:
Worcestershire sauce

Most chili recipes have a good handle on the basics: ground meat, beans, tomatoes, and spices. But the best chili recipes also have a secret weapon: Worcestershire sauce. This one also includes sausage, bacon, and ground mustard to achieve an incredible depth of flavor.

Prep Time: 25 min **Cook Time:** 1 hr 45 min **Serves** 10

3/4 pound Italian sausage links,
   cut into 1/2-inch chunks

3/4 pound ground beef

1 large onion, chopped

1 green bell pepper, seeded and chopped

1 jalapeño pepper, seeded, deveined,
   and minced (wear gloves when handling)

2 garlic cloves, minced

1 cup beef broth

1/2 cup Worcestershire sauce

1 1/2 teaspoons chili powder

1 teaspoon freshly ground black pepper

1 teaspoon ground mustard

1/2 teaspoon celery seed

1/2 teaspoon salt

6 cups chopped fresh plum tomatoes
   (about 2 pounds)

6 bacon strips, cooked and crumbled

1 can (15 1/2 ounces) kidney beans,
   rinsed and drained

1 can (15 ounces) pinto beans,
   rinsed and drained

1 can (15 ounces) chickpeas,
   rinsed and drained

1. In a 4-quart kettle or Dutch oven over medium heat, brown the sausage and beef. Drain, discarding all but 1 tablespoon of the drippings. Set the meat aside.

2. Sauté the onion, bell peppers, jalapeño peppers, and garlic in the drippings until beginning to soften, about 3 minutes. Add the broth, Worcestershire sauce, chili powder, black pepper, mustard, celery seed, and salt. Bring to a boil over medium heat. Reduce the heat, cover, and simmer for 10 minutes.

3. Add the tomatoes, bacon, and sausage and beef, then return to a boil. Reduce the heat, cover, and simmer for 30 minutes.

4. Add the kidney beans, pinto beans, and chickpeas. Simmer until the liquid thickens slightly, about 1 hour, stirring occasionally.

Personalize It!

Chili is easily adaptable. Don't like pinto beans? Use black beans instead. Don't have fresh tomatoes? Use canned diced tomatoes. Like it spicy? Chop 2 jalapeño peppers, leaving in the seeds, and increase the chili powder to 1 tablespoon. ❄

VEGETARIAN CHILI

SECRET INGREDIENT:
chocolate chips

Here's a perfect example of using just a little bit of something to get a lot of flavor in return. Semi-sweet chocolate chips—stirred in at the end of cooking—are the secret to the deep, rich taste of this chili. The chips coax out the best of the other ingredients without overpowering the dish. *See photograph on page 192.*

Prep Time: 10 min   **Cook Time:** 45 min   **Serves** 4

1 tablespoon olive oil

2 garlic cloves, minced

1 1/2 cups chopped onion, divided

1 cup seeded and chopped green bell pepper

1 can (15 ounces) pinto beans,
   rinsed and drained

1 can (15 ounces) black beans,
   rinsed and drained

2 cans (14 1/2 ounces each) diced tomatoes,
   with juice

1 can (8 1/2 ounces) whole-kernel corn,
    rinsed and drained

4 teaspoons chili powder

2 teaspoons ground cumin

2 teaspoons dried oregano

2 tablespoons semi-sweet chocolate chips

1 teaspoon salt

1/4 teaspoon freshly ground black pepper

1/2 cup sour cream

1/2 cup shredded cheddar cheese
    (about 2 ounces)

1. Heat the oil in a large pot over medium-high heat.

2. Add the garlic, 1 1/4 cup of the onions, and the bell pepper. Cook, stirring occasionally, until softened, 6 to 7 minutes.

3. Stir in the pinto beans, black beans, tomatoes (with juice), corn, chili powder, cumin, and oregano. Bring the mixture to a boil, then reduce the heat to medium-low, cover, and simmer, stirring occasionally, until the mixture thickens slightly, 35 to 40 minutes.

4. Remove from the heat and stir in the chocolate chips, salt, and pepper.

5. To serve, spoon the chili into four serving bowls and top each with 2 tablespoons sour cream, 1 tablespoon chopped onion, and 2 tablespoons cheese.

Personalize It!

If you like a little heat to your chili, add a minced jalapeño or serrano pepper in with the vegetables. Don't like pinto or black beans? Substitute your favorite bean. If you prefer a more intense flavor, try making the chili the night before and let the flavors develop while it chills. ✳

BEEF STEW WITH HERBED DUMPLINGS

SECRET INGREDIENT:
potatoes

Beef and potatoes form the basis of beef stew. Usually the potatoes are stewed right along with the beef. But our version adds a delicious new twist in the form of tender, herbed dumplings made with shredded potatoes. They are easily mixed together and dropped into the stew shortly before serving.

Prep Time: 30 min **Cook Time:** 2 hrs 10 min **Serves** 6

STEW

1/4 cup all-purpose flour

3/4 teaspoon salt

1/2 teaspoon freshly ground black pepper

2 pounds beef stew meat, cubed

2 onions, chopped

2 tablespoons vegetable oil

2 cans (10 1/2 ounces each) condensed beef
    broth, undiluted

3/4 cup water

1 tablespoon red-wine vinegar

6 carrots, cut into 2-inch chunks

2 bay leaves

1 teaspoon dried thyme

1/4 teaspoon garlic powder

DUMPLINGS

1 egg

3/4 cup seasoned dry bread crumbs

1 tablespoon all-purpose flour

1 tablespoon minced fresh parsley

1 tablespoon minced onion

1/2 teaspoon dried thyme

1/2 teaspoon salt

1/2 teaspoon freshly ground black pepper

2 1/2 cups finely shredded uncooked potatoes

1. For stew, in a large zip-close bag, combine the flour, salt, and pepper. Add the meat and toss to coat.

2. In a 4-quart kettle or Dutch oven, cook the meat and onions in the oil until the meat is browned and the onions are tender, 6 to 8 minutes. Brown the meat in batches, if necessary, to avoid overcrowding.

3. Stir in the broth, water, vinegar, carrots, bay leaves, thyme, and garlic powder. Bring to a boil, then reduce the heat, cover, and simmer until the meat is almost tender, about 1 1/2 hours. Remove the bay leaves.

4. For dumplings, in a medium bowl, beat the egg, then add the bread crumbs, flour, parsley, onion, thyme, salt, and pepper. Stir in the potatoes and mix well. With floured hands, shape into 1 1/2-inch balls. Dust with flour.

5. Bring the stew to a boil. Drop the dumplings onto the stew in generously rounded tablespoons. Cover and simmer for 30 minutes (do not lift cover). Serve.

One More Notch! Deepen the stew's flavor by replacing half of the carrots with parsnips and replacing the red-wine vinegar with 2 tablespoons Worcestershire sauce.

LOUISIANA BEEF STEW

SECRET INGREDIENT:
molasses

Need sweet, rich flavor? Add molasses. It deepens the taste of barbecue sauces, stews, and desserts. Here, it rounds out the savoriness of beef, potatoes, tomatoes, and carrots in a Southern-style stew.

Prep Time: 20 min   **Cook Time:** 50 min   **Serves** 4

1 tablespoon vegetable oil

2 tablespoons all-purpose flour

1 pound bottom round beef roast, cut into 1/2-inch chunks

1 small onion, finely chopped

2 garlic cloves, minced

2 carrots, thinly sliced

1 pound all-purpose potatoes, peeled and cut into 1/2-inch chunks

2 cans (15 ounces each) diced tomatoes, with juice

3 tablespoons molasses

3 tablespoons red-wine vinegar

3/4 teaspoon ground ginger

3/4 teaspoon salt

1. In a Dutch oven or flame-proof baking dish, heat the oil over medium-high heat. Place the flour in a shallow dish and dredge the beef, shaking off the excess. Add the beef to the pan and cook until lightly browned, about 3 minutes. Transfer to a plate.

2. Reduce the heat to medium, add the onion and garlic, and sauté until tender, 5 minutes.

3. Add the carrots and cook until they begin to soften, about 3 minutes.

4. Add the potatoes, tomatoes (with juice), molasses, vinegar, ginger, and salt. Bring to a boil. Reduce the heat and simmer, covered, until the potatoes are tender, about 30 minutes.

5. Return the beef to the pan and simmer, covered, until cooked through, about 5 minutes.

One More Notch! To fire up the flavor, add 1 teaspoon hot-pepper sauce along with the molasses. A little ground mustard wouldn't hurt either.

NORTH AFRICAN BEEF AND POTATO STEW

SECRET INGREDIENT:
dates

Versions of beef stew are made all over the world, and this one takes its cues from North Africa, with the flavors of cumin, ginger, and cinnamon. To add a touch of sweetness, we included pitted dates. Yams also give the stew a more complex flavor than traditional white potatoes ever could.

Prep Time: 20 min **Cook Time:** 1 hr 30 min **Serves** 4

2 tablespoons olive oil, divided

1 1/2 pounds boneless beef chuck,
    cut into 1 1/2-inch pieces

1 cup coarsely chopped onion

3 garlic cloves, minced

1 can (14 1/2 ounces) diced tomatoes
    with green pepper, celery, and onion

1 teaspoon ground cumin

1/2 teaspoon ground ginger

1/4 teaspoon ground cinnamon

1 cup water

2 yams (about 1 pound), peeled and cut
    into 1-inch pieces

3/4 cup pitted dates, halved crosswise

3 tablespoons chopped fresh cilantro

1/2 teaspoon salt

1. Heat 1 tablespoon of the oil in a large nonstick skillet over medium-high heat. Add half of the beef and cook, turning often, until browned, about 4 minutes. Transfer the beef to a large bowl. Repeat with the remaining oil and beef.

2. Stir the onion and garlic into the pot and cook, stirring, until the garlic is toasted, about 1 minute.

3. Add the beef, tomatoes, cumin, ginger, cinnamon, and water to the pot. Bring to a boil, reduce the heat to medium-low, and simmer, covered, until the onions are soft, about 45 minutes.

4. Add the yams and cook, stirring occasionally, until the beef is very tender and the yams are cooked through, about 25 minutes longer.

5. Stir in the dates and cook 5 minutes. Remove from the heat and stir in the cilantro and salt.

Personalize It!

Not a fan of sweet spices? Just take them out and substitute 1 teaspoon dried oregano and 1 teaspoon dried basil for the ginger and cinnamon. Leave out the dates, add 1/2 teaspoon dried thyme, and substitute parsley for the cilantro for a decidedly Italian-style stew.

CLASSIC VEAL STEW

SECRET INGREDIENT:
beer

Belgians have a way with stew. Their secret? Add beer to the braising liquid. Here's a new twist on traditional Belgian beef carbonnade made with veal. Dark beer enhances the rich flavor of the mushrooms.
See photograph on page 171.

Prep Time: 15 min **Cook Time:** 1 hr 30 min **Serves** 4

1 pound stewing veal, cut into 1-inch pieces

1/4 teaspoon freshly ground black pepper

3/4 teaspoon salt, divided

2 tablespoons vegetable oil

2 portobello mushrooms, stems removed
    and caps cut into 1-inch pieces

8 large shallots, finely chopped

2 tablespoons all-purpose flour

1 bottle (12 ounces) dark beer

1 tablespoon white-wine vinegar

1/2 teaspoon dried thyme

1 pound large carrots, peeled and cut
    into 2-inch lengths

1. Pat the veal dry and season with pepper and 1/4 teaspoon of the salt.

2. Heat the oil in a large saucepan or Dutch oven over high heat. Add the veal and cook until browned on all sides, 3 to 4 minutes. Transfer to a plate.

3. Reduce the heat to medium and add the mushrooms and shallots to the pan. Sauté until the shallots are just golden, about 5 minutes.

4. Stir in the flour. Add the veal, beer, vinegar, thyme, and the remaining salt, then bring to a boil.

5. Add the carrots, reduce the heat, and simmer, covered, until the veal is tender, about 1 1/4 hours.

6. Transfer the veal, carrots, and mushrooms to a warm serving dish. Boil the remaining liquid until reduced to about 1 1/4 cups and pour over the veal.

One More Notch! Cook 4 strips of bacon in the pan and remove to drain on a paper towel–lined plate. Use the drippings to cook the veal and use 1 chopped onion instead of the shallots. Add 1 tablespoon brown sugar along with the beer. Chop the bacon and stir it into the stew toward the end of the cooking time.

ASIAN-STYLE PORK STEW

SECRET INGREDIENT:

cola

With its spicy-sweet caramel flavor, cola has plenty of uses in the kitchen. Here, it enlivens the Asian flavors of a long-simmering pork stew. The best part is that most of the cooking is unattended.

Prep Time: 20 min   **Cook Time:** 1 hr 10 min   **Serves** 6

2 tablespoons peanut oil, divided

2 pounds boneless pork shoulder, cut into 2-inch cubes

2 tablespoons cornstarch

1 can (12 ounces) cola

1 cup chopped onion

5 garlic cloves, minced

2 tablespoons peeled, minced fresh ginger

3 tablespoons soy sauce, divided

2 carrots, thinly sliced

1 cup chopped green onions, divided

12 ounces udon noodles or linguine

1. Heat 1 tablespoon of the oil in a large pot over medium-high heat. In a large bowl, toss the pork with the cornstarch to coat. Add half the pork to the pot and cook, turning occasionally, until browned, about 4 minutes. Transfer the pork to a plate. Repeat with the remaining oil and pork.

2. Add the first batch of pork back into the pot and stir in the cola, onion, garlic, and ginger. Bring to a boil. Reduce the heat to medium-low, cover, and simmer, stirring occasionally, until the onions are tender, about 30 minutes.

3. Stir in 2 tablespoons of the soy sauce, the carrots, and 3/4 cup of the green onions. Cover, return to a simmer, and cook until the pork is very tender, about 40 minutes longer.

4. Meanwhile, cook the noodles according to the package directions, and drain.

5. Divide the noodles among six bowls. Remove the stew from the heat, stir in the remaining soy sauce, and spoon over the noodles. Sprinkle with the remaining green onions.

One More Notch! Add a little earthiness to the stew by adding 4 ounces quartered white mushrooms when you stir in the carrots.

MEXICAN PORK AND CHILI STEW

SECRET INGREDIENT:
tortilla chips

Mexican pork and chili stew, also called *Pozole*, is a traditional dish made with pork that is simmered with pureed chiles. Often served topped with fried tortilla strips, we kick up the flavor by topping it with crumbled chile-lime-flavored tortilla chips. The white hominy adds a subtle aroma of sweet corn.

Prep Time: 20 min **Cook Time:** 1 hr 10 min **Serves** 6

2 tablespoons olive oil, divided

1 boneless pork shoulder (2 pounds), cut into 3-inch pieces

1 cup chopped onion

5 garlic cloves, minced

1 teaspoon dried oregano

2 cans (14 1/2 ounces each) plus 1 cup chicken broth

3 ancho chiles, stems and seeds removed (wear gloves when handling)

Hot water

1 1/2 cups chopped tomatoes

1 can (15 ounces) white hominy, drained and rinsed

1/2 teaspoon salt

2 cups crumbled chili-lime tortilla chips

1 Haas avocado, peeled, pitted, and sliced

1. Heat 1 tablespoon of the oil in a large pot over medium-high heat. Add the pork and cook, turning occasionally, until browned, 4 to 5 minutes. Transfer to a large bowl and set aside.

2. Heat the remaining 1 tablespoon of oil in the pot. Stir in the onion and garlic and cook until it starts to soften, 2 to 3 minutes.

3. Stir in the oregano and cook for 30 seconds. Add 2 cans of the chicken broth and scrape up any browned bits from the bottom of the pot with a wooden spoon.

4. Add the pork, bring to a boil, reduce the heat to medium-low, and cook, partially covered, until very tender, about 1 hour 10 minutes.

5. Meanwhile, add the chiles to a small bowl with enough hot water to cover by 1 inch and soak until softened, about 30 minutes. Transfer the chiles to a blender. Add the remaining 1 cup chicken broth and puree.

6. Transfer the pork into a large bowl. With two forks, shred the pork and return it to the pot with the chili puree, tomatoes, and hominy. Bring to a boil over medium-high heat, then reduce the heat to medium-low, cover, and simmer for 20 minutes. Remove from the heat and stir in the salt.

7. To serve, divide the stew among six bowls and top each with tortilla chips and avocado.

One More Notch! In addition to the tortilla chips and avocado slices, serve the stew with some chopped onion, oregano, lime wedges, radishes, and crushed red-pepper flakes.

MALAY FISH STEW

SECRET INGREDIENT:
coconut milk

Braising is an ideal method for keeping fish moist and succulent. When the simmering liquid includes coconut milk, you get an infusion of intoxicating tropical aroma as well. Serve this stew with noodles or rice to soak up the fragrant broth.

Prep Time: 15 min **Cook Time:** 20 min **Serves** 4

1 tablespoon sunflower oil

4 scallions, chopped

1 red chile pepper, seeded and sliced (wear gloves when handling)

2 celery stalks, sliced

1 red bell pepper, seeded and sliced

1 garlic clove, crushed

1/2 teaspoon fennel seeds

2 teaspoons ground coriander

1/2 teaspoon ground cumin

1/4 teaspoon turmeric

1 can (14 1/2 ounces) chopped tomatoes, with juice

1/2 cup coconut milk

1 1/4 cups fish stock, preferably homemade

2 tablespoons fish sauce or light soy sauce

1 can (6 ounces) sliced bamboo shoots, drained

1 1/2 pounds thick skinless white fish fillet, such as cod or haddock, cut into chunks

16 tiger shrimp, peeled and deveined

Juice of 1/2 lime

2 scallions, chopped

1 tablespoon chopped fresh cilantro

1. In a large nonstick skillet over medium heat, heat the oil. Add the scallions, chile pepper, celery, and red pepper, and sauté until the vegetables are slightly softened, about 5 minutes.

2. Stir in the garlic, fennel seeds, coriander, cumin, and turmeric and sauté until fragrant, 1 minute.

3. Add the tomatoes with juice, coconut milk, stock, and fish sauce or soy sauce. Bring to a boil, reduce the heat, and simmer, covered, for 5 minutes.

4. Stir in the bamboo shoots, fish, and shrimp. Simmer, covered, until the fish flakes easily with a fork and the shrimp are pink and cooked through, about 5 minutes.

5. Stir in the lime juice. Sprinkle with chopped scallions and cilantro before serving.

that's **ingenious**

Not everyone has homemade fish stock on hand (lucky you if you do!). For a simple substitute, combine 3/4 cup bottled clam juice, 2/3 dry white wine, 1/2 cup water, 1/2 cup sliced onion, and 2 to 3 sprigs of parsley in a saucepan. Simmer over medium heat until reduced to about 1 1/4 cups. Strain before using.

ALBUQUERQUE SHRIMP AND TURKEY GUMBO

SECRET INGREDIENT:
salsa

Gumbo is like a classic novel: It's open to interpretation. This version uses salsa and frozen bell pepper strips to streamline prep time while kielbasa and shrimp round out the rich flavors.

Prep Time: 15 min **Cook Time:** 30 min **Serves** 4

1 cup uncooked white rice

2 tablespoons canola oil

1/4 cup all-purpose flour

1 cup chopped onion

1 cup frozen mixed bell pepper strips

1/2 cup chopped celery

1 1/2 cups frozen cut okra

3 cups jarred medium salsa

1 can (14 1/2 ounces) chicken broth

8 ounces turkey kielbasa, cut into
1/4-inch-thick slices

3/4 pound peeled and deveined large shrimp

1. In a small pot, cook the rice according to package directions.

2. Meanwhile, in a large pot over medium-high heat, cook the oil and flour, stirring constantly with a wooden spoon, until starting to brown, 4 to 5 minutes.

3. Stir in the onion, peppers, and celery and cook, stirring often, until beginning to soften, 5 to 6 minutes.

4. Add the okra and cook 4 minutes.

5. Stir in the salsa and cook until the mixture begins to simmer, 2 to 3 minutes.

6. Add the chicken broth and kielbasa and bring to a boil. Reduce the heat to medium-low and simmer, covered, for 15 minutes.

7. Stir in the shrimp, return to a simmer, and cook until the shrimp are pink and cooked through, 3 to 4 minutes.

8. To serve, divide the gumbo among four large serving bowls and place 3/4 cup of the rice in the center of each.

One More Notch! The process of cooking the oil and flour together in this recipe is called making a roux. The longer it cooks, the darker and more flavorful it becomes. However, the longer it cooks, the less thickening power the flour has. For added flavor, keep cooking the roux until it is a dark rust color. To help thicken the gumbo a little more, after adding the kielbasa, simmer it with the lid partially covering the pot.

EASY CIOPPINO

SECRET INGREDIENT:
V8 juice

Cioppino, that wonderful seafood stew made famous in San Francisco, doesn't have to take long to prepare. This version uses V8 juice and clam juice to shorten the soup's ingredient list without losing a bit of flavor. To save even more time, look for Clamato juice, a blend of tomato and clam juices that is available on many grocery store shelves.

Prep Time: 10 min **Cook Time:** 50 min **Serves** 4

1 tablespoon olive oil

4 garlic cloves, minced

1 cup chopped onion

1 cup seeded, chopped green bell pepper

1 can (14 1/2 ounces) Italian-seasoned diced tomatoes

3/4 cup V8 juice

3/4 cup bottled clam juice

16 littleneck clams, scrubbed

12 ounces halibut fillet, cut into
1 1/2-inch pieces

12 ounces peeled and deveined extra-large shrimp

1/2 cup sliced basil leaves

1. Heat the oil in a large pot over medium-high heat.

2. Add the garlic, onion, and bell pepper and cook, stirring occasionally, until starting to soften, 3 to 4 minutes.

3. Pour in the tomatoes, V8, and clam juice and bring to a boil. Reduce the heat to medium-low and simmer, covered, until the flavors have blended, 30 minutes.

4. Add the clams and cook until they open, 12 to 15 minutes.

5. Remove the clams and transfer to four serving bowls. Add the halibut and shrimp and cook until the fish flakes easily with a

fork and the shrimp are pink and cooked through, 3 to 4 minutes.

6. Stir in the basil. Ladle the soup over the clams and serve immediately.

One More Notch! A great addition to this dish is 1 tablespoon roasted red pepper and garlic mayonnaise spooned into each bowl. To make the mayonnaise, puree or very finely chop 1/2 of a jarred roasted red pepper and whisk it together with 1/4 cup mayonnaise and 1 small minced garlic clove.

MEXICAN CHICKEN SOUP WITH CHEESE

SECRET INGREDIENT:
tortillas

In America, we make chicken soup with noodles or rice. Our neighbors to the south use strips of corn tortillas instead. They add delightful crunch to this quick soup flavored with cumin, coriander, and melted Monterey Jack cheese. *See photograph on page 171.*

Prep Time: 15 min **Cook Time:** 10 min **Serves** 4

6 corn tortillas (6-inch), cut into
   1/2-inch-wide strips

2 teaspoons olive oil

1 green bell pepper, seeded and cut
   into 1/2-inch chunks

3 scallions, thinly sliced

3 garlic cloves, minced

2 large tomatoes, seeded and cubed

1 1/2 cups chicken broth

1/2 cup water

1 1/2 teaspoons ground cumin

1 1/2 teaspoons ground coriander

1/2 teaspoon salt

6 ounces skinless, boneless chicken breast,
   cut into thin strips

1/4 cup shredded Monterey Jack cheese
   (about 1 ounce)

1. Preheat the oven to 400°F.

2. Place the tortilla strips on a baking sheet and bake until crisp, about 5 minutes.

3. Meanwhile, heat the oil in a medium nonstick saucepan over medium heat. Add the pepper, scallions, and garlic and sauté until the scallions are tender, about 2 minutes. Stir in the tomatoes and cook until they start to collapse, about 2 minutes.

4. Add the broth, water, cumin, coriander, and salt to the pan and bring to a boil.

5. Add the chicken. Reduce the heat and simmer, covered, until the chicken is cooked through, about 3 minutes.

6. Ladle the soup into four bowls and top with the tortilla strips and cheese.

that's **ingenious**

> If you don't have corn tortillas at home and can't get to the store, check your snack shelf. You can use a few handfuls of tortilla snack chips instead.

TURKEY AND BARLEY SOUP

SECRET INGREDIENT:
chestnuts

Here's the perfect recipe for Thanksgiving leftovers. Simmer the turkey carcass with aromatic vegetables to make a rich stock, then fill out the soup with leeks, Brussels sprouts, parsnips, turkey meat, and a handful of chestnuts for rich flavor and extra chew.

Prep Time: 20 min **Cook Time:** 2 hrs 15 min **Serves** 6

STOCK

1 turkey carcass

1 onion, quartered

1 carrot, chopped

2 celery stalks, chopped

Parsley sprigs

Thyme sprigs

1 bay leaf

SOUP

1 large carrot, chopped

1 large parsnip, peeled and chopped

3 celery stalks, chopped

4 to 6 Brussels sprouts, chopped

1 large leek, chopped

3 1/2 ounces freshly cooked or vacuum-packed
chestnuts, coarsely chopped

2 1/2 ounces pearl barley

3 tablespoons chopped fresh parsley

3 1/2 ounces cooked skinless turkey,
chopped or shredded

Salt and freshly ground black pepper

1. For stock, break up the carcass, discarding any skin, and place it in a very large stock pot. Add the onion, carrot, and celery.

2. Tie the parsley, thyme sprigs, and bay leaf together to make a bouquet garni and add it to the pan. Cover with water and bring to a boil, skimming off any foam. Reduce the heat and simmer, covered, for 1 1/2 hours. Strain the stock into a large heat-proof bowl, discarding the bones, vegetables, and herbs. Wipe out the pan.

3. For soup, measure the stock and, if necessary, add water to make 6 cups. Skim off any fat and pour it into the stock pot.

4. Bring the stock to a boil and add the carrot, parsnip, celery, Brussels sprouts, leek, chestnuts, and barley. Reduce the heat and simmer, covered, until the barley is tender, about 35 minutes.

5. Add the parsley and turkey and simmer until heated through, about 4 minutes. Season with salt and pepper, to taste.

One More Notch! Serve the soup with blue cheese bruschetta. Slice a baguette into rounds, then broil the rounds just until golden. Meanwhile, mix together extra-virgin olive oil, chopped garlic, salt and freshly ground black pepper and brush over the broiled toasts. Top with crumbled blue cheese and heat under the broiler until the cheese begins to melt.

TURKEY NOODLE SOUP

SECRET INGREDIENT:
cloves

There are probably as many recipes for turkey noodle soup as there are cooks in the United States. This one features the distinguishing flavors of sage and cloves.

Prep Time: 15 min **Cook Time:** 1 hr 20 min **Serves** 6

9 cups chicken or turkey stock

4 carrots, peeled and shredded

3 celery stalks, sliced

1 onion, chopped

1 teaspoon rubbed sage

1/2 teaspoon freshly ground black pepper

3 whole cloves

1 bay leaf

2 cups diced cooked turkey

1 cup macaroni

1/4 cup chopped fresh parsley

1. In a large Dutch oven or soup pot over medium-high heat, combine the stock, carrots, celery, onion, sage, and pepper.

2. Make a spice bag by placing the cloves and bay leaf in the center of a small piece of cheesecloth or a clean coffee filter. Bring up the edges and tie securely with cotton string. Add the spice bag to the pot. Bring to a boil, reduce the heat, and simmer, covered, until the carrots are tender, about 1 hour.

3. Add the turkey, macaroni, and parsley and simmer, covered, until the macaroni is tender and the soup is heated through, about 15 minutes. Remove the spice bag before serving.

TOMATO AND LENTIL SOUP

SECRET INGREDIENT:
ground ginger

Here's a classic lentil soup with mushrooms and tomatoes. Our new twist is a kiss of peppery licorice flavor from sweet tarragon and ground ginger.

Prep Time: 10 min	**Cook Time:** 40 min	**Serves** 4

1/4 cup dried porcini or shiitake mushrooms

1 cup hot water

1 tablespoon olive oil

1 large onion, finely chopped

3 garlic cloves, minced

1 can (15 ounces) diced tomatoes (with juice)

1 teaspoon ground ginger

1 teaspoon dried tarragon

Salt

2 cups water

1/2 cup lentils, picked over and rinsed

1. Combine the mushrooms and water in a small bowl. Let stand 20 minutes until softened. With a slotted spoon or your fingers, scoop the mushrooms from the soaking liquid. Strain the liquid through a fine-meshed sieve and set aside. Coarsely chop the mushrooms.

2. Meanwhile, heat the oil in large saucepan over medium heat. Add the onion and garlic, and cook, stirring frequently, until the onion is golden, about 7 minutes.

3. Stir in the mushrooms, the strained liquid, tomatoes (with juice), ginger, tarragon, salt,

and water. Add the lentils and bring the soup to a boil. Reduce to a simmer, cover, and cook until the lentils are tender, about 30 minutes.

One More Notch! Punch up the flavors by cooking 4 strips of bacon in the saucepan before adding the onions. Use the bacon drippings in place of the olive oil. Crumble the bacon over the soup before serving.

PORTUGUESE KALE SOUP WITH BEANS

SECRET INGREDIENT:
pepperoni

Vitamin-rich kale tastes great teamed with sausage, potatoes, and kidney beans. Traditional Portuguese soups include linguiça, a hard-to-find smoked sausage flavored with paprika. Ours uses a mixture of Italian sausage and pepperoni available in any supermarket. *See photograph on page 170.*

Prep Time: 15 min	**Cook Time:** 45 min	**Serves** 6

4 ounces spicy turkey sausage or Italian sausage, casings removed, if necessary

1 1/2 ounces sliced pepperoni, slivered

1 large yellow onion, quartered and thinly sliced

1 celery stalk, coarsely chopped

4 cups chicken stock

4 cups water

8 ounces kale, thick stems removed and leaves sliced, or 2 packages (10 ounces each) frozen kale, thawed and squeezed dry

1 small red bell pepper, seeded and diced

1/2 teaspoon minced garlic

12 ounces red potatoes, halved and sliced

1/2 teaspoon hot red-pepper sauce

1/4 teaspoon salt

1 1/2 cups cooked or canned red kidney beans, cannellini beans, or chickpeas, rinsed and drained if canned

1/4 cup grated Parmesan cheese

1. Crumble the sausage into a soup pot or 5-quart Dutch oven over medium-low heat. Cook, stirring, until no longer pink, about 4 minutes. Add the pepperoni and cook until the fat is rendered, about 2 minutes. Transfer to a paper towel–lined plate to drain. Discard all but 1 teaspoon of drippings from the pot.

2. Add the onion and celery. Reduce the heat, cover, and cook, stirring occasionally, until soft, about 8 minutes. Return the meat to the pot, add the stock, water, kale, bell pepper, and garlic. Bring to a boil, reduce the heat, and simmer, covered, for 10 minutes.

3. Stir in the potatoes, red-pepper sauce, and salt. Simmer, covered, until the potatoes and kale are tender, about 20 minutes. Add the beans and cook until just heated through, 5 minutes. Garnish each serving with cheese.

Personalize It!

Don't like kale? Use spinach or chard instead.

MEDITERRANEAN ROASTED VEGETABLE SOUP

SECRET INGREDIENT:

carrot juice

Roasting vegetables caramelizes their sugars and brings out their sweetness. It's a fantastic technique for intensifying the flavor of a sauce or soup. It also helps to use carrot juice in place of plain old broth as the soup base. *See photograph on page 171.*

Prep Time: 15 min   **Cook Time:** 45 min   **Serves** 4

1 tablespoon olive oil

5 garlic cloves

12 ounces all-purpose potatoes, cut into 1/2-inch chunks

1 green bell pepper, seeded and cut into 1/2-inch squares

1 yellow bell pepper, seeded and cut into 1/2-inch squares

1 teaspoon fresh rosemary, chopped

1 yellow squash, halved lengthwise and cut crosswise into 1/2-inch pieces

1 large red onion, cut into 1/2-inch chunks

1 1/2 cups carrot juice

12 ounces plum tomatoes, seeded and diced

1 teaspoon fresh tarragon

3/4 teaspoon salt

3/4 cup water

1. Preheat the oven to 450°F.

2. In a roasting pan, combine the oil and garlic and roast until the oil begins to sizzle, about 5 minutes.

3. Add the potatoes, bell peppers, and rosemary and toss to coat. Roast until the potatoes begin to color and soften, about 15 minutes.

4. Add the squash and onion and roast until the squash is tender, about 15 minutes longer.

5. In a medium Dutch oven, combine the carrot juice, tomatoes, tarragon, and salt and bring it to boil over medium heat. Add the roasted vegetables.

6. Pour the water into the roasting pan and scrape up any brown bits. Pour the pan juices into the Dutch oven and cook until heated through, about 2 minutes.

that's **ingenious**

To quickly seed a bell pepper, hold it by the stem and stand it upright on your cutting board. Put your knife blade just outside the stem and cut down to remove one quadrant of the flesh from the core. Continue around the pepper, holding the stem and removing the remaining flesh from the core.

PUMPKIN BISQUE

SECRET INGREDIENT:

canned pumpkin

People usually assume that using convenience ingredients means giving up quality. On the contrary, some prepared foods have more desirable qualities than fresh foods. Canned pumpkin, for instance, is made from an extra-creamy breed of pumpkin that is unavailable to consumers. *See photograph on page 171.*

Prep Time: 15 min   **Cook Time:** 45 min   **Serves** 4

1 tablespoon vegetable oil

1 small onion, finely chopped

2 carrots, peeled and finely chopped

2 celery stalks, finely chopped

1/4 cup tomato paste

2 cans (14 1/2 ounces each) chicken broth

1 bay leaf

1/2 teaspoon dried thyme

1 can (15 ounces) solid-pack pumpkin puree

1/4 cup half-and-half

1/4 teaspoon salt

1/4 teaspoon ground white pepper

Sour cream (optional garnish)

Rosemary (optional garnish)

1. In a large saucepan over medium heat, heat the oil. Add the onion, carrots, and celery. Sauté until softened, about 5 minutes.

2. Stir in the tomato paste. Cook for 1 minute.

3. Add the broth, bay leaf, and thyme. Simmer, uncovered, until the vegetables are very tender, about 30 minutes.

4. Stir in the pumpkin. Cook for 5 minutes longer. Remove the bay leaf.

5. In a blender or food processor, puree the soup in batches. Pour the soup back into the saucepan.

6. Add the half-and-half. Bring to a simmer. Add the salt and pepper. If it's too thick, add a little water.

7. Top with the sour cream and rosemary, if using, before serving.

Personalize It!

If you're a fresh pumpkin purist, use about 2 pounds of small pie or sugar pumpkins to replace the canned pumpkin. Quarter the pumpkins and scrape out the strings and seeds (roast the seeds separately, if you like). Put the pumpkin pieces, skin side up, in a roasting pan and add 1/4 inch of water to the pan. Roast at 400°F until tender, about 45 minutes. Scoop the flesh from the skins and puree until smooth.

HARVEST SQUASH SOUP

SECRET INGREDIENT:

applesauce

Applesauce lends body and flavor to this satisfying autumn soup. Serve it with chunks of crusty bread as the first course in a meal featuring roast pork.

Prep Time: 15 min   **Cook Time:** 35 min   **Serves** 10

1 1/2 cups chopped onion

1 tablespoon vegetable oil

4 cups mashed cooked butternut squash

3 cups chicken broth

2 cups unsweetened applesauce

1 1/2 cups milk

1 bay leaf

1 tablespoon lime juice

1 tablespoon sugar

1 teaspoon curry powder

1/2 teaspoon ground cinnamon

1/2 teaspoon salt (optional)

1/4 teaspoon freshly ground black pepper

1/4 teaspoon ground nutmeg

1. In a large saucepan or Dutch oven, sauté the onion in the oil until tender, about 4 minutes.

2. Add the squash, broth, applesauce, milk, bay leaf, lime juice, sugar, curry powder, cinnamon, salt, if using, pepper, and nutmeg. Simmer, uncovered, until the flavors have blended, about 30 minutes.

3. Remove the bay leaf before serving.

that's **ingenious**

To save time, look for frozen butternut squash in the freezer section of well-stocked supermarkets. If you can't find it, peel 2 butternut squash and discard the seeds. Chop and steam over simmering water until tender, about 20 minutes. Mash.

CREAMY BUTTERNUT SQUASH SOUP

SECRET INGREDIENT:
cheddar cheese

With its creamy texture, mild and savory flavor, and gorgeous golden color, it's hard to improve on butternut squash soup. But this version manages to do it. Cheddar cheese melted on top of the soup adds another layer of taste and richness.

Prep Time: 20 min **Cook Time:** 1 hr 20 min **Serves** 4

2 butternut squash (1 1/2 pounds)

1/4 teaspoon salt, divided

1/4 teaspoon freshly ground black pepper, divided

1 teaspoon vegetable oil

4 shallots, finely chopped (about 1/2 cup)

1/4 cup dry white wine or water

1/4 cup chicken or vegetable broth

1 cup milk

4 slices (1/2 inch thick) French or Italian bread

1 cup shredded cheddar or Gruyère cheese (4 ounces)

2 tablespoons snipped fresh chives or minced fresh parsley (optional)

1. Preheat the oven to 400°F.

2. Halve the squash lengthwise and sprinkle with 1/8 teaspoon of the salt and 1/8 teaspoon of the pepper. Place on a baking sheet, cover loosely with foil, and bake until tender, 50 to 60 minutes. Scoop the squash from the shells and transfer the pulp to a food processor or blender. Set aside. Discard the shells.

3. In a small saucepan, heat the oil over medium heat. Add the shallots and sauté, stirring, until softened, about 3 minutes.

4. Add the wine or water and cook, uncovered, until reduced to 2 tablespoons, about 2 minutes.

5. Stir in the broth, milk, the remaining 1/8 teaspoon of the salt, and the remaining 1/8 teaspoon of the pepper. Add the mixture to the food processor with the squash. Whirl until pureed, working in batches, if necessary.

6. Divide half of the soup among four 1 1/2-cup ovenproof bowls or baking dishes or a 2-quart casserole. Place a slice of bread on top of each portion, then sprinkle each with 2 tablespoons of the cheese. Top with the remaining soup and sprinkle with the remaining cheese.

7. Set the bowls on a baking sheet and bake the soup until bubbling, about 25 minutes. Place the soup briefly under a preheated broiler to brown the cheese, then sprinkle with the chives or parsley, if using.

Personalize It!
For a nice flavor change, use acorn squash instead of the butternut. Or try sweet potatoes.

CREAMY POTATO SOUP

SECRET INGREDIENT:
peanut butter

The final swirl of sour cream in this soup may lead your guests into believing that sour cream provides its buttery texture. They'll never guess what's behind those creamy pureed potatoes: peanut butter.

Prep Time: 15 min   **Cook Time:** 20 min   **Serves** 4

1 tablespoon vegetable oil

1 yellow onion, finely chopped

1 garlic clove, finely chopped

2 all-purpose potatoes, peeled and chopped

2 carrots, sliced

1 celery stalk, sliced

3 1/2 cups chicken broth

1/2 cup smooth peanut butter

1/4 teaspoon cayenne pepper

1/4 cup sour cream

1. In a large saucepan, heat the oil over medium heat. Add the onion and garlic; sauté until they begin to soften, about 2 minutes.

2. Stir in the potatoes, carrots, and celery. Add the broth and bring to a boil over high heat. Reduce the heat, cover, and simmer until the vegetables are tender, about 15 minutes.

3. Remove the soup from the heat. Stir in the peanut butter and cayenne until well-mixed. Using a food processor or blender, puree the soup, half at a time, until smooth.

4. Return the soup to a medium saucepan. Reheat over medium heat until it is hot but not boiling. Ladle the soup into serving bowls and swirl a tablespoonful of sour cream into each serving. Serve immediately.

One More Notch! To enhance the savory flavors, simmer a few sprigs of fresh thyme (or 1/2 teaspoon dried) along with the vegetables. Remove the sprigs before pureeing the soup.

WATERCRESS AND PARSLEY SOUP

SECRET INGREDIENT:
evaporated milk

Sometimes simplicity reigns supreme as is the case with this light, refreshing soup. Evaporated milk adds velvety texture without piling on the calories.

Prep Time: 15 min   **Cook Time:** 15 min   **Serves** 4

2 tablespoons unsalted butter or margarine

1 small yellow onion, coarsely chopped (about 1/2 cup)

1/4 cup all-purpose flour

2 1/4 cups low-sodium chicken or vegetable broth

1 can (12 ounces) evaporated milk

2 1/2 cups chopped fresh flat-leaf parsley, divided

2 cups watercress leaves

1/8 teaspoon ground nutmeg

1/8 teaspoon salt

1/4 teaspoon freshly ground black pepper

1. In a large, heavy saucepan, melt the butter or margarine over medium-low heat. Add the onion, cover, and cook until softened, about 5 minutes.

2. Add the flour and cook, stirring, for 2 minutes. Gradually stir in the broth and milk and bring to a boil over medium heat, whisking constantly.

3. Adjust the heat so that the mixture simmers gently, then add 2 cups of the parsley and the watercress, nutmeg, salt, and pepper. Cover and cook until the watercress is wilted, about 5 minutes.

4. Drain the mixture in a large sieve set over a bowl, reserving the liquid. Place the solids, 1 cup of the reserved liquid, and the remaining 1/2 cup of the parsley in a blender or food processor and whirl until pureed, 30 to 40 seconds.

5. Return the puree to the saucepan, add the remaining liquid, and reheat.

One More Notch! To take this soup over the top, replace the evaporated milk with heavy cream or half-and-half.

CREAM OF CRAB SOUP

SECRET INGREDIENT:
curry powder

If you can find fresh crabmeat, that alone will make this soup taste outstanding. Otherwise, use refrigerated lump crabmeat for the best quality. Either way, the curry powder and crab boil seasoning lend so much flavor to this soup, you don't need to add much else.

Prep Time: 5 min   **Cook Time:** 10 min   **Serves** 6

1/2 cup unsalted butter or margarine

1/2 cup all-purpose flour

1 to 2 tablespoons crab boil seasoning, such as Old Bay

1 teaspoon salt

1/2 teaspoon curry powder

4 cups milk

1 pound cooked crabmeat or 3 cans (6 ounces each) crabmeat, drained

2 tablespoons minced fresh parsley

1. Melt the butter or margarine in a 3-quart saucepan. Stir in the flour, seasoning, salt, and curry powder. Cook until thickened and bubbly, about 2 minutes.

2. Gradually add the milk. Cook and stir until the mixture is hot (do not boil), about 2 more minutes.

3. Pick over the crab to remove any cartilage, if necessary. Add the crab and parsley to the soup and stir just until the crab is heated. If desired, thin the soup with additional milk.

One More Notch! To add even more flavor, sauté 2 large chopped shallots in the butter, until soft, about 2 minutes, before stirring in the flour.

CHEDDAR CHEESE AND BROCCOLI SOUP

SECRET INGREDIENT:
evaporated milk

If you love cheese but are watching calories, don't despair. Here's a comforting soup recipe with all the creamy richness of real cheddar cheese and plenty of health-boosting broccoli. Evaporated milk adds body to the soup without adding extra fat. *See photograph on page 171.*

Prep Time: 15 min   **Cook Time:** 20 min   **Serves** 6

1 pound broccoli

1 tablespoon olive oil

1 onion, chopped

1 celery stalk, chopped

2 tablespoons all-purpose flour

1 can (14 1/2 ounces) reduced-sodium chicken broth

1 can (12 ounces) evaporated fat-free milk

1 1/2 cups shredded reduced-fat cheddar cheese (12 ounces)

1/2 teaspoon freshly ground black pepper

1/4 teaspoon nutmeg

Salt

1. Trim and peel the broccoli stems. Cut off 12 small florets. Coarsely chop enough remaining broccoli to equal 2 cups. Blanch the chopped broccoli and florets in boiling water just until bright green, about 2 minutes. Drain and set aside.

2. Heat the oil in a medium saucepan over medium heat. Sauté the onion and celery until soft, about 5 minutes.

3. Whisk in the flour and cook 1 minute. Add the broth and evaporated milk. Cook, stirring constantly, until the mixture simmers and thickens, about 5 minutes.

4. Add the chopped broccoli, cheese, pepper, nutmeg, and salt, to taste. Stir until the cheese melts and the soup is heated through, about 3 minutes. Serve 1 cup per person, topped with the broccoli florets.

Personalize It!

Make the soup with asparagus, trimmed and coarsely chopped, instead of the broccoli.

CREAMY AVOCADO SOUP

SECRET INGREDIENT:

coconut milk

Think of this soup during the dog days of summer. It requires no cooking and features the refreshing flavors of lemon, cilantro, and avocado. Tropical-tasting coconut milk blended with creamy Greek yogurt adds to the silky yet full-bodied texture.

Prep Time: 20 min	**Cook Time:** 0 min	**Serves** 4

1/2 vegetable bouillon cube

Boiling water

Cold water

Small bunch of fresh cilantro, rinsed and dried

2 Haas avocados, halved and pitted

4 green onions, trimmed and chopped

1 large garlic clove, crushed

1 fresh green chile pepper, seeded and chopped
    (wear gloves when handling)

1 cup (8 ounces) natural Greek yogurt or
    plain yogurt

2/3 cup coconut milk

1 tablespoon olive oil

Pinch of sugar

1 tablespoon fresh lemon juice

Salt and freshly ground black pepper

1. Dissolve the bouillon cube in a small amount of the boiling water in a measuring cup, then add enough cold water to make 1 1/4 cups.

2. Roughly chop all but a few leaves of the cilantro. Scoop the avocado flesh into a blender or food processor. Add the broth, onions, garlic, chile peppers, the chopped cilantro, yogurt, coconut milk, oil, sugar, and lemon juice, and process, scraping down the sides once, until velvety and smooth, about 2 minutes.

3. Season with salt, to taste, and chill for at least 3 hours or overnight. Sprinkle with the reserved cilantro and black pepper.

One More Notch! To cool things down even further, place a couple of ice cubes in the soup bowls before serving. This soup tastes best when it's just short of frozen.

CHILLED TROUT SOUP

SECRET INGREDIENT:

horseradish

Silky and elegant in texture with a beguiling pale pink color, this cold soup makes the perfect summer starter. Cream cheese gives it a smooth texture as horseradish kicks up the flavor.

Prep Time: 15 min	**Cook Time:** 35 min	**Serves** 6

1 fennel bulb, quartered lengthwise

2 slices unpeeled beet (about 1/2 inch thick)

2 bay leaves

1/2 teaspoon black peppercorns

1/2 teaspoon salt

1 cup medium-dry white wine

3 1/2 cups cold water

2 sprigs of fresh tarragon

1 large, fresh, cleaned trout (about 12 ounces)

4 ounces cream cheese

1 tablespoon grated horseradish or
    2 tablespoons horseradish sauce

Salt and freshly ground black pepper

3 ounces smoked trout fillet, flaked

1. Put the fennel into a saucepan large enough to hold the trout. Add the beet, bay leaves, peppercorns, salt, wine, and water.

2. Pick the leaves off the tarragon and set aside. Add the tarragon stems to the pan. Bring to a boil, reduce the heat, and simmer until fragrant, about 10 minutes.

3. Add the whole trout to the pan. Bring to a boil, then reduce the heat, and simmer until the flesh is opaque throughout, 7 to 8 minutes. Remove the fish to a plate to cool.

4. Skin and bone the trout, setting aside the flesh and returning the head, tail, skin, and bones to the saucepan. Bring to a boil, reduce the heat, and simmer, partially covered, until the remaining fish meat falls from the bones, about 15 minutes. Strain into a medium bowl and let cool.

5. Puree the reserved trout flesh, cream cheese, and horseradish in a blender or food processor. Transfer to a large bowl and add the strained cooking liquid. Season with salt and pepper, to taste, then chill at least 3 hours or overnight.

6. Ladle the soup into cold soup bowls. Sprinkle with the smoked trout, tarragon leaves, and black pepper.

One More Notch! Top the soup with bits of crumbled cooked bacon to enhance the smokiness of the trout.

CLASSIC GAZPACHO

SECRET INGREDIENT:
bread

Most soups are enriched and thickened with cream or a mixture of butter and flour. Gazpacho achieves its body with a different thickener: bread. The bread is pureed right along with the vegetables in this no-cook soup, creating a satisfying texture as it allows the light, refreshing taste of the vegetables to shine through.

Prep Time: 20 min   **Cook Time:** 0 min   **Serves** 4

SOUP

1 pound fresh tomatoes, quartered and seeded

1/2 cucumber, peeled and coarsely chopped

1 red bell pepper, seeded and coarsely chopped

2 garlic cloves

1 small onion, quartered

1 slice bread, torn into pieces

2 cups low-sodium tomato juice

1 tablespoon tomato puree

2 tablespoons red-wine vinegar

2 teaspoons olive oil

1/4 teaspoon salt

VEGETABLES

1 red bell pepper, seeded and finely diced

4 scallions, thinly sliced

1/2 cucumber, peeled, seeded, and finely diced

2 slices bread, toasted and cut into cubes

1. For soup, mix the tomatoes, cucumber, pepper, garlic, onion, bread, tomato juice, tomato puree, vinegar, oil, and salt in a large bowl. Ladle batches of the mixture into a blender or food processor and puree until smooth. Pour the soup into a large clean bowl, then cover and refrigerate for 2 hours.

2. For vegetables, place the pepper, scallions, cucumber, and bread croutons in separate serving dishes.

3. To serve, ladle the soup into bowls over the vegetables.

Personalize It!

For a milder flavor, use 2 shallots instead of the onion. Or, if you like it spicy, stick with the onion and add 1 seeded, deveined, and diced jalapeño pepper (wear gloves when handling) to the vegetables. In very hot weather, add a few ice cubes to the soup just before serving to keep it well-chilled. ❄

STRAWBERRY-KIWI SOUP

SECRET INGREDIENT:

yogurt

Fruit soup makes a refreshing lunch or first course on a hot summer day. Plus, it's ultra-easy to make. This one gets its body and richness from vanilla-flavored yogurt.

Prep Time: 10 min	**Cook Time:** 0 min	**Serves** 4

2 pints fresh strawberries, hulled

6 kiwifruit, peeled and coarsely chopped

1 tablespoon fresh lime juice

3/4 cup vanilla yogurt

Pinch of ground allspice

1. Combine the strawberries, kiwifruit, lime juice, yogurt, and allspice in a blender or food processor. Process until smooth.

2. Refrigerate the soup for at least 30 minutes or overnight before serving.

that's **ingenious**

> Don't have vanilla yogurt? Don't worry. Mix 1/2 teaspoon vanilla extract and 2 tablespoons honey or brown sugar into plain yogurt.

COOL RASPBERRY SOUP

SECRET INGREDIENT:

white wine

Here's an easy cool-down dish for a steamy summer lunch or dinner. Serve it as a first or last course. White wine gives it a sophisticated flair that trumps ordinary fruit soups.

Prep Time: 15 min	**Cook Time:** 5 min	**Serves** 4

1 1/4 cups water

1 bag (20 ounces) frozen raspberries, thawed

1/4 cup white wine

1 cup cranberry-raspberry juice

1/2 cup sugar

1 1/2 teaspoons ground cinnamon

3 whole cloves

1 tablespoon fresh lemon juice

1 cup raspberry yogurt

1/2 cup sour cream

1. Place the water, raspberries, and wine in a blender or food processor. Cover and puree, scraping down the sides once, until smooth, about 2 minutes.

2. Transfer to a large saucepan and add the cranberry-raspberry juice, sugar, cinnamon, and cloves. Bring just to a boil over medium heat.

3. Remove from the heat, strain into a large bowl (discard the solids), and cool. Whisk in the lemon juice and yogurt. Refrigerate for at least 3 hours or overnight. Top each serving with 2 tablespoons sour cream.

that's **ingenious**

> Turn this into raspberry sorbet by freezing the mixture in an ice cream freezer according to the manufacturer's instructions. Or freeze the mixture in a shallow metal pan until solid then scrape out servings with a spoon.

extraordinary

poultry

main dishes

ROASTED HERB AND GARLIC CHICKEN

SECRET INGREDIENT:
cream cheese

Moisture is the secret to a succulent roast chicken. In this recipe, it comes in the form of herbed cream cheese slathered under the chicken skin so that it slowly melts and keeps the meat continually basted during roasting. A fresh lemon in the cavity of the bird and dry white wine poured over the skin heighten the flavors.

Prep Time: 30 min   **Cook Time:** 2 hr   **Serves** 8

CHICKEN

1 large roasting chicken (about 5 pounds)

1 teaspoon salt, divided

1 teaspoon freshly ground black pepper, divided

2 teaspoons grated lemon zest, divided

1 large lemon, halved

1 cup fresh cilantro leaves

1 cup fresh parsley leaves

2 large garlic cloves

1/2 cup cream cheese

3 tablespoons sour cream

1 cup dry white wine

GRAVY

1 cup chicken broth

2 tablespoons cornstarch

1/4 cup cold water

Lemon slices

Sprigs of fresh cilantro

Parsley

1. Preheat the oven to 425°F.

2. Wash the chicken inside and out with cold running water; discard the giblets and neck. Sprinkle the large cavity with 1/2 teaspoon of the salt and 1/2 teaspoon of the pepper. Sprinkle 1 teaspoon of the lemon zest into the cavity. Holding the chicken on a slant, squeeze the lemon inside the cavity, then stuff the lemon inside.

3. Position the chicken breast side up. Starting at the neck end, ease your fingers gently under the skin to loosen the skin over the breasts and thighs.

4. In a food processor or blender, process the cilantro, parsley, and garlic until finely chopped, 30 seconds.

5. Add the cream cheese, sour cream, the remaining 1/2 teaspoon pepper, the remaining 1/2 teaspoon salt, and the remaining 1 teaspoon lemon zest. Process a few seconds more to mix. Push the herbed cheese mixture under the skin, easing it along so that it covers the breasts and thighs evenly in a thin layer.

6. Truss the chicken and insert a roasting thermometer in the thigh, then place it on the rack in the pan. Pour the wine over the chicken and roast, uncovered, for 30 minutes. Lower the oven temperature to 350°F and continue roasting the chicken, basting frequently with the pan juices, until the thermometer registers 180°F and the juices of the chicken run clear when a thigh is pierced with a fork, about 1 1/2 hours.

7. Carefully lift the chicken from the roasting pan, tilting it so the juices run out of the cavity into the pan. Let it stand on a carving board for 10 minutes.

8. Meanwhile, for gravy, pour the pan drippings into a heat-proof measuring cup and skim off the fat. Add enough chicken broth to make 2 cups liquid and pour the mixture back into the pan. In a cup, dissolve the cornstarch in the water and whisk into the drippings. Bring to a boil over high heat, scraping up the browned bits from the bottom of the pan. Boil until the gravy thickens, about 2 minutes.

9. Carve the chicken. Decorate with the lemons, cilantro, and parsley. Serve with the gravy.

Personalize It!

To vary the flavor, swap the cilantro leaves for tarragon or sage leaves (use a bit less as these are stronger-tasting herbs). Use oranges instead of lemons for zest and juice. ❖

SUPER-MOIST PEPPER CHICKEN

SECRET INGREDIENT:

kosher salt

There are a hundred ways to roast a chicken, and each one claims to be the best. This version might be the only way you'll ever want to roast again. A crust made with kosher salt, pepper, egg whites, and water helps to gently cook the bird while locking in moisture for consistent results every time. You be the judge. *See photograph on page 175.*

Prep Time: 20 min **Cook Time:** 1 hr 45 min **Serves** 4

1 lemon

1 whole chicken (3 1/2 to 4 pounds)

2 boxes (3 pounds each) kosher salt

1/4 cup freshly ground black pepper

3 egg whites

2 cups water

3 rosemary sprigs

1. Preheat the oven to 350°F. Line a roasting pan with enough foil to overlap on all sides.

2. With a fork, prick all over the lemon. Insert the lemon into the cavity of the chicken and close the skin over the opening, securing with toothpicks.

3. Combine the salt, pepper, egg whites, and water in a large bowl. Cover the bottom of the roasting pan with a third of the salt mixture and set the chicken on top of the

salt. Lay the rosemary on top of the breast of the chicken. Carefully spoon the remaining salt over the chicken to completely cover it. Lift the foil near the sides of the pan to keep any salt from spilling out.

4. Roast the chicken for 1 hour 45 minutes. Remove from the oven and let stand 15 minutes. Crack the crust with a hammer or rolling pin and discard.

5. Transfer the chicken to a work surface and brush off any salt that remains. Remove the skin, cut up the chicken, and serve.

Personalize It!

This simple recipe is easy to make your own. Try different herbs in place of the rosemary, and stir your favorite spice mixes into the salt to help perfume the meat. ❖

ORANGE-GLAZED CHICKEN WITH RICE

SECRET INGREDIENT:

currant jelly

Orange juice concentrate provides the citrus flavor in these easy roast chicken pieces, but the secret to their appetizing glaze is a jar of currant jelly. Orange-scented rice rounds out the meal.

Prep Time: 20 min **Cook Time:** 1 hr 15 min **Serves** 4

CHICKEN

1/2 cup currant jelly

1/2 cup cold water, divided

1/4 cup orange juice concentrate

2 tablespoons cornstarch

1 teaspoon dry mustard

Dash of hot-pepper sauce

2 tablespoons vegetable oil

1/2 cup all-purpose flour

1/4 teaspoon salt

1 broiler-fryer chicken (3 1/2 to 4 pounds), cut up

RICE

1 cup diced celery

1/4 cup chopped onion

2 tablespoons unsalted butter or margarine

1 1/3 cups water

1 1/3 cups uncooked instant rice

2 tablespoons orange juice concentrate

1/2 teaspoon salt

1. Preheat the oven to 350°F. Grease a 9 x 13-inch baking dish.

2. For chicken, in a small saucepan, combine the jelly, 1/4 cup of the water, and the orange juice concentrate. Stir on low heat until the jelly is melted, about 2 minutes.

3. Combine the cornstarch and remaining 1/4 cup water in a cup; gradually stir into the jelly mixture along with the mustard and hot-pepper sauce.

4. Bring to a boil over high heat, stirring constantly. Cook about 2 minutes more; remove from the heat and set aside.

5. Add the oil to a large nonstick skillet. Combine the flour and salt in a shallow dish. Dredge the chicken in the flour and brown it in the skillet over medium heat.

6. Place the chicken in the baking dish. Pour the sauce over the chicken. Cover and bake for 20 minutes. Baste with the sauce. Bake, uncovered, until the juices run clear when the chicken is pierced with a fork, 45 minutes longer.

7. Meanwhile, for rice, in a medium saucepan, sauté the celery and onion in the butter or margarine until crisp-tender, about 5 minutes. Add the water and bring to a boil.

8. Stir in the rice, orange juice concentrate, and salt. Cover and remove from the heat; let stand until water is absorbed, 5 to 7 minutes.

9. Serve the chicken over the rice.

Personalize It!

This recipe tastes great with pork, too. Replace the cut-up chicken with 6 bone-in pork loin chops (each about 1 inch thick). Increase the cooking time to about 2 hours, or until the pork juices run clear (about 155°F on an instant-read thermometer). ✳

CHICKEN WITH APPLES

SECRET INGREDIENT:
Calvados

Looking for a meal that can be on the table in 30 minutes yet is elegant enough for a dinner party? This dish looks and tastes like it comes from a fine French bistro, but with far healthier ingredients. A triple shot of apples, apple juice, and Calvados (a French apple brandy) gives it intense autumnal flavors.

See photograph on page 175.

See photograph on page 175.

Prep Time: 10 min	Cook Time: 20 min	Serves 4

2 shallots, finely chopped

2 tart apples, peeled and cut into 1/4-inch slices

1 cup apple juice

3/4 cup reduced-sodium chicken broth

1 tablespoon Calvados

1/4 cup all-purpose flour

Salt

1/2 teaspoon freshly ground black pepper

4 skinless, boneless chicken breast halves (5 ounces each)

2 tablespoons heavy cream

1. Lightly coat a large, heavy nonstick skillet with nonstick cooking spray and set over medium-high heat. Sauté the shallots until soft, about 2 minutes.

2. Add the apples and sauté until lightly browned, about 3 minutes.

3. Add the apple juice, broth, and Calvados. Cook, stirring, until the apples are tender, about 5 minutes. Transfer to a medium bowl. Wipe the skillet clean and set aside.

POULTRY

4. Meanwhile, combine the flour, salt, to taste, and pepper on sheet of wax paper. Coat the chicken breasts with the flour, pressing with your hands so the flour adheres and the chicken is flattened evenly.

5. Lightly coat the skillet again with cooking spray. Cook the chicken over medium-high heat until browned and almost cooked through, about 3 minutes on each side.

6. Return the apple mixture and any juices to the skillet and bring to a boil. Reduce the heat and simmer 2 minutes. Stir in the cream and remove from the heat.

that's **ingenious**

If you can't find Calvados, use applejack, another apple brandy, or apple cider. And if you're tired of chicken breasts, turkey cutlets make a fine substitute here.

EARL GREY CHICKEN

SECRET INGREDIENT:
Earl Grey tea

Chicken breasts dry out easily when cooked. Poaching them in flavored liquid keeps the meat moist and adds subtle aromas. Tea bags are perfect for flavoring the poaching liquid. In this elegant main dish, Earl Grey tea adds the subtle citrus aromas of bergamot, a small sour orange with a wonderfully aromatic peel.

Prep Time: 15 min   **Cook Time:** 25 min   **Serves** 4

6 cups water

8 Earl Grey tea bags

1 tablespoon fresh lemon juice

4 boneless, skinless chicken breasts
(about 1 1/2 pounds)

2 teaspoons olive oil

1/2 cup chopped onion

1 garlic clove, minced

1 cup chicken broth

3/4 cup heavy cream

1/4 teaspoon salt

1/8 teaspoon freshly ground black pepper

1 tablespoon chopped fresh oregano or parsley

1. Put the water in a deep sauté pan and bring to a boil. Turn off the heat and add the tea bags. Let steep for 5 minutes. Remove the bags, squeezing to release any liquid.

2. Add the lemon juice and return to a boil over high heat. Reduce the heat to medium-low, regulating it so that the liquid barely simmers (160° to 170°F).

3. Add the chicken to the liquid, completely submerging it. Cook, uncovered, until the chicken is just barely pink in the center, about 10 minutes. Remove from the heat and let stand for 5 minutes.

4. Meanwhile, heat the oil in a small non-stick skillet over medium heat. Add the onion and garlic and cook until tender, about 4 minutes.

5. Add the broth, cream, and 1/4 cup of the poaching liquid. Raise the heat to high and boil until reduced to about half the original volume, about 5 minutes. Stir in the salt and pepper.

6. Transfer the chicken to a platter or plates and spoon the sauce over the top. Sprinkle with the oregano or parsley.

One More Notch! Serve with coconut rice made by simmering 1 cup rice in 1 1/2 cups water mixed with 1/2 cup canned coconut milk.

CHICKEN AND CASHEW PANCAKES

SECRET INGREDIENT:

orange zest

Chicken stir-fried with cashews, carrots, celery, cabbage, and a touch of sesame makes a delicious filling for thin pancakes. But what really wakes up the flavors is a healthy shot of freshly grated orange zest.

Prep Time: 30 min **Cook Time:** 30 min **Serves** 4

PANCAKES

1/2 cup all-purpose flour

Salt and freshly ground black pepper

1 egg, beaten

1 1/4 cups milk

1 teaspoon canola oil, divided

FILLING

2 ounces unsalted cashews

1 tablespoon canola oil

1/2 pound skinless, boneless chicken breasts, cut into strips

1 garlic clove, crushed

1 teaspoon finely chopped fresh ginger

1 fresh red chile pepper, seeded and finely chopped (wear gloves when handling), optional

2 carrots, cut into matchstick strips

2 celery stalks, cut into matchstick strips

Grated zest of 1/2 orange

1/2 cup shredded Savoy cabbage

1 tablespoon reduced-sodium soy sauce

1 tablespoon toasted sesame oil

1. For pancakes, sift the flour into a large bowl and add a little salt and pepper, to taste. Make a well in the center. Mix the egg with the milk in a measuring cup, then pour into the well. Gradually whisk the flour into the egg and milk to form a smooth batter.

2. Use a little of the oil to lightly grease a medium nonstick skillet and place it over medium heat. Pour in a little of the batter and tilt the pan to distribute the batter evenly across the surface to form a thin pancake (about 8 inches in diameter). Cook until the edges appear dry, about 2 minutes. Turn with a spatula and cook on the other side for about 30 seconds. Slide out onto a plate warmed in the microwave for 15 to 30 seconds and cover with wax paper.

3. Cook the remaining batter in the same way, adding a little more oil to the pan between pancakes, as necessary. Make 8 pancakes total, stacking them up, interspersed with wax paper. Cover the stack with foil, sealing it well. Set aside and keep warm.

4. For filling, heat a wok or large skillet. Add the cashews and stir-fry them over medium heat until golden, a few minutes. Remove to a plate and set aside.

5. Add the oil to the pan, then add the chicken, garlic, ginger, and chile, if using. Stir-fry until the chicken is no longer pink, 3 minutes.

6. Add the carrots and celery and stir-fry for 2 minutes.

7. Add the orange zest and cabbage, and stir-fry for 1 minute.

8. Sprinkle with the soy sauce and oil, and stir-fry for another minute.

9. Return the cashews to the pan and toss to mix.

10. Divide the filling among the warm pancakes and fold them over or roll up. Serve immediately, with a little extra soy sauce, if desired.

that's **ingenious**

To save time, replace the pancakes with store-bought crêpes.

INDIAN-STYLE TANDOORI GRILLED CHICKEN BREASTS

SECRET INGREDIENT:

yogurt

A tandoor is a bell-shaped clay oven heated over coals to a super-high temperature. At home, a charcoal grill or broiler works fine. Yogurt does double duty in this tandoori dish, both as a tenderizer in the spicy chicken marinade and as the base for a refreshing cucumber relish.

Prep Time: 30 min   **Cook Time:** 15 min   **Serves** 6

CHICKEN

1 cup plain low-fat yogurt

2 tablespoons tomato paste

1 tablespoon peeled and grated ginger

1 tablespoon curry powder

2 teaspoons garam masala

1 large garlic clove, minced

6 skinless, boneless chicken breast halves (about 2 pounds)

Canola oil

RAITA

1 large cucumber

1 1/2 cups plain low-fat yogurt

1 large tomato, finely chopped

1 teaspoon ground coriander

1 teaspoon ground cumin

Pinch of cayenne pepper

Pinch of salt

2 large lemons or limes, cut in wedges

Sprigs of fresh coriander

1. For chicken, process the yogurt, tomato paste, ginger, curry powder, garam masala, and garlic in a food processor or blender until blended, about 30 seconds, or simply whisk them in a small bowl. Transfer to a large, shallow bowl that is big enough to hold the chicken breasts in a single layer.

2. Cut 2 slits on each side of the chicken breasts. Place them in the marinade, turning to coat and rubbing the marinade into the slits. Cover with plastic wrap and let marinate in the refrigerator for 30 minutes or overnight.

3. Meanwhile, for raita, cut the cucumber in half lengthwise (do not peel) and remove the seeds with a spoon. Grate the cucumber into a medium bowl and squeeze out as much juice as possible with your hands (discard the juice).

4. Add the yogurt, tomato, coriander, cumin, cayenne, and salt and mix well. Transfer to a serving bowl and keep cold in the refrigerator.

5. Preheat the grill or broiler to high. Remove the chicken from the marinade (discard the marinade). Brush the grill rack with oil, then place the chicken on top. Grill or broil 6 inches from the heat, turning several times, until the juices run clear when the chicken is pierced with a fork, about 12 minutes (the outsides of the chicken may look slightly charred). Transfer to a serving plate.

6. Decorate with the lemon or lime and the coriander. Serve with the raita in a separate serving dish, on the side.

Personalize It!

Turn this dish into tandoori chicken kebabs if you like. Cut the breasts into 1 1/4-inch cubes before placing them in the marinade. Soak 8 bamboo skewers in cold water. Cut 1 large unpeeled zucchini into rounds about 1 inch thick. Seed and cut 1 large red bell pepper and 1 large yellow bell pepper into 1 1/4-inch cubes. Alternately thread the chicken and vegetables on the skewers. Grill or broil the kebabs for 8 to 10 minutes.

OVEN-BAKED BARBECUED CHICKEN

SECRET INGREDIENT:
apple butter

Some barbecue sauces are loaded with butter. This lighter version gets its thick texture from apple butter. Prepared salsa and Worcestershire sauce kick up the flavors. Best of all, the recipe only requires 5 minutes of prep.

Prep Time: 5 min   **Cook Time:** 25 min   **Serves** 4

1/3 cup apple butter

2 tablespoons salsa

2 tablespoons ketchup

1 tablespoon vegetable oil

1/2 teaspoon salt

1/4 teaspoon garlic powder

2 drops Worcestershire sauce

2 drops liquid smoke (optional)

4 boneless, skinless chicken breast halves (about 1 pound)

1. Preheat the oven to 375°F. Grease an 8-inch square baking dish.

2. Combine the apple butter, salsa, ketchup, oil, salt, garlic powder, Worcestershire sauce, and liquid smoke, if using, in a small bowl.

3. Add the chicken to the baking pan. Pour the sauce over the chicken.

4. Bake, uncovered, until the juices run clear when the chicken is pierced with a fork, about 25 minutes.

One More Notch! Flavor up the barbecue sauce even more by adding 2 teaspoons molasses, 1/2 teaspoon ground mustard, and 1/2 teaspoon pure chile powder such as ancho or chipotle.

CURRIED CHICKEN

SECRET INGREDIENT:
raisins

Some curries are smoking hot. Here's a milder, gentler curry that even kids will enjoy. Raisins give the dish a touch of sweetness that adds to the easygoing flavor profile.

Prep Time: 10 min   **Cook Time:** 25 min   **Serves** 4

1 1/3 cups chicken or vegetable broth

1 onion, chopped

2 garlic cloves, chopped

3 tablespoons vegetable oil

3 tablespoons all-purpose flour

2 tablespoons mild curry powder

4 skinless, boneless chicken breast halves (about 1 1/2 pounds), cut into 1-inch cubes

Small handful of fresh coriander, rinsed, dried, and chopped

2 level tablespoons seedless raisins

3 tablespoons sliced almonds

Juice of 1/2 lemon

2 tablespoons plain or Greek yogurt

2 tablespoons heavy cream

Salt and freshly ground black pepper

1. Add the broth to a medium saucepan and bring to a boil.

2. Meanwhile, fry the onion and garlic gently in the oil in a large nonstick skillet over medium-low heat until soft, about 5 minutes.

3. Mix the flour and curry powder in a large bowl, then toss the chicken in the mixture until evenly coated. Add the chicken and any extra flour mixture to the pan and fry over medium heat, stirring, until the chicken is no longer pink, about 3 minutes.

4. Add 1 tablespoon coriander to the chicken along with the raisins and the broth. Bring to a boil, stirring, then reduce the heat and simmer until the liquid reduces slightly, about 10 minutes.

5. Toast the almonds in a small dry nonstick skillet.

6. Remove the chicken from the heat and stir in the almonds, lemon juice, yogurt, cream, and salt and pepper, to taste. Reheat very gently, but do not allow it to boil.

7. Sprinkle with additional coriander before serving.

One More Notch! Enhance the meal by serving the chicken with lemon rice. Add 2 strips of lemon zest, 1/2 teaspoon salt, and a pinch of nutmeg to the water when cooking the rice.

MEXICAN CHICKEN CASSEROLE

SECRET INGREDIENT:

salsa

Here's your answer to the weeknight meal dilemma: Take shortcuts. Pre-cooked chicken cuts your prep and cooking time without sacrificing flavor. Store-bought salsa makes for a quick and delicious sauce. For an authentic Mexican touch, sauté strips of fresh corn tortillas in a little oil as a topping.

Prep Time: 20 min **Cook Time:** 30 min **Serves** 4

1/4 cup canola oil, divided

1 large onion, chopped

3 garlic cloves, minced

2 jalapeño peppers, seeded, deveined, and minced (wear gloves when handling)

1 package (10 ounces) cooked, carved chicken breasts, such as Perdue Shortcuts

1 can (15 ounces) red kidney beans, drained and rinsed

1 jar (16 ounces) purchased mild chunky salsa

2 cups shredded Mexican blend cheese (about 8 ounces)

3 corn tortillas, cut into thin strips

1/3 cup sour cream

1. Preheat the oven to 400°F and coat an 8-inch square baking dish with cooking spray.

2. Heat 1 tablespoon of the oil in a large nonstick skillet over medium-high heat. Add the onion, garlic, and jalapeños and cook, stirring occasionally, until beginning to soften, 3 to 4 minutes.

3. Stir in the chicken and beans and cook until hot, 2 to 3 minutes.

4. Add the salsa and cook 2 minutes longer. Transfer the mixture to the baking dish and sprinkle the top with the cheese.

5. Bake until bubbly and the cheese melts, about 15 minutes.

6. Meanwhile, wipe out the skillet and heat the remaining 3 tablespoons oil over medium-high heat. Add a third of the tortilla strips and cook, turning occasionally, until crisp, 2 to 2 1/2 minutes. Transfer to a paper towel–lined plate to drain. Repeat with the remaining strips.

7. Remove the casserole from the oven and top with the tortilla strips, then drizzle with the sour cream.

that's **ingenious**

Don't have red kidney beans? Substitute black beans or pinto beans. Don't have Mexican blend cheese? Use cheddar, mozzarella, or Colby instead. This versatile dish can stand up to many ingredient changes, so add your favorite salsa or sauce and have fun with it.

HUNTER'S CHICKEN

jarred tomato sauce with mushrooms

Hunter's chicken, also known as chicken cacciatore, is a classic way of braising chicken in a hearty tomato sauce. Mushrooms are usually added for deeper flavor. To get a jump-start on the dish, use bottled tomato sauce with mushrooms. Dinner will be ready in under an hour.

Prep Time: 15 min   **Cook Time:** 45 min   **Serves** 4

2 tablespoons olive oil

3 pounds bone-in chicken parts

3/4 teaspoon salt

1/4 teaspoon freshly ground black pepper

2 cups frozen mixed bell pepper strips

1 onion, sliced

6 garlic cloves, sliced

1 jar (26 ounces) tomato sauce with mushrooms

1. Heat the oil in a large pot over medium-high heat. Sprinkle the chicken with the salt and pepper and add to the pot. Cook, turning occasionally, until the chicken is browned, about 8 minutes. Transfer the chicken to a plate.

2. Add the pepper strips, onion, and garlic to the pot and cook, stirring occasionally, until the vegetables start to soften, 4 to 5 minutes.

3. Add the chicken and sauce. Reduce the heat to medium-low, cover, and simmer until the chicken is very tender, 30 to 35 minutes.

One More Notch! For more kick, stir in a pinch of crushed red-pepper flakes when you sauté the vegetables. Serve with wide egg noodles to round out the meal.

BRAISED CHICKEN AND FENNEL

apricots

Tender and full-flavored chicken thighs taste excellent in casseroles—especially when teamed with sweet apricots and fennel that have been scented with cumin and coriander.

Prep Time: 15 min   **Cook Time:** 50 min   **Serves** 4

2 tablespoons canola oil

8 chicken thighs (about 1 pound)

1 onion, sliced

2 garlic cloves, chopped

2 teaspoons ground cumin

2 teaspoons ground coriander

1 1/4 cups reduced-sodium chicken broth

3 carrots, halved crosswise, then each half cut into 6 to 8 thick fingers

1 bulb of fennel, halved lengthwise, then cut crosswise into slices

5 apricots, pitted and quartered

Salt and freshly ground black pepper

Chopped fennel leaves from the bulb

1. Heat the oil in a large nonstick skillet and sauté the chicken, turning occasionally, until golden brown all over, 5 to 10 minutes. Remove from the pan.

2. Add the onion and garlic to the pan and sauté until soft and golden, about 5 minutes.

3. Stir in the cumin and coriander. Fry for 1 minute, then add the broth.

4. Return the chicken to the pan together with the carrots and fennel. Bring to a boil. Stir well, then reduce the heat, cover, and simmer gently until the chicken is tender, about 30 minutes. Remove the lid. If there is too much liquid, boil to reduce it slightly.

5. Add the apricots to the casserole and stir gently to mix. Simmer over low heat until they soften, 5 minutes longer.

6. Season with the salt and pepper, to taste. Sprinkle with the fennel leaves and serve.

that's **ingenious**

If ripe apricots aren't available, use 1 can (15 ounces) apricot halves in natural juice, drained and cut in half. To round out the meal, serve the chicken with saffron rice.

SPANISH-STYLE CHICKEN

SECRET INGREDIENT:

sausage

Salty black olives, sweet bell peppers, spicy chorizo sausage, and white wine make plain old chicken brand new again. The hint of smoke in the chorizo bolsters the dark taste of chicken thighs. Serve with rice or crusty bread to soak up the juices. *See photograph on page 175.*

| **Prep Time:** 15 min | **Cook Time:** 30 min | **Serves** 4 |

2 tablespoons olive oil

8 skinless, boneless chicken thighs, halved

1 red onion, thinly sliced

1 red bell pepper, seeded and sliced

1 yellow bell pepper, seeded and sliced

1 garlic clove, crushed

1 can (19 ounces) chopped tomatoes (with juice)

2/3 cup dry white wine

1 tablespoon paprika

3 ounces chorizo sausage, cut into thick slices

2 tablespoons pitted black olives (preferably oil-cured), halved

Salt and freshly ground black pepper

Parsley, rinsed, dried, and chopped

1. Heat the oil in a large flame-proof casserole, then fry the chicken over high heat until golden.

2. Add the onion, peppers, and garlic to the chicken. Fry until they are lightly browned and slightly softened, 5 to 7 minutes.

3. Stir in the tomatoes (with juice), wine, and paprika and bring to a boil. Add the sausage, then simmer until the chicken is cooked, 15 minutes.

4. Add the olives to the casserole, then season with salt and pepper, to taste.

5. Add the parsley before serving.

that's **ingenious**

If you can't find Spanish chorizo, a ready-to-eat smoked sausage, use Mexican chorizo or Cajun andouille sausage, but cook the sausage in the pan along with the chicken. You could also use spicy smoked kielbasa or hot Italian sausage the same way.

CHICKEN SLOPPY JOES

SECRET INGREDIENT:
buttermilk biscuit dough

Serving Sloppy Joes on buttermilk biscuits definitely one-ups the more ubiquitous hamburger rolls. Biscuits are sweeter and richer, and the cheese melts right into them.

Prep Time: 10 min **Cook Time:** 20 min **Serves** 4

1 package (16.3 ounces) big buttermilk biscuits, such as Pillsbury Grands

1 cup shredded sharp cheddar cheese (about 4 ounces)

1 tablespoon canola oil

2 garlic cloves, minced

1 cup chopped onion

1 cup seeded and chopped green bell pepper

1 pound ground chicken

1 teaspoon chili powder

1 cup ketchup

2 tablespoons dark brown sugar

1/4 teaspoon salt

1. Prepare the biscuits according to the package directions. Remove the biscuits from the oven and allow to cool for 5 minutes.

2. Split the biscuits in half and arrange the tops on a baking sheet. Sprinkle each top with 2 tablespoons of the cheese and bake until melted, 3 to 4 minutes.

3. Meanwhile, heat the oil in a large non-stick skillet over medium-high heat. Add the garlic, onion, and pepper and cook, stirring occasionally, until they start to soften, 4 to 5 minutes.

4. Stir in the chicken and chili powder and cook until no longer pink, 3 to 4 minutes.

Add the ketchup, brown sugar, and salt and cook, stirring occasionally, until slightly thickened and the chicken is cooked through, 4 to 5 minutes.

5. Divide the chicken mixture among the biscuits and serve immediately.

One More Notch! For more intense flavor, add 1 teaspoon ground cumin, 2 teaspoons Worcestershire sauce, and a shake of ground ancho chili powder.

CRISPY CRUNCHY CHICKEN NUGGETS WITH HONEY MUSTARD

SECRET INGREDIENT:
cashews

It seems that every kid loves chicken nuggets. This version is sure to please the adults, too. Cashews add extra crunch and richness while a shot of maple syrup deepens the flavor of the honey mustard. *See photograph on page 175.*

Prep Time: 15 min **Cook Time:** 20 min **Serves** 4

1/3 cup Dijon mustard

4 teaspoons honey

4 teaspoons maple syrup

1/2 cup all-purpose flour, divided

1 teaspoon garlic powder

1 teaspoon ground cumin

1/2 teaspoon onion powder

1/2 teaspoon salt

1/4 teaspoon cayenne pepper

2 eggs, lightly beaten

1 1/2 cups cashews, very finely chopped

4 boneless, skinless chicken breasts (about 1 pound), cut into 10 chunks each

4 cups canola oil

1. Preheat the oven to 250°F.

2. Combine the mustard, honey, and syrup in a small bowl. Mix well and set aside.

3. Combine 1/4 cup of the flour, the garlic powder, cumin, onion powder, salt, and cayenne in a shallow bowl; mix well.

4. Place the eggs in a separate shallow bowl.

5. Combine the remaining 1/4 cup flour and the cashews in a third shallow bowl.

6. Add the chicken, a few pieces at a time, to the flour and toss to coat. Shake off the excess flour and dip in the eggs to coat. Shake off the excess egg then dip in the cashew mixture to coat. Place on a baking sheet.

7. Pour the oil in a 3-quart saucepan and heat to 340°F on a deep fry thermometer over medium heat. Add the chicken, 10 pieces at a time, and fry until golden brown and cooked through, about 4 minutes. Transfer to a paper towel–lined baking sheet to drain. Keep warm in the oven. Make sure the oil has returned to temperature before frying the next batch of chicken.

8. Serve with the mustard sauce for dipping.

Personalize It!

If you're not a fan of honey mustard, try this: Mix together 1/4 cup buttermilk, 1/4 cup sour cream, and 3 tablespoons chopped fresh chives. Or use a creamy salad dressing like blue cheese or ranch. Even onion dip will work in a pinch. ❄

STUFFED GLAZED CORNISH HENS

SECRET INGREDIENT:
apricot preserves

Filled with a mushroom and sage bread stuffing, these savory hens make perfect individual servings for an autumn meal. The glaze couldn't be easier: a jar of apricot preserves brushed over the skin during roasting.

Prep Time: 20 min **Cook Time:** 1 hr 30 min **Serves** 4

3 tablespoons chopped celery

3 tablespoons chopped onion

1/4 cup unsalted butter or margarine

3 cups dry bread cubes

1 can (4 ounces) mushroom stems and pieces, drained

1 1/2 teaspoons poultry seasoning

1/2 teaspoon rubbed sage

1/4 teaspoon salt

1/4 teaspoon freshly ground black pepper

1/4 to 1/3 cup chicken broth

4 Cornish game hens (1 pound each)

1 jar (12 ounces) apricot preserves, warmed

Fresh rosemary sprigs (optional)

1. Preheat the oven to 350°F.

2. In a large nonstick skillet, sauté the celery and onion in the butter or margarine until tender, about 5 minutes; remove from heat.

3. Add the bread, mushrooms, poultry seasoning, sage, salt, and pepper and mix well. Toss with enough broth to just moisten.

4. Stuff the hens with the bread mixture, then tie the drumsticks together with cotton string. Place on a rack in a large shallow baking pan. Cover and bake for 1 hour.

5. Remove from the oven and brush with the preserves. Bake, uncovered, until the juices run clear when the hens are pierced

with a fork, 30 to 45 minutes longer, basting every 10 to 15 minutes.

6. Garnish the serving platter with rosemary sprigs, if using.

One More Notch! Jazz up the glaze by mixing 1/2 teaspoon ground ginger and 1/4 teaspoon grated nutmeg right into the preserves.

CORNISH HENS WITH HAM AND WILD RICE STUFFING

SECRET INGREDIENT:

orange zest

Wild rice stuffing makes the ideal accompaniment to these simply roasted birds. With savory mushrooms, pecans, ham, and thyme in the stuffing, grated orange zest adds a refreshing burst of citrus.

Prep Time: 20 min **Cook Time:** 1 hr 40 min **Serves** 4

3/4 cup uncooked wild rice

1 1/2 cups broth

1 tablespoon unsalted butter or margarine

1 cup sliced fresh mushrooms

1 yellow onion, chopped

1/4 cup diced cooked ham

1 teaspoon dried thyme

1 teaspoon dried marjoram

1 teaspoon grated orange zest

1/4 cup toasted chopped pecans (optional)

Salt and freshly ground black pepper

2 Cornish game hens (1 1/2 to 2 pounds each)

1. Place the rice in a mesh strainer. Run cold water through the rice and clean thoroughly. In a small saucepan, bring the broth to a boil. Stir in the rice and return to a boil.

Lower the heat and simmer, covered, until the broth is absorbed, about 40 minutes.

2. Meanwhile, in a medium saucepan, melt the butter or margarine over medium heat. Add the mushrooms and onion and cook until tender, about 5 minutes.

3. In a large bowl, combine the rice, mushroom mixture, ham, thyme, marjoram, orange zest, and pecans, if using. Add salt and pepper, to taste, and set aside.

4. Preheat the oven to 375°F. Lightly grease a 1 1/2-quart casserole.

5. Rinse and drain the hens, then pat dry. Remove the giblets and neck. Stuff the hens with the rice mixture then tie the legs together with cotton string. Place the hens, breast side up, on a rack in a roasting pan. Cover the hens loosely with foil. Spoon the remaining stuffing into a casserole dish, then cover and refrigerate.

6. Roast the hens for 30 minutes. Uncover and roast until the hens are cooked through, basting occasionally with pan drippings, 30 to 45 minutes longer.

7. Bake the covered casserole of stuffing alongside the hens during the last 20 minutes of roasting.

8. To serve, halve the hens lengthwise.

One More Notch! To further flavor the birds, combine softened butter, parsley, salt, and pepper in a small bowl. Ease your fingers under the skin of the hens, separating the skin from the meat. Rub the butter mixture all over the birds underneath the skin.

POULTRY

ORANGE-ROSEMARY CORNISH HENS

SECRET INGREDIENT:
Earl Grey tea

Rock Cornish hens are a cross between two different breeds of chicken, and typically weigh just over a pound—perfect for individual servings. In this recipe, the roasting hens are brushed with a delicious orange marmalade glaze. Earl Grey tea in the glaze enhances the orange aromas. *See photograph on page 175.*

Prep Time: 20 min **Cook Time:** 1 hr 5 min **Serves** 4

1 tea bag, such as Earl Grey

1/4 cup boiling water

Juice from 1 orange

1/2 cup orange marmalade

4 Rock Cornish hens (1 pound each), thawed if frozen

1/2 teaspoon freshly ground black pepper

Salt

1 orange (unpeeled), cut into quarters

2 onions, sliced

8 sprigs fresh rosemary, divided

8 sprigs fresh thyme, divided

1. Preheat the oven to 375°F. Fit a roasting pan with rack.

2. In a small saucepan, steep the tea bag in the water for 5 minutes. Remove the bag, squeezing to release any liquid. Add the orange juice, then stir in the marmalade until melted. Keep warm over low heat.

3. Remove and discard the giblets and neck from hens. Wash the hens and dry thoroughly, and then add the pepper to the cavity and sprinkle lightly with salt. Loosen the breast skin slightly. Stuff the large cavity of each hen with 1 orange quarter, one-fourth of the onion slices, 1 rosemary sprig, and 1 thyme sprig. Tie the legs together with cotton string.

4. Place the hens, breast side up, on the rack in the roasting pan. Brush the hens under and over the skin with about one-fourth of the glaze. Pour enough water into the pan to cover the bottom but not enough to touch the rack.

5. Roast in the center of the oven, basting over and under the skin every 20 minutes with the remaining glaze, until browned and the juices run clear when the hens are pierced with a fork, about 1 to 1 1/4 hours. Remove from the oven and let stand for 10 minutes.

6. Discard the rosemary, thyme, onions, and orange from the cavities of the hens. Dress up the hens with the remaining rosemary and thyme sprigs. Discard the skin before eating.

Personalize It!

For a family-style presentation of a single bird, replace the Cornish hens with a whole roasting chicken (about 3 pounds). Roast the chicken at 400°F until the juices run clear, 1 to 1 1/2 hours.

BROILED JAVA TURKEY

SECRET INGREDIENT:
coffee

Boneless, skinless turkey breast halves are readily available in most supermarket meat departments. Often labeled "turkey London broil," they make a great canvas to paint with flavor. Brewed coffee creates a hearty marinade here that imparts tons of flavor in a short time. *See photograph on page 173.*

Prep Time: 10 min   **Cook Time:** 35 min   **Serves** 6

3/4 cup brewed coffee

2 tablespoons balsamic vinegar

2 garlic cloves, minced

2 tablespoons sugar

1 tablespoon olive oil

1 teaspoon Worcestershire sauce

1/8 teaspoon ground cinnamon

1 1/2 pounds boneless skinless turkey breast "London broil"

1/2 teaspoon salt

1/4 teaspoon freshly ground black pepper

1. In a medium bowl, combine the coffee, vinegar, garlic, sugar, olive oil, Worcestershire sauce, and cinnamon. Transfer to a large zip-close bag and add the turkey. Refrigerate at least 2 hours, or overnight, turning occasionally.

2. Preheat the oven to 425°F. Coat a rimmed baking sheet with cooking spray.

3. Remove the turkey from the marinade, reserving marinade, and sprinkle with the salt and pepper. Place the turkey on a wire rack on the baking sheet.

4. Roast, brushing with reserved marinade every 10 minutes, until an instant-read thermometer inserted into the thickest part of the breast registers 165°F, about 30 minutes. Remove from the oven.

5. Preheat the broiler.

6. Broil the turkey 5 inches from the heat until nicely browned, 1 to 2 minutes. Let stand for 5 minutes before slicing.

One More Notch! Serve this with olive-oil mashed potatoes. Boil 1 1/2 pounds peeled potatoes in water until tender. Drain the potatoes then mash them with 1/4 cup extra-virgin olive oil and 1/4 cup milk.

JERK TURKEY BREAST WITH GINGER BARBECUE SAUCE

SECRET INGREDIENT:
ginger ale

Store-bought barbecue sauces are a great convenience to have around. But because they have such a distinctive taste, they work well only in certain dishes. Adding ginger ale to the sauce creates the perfect sauce for Jamaican jerk turkey. *See photograph on page 174.*

Prep Time: 20 min   **Cook Time:** 1 hr 40 min   **Serves** 6

5 green onions, chopped

4 garlic cloves

1 onion, quartered

2 jalapeño peppers, seeded and deveined (wear gloves when handling)

1 piece (1/2 inch) fresh ginger, peeled

1/4 cup canola oil

2 tablespoons soy sauce

2 teaspoons allspice

1 teaspoon dried thyme

1 bone-in turkey breast (5 to 6 pounds)

1 1/2 teaspoons salt

1 cup ginger ale

1 cup prepared barbecue sauce

1. In a blender, combine the green onions, garlic, onion, jalapeños, ginger, oil, soy sauce, allspice, and thyme. Blend until a thick paste forms, then transfer to a large bowl.

2. With the tip of a sharp knife make several slits all over the turkey breast. Add the turkey to the green onion mixture, turning to coat the breast. Refrigerate for at least 4 hours, or overnight, turning occasionally.

3. Preheat a gas grill on high until the thermometer reaches the maximum temperature. Turn off one of the burners and reduce the heat on the other burner(s) to medium. Remove the turkey from the marinade and sprinkle with the salt. On a lightly oiled grill rack, grill the turkey breast, skin side down, over the unlit burner, using indirect heat, turning every 20 minutes until an instant-read thermometer inserted into the thickest part of the breast registers 160°F, about 1 hour 40 minutes. Remove to a cutting board and let rest for 10 minutes before slicing.

4. Meanwhile, combine the ginger ale and barbecue sauce in a small pot and bring to a boil over medium-high heat. Reduce the heat to medium-low and simmer until thickened and reduced to about 1 3/4 cups, 18 to 20 minutes.

One More Notch! Traditionally jerk is made using habañero or scotch bonnet peppers, two of the hottest peppers in the world. To kick the spice on this marinade to intensely hot, substitute 1 habañero or scotch bonnet for the jalapeño peppers. Make sure you handle the peppers while wearing rubber gloves, being careful to not touch your eyes, nose, or mouth.

LIGURIAN HOLIDAY TURKEY WITH HERBED GRAVY

SECRET INGREDIENT:
pesto sauce

Roast turkey lends itself well to rubs and pastes because the slow cooking gives the flavors time to permeate the meat. Store-bought pesto saves loads of prep time and imparts a fresh herb and garlic flavor to turkey. Just slather it under the skin and enjoy the results.

Prep Time: 40 min **Cook Time:** 3 hr 20 min **Serves** 8

1 whole turkey (12 to 14 pounds)

1/2 cup plus 1/4 cup prepared pesto sauce, divided

1 onion, quartered

1 lemon, halved

1 tablespoon olive oil

1 teaspoon salt

1/4 teaspoon freshly ground black pepper

1 cup chopped onion

1/2 cup chopped celery

1/2 cup chopped carrots

2 cans (14 1/2 ounces each) low-sodium chicken broth, divided

4 cups plus 1 tablespoon water

4 teaspoons cornstarch

1. Preheat the oven to 425°F. Coat a roasting pan and rack with cooking spray.

2. Remove the giblets and neck from the turkey. Carefully slide your fingers under the turkey skin and separate it from the breast, thighs, and legs of the turkey. Rub 1/2 cup of the pesto under the skin over the breast meat, legs, and thighs and in the cavity of the turkey. Stuff the onion and lemon in the cavity of the turkey. Truss the legs with cotton string and tuck the wing tips under the bird.

3. Set the turkey, breast side up, on the rack. Rub the skin with the oil and sprinkle with the salt and pepper.

4. Place the turkey neck, onion, celery, carrots, 1 can of the chicken broth and 4 cups of the water in the bottom of the roasting pan.

5. Place the turkey on the rack in the roasting pan in the lower third of the oven and cook 20 minutes. Loosely cover the turkey with foil and reduce the oven temperature to 350°F. Continue roasting the turkey, adding water to the pan as it evaporates, until an instant-read thermometer inserted into the thickest part of the thigh registers 175°F, about 3 hours 15 minutes. Remove from the oven, then transfer the turkey to a serving platter and loosely cover with foil.

6. Remove the rack from the roasting pan and pour off the liquid into a measuring cup, skimming off any fat. Discard the solids from the pan and set it over 2 burners on low heat.

7. Pour in the pan juices and, with a wooden spoon, scrape up any browned bits. Add enough chicken broth to make the liquid equal 2 cups. Transfer the mixture to a small pot over medium-high heat and bring to a boil. Stir in the remaining 1/4 cup pesto. Return to a boil. In a glass measure, stir together the cornstarch and the remaining 1 tablespoon water until the cornstarch is dissolved. Add to the pot and cook until the gravy thickens, about 1 minute.

One More Notch! To boost the flavor in the gravy, omit the cornstarch and instead sauté 2 tablespoons flour in 2 tablespoons of the turkey fat in the small pot before adding the liquid. Once the gravy thickens, remove from the heat and swirl in 2 tablespoons unsalted butter.

TURKEY MOLE

SECRET INGREDIENT:
chocolate

Derived from the word *molli* (concoction), this spicy Mexican sauce is a rich blend of onions, garlic, and chile peppers. The signature dark taste and color come from chocolate, which adds sweetness and a bitter edge that balances the other flavors. *See photograph on page 192.*

Prep Time: 15 min　**Cook Time:** 30 min　**Serves** 4

2 teaspoons canola oil

2 large onions, chopped

2 large garlic cloves, minced

1 1/2 tablespoons chili powder

1 tablespoon sesame seeds

1 small red chile pepper, seeded, deveined, and minced (wear gloves when handling)

1 pound skinless, boneless turkey breast fillets, cut into 1-inch-wide strips

1/2 teaspoon salt

1 can (14 ounces) whole tomatoes (with juice)

1 cup raisins

1/2 teaspoon ground cloves

1 cup low-fat, reduced-sodium chicken broth

3 tablespoons chopped bittersweet chocolate

1/4 cup toasted sliced almonds

2 tablespoons chopped fresh cilantro

Sprigs of fresh cilantro

1. Heat the oil in a large nonstick skillet over medium-high heat. Add the onions, garlic, chili powder, sesame seeds, and chile pepper. Sauté until the onions are soft and the sesame seeds are fragrant and toasted, about 10 minutes.

2. Sprinkle the strips of turkey with the salt. Add the turkey to the skillet and toss with the onion mixture. Stir in the tomatoes (with juice) and raisins. Sprinkle in the cloves.

3. Pour in the broth and bring to a full boil. Reduce the heat to medium-low, cover the

POULTRY

skillet, and simmer gently until the turkey is no longer pink, about 10 minutes.

4. Add the chocolate, almonds, and chopped cilantro, and stir until the chocolate has melted. Spoon into a serving dish and decorate with sprigs of cilantro.

Personalize It!

Serve this as a taco dinner. Just extend and firm up the sauce. Dissolve 2 teaspoons cornstarch and 1/4 cup cold water in a measuring cup and whisk the mixture into the pan after the turkey is cooked but before adding the chocolate. Bring to a boil and cook until the sauce thickens, about 2 minutes. Then serve as a filling for tacos, along with lettuce, tomatoes, onions, avocado, and cheese. ❖

TURKEY AND SPINACH SPIRALS

SECRET INGREDIENT:

potatoes

When sliced, this turkey roll reveals a pretty spiral of green spinach. Instead of serving potatoes on the side, Parmesan mashed potatoes are rolled right into the filling.

Prep Time: 20 min **Cook Time:** 1 hr 15 min **Serves** 6

2 all-purpose potatoes (12 ounces), peeled and cut into 1-inch cubes

3 garlic cloves

1/4 cup freshly grated Parmesan cheese

1 large egg white

1/4 teaspoon freshly ground black pepper

1/8 teaspoon ground nutmeg

1/2 skinless, boneless turkey breast (2 1/2 pounds)

1 package (10 ounces) frozen chopped spinach, thawed and squeezed dry

2 teaspoons olive oil

1/4 teaspoon salt

1. In a large saucepan, boil the potatoes and garlic in water until the potatoes are tender, about 15 minutes. Remove 2 tablespoons of the cooking water to a cup, then drain the potatoes. Return the potatoes, garlic, and the reserved cooking water to the saucepan and mash them with a potato masher or an electric mixer on low speed until smooth.

2. Stir in the Parmesan, egg white, pepper, and nutmeg and combine well, then set aside.

3. Preheat the oven to 400°F. Lightly grease a roasting pan.

4. Place the turkey breast on a cutting board with one of the short ends facing you. Using a sharp knife, beginning at one of the long sides, split the turkey breast almost in half, leaving just 1/2 inch uncut at the other long side. Open the breast up like a book so that you have one thin rectangular piece of meat.

5. Cover the turkey with the spinach and spread the potato mixture on top.

6. Starting at one of the long sides, roll up the turkey breast, jelly roll–style. Tie with cotton string about every 2 inches to prevent the stuffing from coming out.

7. Place the turkey roll, seam side down, on the roasting pan, brush it with the oil, and sprinkle with the salt.

8. Roast until the meat is no longer pink, about 1 hour. Let stand for 10 minutes before slicing.

One More Notch! For more flavor and color in the filling, spread the turkey with pesto before adding the spinach. Layer on some roasted red peppers after spreading on the potato mixture.

CRUNCHY TURKEY CUTLETS WITH CHERRY SAUCE

SECRET INGREDIENT:
honey mustard pretzels

Turkey cutlets are tailor-made for quick-and-easy weeknight dinners. Honey-mustard pretzels keep these cutlets from tasting like the same old dish. The crushed nuggets pack a lot of seasoning and make an ideal crunchy breading.

Prep Time: 20 min   **Cook Time:** 10 min   **Serves** 4

1 1/2 cups honey mustard pretzel nuggets

3 tablespoons all-purpose flour

1 teaspoon salt, divided

1/4 teaspoon freshly ground black pepper, divided

1 large egg, lightly beaten

4 turkey cutlets (about 1 pound)

2 tablespoons olive oil

2 tablespoons unsalted butter, divided

3 tablespoons chopped shallot

1 tablespoons red-wine vinegar

1/3 cup cherry preserves

1. Place the pretzels in a zip-close bag and set on a work surface. Crush the pretzels with a rolling pin until they mostly resemble coarse crumbs. Transfer to a shallow bowl.

2. Combine the flour, 1/2 teaspoon of the salt, and 1/8 teaspoon of the pepper in a shallow bowl. Place the egg in a separate shallow bowl.

3. Working one at a time, dredge both sides of a turkey cutlet in the flour. Shake off the excess and dip both sides into the egg to coat, shaking off any excess. Dredge the cutlet in the pretzel crumbs to coat and transfer to a clean plate. Repeat with the remaining three cutlets.

4. Heat the oil in a large nonstick skillet over medium-high heat. Add the cutlets and cook until lightly golden and cooked through, 2 to 3 minutes per side. Transfer to a plate warmed in the microwave for 15 to 30 seconds and cover with foil to keep warm.

5. Wipe out the skillet and return to the stove over medium-high heat. Melt 1 tablespoon of the butter and add the shallot and cook for 1 minute. Add the vinegar and cook until nearly evaporated, 30 seconds. Stir in the preserves and cook for 1 minute. Remove from the heat and swirl in the remaining 1 tablespoon butter, the remaining 1/2 teaspoon salt, and the remaining 1/8 teaspoon pepper.

6. Serve the cutlets with the sauce.

One More Notch! For extra zing, swirl 1 tablespoon Dijon mustard into the coating for the cutlets.

TURKEY VEGETABLE POTPIE

SECRET INGREDIENT:
cream of mushroom soup

Why leave canned soup and frozen mixed vegetables on your B-list of pantry items? Canned cream of mushroom soup is extremely versatile and can be used on pastas or as the sauce base for casseroles like this one. Frozen mixed vegetables further cut prep time, and add both color and flavor.

Prep Time: 10 min   **Cook Time:** 25 min   **Serves** 4

1 can (10 3/4 ounces) cream of mushroom soup

1 package (10 ounces) frozen mixed vegetables

2 cups diced cooked turkey

1/2 cup milk

1 tablespoon Dijon mustard

1 teaspoon Worcestershire sauce

1 sheet frozen puff pastry
(half of 17.3-ounce package), thawed

1. Preheat the oven to 400°F. Coat a 6-cup, preferably oval, baking dish with cooking spray.

2. In a medium pot, combine the soup, vegetables, turkey, milk, mustard, and Worcestershire sauce over medium-high heat and cook, stirring occasionally, until hot, 5 to 6 minutes. Pour the turkey mixture into the baking dish.

3. On a lightly floured surface, roll the puff pastry out so that it is slightly larger than the baking dish. Lay the puff pastry over the baking dish and trim the sides of the dough so that the overhang is not longer than 1 inch in any spot. Firmly press the overhang against the sides of the baking dish.

4. Bake until golden brown and the filling is bubbling, 20 to 25 minutes.

One More Notch! Serve with sautéed spinach with garlic. Heat 2 tablespoons of extra-virgin olive oil in a large nonstick skillet and add 3 sliced garlic cloves. Cook the garlic until lightly browned, then add 2 large bunches of trimmed, cleaned spinach in batches, adding the next batch when the previous batch wilts enough to allow room for more.

SWISS TURKEY BURGER

bread and butter pickle chips

The right condiment, such as a crispy pickle, can make a good burger a whole lot better. Unfortunately, the pickles tend to slide out of the bun when you bite into the sandwich. This burger solves the problem by wrapping the burger around the pickle!

Prep Time: 15 min   **Cook Time:** 10 min   **Serves** 4

1 pound ground turkey

4 ounces Swiss cheese, chopped

1/4 teaspoon salt

8 bread and butter pickle chips

4 hamburger buns

4 romaine lettuce leaves, trimmed

4 tomato slices

4 thin red onion slices

1/4 cup ketchup

1. Preheat the broiler with an oven rack positioned 5 inches below. Coat a broiler pan with cooking spray.

2. In a medium bowl, gently mix together the turkey, cheese, and salt. Divide the mixture into four. Working a portion at a time, slightly flatten the turkey into a rough disk shape. Place two pickle chips on top and fold the meat around them to seal them in the center, then form the meat into a 3 1/2-inch disk. Repeat with the remaining ingredients.

3. Place the burgers on the broiler pan and broil the burgers until browned and cooked through, 4 to 5 minutes per side.

4. To assemble, place the bottom of each hamburger bun on a serving plate. Top each with 1 lettuce leaf, 1 burger, 1 tomato slice,

1 red onion slice, and 1 tablespoon of the ketchup. Add the top buns and serve.

that's **ingenious** !

To make prepping even faster, try dicing the pickles and mixing them in with the turkey, cheese, and salt. Then just form the burgers and broil.

ROAST DUCK WITH COUSCOUS AND RED WINE

SECRET INGREDIENT:

figs

This recipe is a play on sweet and savory. Whole duck is roasted with a spice rub of cinnamon, salt, pepper, and allspice, then stuffed with savory couscous studded with chunks of wine-soaked figs. The succulent figs perfectly match the rich and tender roast duck meat.

Prep Time: 20 min **Cook Time:** 1 hr 45 min **Serves** 6

1 duck (3 1/2 pounds), tail, wing tips, and visible fat removed

1/2 teaspoon salt

1/2 teaspoon ground cinnamon

1/4 teaspoon freshly ground black pepper

1/8 teaspoon ground allspice

6 ounces dried figs, quartered

1 cup dry red wine or low-sodium chicken broth

2 tablespoons sugar

3/4 teaspoon dried thyme

3/4 cup boiling water

1/2 cup instant couscous

1. Using a fork, prick the skin of the duck all over. In a small bowl, mix together the salt, cinnamon, pepper, and allspice. Rub the mixture onto the skin and into the cavity of the duck.

2. In a Dutch oven large enough to hold the duck on a rack, bring 2 inches of water to a boil on the stovetop. Lightly grease the rack and adjust it so that the duck will sit above the water. Place the duck in the Dutch oven, adjust the heat so that the water simmers, and cook, covered, until an instant-read thermometer reads 175°F when inserted in a thigh, about 1 hour. Remove the duck, pat dry, then air-dry for 30 minutes.

3. Preheat the oven to 400°F.

4. Meanwhile, in a medium saucepan, combine the figs, wine or broth, sugar, and thyme and bring to a boil over medium heat. Adjust the heat so that the mixture simmers, and cook, covered, until the figs are soft, about 10 minutes.

5. In a medium bowl, pour the water over the couscous and let stand for 5 minutes.

6. Using a slotted spoon, remove the figs from the saucepan, reserving the wine mixture, and stir them into the couscous. Spoon the couscous mixture into the duck cavity and brush the duck with a little of the reserved wine mixture.

7. Place the duck on a rack in a roasting pan. Roast, basting every 10 minutes with the wine mixture, until the skin is crisp and a leg moves easily in its socket, about 30 minutes.

One More Notch! Stir 1/2 cup pistachios into the couscous along with the figs for a flavor surprise.

FIVE-SPICED STIR-FRIED DUCK

SECRET INGREDIENT:

pears

Five-spice powder contains equal parts cinnamon, cloves, fennel seed, star anise, and peppercorns—an ideal seasoning for strips of duck breast meat. The strips are stir-fried with vegetables and, for a delightfully sweet touch, chunks of juicy fresh pear.

Prep Time: 20 min   **Cook Time:** 10 min   **Serves** 6

1 1/2 pounds boneless duck breasts

2 teaspoons Chinese five-spice powder

3 tablespoons rice vinegar or sherry vinegar

3 tablespoons low-sodium soy sauce

2 tablespoons honey

2 tablespoons canola oil

4 celery stalks, thinly sliced

8 ounces small white onions, thinly sliced

2 large juicy pears, peeled, cored, and cut into bite-size pieces

1 cup sliced canned water chestnuts, drained

1/2 pound bok choy, shredded

1 1/2 cups bean sprouts, washed and drained

Celery leaves

6 cups cooked Chinese noodles or spaghetti (optional)

1. Remove the skin and all visible fat from the duck breasts, then cut them across the grain into long strips, 1 inch wide. Sprinkle with the five-spice powder and toss to coat, then set aside.

2. In a cup, whisk together the vinegar, soy sauce, and honey and set aside.

3. Heat a wok or heavy skillet over high heat until hot. Add the oil, swirling the wok to coat the bottom and sides. Add the duck breasts and stir-fry for 2 minutes.

4. Add the celery and onions and continue to stir-fry until the celery and onions have softened, about 3 minutes.

5. Add the pears and water chestnuts and stir to just mix.

6. Add the soy sauce mixture to the wok. Heat until the liquid is bubbling and stir-fry for 2 minutes longer.

7. Add the bok choy and bean sprouts and stir-fry until the bok choy and sprouts just wilt, about 1 minute longer.

8. Decorate with the celery leaves and serve with the Chinese noodles, if using.

Personalize It!

Replace the duck with strips of rabbit, turkey, or chicken meat if you like. ✳

EASY PEKING DUCK

SECRET INGREDIENT:

flour tortillas

Recipes for traditional Peking duck typically require two days. Boneless duck breasts, now widely available in supermarkets, save time and avoid waste. You only cook as much duck as you need, get plenty of crispy skin, and best of all, it only takes a few minutes.

Prep Time: 10 min   **Cook Time:** 15 min   **Serves** 4

2 boneless, skin-on duck breast halves (about 3/4 pound)

1/2 teaspoon salt

1/4 teaspoon freshly ground black pepper

8 store-bought crêpes

3/4 cup hoisin sauce

1/2 cucumber, peeled, seeded, and cut into 1/4-inch-thick strips

2 green onions, cut into 8 pieces

1. Preheat the oven to 400°F.

2. Score the skin of each duck breast in a crosshatch pattern with a sharp knife and sprinkle with the salt and pepper. Heat an oven-proof medium skillet over medium-high heat and add the duck breasts, skin side down. Cook until browned, 6 to 8 minutes, pouring off excess fat as needed. Turn the breasts over and cook 2 minutes longer.

3. Transfer the skillet to the oven and cook until a thermometer inserted into the thickest part of the breast registers 130° to 135°F for medium-rare. Cover the pan loosely with foil and let stand for 3 minutes.

4. Warm the crêpes according to the package directions.

5. Spread the center of each crêpe with 1 1/2 tablespoons of the hoisin. Top with the cucumbers and green onions. Slice the duck into scant 1/4-inch-thick slices and arrange over the vegetables. Fold the crêpe over the filling. Serve immediately.

One More Notch! To take the flavor over the top, marinate the duck breasts for a few hours in 2 tablespoons soy sauce, 2 tablespoons orange juice, and 1/2 teaspoon Chinese five-spice powder.

extraordinary
meat
main dishes

BROILED SPICY STEAKS

SECRET INGREDIENT:
coffee

Most spice producers make at least one commercial spice rub for beef. But you won't find our flavor combination anywhere on grocery store shelves. Mixing a bit of coffee into the rub creates a rich, aromatic flavor.
See photograph on page 173.

Prep Time: 5 min   **Cook Time:** 10 min   **Serves** 4

4 bone-in Delmonico or strip steaks
    (about 2 pounds), trimmed of excess fat

3 tablespoons finely ground espresso or dark
    roast coffee

1 tablespoon chili powder

1 teaspoon sugar

1/2 teaspoon salt

1/2 teaspoon freshly ground black pepper

1. Pat the steaks dry with paper towels.

2. Mix the espresso or coffee, chili powder, sugar, salt, and pepper in a small bowl. Sprinkle the spice mix over the steaks, patting it in with your fingers. Let rest at room temperature for 30 minutes.

3. Preheat the broiler. Put the steaks on a broiler pan and broil 4 to 6 inches from the heat until darkly crusted on the surface, 4 to 6 minutes per side for medium-rare to medium (145°F to 155°F on an instant-read thermometer).

4. Remove and let rest for 5 minutes to redistribute the juices.

One More Notch! Serve the steak with a pat of butter melted over the top for an even richer, fuller flavor, or serve with your favorite steak sauce.

SIRLOIN STEAKS WITH PORT SAUCE

SECRET INGREDIENT:
Dijon mustard

Port makes a fantastic sauce for beef when mixed into the juices from pan-seared steaks. But the real surprise here is a sauté of mushrooms, peppers, potatoes, and sugar snap peas. Dijon mustard mixed with Worcestershire perks up the veggies and pairs well with the beef.
See photograph on page 177.

Prep Time: 20 min   **Cook Time:** 20 min   **Serves** 4

STEAKS

1 pound small new potatoes, scrubbed

1 teaspoon olive oil

1 cup large mushrooms, quartered

1 cup sugar snap peas

1 large red bell pepper, seeded and cut
    into thin strips

2/3 cup low-fat, reduced-sodium beef or
    vegetable broth, divided

1 tablespoon Worcestershire sauce

1 teaspoon Dijon mustard

1 teaspoon dark brown sugar

4 thin sirloin steaks (5 ounces each),
    trimmed of fat

1 teaspoon unsalted butter

Salt and freshly ground black pepper

SAUCE

1 shallot, finely chopped

2 garlic cloves, crushed

1/4 cup port

 Salt and freshly ground black pepper

1. For steaks, place the potatoes in a medium saucepan and cover with water. Bring to a boil, then reduce the heat, and simmer until tender, 10 to 12 minutes.

2. Meanwhile, heat the oil in a large non-stick skillet over medium-high heat. Add the mushrooms, peas, and pepper strips, and stir-fry for 1 minute.

3. In a small bowl, mix half of the broth with the Worcestershire sauce, mustard, and brown sugar, and stir into the vegetables. Reduce the heat and simmer gently until the vegetables are just tender, 3 minutes, stirring frequently.

4. Drain the potatoes and add them to the vegetables. Stir gently, then cover and keep over very low heat until ready to serve.

5. Heat a cast-iron grill pan. Add the butter to the grill pan and turn up the heat to high. Season the steaks on both sides with salt and pepper. As soon as the butter sizzles and starts to foam, add the steaks. Cook until an instant-read thermometer inserted through the side of a steak registers 145°F for medium-rare, 3 to 5 minutes per side. Remove the steaks to dinner plates warmed in the microwave for 15 to 30 seconds. Keep warm while making the sauce.

6. For sauce, add the shallot and garlic to the cooking juices in the pan and cook, stirring, over low heat for 1 minute.

7. Pour in the port and increase the heat so the sauce is bubbling. Cook for about 1 minute, stirring.

8. Pour in the remaining broth and any steak juices from the plates. Boil 1 minute, then add salt and pepper, to taste.

9. Spoon the sauce over the steaks and serve immediately with the vegetables.

that's **ingenious** !

If you don't have port, use Madeira, sherry, dry vermouth, or 1/4 cup dry red wine mixed with 1/2 teaspoon brown sugar.

FLANK STEAK SANTA FE

SECRET INGREDIENT:
croutons

Stuffed and rolled flank steak makes a great presentation when sliced. And it's a cinch to put together. Croutons add body to the sausage in our flank steak filling, and picante sauce kicks up the heat.

Prep Time: 15 min **Cook Time:** 1 hr 40 min **Serves** 6

3/4 pound spicy sausage or chorizo, casings removed, if necessary

2 eggs, beaten

1 1/2 cups unseasoned croutons

1/3 cup sliced green onions

1/3 cup minced fresh parsley

1 flank steak (1 1/2 to 2 pounds)

3 tablespoons vegetable oil

1 jar (16 ounces) picante sauce or salsa verde

1. In a large nonstick skillet, crumble and brown the sausage; drain.

2. Add the eggs, croutons, onions, and parsley. Mix well.

3. Slice the steak in half horizontally to within 1/2 inch of the end. Open the steak like a book and pound to 1/2-inch thickness. Spread with the sausage mixture. Roll up, jelly roll–style, beginning at a short end, and tie with cotton string.

4. Preheat the oven to 350°F.

5. In a large nonstick skillet, brown the steak in the oil, 5 to 8 minutes. Place in a 9 x 13-inch baking dish. Spread the picante sauce or salsa verde over the steak. Cover and bake until tender, 1 1/2 to 1 3/4 hours.

One More Notch! For even more richness and taste, add 1/2 cup shredded Monterey Jack or dry Jack cheese to the filling. If you like, serve with additional picante sauce or salsa, too.

MEAT

BARBECUED CHUCK ROAST

SECRET INGREDIENT:
applesauce

A chuck roast requires long, gentle grilling over indirect heat and basting often to make it tender and moist. Our barbecue baste includes applesauce to balance the acidity of vinegar and create a thicker glaze.

Prep Time: 10 min **Cook Time:** 1 hr 35 min **Serves** 6

1/3 cup apple-cider vinegar

1/4 cup ketchup

2 tablespoons vegetable oil

2 tablespoons soy sauce

1 tablespoon Worcestershire sauce

1 teaspoon garlic powder

1 teaspoon mustard powder

1 teaspoon salt

1/4 teaspoon freshly ground black pepper

1 boneless beef chuck roast (2 1/2 to 3 pounds)

1/2 cup applesauce

1. In a large zip-close bag or shallow glass container, combine the vinegar, ketchup, oil, soy sauce, Worcestershire sauce, garlic powder and mustard powder, salt, and pepper. Mix well.

2. Add the roast and turn to coat. Seal the bag or cover the container and refrigerate for at least 3 hours, turning occasionally.

3. Pour the marinade into a small saucepan. Bring to a boil, then reduce the heat and simmer for 15 minutes.

4. Preheat the grill to medium (350°F). If using charcoal, spread the coals to opposite sides, leaving an empty unheated space in the middle. On a gas grill, turn off the middle burner. Put the roast over the unheated part of the grill, cover, and cook by indirect heat for 20 minutes, turning occasionally.

5. Add the applesauce to the marinade and brush over the roast. Continue basting and turning the roast several times until the meat reaches the desired doneness (for rare, a meat thermometer should read 140°F; medium, 160°F; well-done, 170°F), 1 to 1 1/2 hours.

One More Notch! For a smoky-tasting roast, soak 2 cups wood chips or chunks in water for 30 minutes then toss them onto the hot coals before adding the roast. On a gas grill, wrap the wood in foil, poke holes in the foil, and put it directly over one of the heated burners until you see smoke.

SLOW-BRAISED BEEF AND BARLEY

SECRET INGREDIENT:
juniper berries

Juniper berries give this dish the distinctive flavor of gin. The beef is slowly simmered until meltingly tender, as barley soaks up some of the juices and thickens the rich gravy to make a hearty casserole. Serve with a green vegetable such as French-cut green beans. *See photograph on page 176.*

Prep Time: 20 min **Cook Time:** 2 hr **Serves** 4

1 pound beef chuck or lean braising steak, trimmed and cut into 2-inch cubes

2 garlic cloves, halved

3 bay leaves

6 juniper berries, lightly crushed

Sprig of fresh thyme

1 cup full-bodied red wine

12 pearl onions

Boiling water

1 tablespoon olive oil

1/2 cup pearl barley

1 1/2 cups low-fat, reduced-sodium beef broth

Salt and freshly ground black pepper

3 large carrots, cut into large chunks

2 celery stalks, sliced

1. Place the beef in a large bowl with the garlic, bay leaves, juniper berries, and thyme. Pour the wine over the top, then cover and let marinate in the refrigerator for 8 hours or overnight.

2. Preheat the oven to 325°F.

3. Place the onions in a small bowl and add enough water to cover. Let stand for 2 minutes, then drain. When cool enough to handle, peel off the skins, then set aside.

4. Remove the beef from the marinade and pat dry on a paper towel, reserving the marinade. Heat the oil in a large flame-proof casserole over medium heat. Add the beef and brown it on all sides. Work in batches, if necessary, to avoid overcrowding. Remove the beef and set aside on a plate.

5. Add the onions to the casserole and cook gently until lightly colored all over, 3 to 4 minutes.

6. Add the barley and cook for 1 minute, stirring, then return the beef and any juices to the casserole. Pour in the broth and bring to a simmer.

7. Strain the marinade into the casserole, and add the bay leaves and sprig of thyme. Season lightly with salt and pepper, to taste. Cover with a tight-fitting lid, transfer to the oven, and braise for 45 minutes.

8. Add the carrots and celery. Stir to mix. Cover again, and braise until the beef, barley, and vegetables are tender, 1 to 1 1/4 hours. Remove the bay leaves and thyme before serving.

Personalize It!

This recipe makes a thick, rich gravy. If you prefer sauces on the thinner side, stir in an extra 1/2 cup beef broth about 20 minutes before the end of the cooking time. ❄

SPICED POT ROAST

SECRET INGREDIENT:
chutney

Here's your antidote to boring pot roasts. This Indian-style roast features ginger, curry powder, and raisins with a few big spoonfuls of chutney to deepen the spicy sweetness. Mango chutney works well, but almost any chutney will do.

Prep Time: 15 min   **Cook Time:** 3 hr   **Serves** 6

1/3 cup all-purpose flour

1 teaspoon salt

1/4 teaspoon freshly ground black pepper

2 tablespoons vegetable oil

1 boneless beef rump roast or chuck roast (about 3 pounds)

1 1/2 cups beef broth

1/2 cup chutney

1/2 cup raisins

1/2 cup chopped onion

1 1/2 teaspoons curry powder

1/2 teaspoon garlic powder

1/2 teaspoon ground ginger

1. Preheat the oven to 325°F.

2. Combine the flour, salt, and pepper in a small bowl and rub over the entire roast.

3. In a large Dutch oven, heat the oil over medium-high heat. Add the roast and brown it on all sides, 5 to 7 minutes.

4. Combine the broth, chutney, raisins, onion, curry powder, garlic powder, and ginger in a medium bowl. Pour the mixture over the roast. Cover and bake until the meat is tender, about 3 hours.

Personalize It!

The pot roast tastes great using the pan juices for gravy, but if you prefer a thicker sauce, remove the roast to a platter, then place the pan with the juices over medium heat. Dissolve 1 teaspoon cornstarch in 1 tablespoon cold water in a cup, then stir into the juices until thickened, about 2 minutes. Repeat if you like an even thicker sauce. ❄

MEAT

BEEF STROGANOFF

SECRET INGREDIENT:
pickles

Here's a classic stroganoff, rich with sour cream, mushrooms, and thinly sliced beef tenderloin. So what's new? The addition of chopped pickles to perk up the sauce. One bite and you'll never go back to your old recipe!

Prep Time: 30 min | **Cook Time:** 20 min | **Serves** 4

3 tablespoons unsalted butter, divided

1 large red onion, thinly sliced

1/2 pound small chestnut mushrooms, clean and halved

1 1/4 pounds beef filet

2 teaspoons fresh green peppercorns in brine or dry black peppercorns, crushed

Salt

2 tablespoons Dijon mustard

1 1/4 cups sour cream

8 small drained cocktail gherkins, chopped

Small bunch of chives

1. Heat a tablespoon of the butter in a large nonstick skillet. Add the onions over medium heat until slightly softened, 2 to 3 minutes.

2. Add the mushrooms to the pan. Increase the heat to medium-high and cook, stirring, until they have softened and most of the liquid has evaporated, about 5 minutes.

3. While the mushrooms are cooking, slice the beef filet very thinly, then cut it across the grain into thin strips (piling several slices on top of one another will speed up this process).

4. Place the mushrooms and onions in a large bowl and set aside.

5. Add another tablespoon of butter to the pan and increase the heat to high. Add half the beef and stir-fry until very lightly browned, 2 to 3 minutes, then remove it. Heat the remaining tablespoon of butter and cook the rest of the beef the same way.

6. Return the onion, mushrooms, and the first batch of beef with any juices to the skillet.

7. Add the peppercorns to the pan with salt, to taste, and heat through for 1 to 2 minutes.

8. Blend the mustard and sour cream together in a small bowl. Stir into the beef with the gherkins. Heat through gently, without boiling.

9. Trim, rinse, and dry the chives, then snip them over the top and serve.

Personalize It!

Watching calories? Lighten the stroganoff by using reduced-fat sour cream and olive oil instead of butter.

STUFFED MEAT LOAF

SECRET INGREDIENT:
frozen shredded hash browns

It's sounds time-consuming, but this delicious stuffed meat loaf takes only 15 minutes to put together thanks to frozen shredded hash browns. Meat and potatoes—all in one dish!

Prep Time: 15 min | **Cook Time:** 50 min | **Serves** 8

MEAT LOAF

1 cup soft bread crumbs

1/2 cup beef broth

1 egg, beaten

4 teaspoons dried minced onion

1 teaspoon salt

1/4 teaspoon Italian seasoning

1/4 teaspoon freshly ground black pepper

1 1/2 pounds ground beef

4 cups frozen shredded hash browns, thawed

1/3 cup grated Parmesan cheese

1/4 cup minced fresh parsley

1 teaspoon onion salt

MEAT

1 can (8 ounces) tomato sauce

1/4 cup beef broth

2 teaspoons prepared mustard

Parmesan cheese (optional)

1. Preheat oven to 375°F.

2. For meat loaf, in a large bowl, combine the bread crumbs, broth, egg, minced onion, salt, Italian seasoning, and pepper. Let stand for 2 minutes.

3. Add the beef and mix well. On a piece of wax paper, pat the meat mixture into a 10-inch square.

4. Combine the hash browns, Parmesan, parsley, and onion salt in a large bowl. Spoon over the meat. Roll up, jelly roll–style, removing the wax paper as you roll. Pinch the edges and ends to seal.

5. Place, seam side down, in an ungreased shallow baking pan. Bake until the meat is no longer pink, 40 minutes.

6. For sauce, combine the tomato sauce, broth, and mustard in a small bowl, then spoon over the meat loaf. Return to the oven for 10 minutes.

7. Sprinkle with Parmesan, if using, before serving.

One More Notch! Give the meat loaf more flavor by using a mixture of ground beef, ground pork, and ground veal. Some markets sell this ready-made combination as "meat loaf mix".

PESTO MEAT LOAF

SECRET INGREDIENT:

salsa

This may soon become your favorite meat loaf recipe! It features several unique twists that add flavor and moisture. The pesto itself is rich in flavor but it also includes cooked rice for extra body and cheddar cheese to complement the beef. The meat loaf gets just the right amount of tang from a common pantry ingredient: salsa.

Prep Time: 15 min   **Cook Time:** 50 min   **Serves** 8

PESTO

2 garlic cloves

1/3 cup olive oil or vegetable oil

1 cup packed fresh basil leaves

3/4 cup cooked long-grain rice

1/4 cup chopped walnuts

1/4 cup shredded sharp cheddar cheese

1/4 teaspoon salt

MEAT LOAF

1/2 cup quick-cooking oats

1/2 cup finely chopped green onions

1 egg, beaten

1/4 cup salsa

2 garlic cloves, minced

1/2 teaspoon salt

2 pounds lean ground beef

1. Preheat oven to 350°F.

2. For pesto, place the garlic, olive oil or vegetable oil, basil, rice, walnuts, cheese, and salt in a food processor or blender. Cover and process on low speed until a paste forms.

3. For meat loaf, in a large bowl, combine the oats, green onions, egg, salsa, garlic, and salt. Add the pesto and stir to combine.

4. Add the beef and mix well. Transfer to a greased 9 by 5-inch loaf pan and gently form into a loaf shape. Bake until no longer

MEAT

pink, for 50 to 60 minutes, draining off fat as necessary.

5. Remove from the oven and let stand in the pan for 10 minutes before slicing.

One More Notch! For extra zip, spread another 1/2 cup salsa over the top of the meat loaf before baking.

NO-NOODLE LASAGNA

SECRET INGREDIENT:
French bread

Lasagnas can be made with sheets of ribboned pasta, egg roll wrappers, and even sheets of sliced vegetables like zucchini or eggplant. But with slices of bread? Just wait until you try it. It's like a layered pizza casserole with seasoned ground beef!

Prep Time: 20 min   **Cook Time:** 50 min   **Serves 8**

1 pound ground beef

1/3 cup chopped onion

1/3 cup chopped celery

2 garlic cloves, minced

14 slices French bread (1/2 inch thick), toasted, divided

4 large tomatoes, cut into 1/2-inch-thick slices, divided

1 teaspoon dried basil

1 teaspoon dried parsley flakes

1 teaspoon dried oregano

1 teaspoon crushed dried rosemary

1 teaspoon garlic powder

3/4 teaspoon salt

1/2 teaspoon freshly ground black pepper

2 teaspoons olive oil or vegetable oil, divided

3 tablespoons unsalted butter or margarine

3 tablespoons all-purpose flour

1 1/2 cups milk

1/3 cup grated Parmesan cheese

2 cups shredded mozzarella cheese (8 ounces)

1. Preheat the oven to 350°F.

2. In a large nonstick skillet, brown the beef, onion, celery, and garlic over medium-high heat. Drain and set aside.

3. Line the bottom of an ungreased 13 x 9-inch baking dish with 10 slices of the bread.

4. Top with half of the meat mixture and half of the tomatoes.

5. Combine the basil, parsley, oregano, rosemary, garlic powder, salt, and pepper in a cup. Sprinkle half the seasoning over the tomatoes. Drizzle with 1 teaspoon of the olive or vegetable oil. Crumble the remaining bread over the top. Repeat with another layer of meat, tomatoes, seasonings, and oil.

6. In a small saucepan over medium heat, melt the butter. Stir in the flour until smooth. Gradually stir in the milk and bring to a boil. Cook and stir until thickened and bubbly, about 2 minutes.

7. Remove from the heat and stir in the Parmesan. Pour over the casserole, then top with the mozzarella.

8. Bake, uncovered, until bubbly and the cheese is golden brown, 40 to 45 minutes.

that's **ingenious**

To save time, replace the basil, parsley, oregano, and rosemary with 4 teaspoons Italian seasoning.

MEAT

SOUTHWESTERN LASAGNA

SECRET INGREDIENT:
canned enchilada sauce

In Italy, they make lasagna with pasta. But in the Southwest United States, they make it with corn tortillas. The results are delicious and the dish is easy to make if you use canned enchilada sauce to get a jump on things. *See photograph on page 177.*

Prep Time: 25 min   **Cook Time:** 1 hr   **Serves** 6

1 1/2 pounds ground beef

1 onion, chopped

1 can (15 ounces) enchilada sauce

1 can (14 1/2 ounces) diced tomatoes (with juice)

1 can (2 1/4 ounces) sliced ripe olives, drained

1 teaspoon salt

1/4 teaspoon garlic powder

1/4 teaspoon freshly ground black pepper

1 cup small-curd cottage cheese

1 egg

1/2 pound Monterey Jack cheese, thinly sliced

8 corn tortillas (8-inch), halved

1/2 cup shredded cheddar cheese (2 ounces)

1. In a large nonstick skillet, brown the beef and onion; drain.

2. Stir in the enchilada sauce, tomatoes (with juice), olives, salt, garlic powder, and pepper. Bring to a boil. Reduce the heat and simmer, uncovered, until the liquid reduces slightly, about 20 minutes.

3. In a small bowl, combine the cottage cheese and egg; set aside.

4. Preheat oven to 350°F. Grease a 9 x 13-inch baking dish.

5. Spread one-third of the meat sauce in the baking dish. Top with half the Monterey Jack, half the cottage cheese mixture, and half the tortillas. Repeat the layers, ending with meat sauce. Sprinkle with the cheddar cheese.

6. Cover and bake for 20 minutes. Uncover and bake until bubbly and golden brown, 10 minutes longer.

One More Notch! For bolder flavor, use a mixture of ground beef and ground pork for the sauce and crumble in 4 ounces spicy chorizo sausage, too.

SHEPHERD'S PIE

SECRET INGREDIENT:
ground mustard

Shepherd's pie is traditionally made with lamb (shepherds really did make it!), but Americans often use ground beef instead. To give the beef more oomph, we include ground mustard in the mix. A little horseradish brightens things up, too.

Prep Time: 20 min   **Cook Time:** 1 hr   **Serves** 4

8 potatoes (2 pounds), peeled and cubed

1 pound ground beef

3/4 cup chopped onion

2 garlic cloves, minced

3 tablespoons vegetable oil, divided

1 cup chopped fresh mushrooms

1 tablespoon tomato paste

1/2 cup beef broth

2 teaspoons prepared horseradish

1 teaspoon ground mustard

1 1/2 teaspoons salt, divided

1/4 teaspoon freshly ground black pepper

1/2 cup seeded and diced green bell pepper

1/2 cup seeded and diced red bell pepper

1/3 cup milk

1 cup shredded cheddar cheese (4 ounces)

2 egg whites

1. Preheat the oven to 425°F. Grease an 11 x 7-inch baking pan.

2. Cook the potatoes in boiling salted water until tender, 15 to 20 minutes. Drain, then transfer to a large bowl.

3. In a large nonstick skillet, brown the beef, onion, and garlic in 2 tablespoons of the oil. Add the mushrooms. Cook and stir until the mushrooms begin to release their juice, 3 minutes; drain.

4. Place the tomato paste in a small bowl. Gradually whisk in the broth until smooth. Stir in the horseradish, mustard, 1 teaspoon of the salt, and the pepper.

5. Add to the meat mixture. Pour into the baking pan and set aside.

6. In the same skillet, sauté the peppers in the remaining oil until tender, about 3 minutes. Drain and spoon over the meat mixture.

7. Warm the milk in the microwave for 30 seconds. Add it to the potatoes, along with the cheese and the remaining salt.

8. Beat the egg whites in a small bowl until stiff peaks form. Gently fold them into the potatoes. Spoon over the peppers.

9. Bake, uncovered, for 15 minutes. Reduce the heat to 350°F and bake until bubbly, about 20 minutes longer.

One More Notch! For a richer potato topping, use heavy cream instead of milk. You can also save the egg yolks and mix them into the potatoes along with the cheese and salt.

RUTABAGA BEEF PIE

SECRET INGREDIENT:
steak sauce

When cold weather rolls in, let this hearty pie warm up your kitchen and satisfy your hunger. Steak sauce adds a spicy taste to the beef and complements the slightly sweet flavor of the rutabagas.

Prep Time: 20 min **Cook Time:** 1 hr 5 min **Serves** 6

3 cups diced peeled rutabagas

2 cups diced peeled potatoes

1 pound ground beef

1/2 cup chopped onion

1/2 cup sliced celery

1/4 cup steak sauce

1 teaspoon salt

1/4 teaspoon freshly ground black pepper

Pastry for double-crust pie (9 inches)

1. Preheat the oven to 425°F.

2. In a large saucepan, cook the rutabagas and potatoes in boiling salted water just until tender, 15 to 20 minutes. Drain and set aside.

3. In a large nonstick skillet over medium heat, cook the beef, onion, and celery until the meat is browned and vegetables are tender, 5 to 8 minutes; drain.

4. Add the rutabagas and potatoes, steak sauce, salt, and pepper.

5. Line a 9-inch pie plate with the bottom pastry. Fill with the rutabaga mixture. Top with the remaining pastry. Flute the edges and cut slits in the top.

6. Bake for 10 minutes. Reduce the heat to 350°F and bake until the crust is golden, 35 to 40 minutes longer.

One More Notch! Cook 4 chopped strips of bacon in the skillet until crisp. Sauté the onion and celery in the bacon drippings, then add the beef.

GRILLED PORK ROAST WITH TANGY MUSTARD SAUCE

SECRET INGREDIENT:
apricot preserves

This recipe takes minimal effort but it explodes with flavor. Horseradish, mustard, and apricot preserves make a remarkable glaze for pork. To enhance the smoky aromas, soak a few handfuls of wood chips or chunks in water for 20 minutes then toss them onto the hot coals of the grill before adding the pork.

Prep Time: 10 min **Cook Time:** 1 hr 15 min **Serves** 10

ROAST

1 1/4 teaspoons ground mustard

3/4 teaspoon garlic powder

1/4 teaspoon ground ginger

1 boneless pork loin roast (2 1/2 to 3 pounds)

2 teaspoons olive oil or vegetable oil

SAUCE

1/2 cup horseradish mustard

1/2 cup apricot preserves

1. For roast, combine the mustard, garlic powder, and ginger in a cup.

2. Rub the roast with the olive or vegetable oil, then rub it with the spice mixture. Place the roast in a large zip-close bag or shallow glass container. Seal the bag or cover the container and refrigerate for 6 hours or overnight.

3. Preheat a grill to medium (350°F). If using charcoal, spread coals to opposite sides, leaving an empty unheated space in the middle. On a gas grill, turn off the middle burner.

4. Put the pork over the unheated part of grill, cover, and cook by indirect heat for 60 minutes.

5. For sauce, combine the horseradish mustard and preserves in a small bowl.

6. Continue grilling the pork until a meat thermometer reads 160°F to 170°F, 15 to 30 minutes, basting twice with sauce.

7. Remove from the grill and let stand for 10 minutes before slicing. Heat the remaining sauce to serve with the roast.

that's **ingenious**

If you don't have horseradish mustard, simply combine 1/4 cup spicy brown mustard and 1/4 cup prepared horse-radish to create your own. You could also replace the apricot preserves with pineapple preserves or apple butter. If you're using a gas grill, enhance the smokiness by wrapping water-soaked wood chips in foil, poking holes in the foil, and putting the packet directly on one of the heated burners.

APPLE-CARDAMOM ROAST PORK

SECRET INGREDIENT:
cranberries

Here's a fabulous roast to serve to company. It features the time-honored pairing of pork and apples spiced with the heady aroma of cardamom. Cranberries add a shot of color and a tart counterpoint to the sweet apples, balancing all of the flavors.

Prep Time: 10 min **Cook Time:** 2 hr 30 min **Serves** 8

1 boneless pork loin roast (3 to 3 1/2 pounds), trimmed

1/2 teaspoon poultry seasoning

1 jar (10 ounces) apple jelly

1 cup apple juice

1/2 teaspoon ground cardamom

1 cup peeled, seeded, and chopped fresh or dried tart apples

3 tablespoons chopped fresh or dried cranberries

5 teaspoons cornstarch

2 tablespoons water

MEAT

1. Preheat the oven to 325°F.

2. Place the roast on a rack in a shallow roasting pan and rub with the poultry seasoning. Bake, uncovered, until a meat thermometer reads 160°to 170°F, about 2 1/2 hours.

3. Meanwhile, combine the jelly, apple juice, and cardamom in a large saucepan. Cook and stir over low heat until smooth, about 1 minute.

4. Add the apples and cranberries and cook until tender, 5 to 10 minutes.

5. Combine the cornstarch and water in a cup. Stir into the apple mixture, then bring to a boil. Cook and stir over medium heat until thickened, 1 to 2 minutes.

6. Remove the roast from oven and let stand for 10 minutes before slicing. Serve with apple topping.

Personalize It!

If you don't need a big roast, use the topping with pork chops or sausages. ❖

PORK MEDALLIONS WITH PEPPERS

SECRET INGREDIENT:

orange juice

Here's a quick dinner-party dish featuring the bold Sicilian flavors of sweet-tart balsamic vinegar, salty olives, and refreshing orange juice. With vegetables, pork, and rice, this dish makes a satisfying meal by itself, but roasted asparagus would fill out the menu nicely. *See photograph on page 182.*

Prep Time: 20 min   **Cook Time:** 30 min   **Serves** 4

1 cup mixed basmati and wild rice

2 cups plus 2 tablespoons water, divided

2 oranges, peeled

1 tablespoon olive oil

1 pork tenderloin filet (about 12 ounces), sliced crosswise into 1/2-inch-thick medallions

1 large sweet Vidalia onion or red onion, halved lengthways and thinly sliced into half rings

1 red bell pepper, seeded and sliced into strips

1 yellow bell pepper, seeded and sliced into strips

1 large carrot, grated

1 garlic clove, finely chopped

1/2 cup fresh orange juice

3 tablespoons balsamic vinegar

1/4 cup pitted chopped black olives

10 basil leaves

Salt and freshly ground black pepper

1. Put the rice and 2 cups of the water in a saucepan. Bring to a boil, then reduce the heat to low. Cover and simmer according to the package instructions, until the rice is tender and all the water has been absorbed, about 15 minutes. Cut the oranges crosswise into 1/2-inch-thick slices, then into quarters. Set aside.

2. Heat the oil in a large nonstick skillet over medium-high heat. Cook the pork medallions, in batches, for 2 to 3 minutes on each side. Remove the meat with a slotted spoon and set aside.

3. Reduce the heat to medium and add the onion, peppers, carrot, and garlic to the pan. Cover and cook, stirring frequently, until the vegetables start to soften, 5 to 6 minutes.

4. Add the remaining 2 tablespoons of water, the orange juice, and vinegar. Stir to mix well. Cover and cook until the vegetables are tender, 3 to 4 minutes.

5. Return the pork to the pan. Add the olives, oranges and their juice, and the basil leaves. Cook for 1 minute to reheat the pork, stirring well. Add salt and pepper, to taste.

6. To serve, divide the rice among four plates warmed in the microwave for 15 to

30 seconds and place the pork medallions and vegetables on top. Drizzle with any juices remaining in the pan and serve immediately.

Personalize It!

For a change of pace from pork, use boneless lamb leg steaks instead. Pound them to about 1/2-inch thickness and replace the basil in the recipe with 2 teaspoons chopped fresh rosemary.

JERK PORK TENDERLOIN UNDER WRAPS

SECRET INGREDIENT:

maple syrup

Pork tenderloin is quick-cooking and versatile, but its leanness makes it susceptible to dryness. Wrapping the tenderloin with bacon slices keeps the meat moist and adds richness to the Caribbean seasonings. Maple syrup also adds deep flavor, a kiss of sweetness, and perfectly complements the bacon.

Prep Time: 15 min **Cook Time:** 25 min **Serves** 4

1 boneless pork tenderloin (1 to 1 1/4 pounds), trimmed

2 tablespoons maple syrup, divided

2 teaspoons Caribbean jerk seasoning

1/2 teaspoon salt

6 to 8 slices bacon

1. Preheat the oven to 425°F and coat a baking sheet with cooking spray.

2. Pat the pork dry with paper towels and brush it with 1 tablespoon of the maple syrup. Rub the jerk seasoning and salt over the pork.

3. Working 1 slice at a time, wrap the pork with the bacon slightly overlapping the slices.

4. Heat a large nonstick skillet over medium-high heat. Add the pork and cook until browned, turning occasionally, about 2 minutes per side.

5. Transfer to the baking sheet and roast until a thermometer inserted into the center of the pork registers 160°F, 20 to 22 minutes. Remove from the oven and let stand for 5 minutes before slicing.

Personalize It!

If you don't like the spiciness of jerk seasoning, try a milder spice blend or make your own using your favorite herbs and spices.

PORK MEDALLIONS WITH MUSHROOM SAUCE

SECRET INGREDIENT:

sour cream

Cutting the tenderloin into medallions and baking them in a creamy bath is a great way of overcoming the meat's inherent dryness. Sour cream provides plenty of moisture and richness here, serving as the ideal flavor vehicle for sliced fresh mushrooms.

Prep Time: 20 min **Cook Time:** 1 hr 10 min **Serves** 6

2 boneless pork tenderloins (about 2 pounds)

1 egg

1 tablespoon water

1/2 teaspoon crushed dried rosemary

1/4 teaspoon freshly ground black pepper

Dash of garlic powder

1 cup seasoned dry bread crumbs

3 tablespoons vegetable oil

1/2 pound fresh mushrooms, sliced

2 tablespoons unsalted butter or margarine

1 can (10 3/4 ounces) cream of chicken soup, undiluted

1 cup (8 ounces) sour cream

1/4 cup chicken broth

1. Preheat the oven to 325°F.

2. Cut each tenderloin into 8 pieces. Place each piece between two pieces of plastic wrap or wax paper and pound to 3/4-inch thickness.

3. In a shallow dish, combine the egg, water, rosemary, pepper, and garlic powder. Pour the bread crumbs onto a plate. Dip the pork into the egg mixture, then into the bread crumbs.

4. In a large skillet over medium heat, brown the pork in the oil for 5 minutes on each side. Remove to a 9 x 13-inch baking dish; keep warm in the oven.

5. In the same skillet, sauté the mushrooms in the butter or margarine until tender, 4 to 5 minutes. Stir in the soup, sour cream, and broth. Pour over the pork.

6. Cover and bake until the pork is tender and the juices run clear when the pork is pierced with a fork (about 155°F), about 1 hour.

Personalize It!

Try this recipe with chicken or turkey cutlets in place of the pork (reduce the cooking time slightly). You could even use beef steaks, if you like. ❄

MARINATED PORK STRIPS

SECRET INGREDIENT:
lemon-lime soda

Recipes don't come much easier than this one. If you use pre-chopped garlic, you won't have to cut anything but the pork. Lemon-lime soda lends just the right flavor and sweetness to the Asian-style marinade.

Prep Time: 10 min   **Cook Time:** 15 min   **Serves** 6

5 tablespoons soy sauce

1/4 cup ketchup

3 tablespoons vinegar

3 tablespoons chili sauce

3 tablespoons sugar

2 teaspoons salt

1/8 teaspoon freshly ground black pepper

3 garlic cloves, minced

2 cans (12 ounces each) lemon-lime soda

2 pork tenderloins (about 2 pounds), cut lengthwise into 1/2-inch strips

1. In a large zip-close bag or shallow glass container, combine the soy sauce, ketchup, vinegar, chili sauce, sugar, salt, pepper, garlic, and soda.

2. Add the pork and turn to coat. Seal the bag or cover the container and refrigerate for 4 hours or overnight.

3. Preheat a grill to medium-high. Drain and discard the marinade. Thread the pork onto metal or soaked bamboo skewers. Grill until browned and the juices run clear, about 12 minutes.

One More Notch! Serve these pork skewers with a spicy peanut dip made by whisking together 3/4 cup chicken broth, 1/2 cup peanut butter, 2 tablespoons teriyaki sauce or soy sauce, 1 teaspoon toasted sesame oil, and 1 1/2 teaspoons hot-pepper sauce.

SWEET-AND-SOUR PORK

SECRET INGREDIENT:
ketchup

This lighter version of the favorite Asian stir-fry puts the spotlight on the fresh flavors of pineapple, scallions, carrots, and bean sprouts. Ketchup and soy sauce create a foolproof sauce that glazes the pork, the vegetables, and the Chinese egg noodles that make it a complete meal. *See photograph on page 177.*

Prep Time: 30 min   **Cook Time:** 15 min   **Serves** 4

PORK

1 pork tenderloin filet or boneless pork shoulder (12 ounces), trimmed of fat and cut into 2-inch strips

1 tablespoon low-sodium soy sauce

Freshly ground black pepper

2 teaspoons flour

8 ounces Chinese egg noodles

1 1/2 teaspoons canola oil, divided

8 baby corn, quartered lengthwise

2 carrots, julienned

1 large garlic clove, finely chopped

1 tablespoon finely diced peeled fresh ginger

1 can (15 ounces) pineapple slices in natural juice, drained (juice reserved) and chopped

1 cup bean sprouts

4 scallions, sliced diagonally

1/2 teaspoon toasted sesame oil

SAUCE

1 tablespoon flour

1 tablespoon sugar

1 tablespoon rice-wine vinegar

2 tablespoons rice wine or dry sherry

2 tablespoons ketchup

3 tablespoons low-sodium soy sauce

1. For pork, place the pork strips in a large bowl. Add the soy sauce and pepper, to taste. Stir to coat the meat. Sprinkle with the flour and stir again. Cover and set aside.

2. For sauce, mix together the flour, sugar, vinegar, wine or sherry, ketchup, soy sauce, and reserved pineapple juice in a small bowl. Set aside.

3. Cook the noodles in a saucepan of salted boiling water, according to the package directions. Drain well and set aside.

4. Heat a wok or heavy skillet until really hot, then add half the oil and swirl to coat the wok. Add the pork and leave for 1 minute to brown, then stir-fry over high heat for 3 to 4 minutes. Remove the pork with a slotted spoon and set aside.

5. Heat the remaining oil in the wok, then add the corn and stir-fry for 1 minute.

6. Add the carrots, garlic, and ginger, and stir-fry for another minute. Sprinkle with a few tablespoons water and let the vegetables steam for 2 to 3 minutes.

7. Pour in the sauce mixture, stir well, and bring to a boil. Add the meat back in the wok and add the noodles, pineapple, and bean sprouts. Heat through.

8. Add the scallions and sesame oil and serve.

One More Notch! Spice up the stir-fry by adding 1 small seeded, deveined, and finely chopped red chile pepper (wear gloves when handling), to the sauce.

MEAT

PORK CHOPS WITH DARK BUTTER SAUCE

SECRET INGREDIENT:
balsamic vinegar

Balsamic vinegar typically ends up on salads, but it has plenty of other uses. Boil it for a minute or two, and its vinegary flavor dissipates, leaving a rich, concentrated sweetness. When mixed with browned butter, the vinegar creates an irresistible sauce that perfectly dresses up sautéed pork chops.

Prep Time: 10 min   **Cook Time:** 20 min   **Serves** 4

4 boneless 1-inch-thick center-cut pork loin chops (about 2 pounds)

2 teaspoons paprika

1 teaspoon salt

1/2 cup (1 stick) unsalted butter, divided

3 tablespoons good-quality balsamic vinegar

1. Pat the pork chops dry with paper towels. Sprinkle on all sides with the paprika and salt. Let rest at room temperature for 20 minutes.

2. Heat 1 tablespoon of the butter in a large nonstick skillet over medium-high heat. Add the pork chops and cook until browned, about 2 minutes per side. Reduce the heat to medium-low and cook for 4 to 6 minutes per side for medium (135° to 140°F). Let rest, loosely covered with foil, for 5 minutes.

3. Meanwhile, melt the remaining butter in a medium nonstick skillet over medium heat. When the butter foams, reduce the heat to medium-low and cook until it turns from yellow to medium brown, but not black, 5 to 7 minutes. Watch carefully so that the butter doesn't burn. Pour into a small heat-proof bowl or glass measure and set aside.

4. Add the balsamic vinegar to the skillet and raise the heat to medium. Stir until the vinegar is boiled down to about half its original volume. Remove from the heat and stir the browned butter back into the pan to combine.

5. Pour over the pork chops and serve.

One More Notch! Take the flavor to the next level by sprinkling the pork chops with crumbled blue cheese and chopped fresh parsley before drizzling on the sauce.

BBQ PULLED PORK

SECRET INGREDIENT:
beer

Great barbecue takes time to make. But a pressure cooker can shorten the cooking time and still turn out tender and moist pulled pork. Another success secret: bottled barbecue sauce doctored up with spices and beer to balance the flavors and keep the pork moist.

Prep Time: 10 min   **Cook Time:** 50 min   **Serves** 8

1 tablespoon ground cumin

2 teaspoons chili powder

1 tablespoon dark brown sugar

2 teaspoons garlic powder

1/2 teaspoon dry mustard

1/2 teaspoon dried thyme

3 pound boneless pork shoulder (2 1/2 pounds), trimmed and cut into 2-inch chunks

1 bottle (16 ounces) barbecue sauce

8 ounces beer

1/2 teaspoon salt

8 soft sandwich rolls

Pickle chips (optional)

1. Combine the cumin, chili powder, brown sugar, garlic powder, mustard, and thyme in a large bowl. Add the pork and toss to coat.

2. Transfer the pork to a pressure cooker and stir in the barbecue sauce and beer. Lock the lid onto the cooker and set over medium-high heat until pressurized, 8 to 10 minutes.

Adjust the temperature to maintain the pressure according to the manufacturer's directions. Cook for 40 minutes, remove from the heat and depressurize the cooker according to the manufacturer's directions.

3. Carefully remove the lid and with 2 forks, pull the meat into shreds. Stir in the salt.

4. Fill each roll with a generous 1/2 cup of the pork and 2 to 3 tablespoons of the sauce. Top with pickle chips, if using.

One More Notch! For a little more oomph, stir in 1 cup finely chopped onion and 1/4 teaspoon ground chipotle chile pepper before cooking the pork. After shredding it, stir in 3 tablespoons chopped fresh cilantro.

BOSTON PORK AND BEANS

SECRET INGREDIENT:
beer

In New England, pork and beans are traditionally simmered slowly in an earthenware casserole dish. This version also includes dark beer to deepen the flavor of the sauce.

Prep Time: 15 min **Cook Time:** 2 hr 10 min **Serves** 4

1 cup dried white beans, soaked overnight in cold water

1 tablespoon canola oil

4 lean bone-in pork loin chops (4 to 6 ounces each), trimmed of fat

1 onion, chopped

8 ounces beer, such as dark ale

1 can (24 ounces) chopped tomatoes (with juice)

2 teaspoons Worcestershire sauce

2 tablespoons dark brown sugar

3 allspice berries

2 tablespoons Dijon mustard

2 slices bacon, cut into bite-size pieces

1 teaspoon apple-cider vinegar

1. Drain and rinse the beans, then place them in a large saucepan and cover with enough cold water to come up to about twice the depth of the beans. Cover the pan with a lid and bring to a boil. Skim off any scum, then reduce the heat, cover the pan again, and cook the beans over low heat until they are just tender, 45 to 60 minutes.

2. Meanwhile, heat the oil in a deep flame-proof casserole or cast-iron pot, add the pork chops and onion, and sear the chops until they are browned on both sides, 3 to 4 minutes per side.

3. Pour in the beer and tomatoes (with juice), then add the Worcestershire sauce, brown sugar, and allspice. Reduce the heat, cover, and cook until the meat is very tender, about 1 hour. Add water, if necessary, to keep the pork moist.

4. Drain the beans and add to the pork chops. Add the mustard, bacon, and vinegar and stir to mix well.

5. Cook, covered, over low heat until both the beans and the pork are very tender, about 1 hour.

One More Notch! To spice things up, make Tuscan-style beans instead. Use Italian sausages, cut into bite-size pieces, instead of pork chops. Brown the sausages and onion in a deep, nonstick skillet, then remove and set aside. Pour the fat from the pan, then add 1/2 cup dry red wine, 1 cup chicken or vegetable stock, 1 can (24 ounces) chopped tomatoes (with juice), 6 chopped fresh sage leaves, 2 bay leaves, 2 crushed garlic cloves, and salt and freshly ground black pepper, to taste. Cook, uncovered, over low heat for 30 minutes. Add the sausage mixture and 1 can (15 ounces) cannellini beans, drained and rinsed, and simmer for 15 minutes. Remove the bay leaves before serving.

ZESTY GLAZED RIBS

SECRET INGREDIENT:
root beer

Barbecued ribs are easy to make and supremely satisfying when they come straight off the grill. Adding root beer to the glaze lends a zesty sweetness that tastes nothing like soda, especially when combined with the deep smokiness of bourbon.
See photograph on page 177.

Prep Time: 10 min **Cook Time:** 1 hr 50 min **Serves** 6

1/2 cup plus 2 tablespoons firmly packed dark brown sugar

1 tablespoons paprika

1 tablespoon chili powder

1 tablespoon salt

2 teaspoons garlic powder

1 teaspoon onion powder

1/2 teaspoon cayenne pepper

5 to 6 pounds pork spare ribs

2 cups root beer

1/2 cup bourbon

1/2 cup fresh orange juice

1 teaspoon hot-pepper sauce

1. Heat a grill to medium-low.

2. Combine 2 tablespoons of the brown sugar, paprika, chili powder, salt, garlic powder, onion powder, and cayenne in a small bowl. Rub the mixture over both sides of the ribs and place the ribs, meat side down, on a well-oiled grill rack. Cook, on a covered grill, until the meat begins to shrink away from the ends of the bones, about 1 1/2 hours, turning every 30 minutes.

3. Meanwhile, combine the root beer, bourbon, orange juice, and hot-pepper sauce in a medium saucepan over medium-high heat. Bring to a boil, reduce the heat to medium, and simmer until the mixture is a syrupy glaze, 35 to 40 minutes.

4. Brush the ribs with half of the glaze and grill for 15 minutes longer. Brush the ribs again and grill for 2 minutes longer. Flip the ribs, brush them with the glaze, and grill until they are nicely glazed, 2 minutes longer.

5. Transfer to a cutting board and cut into individual ribs for serving.

that's **ingenious**

Make the ribs ahead of time. Remove from the grill before glazing and cool to room temperature. Refrigerate the ribs for up to 2 days. Allow an extra 10 minutes for the ribs to get to temperature before you glaze them.

MAPLE-GLAZED HAM WITH RAISIN SAUCE

SECRET INGREDIENT:
apple-cider vinegar

Look no further for the perfect holiday ham. Crowd-pleasing, pretty, and easy to make, this clove-studded ham is glazed with a winning maple-allspice mixture. The accompanying sauce gets sweetness from raisins, apple juice, and orange juice, tempered by the acidic tang of apple-cider vinegar.

Prep Time: 15 min **Cook Time:** 1 hr 30 min **Serves** 10

HAM

1 cooked ham, shank portion (4 to 4 1/2 pounds)

2 tablespoons whole cloves

GLAZE

1/4 cup maple syrup

1 tablespoon unsalted butter or margarine

1 tablespoon light corn syrup

1 tablespoon fresh orange juice

1/8 teaspoon ground allspice

Dash of ground cloves

1/4 cup firmly packed light brown sugar

2 tablespoons cornstarch

1 1/2 cups apple juice

1 cup raisins

3 tablespoons fresh orange juice

1 tablespoon apple-cider vinegar

1 teaspoon grated orange zest

1/8 teaspoon ground allspice

1. Preheat the oven to 325°F.

2. For ham, score the top of the ham into diamonds, then stud with the cloves.

3. Place the ham on a rack in a large shallow baking pan. Insert a roasting thermometer in the center of the thickest part without touching the bone. Bake until heated through, 1 1/4 hours.

4. For glaze, in a small saucepan, combine the maple syrup, butter or margarine, corn syrup, orange juice, allspice, and cloves. Bring to a boil, then remove the pan from the heat.

5. Brush the ham with some of the maple glaze. Bake until a thermometer registers 135°F, about 15 minutes more, brushing once or twice with the remaining glaze. Cover the ham with foil and let stand for 15 minutes before carving.

6. Meanwhile, for sauce, in a medium saucepan, combine the brown sugar and cornstarch. Stir in the apple juice, raisins, orange juice, vinegar, orange zest, and allspice.

7. Cook over medium heat, stirring constantly, until the mixture starts to thicken, 1 to 2 minutes. Cook and stir until completely thickened, 1 to 2 minutes longer. Serve with the ham.

One More Notch! Give the sauce a gorgeous pink hue by replacing 1/2 cup of the apple juice with pomegranate juice.

ROAST LEG OF LAMB

SECRET INGREDIENT:
red currant jelly

Mint jelly is often used in lamb dishes. Here, we switch things up by mixing red currant jelly into the drippings along with red wine to make a fabulous sauce.

Prep Time: 30 min	**Cook Time:** 2 hr	**Serves** 10

1 whole leg of lamb (about 7 pounds), trimmed

8 large garlic cloves, slivered

4 teaspoons snipped fresh rosemary or
   1 1/2 teaspoon dried rosemary leaves, divided

1 tablespoon minced fresh mint

2 teaspoons dry mustard

1 1/2 teaspoons salt, divided

1/4 teaspoon freshly ground black pepper

1/2 cup plus 1 tablespoon cold water

3 pounds unpeeled red-skinned potatoes,
   cut into 1-inch chunks

1 pound baby carrots, peeled

2 tablespoons olive oil

3 cups cooked fresh or thawed frozen peas

1 cup dry red wine or low-sodium beef broth

2 tablespoons cornstarch

1/2 cup red currant jelly

1. Preheat the oven to 350°F.

2. Place the lamb, fat side up, on a rack in a large roasting pan. Using a small pointed knife, insert the garlic slivers into the meat.

3. In a small bowl, combine 3 teaspoons of the rosemary, the mint, mustard, 1 teaspoon of the salt, the pepper, and 1 tablespoon of the water, then spread over the lamb.

4. Roast, uncovered, basting with the drippings, until the meat is the way you like it (155°F for medium), for about 2 hours.

5. After the lamb has been roasting for about 15 minutes, toss the potatoes with the carrots, oil, the remaining 1 teaspoon rosemary, and the remaining 1/2 teaspoon salt in a 9 x 13-inch baking pan.

6. Roast, uncovered, in the same oven with the lamb for 1 1/2 hours. Stir in the peas and roast for 10 minutes longer. When the lamb and vegetables are done, arrange on a platter, turn off the oven, and keep the platter warm in the oven.

7. Pour the drippings from the lamb into a small saucepan, skimming the fat.

8. In a cup, stir together the wine or broth, the remaining 1/2 cup water, and the cornstarch. Add to the drippings with the jelly.

9. Bring to a boil over medium heat and boil for 1 minute, whisking constantly. Pour into a gravy boat and serve with the lamb.

that's ingenious

> If you can't find red currant jelly, replace it with a mixture of 1/4 cup grape jelly and 1/4 cup orange marmalade.

VENISON-MUSHROOM PIE

SECRET INGREDIENT:
sweet potatoes

Red wine, mushrooms, and fresh thyme flavor this hearty venison pie. The filling is topped not with a pastry crust but a golden blanket of mashed sweet potatoes scented with orange.

Prep Time: 30 min **Cook Time:** 1 hr 20 min **Serves** 4

2 tablespoons extra-virgin olive oil

7 ounces whole pearl onions

1 pound boneless haunch of venison or venison shoulder, diced

5 1/2 ounces baby button mushrooms

3 celery stalks, thickly sliced

1 tablespoon fresh thyme leaves

10 ounces full-bodied red wine

5 ounces strong beef stock

1 1/2 pounds sweet potatoes, cubed

1 tablespoon whole-grain mustard

Grated zest and juice of 1 orange

Salt and freshly ground black pepper

1 1/2 tablespoons cornstarch

2 tablespoons cold water

1. Heat the oil in a large saucepan and add the onions. Cover and cook over low heat until the onions are lightly browned all over, 8 to 10 minutes. Move the onions to a plate.

2. Add the venison to the pan and cook, uncovered, over medium-high heat until the meat is well-browned, 2 to 3 minutes.

3. Add the onions, mushrooms, celery, and thyme. Pour in the wine and stock. Bring to a boil, then reduce the heat. Cover and simmer until the venison is tender, about 45 minutes.

4. Meanwhile, steam the sweet potatoes until tender, about 25 minutes. Alternatively, cook them in boiling water for 15 minutes, then drain.

5. Preheat the oven to 375°F.

6. Place the sweet potatoes in a large bowl and mash with the mustard, orange zest and juice, and salt and pepper, to taste. Set aside.

7. Blend the cornstarch with the water in a cup. Stir into the venison mixture and cook, stirring, until lightly thickened, about 2 minutes. Season to taste.

8. Spoon the venison into a 9-inch pie plate. Spread the sweet potatoes over the venison to cover it completely. Bake until golden and bubbly, about 20 minutes. Serve hot.

Personalize It!
If venison is unavailable (or if you don't care for it), use 1 pound boneless bison or beef chuck.

extraordinary
seafood
main dishes

SHRIMP PROVENÇAL

SECRET INGREDIENT:
fennel seeds

The cooking of southern France often features the subtle, licorice-like flavors of fresh fennel. To enhance the aromas, this light shrimp dish includes both chopped fennel and fennel seeds. The shrimp are served with saffron-scented rice to soak up the flavorful sauce. *See photograph on page 179.*

Prep Time: 15 min   **Cook Time:** 30 min   **Serves** 4

1 tablespoon olive oil

1 large onion, chopped

1 fennel bulb, chopped

1 large garlic clove, crushed

1 can (14 ounces) chopped tomatoes (with juice)

1/2 cup reduced-sodium vegetable broth

1 tablespoon fennel seeds

Finely grated zest and juice of 1 orange

Salt and freshly ground black pepper

Pinch of saffron threads

2 cups water

1 cup long-grain rice

1 pound large shrimp, peeled and deveined

Fresh basil leaves

1. Heat the oil in a large nonstick skillet with a tight-fitting lid. Add the onion, chopped fennel, and garlic and cook over medium heat, stirring occasionally, until softened but not browned, about 5 minutes.

2. Add the tomatoes (with juice), broth, fennel seeds, orange zest, and orange juice. Season lightly with salt and pepper. Bring to a boil, stirring, then reduce the heat to low and half-cover the pan. Simmer until the liquid reduces slightly, about 12 minutes.

3. Meanwhile, crumble the saffron into the water in a medium saucepan. Bring to a boil. Add the rice, return to a boil, then reduce the heat to low, cover, and simmer until tender, 15 to 20 minutes.

4. Bring the tomato sauce back to a boil. Place the shrimp on top of the sauce, cover the pan tightly, and cook over low heat until the shrimp are pink and cooked through, 3 to 4 minutes. Do not boil the mixture or the shrimp may toughen.

5. Drain the rice and divide among serving bowls. Top with the shrimp, tomato sauce, and basil and serve immediately.

Personalize It!

If you prefer, make tuna provençal: Omit the shrimp and saffron rice. Instead, make the tomato sauce then stir in 2 cans (3 ounces each) drained and flaked tuna. Serve over cooked pasta shells and garnish with chopped fresh dill.

CRISPY CARIBBEAN SHRIMP

SECRET INGREDIENT:
sweetened coconut flakes

Shrimp have an inherent sweetness that comes to the forefront when they are deep-fried. Add some sweetened coconut flakes to the batter and the crispy results are sublime. This dish makes a great appetizer, but it's even better as a main course.

Prep Time: 20 min   **Cook Time:** 5 min   **Serves** 4

1/2 cup mayonnaise

1/4 cup prepared mango chutney

1/4 teaspoon curry powder

1 cup all-purpose flour

1 tablespoon sugar

1/2 teaspoon salt

1 cup milk

2 cups sweetened coconut flakes

6 cups canola oil

24 peeled and deveined jumbo (16-20 per pound) shrimp

SEAFOOD

1. Combine the mayonnaise, chutney, and curry powder in a small bowl. Mix well and set aside.

2. Combine the flour, sugar, and salt in a medium bowl. Whisk in the milk until smooth.

3. Pour the coconut into a shallow bowl.

4. In a large pot, heat the oil over medium heat to 360°F on a deep-fry thermometer or until a cube of bread dropped in the oil takes about 40 seconds to brown.

5. Drop 8 shrimp into the batter and turn to coat, then, working one at a time, dip each shrimp into the coconut to coat. Drop the shrimp into the oil and cook, turning frequently, until golden brown and cooked through, about 2 minutes.

6. Remove the shrimp from the oil with a slotted spoon and transfer to a paper towel–lined baking sheet. Repeat with the remaining shrimp, returning the oil to 360°F between each batch.

7. Serve immediately with the mayonnaise mixture.

Personalize It!

If you're not a fan of mayonnaise, serve the shrimp with a creamy yogurt dressing or fresh fruit salsa. They're also great on their own, without any sauce or dip.

CREOLE SHRIMP

SECRET INGREDIENT:
bottled Caesar salad dressing

Creole-style shrimp is a classic dish with as many variations as there are families in Louisiana. The recipe is usually quite long but the complex flavor of Caesar salad dressing allowed us to shorten the ingredient list without sacrificing taste.
See photograph on page 178.

Prep Time: 10 min   **Cook Time:** 15 min   **Serves** 4

1 cup long-grain white rice

3 tablespoons unsalted butter

1 cup chopped onion

1 cup seeded and chopped red or orange bell pepper

1 cup chopped tomato

1/2 cup bottled Caesar salad dressing

1 teaspoon Worcestershire sauce

1 1/2 pounds peeled and deveined large shrimp

1/4 cup chopped parsley

1. In a small pot, cook the rice according to the package directions.

2. Meanwhile, heat the butter in a large nonstick skillet over medium-high heat. When melted and hot, add the onion, pepper, and tomato and cook, stirring occasionally, until softened, 6 to 7 minutes.

3. Stir in the Caesar dressing and Worcestershire sauce and cook for 30 seconds. Add the shrimp and cook, turning once, until pink and just cooked through, 3 to 4 minutes.

4. Remove from the heat and stir in the parsley. Serve over the rice.

One More Notch! To give this dish a nice little bite, stir in a dash or two of red-pepper sauce at the end of cooking just before serving.

SEAFOOD

SHRIMP SHAWARMA

peanut butter

Why limit peanut butter to sandwiches? Mixed with lemon juice, it creates a nutty-tart sauce that really livens up shrimp.

Prep Time: 20 min **Cook Time:** 5 min **Serves** 4

6 tablespoons creamy peanut butter

3 tablespoons fresh lemon juice

2 tablespoons plain yogurt

1 garlic clove, minced

Water

1 pound peeled and deveined
    large shrimp

1 tablespoon olive oil

1/2 teaspoon salt

1/4 teaspoon freshly ground black pepper

4 pita breads

2 cups chopped romaine lettuce

1/2 cup chopped tomato

1/2 cup chopped cucumber

1/2 cup chopped green onion

1. In a small bowl, whisk together the peanut butter, lemon juice, yogurt, garlic, and enough water to make the mixture pourable, 1 to 2 tablespoons.

2. In a medium bowl, toss the shrimp with the oil, salt, and pepper.

3. Heat a lightly oiled grill pan over medium-high heat. Add the shrimp and cook until pink and cooked through, 1 1/2 to 2 minutes per side. Transfer the shrimp to a plate.

4. With a sharp knife, slice off the top fourth of the pita breads. Fill each with 1/2 cup of the lettuce, 2 tablespoons of the tomatoes, 2 tablespoons of the cucumber, 2 tablespoons of the green onion, and a quarter of the shrimp.

5. Drizzle each sandwich with 2 tablespoons of the sauce and serve immediately.

that's **ingenious** !

Pre-cooked shrimp make a great and quick alternative if you don't feel like cooking. Look for them at your supermarket's seafood counter and substitute 12 ounces of cooked shrimp for the 1 pound uncooked. For a flavor boost, toss the shrimp with 1 tablespoon olive oil, 1/4 teaspoon salt, 1/8 teaspoon freshly ground black pepper, and a little lemon juice.

BALTIMORE SEAFOOD CAKES

almonds

These rich crab and shrimp cakes are spiced with mustard, Worcestershire sauce, and a little cayenne pepper. Coated in bread crumbs, the cakes are fried until the outside is a crunchy golden brown. Additional crunch comes from chopped almonds mixed right into the cakes. *See photograph on page 179.*

Prep Time: 15 min **Cook Time:** 5 min **Serves** 4

2 slices dry bread

1/2 cup milk

2 cans (4 ounces each) fresh crabmeat

1/2 pound cooked shrimp, peeled, deveined,
    and chopped

2 large eggs, separated

2 teaspoons Dijon mustard

1 tablespoon Worcestershire sauce

1/2 cup ground almonds

Pinch of cayenne pepper

1 tablespoon mayonnaise

Handful of fresh parsley, rinsed, dried, and chopped

1 1/2 cups dried bread crumbs

1/3 cup all-purpose flour

1 tablespoon water

Sunflower or canola oil

1. Soak the bread in the milk in a small bowl for 5 minutes.

2. Pick over the crab to remove any cartilage. Flake the crabmeat into a medium bowl and add the shrimp.

3. Add the egg yolks, mustard, Worcestershire sauce, almonds, cayenne, and mayonnaise to the crab. Add 1 tablespoon of the parsley to the bowl.

4. Squeeze the bread dry, add it to the crab, and stir until soft but not sloppy. Add some dried bread crumbs if the mixture is too moist.

5. Put the flour onto one plate and the bread crumbs onto another. Whisk the water into the egg whites in a shallow bowl.

6. Divide the crab mixture into 8 portions and shape into cakes. Dip them into the flour, shake off the excess, then dip them into the egg whites, and coat with the bread crumbs.

7. Heat 1/2 inch of oil in a skillet over fairly high heat. Fry the cakes until they are crisp and golden, 2 to 3 minutes on each side, then drain them on a paper towel–lined plate and serve two per person.

One More Notch! Make a spicy sandwich by serving the cakes on buns with tartar sauce, lettuce, and salsa.

SEAFOOD POTPIE

SECRET INGREDIENT:
saltine crackers

The key to a great potpie is a tasty crust. But who wants to make pie dough from scratch? And yet prepared pie doughs can be unsatisfying, too. The solution: Saltine crackers. When mixed with a little melted butter, they make an easy and delicious alternative. The best part is crushing the crackers for the recipe—it's a great stress reliever!

Prep Time: 15 min   **Cook Time:** 50 min   **Serves** 4

6 slices bacon, cut into 1-inch pieces

3/4 pound bay scallops

3/4 pound peeled and deveined medium shrimp

6 tablespoons unsalted butter, divided

1 1/2 cups chopped onion

3/4 cup chopped carrots

3/4 cup chopped celery

2 teaspoons dried tarragon

2 garlic cloves, minced

1/4 cup dry vermouth

1 1/2 cups reduced-sodium chicken broth

1 cup heavy cream

1 tablespoon cornstarch

1 tablespoon water

3/4 cup frozen peas

1/4 teaspoon salt

1/4 teaspoon freshly ground black pepper

25 saltine crackers, coarsely crushed (about 1 1/4 cups)

1. Preheat the oven to 400°F. Coat a 9-inch deep-dish pie plate with cooking spray.

2. Heat a large nonstick skillet over medium-high heat and cook the bacon until crisp, 5 to 6 minutes. Transfer with a slotted spoon to a paper towel–lined plate to drain.

3. Add half the scallops to the skillet and cook until opaque and almost cooked through, 2 to 3 minutes. Transfer to a medium bowl and repeat with the remaining scallops.

4. Add the shrimp to the skillet and cook until pink, 1 minute per side; transfer to the bowl with the scallops.

5. Pour off any remaining bacon fat and wipe out the skillet with paper towels. Return the skillet to the stove over medium heat and melt 3 tablespoons of the butter. Add the onions, carrots, celery, tarragon, and garlic and cook, stirring occasionally, until softened, 8 to 10 minutes. Increase the heat to medium-high and add the vermouth. Cook until almost evaporated, about 1 minute.

6. Stir in the broth and cream. Bring to a boil and cook until reduced by almost half, 5 to 7 minutes.

7. Combine the cornstarch and water in a cup. Add to the broth mixture and cook, stirring, until thickened, about 1 minute. Remove from the heat and stir in the bacon, scallops, shrimp, peas, salt, and pepper. Transfer to the pie plate.

8. Melt the remaining 3 tablespoons butter and toss with the crackers in a large bowl until well-coated. Sprinkle over the scallop mixture.

9. Bake until the top is golden and the filling bubbly, about 20 minutes. Let stand for 5 minutes before serving.

that's **ingenious**

Potpies are one of those make-ahead dishes that you can store in the freezer and pop in the oven at a moment's notice. To make this one ahead, prepare the dish as directed up to the point of topping with the crackers. Cool completely to room temperature then wrap in a double layer of plastic and freeze for up to 1 month. For the best results, thaw the potpie in the refrigerator, then bake in the oven as directed, adding an extra 10 to 15 minutes to the total baking time.

SCALLOP PAELLA

SECRET INGREDIENT:

orzo

Classic Spanish paella can be tricky to make because the rice often ends up undercooked and chewy, or overcooked and mushy. This aromatic version uses orzo instead of rice for foolproof results and about an hour of saved time.

Prep Time: 15 min **Cook Time:** 20 min **Serves** 4

8 ounces orzo

2 tablespoons extra-virgin olive oil, divided

1 pound sea scallops

1/2 teaspoon salt, divided

1/4 teaspoon freshly ground black pepper, divided

1 cup chopped onion

3 garlic cloves, minced

3 chorizo sausages (about 8 ounces), cut into 1/4-inch-thick slices

1/2 teaspoon paprika

1/4 teaspoon saffron threads, lightly crushed

1 jar (7 ounces) roasted red peppers, drained and cut into strips

1/2 cup chicken broth

1/3 cup pimiento-stuffed olives, halved

3 tablespoons chopped fresh cilantro

1. Bring a large pot of salted water to a boil over high heat. Add the pasta and cook according to the package directions. Drain, then rinse under cold water and drain again.

2. Heat 1 tablespoon of the oil in a large nonstick skillet over medium-high heat. Sprinkle the scallops with 1/4 teaspoon of the salt and 1/8 teaspoon of the black pepper and cook until browned, 2 minutes per side. Transfer to a plate.

3. Heat the remaining 1 tablespoon oil in the same skillet, add the onion and garlic and cook, stirring occasionally, until fragrant, about 1 minute.

4. Add the sausage, paprika, and saffron. Cook, stirring occasionally, until the sausage starts to brown, 3 to 4 minutes.

5. Add the red peppers and cook until they begin to soften, about 2 minutes.

6. Stir in the broth and the orzo and cook for 1 minute. Add the scallops and olives and cook until hot, 1 to 2 minutes.

7. Remove from the heat and stir in the cilantro and the remaining 1/4 teaspoon salt and the remaining 1/8 teaspoon pepper.

Personalize It!

If you don't care for saffron or don't have any on hand, use a pinch of turmeric for that golden glow.

SCALLOP AND SCALLION FRIED BROWN RICE

SECRET INGREDIENT:

pineapple

Fried rice is an easy dish to throw together but it sometimes lacks pizzazz. Pineapple and fresh ginger change all that, giving the dish a spicy-sweet Polynesian slant.

| **Prep Time:** 15 min | **Cook Time:** 35 min | **Serves** 4 |

1 cup instant brown rice

3 tablespoons peanut oil, divided

2 large eggs, lightly beaten

1 pound bay scallops

2 cups fresh pineapple chunks (1/2 inch)

1 tablespoon peeled and minced fresh ginger

2 garlic cloves, minced

1 cup frozen mixed bell pepper strips

1 cup chopped green onions

3 tablespoons reduced-sodium soy sauce

1 tablespoon rice vinegar

1. Cook the rice according to the package directions, omitting any fat. Transfer the rice to a large baking sheet and spread into a single layer. Let stand for 1 hour at room temperature or in the refrigerator overnight.

2. Heat 1 tablespoon of the oil in a large nonstick skillet over medium-high heat. Add the eggs and cook, stirring, until set, 1 to 2 minutes. Transfer to a medium bowl.

3. Heat 1 tablespoon of the remaining oil in the skillet and add half of the scallops. Cook, stirring occasionally, until lightly browned, 3 to 4 minutes. Transfer to the bowl with the eggs, then return the skillet to the stove and cook the remaining scallops.

4. Heat the remaining 1 tablespoon oil in the skillet. Add the pineapple and cook until it starts to brown, 3 to 4 minutes.

5. Stir in the ginger, garlic, pepper strips, and green onions and cook until the peppers soften, 3 minutes.

6. Add the rice and cook until hot, 2 minutes.

7. Add the eggs and scallops and cook until hot, 1 minute.

8. Stir in the soy sauce and vinegar and cook for 30 seconds.

One More Notch! Give the rice a bit of crunch by stirring in some toasted chopped cashews.

GOLDEN COOKIE-CRUSTED CALAMARI WITH GARLIC-LEMON MAYONNAISE

SECRET INGREDIENT:
graham crackers

Fried calamari is a favorite restaurant appetizer—yet making it at home is far easier than many realize. The key to a great calamari dish is in the coating. Graham cracker crumbs mixed with flour and salt creates a crust with the perfect blend of sweet and savory flavors.

Prep Time: 15 min **Cook Time:** 5 min **Serves** 4

1/2 cup mayonnaise

1 garlic clove, minced

2 teaspoons fresh lemon juice

1 teaspoon grated lemon rind

1 teaspoon drained capers, chopped

1/4 teaspoon red-pepper sauce

1 cup graham cracker crumbs

3/4 cup all-purpose flour

1 teaspoon salt

3/4 cup buttermilk

1 pound cleaned squid bodies, cut into 1/4-inch-thick rings

4 cups canola oil

1. In a small bowl, stir together the mayonnaise, garlic, lemon juice, lemon rind, capers, and red-pepper sauce. Set aside.

2. Whisk together the graham crackers, flour, and salt in a medium bowl.

3. In a medium bowl, combine the buttermilk and squid rings.

4. In a medium pot, heat the oil over medium heat to 360°F on a deep-fry thermometer or until a cube of bread dropped into the oil takes about 40 seconds to brown. Transfer the squid to a mesh strainer and shake to remove the excess buttermilk. Add to the graham cracker crumb mixture and toss well to coat.

5. In batches, add the coated squid to the hot oil and cook until golden and crisp, about 1 minute. Quickly remove the squid from the oil with a slotted spoon and transfer to a paper towel–lined baking sheet. Return the oil to temperature and repeat with the remaining squid.

6. Serve the calamari immediately with the mayonnaise.

Personalize It!

If you are more of a traditionalist, serve the calamari with lemon wedges and a thick hearty marinara or cocktail sauce.

NEW HAVEN–STYLE CLAM PIZZA

SECRET INGREDIENT:
canned chopped clams

New Haven, Connecticut, is famous throughout the Northeast for its pizza. None is more coveted than the clam pizza. In making a version at home, the trick to keeping it simple is using canned chopped clams, which have a mild flavor that blends perfectly with ricotta and mozzarella cheeses.

Prep Time: 10 min **Cook Time:** 20 min **Serves** 4

4 slices bacon, cut into 1-inch pieces

3 garlic cloves, minced

1 large onion, thinly sliced

1 prepared pizza crust (14 ounces), such as Boboli

1 cup part-skim ricotta cheese

1 cup grated mozzarella cheese

1 can (6 1/2 ounces) chopped clams, drained

1 teaspoon dried oregano

1. Preheat the oven to 450°F.

2. Heat a medium nonstick skillet over medium-high heat. Add the bacon and cook

until crisp, 4 to 5 minutes. Remove with a slotted spoon to a paper towel–lined plate to drain.

3. Add the garlic and onion to the skillet and cook, stirring occasionally, until softened, about 5 minutes. Transfer the onion mixture to a large bowl.

4. Set the pizza crust on a baking sheet and spread with the ricotta, leaving a 1/2-inch border.

5. Top with the mozzarella, onion mixture, bacon, and clams. Sprinkle with the oregano.

6. Bake until the cheese melts and the edges of the crust are golden, 10 to 12 minutes. Cut into 4 wedges and serve.

Personalize It!

Okay, so clams aren't your thing? Try topping the pizza with some sautéed medium shrimp or bay scallops. Or omit the seafood all together and add grated Romano cheese.

BELGIAN-STYLE STEAMED MUSSELS WITH GARLIC CRISPS

SECRET INGREDIENT:

beer

In this recipe, beer imparts a slight malt flavor and a touch of bitterness that perfectly complements the briny sharpness of mussels. Soft margarine helps to make the crisped garlic toasts a snap to prepare.

Prep Time: 15 min   **Cook Time:** 15 min   **Serves** 4

1 tablespoon softened margarine

1/2 teaspoon garlic powder

1/3 cup plus 2 teaspoons chopped fresh parsley

1/2 of a small baguette (about 4 ounces), cut on a very sharp angle into 8 slices

2 tablespoons extra-virgin olive oil

1 cup chopped onion

1 cup chopped tomato

1/2 cup chopped celery

4 garlic cloves, minced

1 bottle (8 ounces) light-colored beer, such as pilsner or lager

2 pounds mussels, scrubbed and debearded

1/3 cup heavy cream

1/2 teaspoon salt

1/8 teaspoon freshly ground black pepper

1. Preheat the oven to 400°F. Coat a baking sheet with cooking spray.

2. In a small bowl, stir together the margarine, garlic powder, and 2 teaspoons of the parsley. Spread the mixture on 1 side only of each slice of the bread. Arrange the bread in a single layer on the baking sheet.

3. Bake the bread until crisp and golden, 6 to 7 minutes. Remove from the oven and cool.

4. Heat the oil in a large pot over medium-high heat. Stir in the onion, tomato, celery, and garlic and cook until starting to soften, 4 to 5 minutes.

5. Add the beer and bring to a boil. Add the mussels, cover, and cook until the mussels open, 4 to 5 minutes.

6. Transfer the mussels to a large bowl, discarding any that did not open.

7. Add the cream, salt, and pepper to the pot. Bring to a boil and cook for 1 minute. Stir in the remaining 1/3 cup parsley.

8. Divide the mussels into four large serving bowls and top each with some of the broth and 2 garlic crisps.

Personalize It!

If you don't care for beer, substitute 1/2 cup wine and 1 cup clam juice.

AMAZINGLY MOIST SALMON

SECRET INGREDIENT:

mayonnaise

A light coating of mayonnaise and Dijon mustard creates a protective coating that seals in the moisture of salmon while lending rich flavor. Of course, it's still important to avoid overcooking the fish, but you'll be amazed how such a simple technique yields such big rewards.

Prep Time: 5 min   **Cook Time:** 15 min   **Serves** 4

3 tablespoons mayonnaise

1 tablespoon Dijon mustard

2 tablespoons chopped fresh parsley

1 teaspoon grated orange rind

4 salmon fillets (about 1 1/2 pounds)

1/2 teaspoon salt

1/8 teaspoon freshly ground black pepper

1. Preheat the oven to 500°F. Coat a baking sheet with cooking spray.

2. In a small bowl, whisk together the mayonnaise, mustard, parsley, and orange rind.

3. Sprinkle the salmon with the salt and pepper. Coat each fillet with some of the mayonnaise mixture and set on the baking sheet.

4. Roast until the salmon flakes easily with a fork, 10 to 12 minutes.

Personalize It!

Tired of overcooked chicken breasts or pork chops? This technique works just as well on chicken, pork, and other types of fish. Adjust the seasonings, as desired; add garlic and rosemary for the chicken and try chopped sage for the pork. ❋

GRILLED SALMON WITH PEPPER-CORN RELISH

SECRET INGREDIENT:

cardamom

Cardamom distinguishes the flavor of many Indian and Moroccan dishes, but it's rarely used with America's favorite fish: salmon. Here, it combines with coriander and cinnamon in a terrific spice rub that perks up grilled salmon steaks topped with a colorful relish of summer vegetables. *See photograph on page 179.*

Prep Time: 15 min   **Cook Time:** 15 min   **Serves** 4

1/4 teaspoon plus 2 tablespoons sugar

1 teaspoon ground coriander

Salt

1/2 teaspoon ground cinnamon

1/4 teaspoon ground cardamom

1/4 teaspoon freshly ground black pepper

4 salmon steaks (about 1 1/2 pounds)

1/2 teaspoon yellow mustard seeds

1/3 cup distilled white vinegar

1 zucchini, cut into 1/4-inch pieces

1 orange bell pepper or red bell pepper, cut into 1/4-inch pieces

1 cup corn kernels, fresh or thawed frozen

1. Preheat the grill to medium-high.

2. Combine 1/4 teaspoon of the sugar, coriander, salt, cinnamon, cardamom, and black pepper in small saucepan. Rub 1 1/4 teaspoons of the mixture into one side only of each salmon steak.

3. Add the remaining 2 tablespoons sugar, mustard seeds, and vinegar to the saucepan and bring to a boil over medium heat.

4. Add the zucchini, bell pepper, and corn, and cook until the bell pepper is crisp-tender, about 4 minutes.

5. Place salmon, spice side down, on the grill and cook, without turning, until just done, about 5 minutes.

6. Serve topped with the relish.

One More Notch! Add more flavor by mixing 1/8 to 1/4 teaspoon cayenne pepper, 1/4 teaspoon ground cumin, and 1/4 teaspoon ground ginger into the spice rub.

POACHED SALMON WITH CREAMY DILL SAUCE

SECRET INGREDIENT:
cucumbers

Cool and refreshing, this recipe tastes like springtime on a plate. Diced cucumbers add juicy crunch to the sour cream dill sauce that's dolloped over salmon poached in white wine. For the richest flavor, buy wild Alaskan salmon in season from May to September.

Prep Time: 15 min **Cook Time:** 10 min **Serves** 4

1 1/2 cups water

1 cup dry white wine or low-sodium chicken broth

2 scallions, sliced

8 black peppercorns

4 salmon fillets (about 1 1/2 pounds)

3/4 cup sour cream

1/3 cup peeled, diced cucumber

2 tablespoons snipped fresh dill

1 tablespoon fresh lemon juice

1/4 teaspoon salt

1/8 teaspoon freshly ground black pepper

Fresh dill sprigs

1. Pour the water into a large nonstick skillet. Stir in the wine or broth, scallions, and peppercorns. Put the salmon in the skillet in a single layer. Bring to just a boil over high heat.

2. Reduce the heat to medium-low, cover, and simmer until the fish flakes easily with a fork, about 6 minutes.

3. Meanwhile, stir the sour cream, cucumber, snipped dill, lemon juice, salt, and pepper in a medium bowl. Refrigerate if not serving immediately.

4. Carefully transfer the fish with a slotted spatula to a large platter. Add the dill sprigs. Serve hot or chilled with sauce.

One More Notch! Stir 2 teaspoons prepared horseradish into the sauce for extra zing.

BAKED SKATE

SECRET INGREDIENT:
pickles

Mild and tender, skate wings benefit from a good dose of acidity. In this simple dish, extra flavor comes from balsamic vinegar, capers, butter, shallots, and something your guests will marvel at: pickles.

Prep Time: 15 min **Cook Time:** 20 min **Serves** 4

5 tablespoons unsalted butter

2 large skate wings (about 2 pounds), rinsed

2 shallots, chopped

2 tablespoons balsamic or sherry vinegar

Salt and freshly ground black pepper

2 tablespoons whole capers

3 small gherkins, chopped

1. Preheat the oven to 375°F.

2. Use a little of the butter to grease a shallow baking dish, which must be large enough to hold the skate flat in a single layer. Cut each skate wing into 2 pieces, place them in the baking dish, and dot them with the remaining butter.

3. Sprinkle the fish with the shallots and the balsamic or sherry vinegar and season with salt and pepper, to taste. Bake the skate, uncovered, until the thickest part of the skate wing flakes easily with a fork, about 20 minutes.

4. Sprinkle the fish with the capers and pickles and baste with the cooking juices just before serving.

One More Notch! Fill out the meal by adding some small tomato halves to the baking dish and roasting new potatoes in the oven alongside the fish.

CRUNCHY FLOUNDER WITH PINEAPPLE SALSA

SECRET INGREDIENT:
macadamia nuts

Fried fish is a great American dish and every region seems to have its own version. Macadamia nuts and pineapple salsa make this one taste like the islands of Hawaii.

Prep Time: 20 min   **Cook Time:** 15 min   **Serves** 4

2 cups finely diced pineapple

1/3 cup finely chopped red onion

2 tablespoons chopped fresh cilantro

1 tablespoon fresh lime juice

1 1/2 teaspoons salt, divided

1/4 cup all-purpose flour, divided

2 egg whites, lightly beaten

1/2 cup macadamia nuts

1/2 cup plain dried bread crumbs

4 skinless flounder fillets
    (about 1 1/2 pounds)

1/2 teaspoon garlic powder

1/4 teaspoon freshly ground black pepper

1/4 cup (1/2 stick) unsalted butter

1. Combine the pineapple, onion, cilantro, lime juice, and 1/2 teaspoon of the salt in a medium bowl. Mix well and set aside.

2. Place 3 tablespoons of the flour in a shallow bowl and the egg whites in another shallow bowl.

3. Combine the macadamia nuts and the remaining 1 tablespoon flour in a food processor and pulse until finely chopped. Transfer to a shallow bowl and stir in the bread crumbs.

4. Sprinkle the flounder with the remaining 1 teaspoon salt, garlic powder, and pepper.

5. Working 1 fillet at a time, dip both sides into the flour, shaking off any excess, then into the egg whites and finally the macadamia nut mixture. Place on a clean plate and repeat with the remaining fillets.

6. Melt 2 tablespoons of the butter in a large nonstick skillet over medium-high heat. Add 2 fillets and cook, turning once, until golden and the fish flakes easily with a fork, 3 minutes per side.

7. Transfer to a serving plate and keep warm. Repeat with the remaining butter and fillets. Serve with the salsa.

that's **ingenious**

Don't have bread crumbs? Don't fret. Take 2 to 3 white bread slices and pulse them in a food processor to make coarse crumbs. Spread them on a baking sheet and toast them in a 325°F oven until crisp.

SEAFOOD

GRILLED TUNA WITH HOT-PEPPER SPREAD

SECRET INGREDIENT:
bread

A richly flavored, spicy puree of char-grilled bell peppers, chiles, onion, and garlic makes the perfect partner for grilled meaty fish steaks. A single slice of bread gives the pepper puree great body and mouthfeel.

Prep Time: 20 min · **Cook Time:** 15 min · **Serves** 4

1 onion (unpeeled), halved

2 red bell peppers, seeded and halved lengthwise

2 garlic cloves (unpeeled)

1 small red chile pepper, seeded, deveined, and chopped (wear gloves when handling)

1 large slice whole-wheat bread, torn into pieces

1 tablespoon tomato puree

1/4 cup olive oil, divided

Grated rind and juice of 1 lime, divided

Salt and freshly ground black pepper

4 tuna steaks (about 1 1/2 pounds)

1. Preheat a grill to high. Put the onions and peppers onto the grill, skin side up, along with the garlic. Grill, turning occasionally, until the skins are slightly charred, about 10 minutes. Remove from the grill to cool.

2. When the vegetables are cool enough to handle, peel them and put the flesh into a food processor with the chile pepper, bread, tomato puree, and 3 tablespoons of the oil.

3. Add half the lime rind and lime juice. Process the mixture to a puree, then season to taste with salt and black pepper. Transfer the sauce to a serving bowl and set aside.

4. Rub the remaining oil over the fish then season with salt and pepper, to taste. Grill until golden brown on the outside and still pink in the middle, turning once, 4 to 6 minutes.

5. Sprinkle the steaks with the remaining lime rind and lime juice and serve with the sauce.

Personalize It!
If tuna isn't fresh at your market, use swordfish, shark, or mahi-mahi instead. To save time, use jarred roasted peppers. ❊

CRISPY TUNA STEAKS IN CITRUS SAUCE

SECRET INGREDIENT:
cornmeal

Their beefy texture makes tuna steaks a favorite with confirmed meat eaters. In this tangy recipe, the seasoned cornmeal seals in the tuna's juicy flavor. Who could resist? *See photograph on page 179.*

Prep Time: 15 min · **Cook Time:** 9 min · **Serves** 4

SAUCE

1 1/2 cups fresh orange juice

2 tablespoons dry white wine (optional)

2 tablespoons cornstarch

2 large oranges, peeled and sectioned

TUNA

2 tablespoons chopped fresh cilantro

2 tablespoons cornmeal

Salt

1/4 teaspoon freshly ground black pepper

4 tuna steaks (1/2 inch thick, 6 ounces each)

4 teaspoons olive oil, divided

1. For sauce, whisk the orange juice, wine (if using), and cornstarch in small saucepan until smooth. Bring to a boil over medium-high heat and cook, stirring, until it boils and thickens, about 2 minutes. Remove from heat the and stir in the orange sections. Keep warm.

2. For tuna, mix the cilantro, cornmeal, salt, to taste, and pepper in pie plate. Coat both sides of the tuna steaks with the cornmeal mixture, pressing firmly so it adheres.

3. Heat 2 teaspoons of the oil in large cast-iron skillet over medium-high heat until hot but not smoking. Sear the tuna until done to taste, 2 to 3 minutes on each side for medium-rare. Add the remaining 2 teaspoons of oil just before turning fish. Serve with the sauce.

Personalize It!

Of the many varieties of tuna, the most common kind sold fresh is yellowfin. It's a good choice for this recipe because it holds its shape and is flavorful enough to stand up to the seasonings in the crust and sauce. For variety, try this recipe with salmon, swordfish, or mahi-mahi. ✳

SAUTÉED GROUPER WITH CRUNCHY BREADING

SECRET INGREDIENT:

potato chips

Why leave potato chips to the chip and dip bowl? Crushed chips make a terrific alternative to bread crumbs for coating sautéed fish. The second secret ingredient here is milk, which balances the spicy flavor of the seasoning.

Prep Time: 20 min   **Cook Time:** 10 min   **Serves** 4

1 cup milk

4 grouper fillets (about 1 1/2 pounds)

2 teaspoons crab boil seasoning, such as Old Bay

2 eggs, beaten

1 1/2 cups finely crushed potato chips

2 tablespoons vegetable oil

1. Pour the milk into a large zip-close bag. Add the fish, press out the air, seal, and let rest at room temperature for 30 minutes to 1 hour.

2. Remove the fish to a large piece of foil and sprinkle all over with the seasoning.

3. Add the eggs in a wide shallow baking dish. Put the crushed chips in a similar dish.

4. Use tongs to dip the fish into the eggs, then into the crushed chips, gently pressing in the chips with your fingertips.

5. Heat the oil in a large heavy nonstick skillet over medium heat. Add the fish and cook until the fish is just a bit moist and filmy in the center, about 5 minutes per side, turning with a long, wide spatula. Cook in batches, if necessary.

One More Notch! To intensify the flavor, use flavored potato chips such as sour cream and onion or barbecue.

INDIAN-INSPIRED WHOLE-ROASTED RED SNAPPER

SECRET INGREDIENT:

yogurt

One of the best ways to cook a fish is to roast it whole. With the skin on and the bones intact, the fish stays moist and flavorful. Marinating the fish in spiced-up yogurt helps the fish to stay even more moist as it bakes and allows the fragrant perfume of the spices to permeate the fish.

Prep Time: 10 min   **Cook Time:** 30 min   **Serves** 2

1 cup plain yogurt

2 tablespoons minced peeled fresh ginger

4 garlic cloves, minced

1 teaspoon paprika

1 jalapeño pepper, seeded, deveined, and minced (wear gloves when handling)

1 teaspoon ground cumin

1/2 teaspoon ground coriander

2 whole red snappers (1 1/4 to 1 1/2 pounds), cleaned and scaled

1 teaspoon salt

1/2 teaspoon freshly ground black pepper

1. Combine the yogurt, ginger, garlic, paprika, jalapeño pepper, cumin, and coriander in a medium bowl and mix well.

2. With a sharp knife, make 3 deep cuts (down to the bone) crosswise on each side of the fish. Rub the yogurt mixture over the outside and inside the fish. Place the fish in a glass baking dish and refrigerate for 1 hour.

3. Preheat the oven to 400°F. Coat a large baking sheet with cooking spray.

4. Sprinkle the fish with salt and pepper and set on the baking sheet. Roast until the fish flakes easily with a fork, 30 to 35 minutes.

One More Notch! Intensify the aromatics in this dish by filling the fish cavity with fresh cilantro, parsley, and oregano, and squeezing some fresh lemon juice into the marinade.

MAHI-MAHI TACOS

SECRET INGREDIENT:

cocoa powder

Fish tacos make a light, refreshing entrée. Adding cocoa powder to prepared Mexican seasoning deepens the flavor without fuss, and briefly simmering the fish in bottled picante sauce keeps it moist.

Prep Time: 15 min   **Cook Time:** 15 min   **Serves** 4

4 skinless mahi-mahi fillets (about 1 pound), halved lengthwise

1 tablespoon Mexican seasoning, such as McCormick's

1 teaspoon unsweetened cocoa powder

1 tablespoon olive oil

1 cup medium spicy picante sauce

3/4 cup thinly sliced Vidalia or other sweet onion

1 tablespoon chopped fresh cilantro

1 tablespoon fresh lime juice

1/8 teaspoon salt

8 fresh corn tortillas (6-inch)

1/2 cup sour cream

1. Combine the fish, seasoning, and cocoa powder in a large bowl and toss well to coat.

2. Heat the oil in a large nonstick skillet over medium-high heat. Add the fillets, skinless side up, and cook until lightly browned, turning once, 4 minutes. Stir in the picante sauce and reduce the heat to medium; simmer, turning occasionally, until the fish flakes easily with a fork, 6 to 8 minutes.

3. Meanwhile, combine the onion, cilantro, lime juice, and salt in a small bowl and mix well.

4. Heat the tortillas according to the package directions. Place 1 piece of fish, 1 tablespoon of the sauce, and a quarter of the onion mixture on each tortilla. Top each with 1 tablespoon sour cream.

One More Notch! For added richness and color, top each taco with 1 tablespoon shredded cheddar cheese. Or, to help the cheese melt, scatter it over the warm tortilla and then top with the hot fish.

ASIAN GRILLED MAHI-MAHI

SECRET INGREDIENT:
hoisin sauce

Brushing sauces on seafood during the cooking process is an ideal way to add flavor without overpowering the fish. Hoisin sauce, a popular Asian condiment, makes a fabulous base for barbecue sauce that breathes life into grilled fish with salty-sweet contrasts.

Prep Time: 15 min   **Cook Time:** 10 min   **Serves** 4

3 tablespoons reduced-sodium soy sauce

1 tablespoon peeled minced fresh ginger

3 garlic cloves, minced

4 skinless mahi-mahi fillets (about 1 1/2 pounds)

3 tablespoons hoisin sauce

2 tablespoons ketchup

1 teaspoon fresh lemon juice

1 teaspoon honey

1. Combine the soy sauce, ginger, and garlic in a shallow baking dish. Add the mahi-mahi and turn to coat. Refrigerate, turning occasionally, for 20 minutes.

2. Meanwhile, combine the hoisin, ketchup, lemon juice, and honey in a small bowl.

3. Heat a well-oiled grill pan over medium-high heat. Remove the mahi-mahi from the marinade and place on the grill pan, skinless side up. Cook for 3 minutes, then turn and brush with some of the hoisin mixture. Cook 3 minutes longer, then turn and brush again. Cook for 1 minute. Turn the fillets one last time and brush with the remaining hoisin mixture. Cook until the fish flakes easily with a fork, 2 to 3 minutes longer.

Personalize It!

If mahi-mahi isn't fresh at your market, use salmon, swordfish, tuna steaks, or any other firm-fleshed fish. This sauce tastes terrific on pork and chicken, too.

SMOKED HADDOCK AND POTATO PIE

SECRET INGREDIENT:
cornmeal

Fish pies often include butter and cream in the filling. This one cuts back on calories by using milk that is thickened with cornmeal, which adds a delightfully nutty flavor as well. Sliced potatoes and cheddar cheese make a wonderfully crisp topping.

Prep Time: 30 min   **Cook Time:** 55 min   **Serves** 6

2 1/4 cups plus 3 tablespoons milk

1 pound smoked haddock fillets

1 bay leaf

1 large leek, halved lengthwise and sliced

1 pound russet potatoes, peeled and cut into 1/4-inch-thick slices

Boiling water

3 tablespoons cornmeal

2 cups watercress, thick stalks removed

Salt and freshly ground black pepper

1/2 cup coarsely grated cheddar cheese (about 2 ounces)

Chopped parsley

1. Pour 2 1/4 cups milk into a 12-inch skillet. Add the haddock and bay leaf. Bring to a gentle simmer, then cover and cook until the haddock is just cooked, about 5 minutes.

2. Lift out the fish with a slotted spoon and allow to cool slightly, then peel off the skin and break the flesh into large flakes. Set aside.

3. Strain the milk, reserving 2 cups of the liquid and the bay leaf.

4. Place the leek in the skillet and add the reserved milk and bay leaf. Cover and simmer until the leek is tender, about 10 minutes.

5. Meanwhile, cook the potatoes in a saucepan, adding enough water to cover them. Boil until they are just tender, about 8 minutes. Drain gently.

6. Preheat the oven to 375°F.

7. Remove the bay leaf from the leeks and discard.

8. Mix the cornmeal with the remaining 3 tablespoons milk in a cup to make a smooth paste. Add to the leek mixture and cook gently, stirring, until slightly thickened, 2 to 3 minutes

9. Remove the skillet from the heat and stir in the watercress, allowing it to wilt. Season lightly with salt and pepper. Add the haddock, folding it in gently. Transfer the mixture to a 9-inch pie plate.

10. Arrange the potatoes on top of the fish mixture, overlapping them slightly. Season with salt and pepper, to taste, then sprinkle with the cheese.

11. Bake until the filling is bubbly and the topping is golden, 25 to 30 minutes.

12. Sprinkle with the parsley and let stand for about 5 minutes before serving.

Personalize It!

To make spinach fish pie, use 2 sliced leeks and replace the watercress with baby spinach leaves. Add the spinach to the potato slices for the last 1 to 2 minutes of the boiling time. Drain well. Make a layer of the potatoes and spinach on the bottom of the pie dish. Spoon the hot fish and leek filling over the top and bake for 25 minutes, reserving the cheddar. Sprinkle with the cheese, and broil until bubbly and golden, for 5 to 10 minutes.

PAN-GRILLED HALIBUT STEAKS WITH RED PEPPER SALSA

SECRET INGREDIENT:
balsamic vinegar

With its slightly sweet flavor and large flakes, halibut takes well to pan-grilling. This 30-minute meal is served with a vibrant Italian-style salsa that forgoes the familiar cilantro-lime combination for a more exciting mixture of orange juice, basil, and sweet balsamic vinegar. *See photograph on page 179.*

Prep Time: 15 min	**Cook Time:** 10 min	**Serves** 4

4 halibut steaks (about 1 1/4 pounds)

1 tablespoon extra-virgin olive oil

Juice of 2 small oranges, divided

1 garlic clove, crushed

Salt and freshly ground black pepper

1/2 pound ripe plum tomatoes, diced

1 red bell pepper, seeded and diced

1 small red onion, finely chopped

2 tablespoons chopped fresh basil

1 tablespoon balsamic vinegar

1 teaspoon sugar

1 orange, cut into wedges

1. Place the halibut in a shallow non-metallic dish.

2. In a small bowl, mix together the oil, juice from 1 orange, and garlic and season lightly with salt and pepper. Spoon the mixture over the fish steaks.

3. Combine the tomatoes, bell pepper, onion, juice from 1 orange, basil, vinegar, and sugar in a small bowl. Season lightly with salt and pepper. Spoon into a serving bowl and set aside.

4. Heat a ridged grill pan or heavy skillet coated with cooking spray over high heat.

Place the fish steaks on the grill pan or in the skillet and cook until the fish flakes easily, about 2 to 3 minutes on each side, basting from time to time with the oil mixture.

5. Place the fish steaks on warm serving plates and sprinkle with pepper, to taste. Serve with the oranges and salsa.

One More Notch! In the summertime, grill the halibut steaks over charcoal for a hint of smoke flavor. Use a fish grill basket to easily turn the grilled fish and keep it from falling apart. Or use Pacific halibut, which is a bit firmer than Atlantic halibut and holds up well on the grill without a fish basket.

FILLET OF SOLE KIEV

SECRET INGREDIENT:

crabmeat

Traditionally, Kiev is made by wrapping chicken breasts around cold butter then breading and frying. Here's a modern and slightly less rich but no-less-satisfying version that uses fillet of sole instead of chicken and rolls the sole around fresh crabmeat. Yum!

Prep Time: 20 min   **Cook Time:** 10 min   **Serves** 4

6 ounces claw or lump crabmeat

3 tablespoons mayonnaise

3/4 teaspoon crab boil seasoning, such as Old Bay

3 tablespoons chopped green onions

4 skinless sole fillets (about 1 1/2 pounds)

1/2 teaspoon salt

1/4 teaspoon freshly ground black pepper

3 tablespoons flour

2 large eggs

2 tablespoons milk

1 cup plain dry bread crumbs

3 cups canola oil

1. Pick over the crabmeat to remove any cartilage. Combine the crabmeat, mayonnaise, seasoning, and green onions in a medium bowl and mix well.

2. Sprinkle the sole fillets, skinless side up, with the salt and pepper. Place 1/4 cup of the crab mixture on each fillet near the narrower end and roll up each fillet around it. Secure each roll, including the sides, with toothpicks to be sure to enclose the crab mixture completely.

3. Spread the flour in a shallow bowl. Beat the eggs and milk together in a separate shallow bowl, and add the bread crumbs to a third shallow bowl.

4. Dip each roll in the flour, shaking off the excess, dip it in the egg mixture, shaking off excess, and then dip in the bread crumbs to coat completely. Transfer the rolls to a plate.

5. Heat the oil in a Dutch oven until a cube of bread dropped into the oil takes about 40 seconds to brown. Add the fish rolls and cook, turning them carefully, until the fish is cooked through and the coating is crisp, 7 to 10 minutes. Transfer the rolls with a slotted spoon to a paper towel–lined plate to drain.

One More Notch! As with most seafood dishes, this one tastes great served with lemon wedges for squeezing. To take it to the next level, whip up a remoulade sauce to serve on the side. Mix together 1/2 cup mayonnaise, 1 tablespoon drained chopped capers, 3 tablespoons finely minced onion, and 1 to 2 tablespoons fresh lemon juice.

extraordinary
cereal

Cereal on ice cream? You bet! In fact, there are countless ways to use everyday cereal in your cooking. From multi-grain granolas to simple cornflakes, cereals add crunch, health, and surprise to all sorts of dishes, be it fancy entrées or simple breakfast parfaits. *clockwise:* **Glazed Apple Tart** page 275; **Warm Sesame-Chicken Salad,** page 72; **Crunchy Breakfast Parfait,** page 25; **Ham 'n' Cheese Strata,** page 21

161

extraordinary
breakfasts

Fluff up pancakes with **ricotta cheese**

Transform smoothies with **avocado**

Light and Fluffy Lemon Pancakes, page 11 **and Mango Surprise Smoothie,** page 246

Make frittatas fabulous with **cashews**

clockwise: **Huevos Rancheros,** page 15; **Spinach and Mushroom Frittata,** page 19; **Smoked Haddock Soufflé,** page 20; **Southern Breakfast Skillet,** page 23; **Pumpkin Spice Waffles,** page 13

 163

extraordinary
breads, rolls,
and muffins

Embolden the flavor with **tea leaves**

Make muffins merrier with **applesauce**

Add moisture with **bananas**

clockwise: **Lemon Pound Cake Muffins,** page 42; **Cinnamon Streusel-Topped Muffins,** page 43; **Enlightened Blueberry Muffins,** page 42

Boost richness with **eggnog**

clockwise: **Peaches-and-Cream Quick Bread,** page 30; **Old-Fashioned Glazed Gingerbread,** page 36; **Triple Chocolate Quick Bread,** page 30; **Braided Cranberry Bread,** page 32; **Southern Nut Bread,** page 28; **Blueberry Swirl Coffeecake,** page 37

extraordinary
appetizers
and snacks

Add a tropical twist with **beer**

Make salsa surprising with **pineapple**

Nachos Grande, page 55 and **Cuban Summer Sipper,** page 249

Bolster burgers with **carrots**

clockwise: **Gingered Crab Phyllo Dumplings,** page 53; **Falafel Pitas,** page 58; **Bacon-Cheddar Toasts,** page 57; **Easy Jalapeño Poppers,** page 55; **Lamb Burgers with Fruit Relish,** page 46

167

extraordinary
salads
and dressings

Spark iced tea with **frozen lemonade** concentrate

Sweeten salads with **maple syrup**

Wow breads with **Parmesan cheese**

Cobb Salad with Warm Bacon Dressing, page 62;
Garlic Bread Muffins, page 40; Iced Tea Ade, page 249

Add flavor to
barley with
carrot juice

clockwise: **Apple and Date Salad,** page 76; **Barley, Black Bean, and Avocado Salad,** page 69;
Sweet-and-Sour Duck Salad, page 73; **Crunchy Nut Coleslaw,** page 76;
Summertime Spinach Salad, page 70

extraordinary
soups and stews

Spice up soup with **pepperoni**

Portuguese Kale Soup with Beans, page 90

Add richness with **evaporated milk**

clockwise: **Mexican Chicken Soup with Cheese,** page 88; **Pumpkin Bisque,** page 92; **Classic Veal Stew,** page 83; **Mediterranean Roasted Vegetable Soup,** page 91; **Cheddar Cheese and Broccoli Soup,** page 95

171

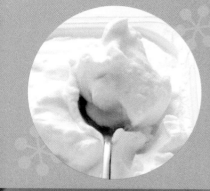

extraordinary
sour cream

Sure, sour cream shows up in lots of baking recipes. But this tart-yet-rich dairy favorite can add a unique dash of flavor to a host of dishes, including salads, pork dishes, and even pasta. *clockwise:* **Carrot and Ginger Salad,** page 69; **Heavenly Deviled Eggs,** page 50; **Triple Chocolate Cookies,** page 254; **Tomato and Pecorino Cheese Pudding,** page 24

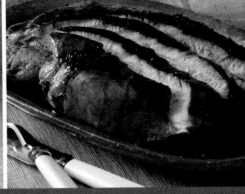

extraordinary coffee

Who knew that coffee could make steak, cake, turkey, ham, soup, cupcakes, barbecue sauce, even gelatin dessert taste so great? Whether its ground coffee or brewed, a surprising number of dishes can be transformed using this worldwide-favorite drink as an ingredient. *clockwise:* **Espresso Biscotti**, page 257; **Seattle Chiffon Cake**, page 268; **Broiled Java Turkey**, page 114; **Broiled Spicy Steak**, page 124, **with Extra-Bold Barbecue Sauce**, page 236

extraordinary
poultry
main dishes

Sweeten salads with **raisins**

Give zest to sauce with **ginger ale**

Jerk Turkey Breast with Ginger Barbecue Sauce, page 114
and Roasted Sweet Potato Salad with Orange Dressing, page 70

Add orange flavor with **Earl Grey tea**

clockwise: **Super-Moist Pepper Chicken,** page 101, **with Sautéed Brussels Sprouts,** page 226; **Crispy Crunchy Chicken Nuggets with Honey Mustard,** page 110; **Chicken with Apples,** page 102; **Spanish-Style Chicken,** page 109; **Orange-Rosemary Cornish Hens,** page 113

Jazz up beef with **juniper berries**

Slow-Braised Beef and Barley, page 126

Make steak sauce sing with **Dijon mustard**

Add surprise to ribs with **root beer**

clockwise: **Sweet-and-Sour Pork,** page 137; **Sirloin Steaks with Port Sauce,** page 124;
Southwestern Lasagna, page 131; **Zesty Glazed Ribs,** page 140,
with Feta-Barley Salad with Citrus Dressing, page 66

177

extraordinary
seafood
main dishes

Fire up corn muffins with **ground chipotle chile peppers**

Create a flavor explosion with **bottled Caesar salad dressing**

Creole Shrimp, page 145, with Smoky Corn Muffins, page 41

Add a crunchy coating to tuna with **cornmeal**

clockwise: **Cod with Gremolata Crust,** page 193; **Pan-Grilled Halibut Steaks with Red Pepper Salsa,** page 159; **Crispy Tuna Steaks in Citrus Sauce,** page 155; **Baltimore Seafood Cakes,** page 146; **Shrimp Provençal,** page 144; **Grilled Salmon with Pepper-Corn Relish,** page 152

extraordinary
pasta, beans, and rice
main dishes

Add depth
to red sauces
with
cinnamon

x

z

Baked Rigatoni Ragu, page 201

extraordinary
pasta, beans, and rice
main dishes

Add depth
to red sauces
with
cinnamon

180

Baked Rigatoni Ragu, page 201

Improve mac 'n' cheese with **potato chips**

Transform burritos with **orange zest**

clockwise: **Golden-Topped Macaroni and Cheese Casserole**, page 200; **Tortellini Carbonara**, page 207; **Thai Shrimp Fried Rice**, page 217; **Cuban Bean Burritos**, page 216

181

extraordinary
orange juice

Use it in soups, sauces, and marinades. Add it to pies, cakes, and ice creams. You can even cook rice with it! Orange juice is one of the most diverse and flavorful drinks in your kitchen, with limitless uses in your daily cooking. *clockwise:* **Baked Trout with Cucumber Sauce,** page 196; **Pork Medallions with Peppers,** page 134; **Banana Cream Pie with Honey-Wafer Crust,** page 273; **Brandied Chestnut and Mushroom Terrine,** page 50

extraordinary
peanut butter

Peanut butter and jelly sandwiches may be an American favorite, but you're missing something wonderful if you don't also use peanut butter in your cooking! It's the perfect ingredient for Asian-inspired sauces as well as for soups, in muffins, even as a glaze for ham. *clockwise:* **Cold Sesame Noodles and Vegetables,** page 213; **Chocolate Ice Cream Cake,** page 278; **Asian Chicken Salad,** page 71

extraordinary
vegetable
and side dishes

Perk up mashed potatoes with **bacon**

Country-Style Mashed Potatoes, page 221

Turn beets into a treat with **cranberry sauce**

Make french fries out of **polenta**

clockwise: **Leek and Cheddar Cheese Tart**, page 233; **Spiced Red Beets and Cabbage**, page 227;
Roasted Cauliflower with Parmesan and Almonds, page 228; **Quinoa Pilaf**, page 224;
Sneaky Fries with Chipotle Ketchup, page 224

extraordinary
sauces, dips,
and spreads

Transform guacamole with **yogurt**

Guacamole with a Kick, page 241

clockwise: **Lemon Butter Spread**, page 243; **Gulf Coast Hot Crab Dip**, page 240; **Moroccan Carrot Dip**, page 239; **Cheesy Pesto Spread**, page 243, **with Rosemary Focaccia**, page 34

187

extraordinary
beverages

Punch up punch with **black pepper-corns**

Warm Pineapple-Ginger Punch, page 250

Reinvent root beer with **heavy cream**

Spice cocoa with **ancho chile pepper**

clockwise: **Strawberry-Yogurt Smoothies,** page 246; **Cuban Summer Sipper,** page 249;
Not-Your-Average-Root-Beer Float, page 248; **Creamsicle Shake,** page 247;
South-of-the-Border Hot Chocolate, page 251, **with Kickin' Kettle Corn,** page 288

189

extraordinary
desserts

Make cake
unique with
**tomato
juice**

Red Velvet Devil's Cake, page 264

Boost brownies with **mini marsh-mallows**

Balance sweet and tart with **lemon zest**

clockwise: **Rocky Road Brownies,** page 258; **Baked Almond-Stuffed Peaches,** page 285; **Raspberry and Vanilla Risotto,** page 286; **Blueberry-Orange Tart,** page 276

extraordinary
chocolate

Chocolate, eaten straight up, is healthy, creamy, romantic, sweet, and oh-so-delicious. But did you know chocolate is also an amazing cooking ingredient? You can easily transform stews, sauces, and almost any dessert with this beloved, ancient flavor.

clockwise: **Vegetarian Chili,** page 80, **with Spicy Surprise Biscuits,** page 35; **Homemade Ice Cream Sandwiches,** page 279; **Turkey Mole,** page 116; **Chestnut Brandy Mousse,** page 287

CRUSTED PAN-SEARED COD WITH TARTAR SAUCE

SECRET INGREDIENT:
Ritz crackers

Cod, a very mild-flavored fish, is often over-whelmed by highly seasoned spice rubs or flavored bread crumbs. Our secret ingredient—rich-tasting Ritz crackers—has a mild, sweet flavor that creates a crunchy crust on the fish without overwhelming the cod's great taste.

Prep Time: 20 min   **Cook Time:** 10 min   **Serves** 4

1/2 cup mayonnaise

2 tablespoons sweet pickle relish

1 teaspoon drained chopped capers

3 tablespoons all-purpose flour

1 large egg, lightly beaten

3 tablespoons milk

20 Ritz crackers, crushed (about 1 1/2 cups)

4 cod fillets (about 1 1/2 pounds)

1/2 teaspoon salt

1/8 teaspoon freshly ground black pepper

1/4 cup canola oil

1. In a small bowl, stir together the mayonnaise, relish, and capers. Set aside.

2. Place the flour in a large shallow bowl. In another large shallow bowl, whisk together the egg and milk. Add the crackers to a third shallow bowl.

3. Sprinkle the cod with the salt and pepper. Working 1 fillet at a time, dredge both sides in the flour, shaking off any excess. Dip the same fillet into the egg mixture, then shake off any excess and dredge in the cracker crumbs to coat. Place the fillet on a clean plate and repeat with the remaining fillets.

4. Heat the oil in a large nonstick skillet over medium-high heat. Add the cod fillets and reduce the heat to medium. Cook until the fillets are golden brown, about 5 minutes. Turn over and cook until golden and the fish flakes easily with a fork, 4 to 5 minutes longer.

5. Serve each fillet with 2 tablespoons of tartar sauce.

that's **ingenious** !

If you don't want to spend the time stirring together the tartar sauce, store-bought makes a good alternative.

COD WITH GREMOLATA CRUST

SECRET INGREDIENT:
mustard

Here's a great way to jazz up plain cod fillets. Gremolata is an Italian mixture of parsley, lemon zest, and garlic (and sometimes chopped anchovy). We add bread crumbs to the gremolata, which bakes into a layer of coarse-grain mustard slathered over the fish and creates a tasty topping.
See photograph on page 179.

Prep Time: 20 min   **Cook Time:** 25 min   **Serves** 4

2 lemons, divided

1/2 cup white bread crumbs

3 tablespoons chopped parsley

2 garlic cloves, crushed

Salt and freshly ground black pepper

4 skinless cod fillets (about 1 pound)

2 teaspoons coarse mustard

3 plum tomatoes, quartered

1 large zucchini, thinly sliced diagonally

1 tablespoon olive oil

1 pound potatoes, peeled and cut into chunks

Boiling water

1 teaspoon saffron threads

3 tablespoons 1% milk, warmed

1. Preheat the oven to 400°F. Coat a large oven-proof dish with cooking spray.

2. Finely grate the zest from one of the lemons in a medium bowl. Mix with the bread crumbs, parsley, and garlic, and season lightly with salt and pepper.

3. Place the fillets in the baking dish, then spread the mustard evenly over the top and sprinkle with the juice from 1 lemon. Arrange the tomatoes and zucchini around the fish.

4. Cut the remaining lemon into 4 wedges and put them into the dish.

5. Spoon the bread-crumb mixture over the fish and press down lightly. Drizzle with the oil.

6. Bake the fish until it flakes easily with a fork and the topping is crisp, about 25 minutes.

7. Meanwhile, place the potatoes in a medium saucepan, cover with the water, and add the saffron. Cook the potatoes until tender, 15 to 20 minutes. Drain the potatoes and mash with a potato masher or electric mixer on low speed with the milk. Season lightly with salt and pepper.

8. Serve the fish with the potatoes, tomatoes, and zucchini.

that's **ingenious**

Crushing garlic releases more of its essential oils and results in a sharper flavor. First mince the garlic, then sprinkle it with a little salt. Put your knife blade flat over the pile and starting at one end of the pile, press down with the flat edge of the knife, pushing and scraping the blade across the pile. Repeat until the garlic flattens and releases its juices. The salt helps to keep the garlic bits from popping all over the kitchen as you work.

NEW ENGLAND COD CAKE BURGERS

SECRET INGREDIENT:
instant mashed potatoes

Traditionally, fish cakes are made with mayonnaise to bind the ingredients together. To lighten the texture (and the calorie count), use prepared instant mashed potatoes, which give the fish cakes a lighter, fluffier consistency.

Prep Time: 15 min	Cook Time: 30 min	Serves 6

1/2 cup mayonnaise

3 tablespoons sweet pickle relish

1/8 teaspoon cayenne pepper

3/4 cup plain dry bread crumbs, divided

1 pound skinless cod fillets

1 1/2 cups prepared instant mashed potatoes

3 tablespoons canola oil, divided

4 garlic cloves, minced

1/3 cup finely chopped red onion

1 teaspoon dried basil

1/2 cup chopped green onions

2 teaspoons grated lemon zest

1 large egg, lightly beaten

1 teaspoon salt

1/4 teaspoon freshly ground black pepper

6 hamburger rolls

1. Combine the mayonnaise, relish, and cayenne in a small bowl and mix well.

2. Spread 1/2 cup of the bread crumbs in a shallow bowl and set aside.

3. Fill a large skillet 2/3 full with lightly salted water and bring to a boil over medium-high heat. Add the cod, reduce the heat to medium, and simmer gently until the fish flakes easily with a fork, 8 to 10 minutes. Remove the fish with a slotted spoon and drain well.

4. Transfer to a large bowl, break into smaller pieces, and stir in the mashed potatoes.

5. Heat 1 tablespoon of the oil in a medium nonstick skillet over medium-high heat. Add the garlic, red onion, and basil and cook, stirring occasionally, for 2 minutes.

6. Stir in the green onions and cook 1 minute longer. Remove from the heat and add to the cod mixture.

7. Stir in the remaining 1/4 cup bread crumbs, lemon zest, egg, salt, and pepper and mix gently until well-combined.

8. Divide the mixture into six portions and form each into a 1/2-inch-thick patty. Roll each patty in the bread crumbs to coat.

9. Heat 1 tablespoon of the remaining oil in a large nonstick skillet over medium heat. Add the 4 cod cakes to the pan and cook until golden and heated through, about 5 minutes per side. Transfer to a plate and keep warm. Heat the remaining 1 tablespoon oil and repeat with the remaining cod cakes.

10. To serve, place a cod cake on each roll and top with some of the mayonnaise mixture.

One More Notch! Top the burgers with sliced red onions, tomatoes, and lettuce. For an extra treat, serve dill pickle wedges on the side.

FISH AND CHIPS

SECRET INGREDIENT:

beer

Making a batter for fish is simple, but the batter takes on new life with the addition of dark beer. The natural carbonation of beer creates a lighter batter while the stout's hearty flavor stands up to the frying process.

Prep Time: 10 min   **Cook Time:** 20 min   **Serves** 4

3/4 cup prepared tartar sauce

3/4 teaspoon crab boil seasoning, such as Old Bay

5 to 6 cups canola oil

1 1/2 cups all-purpose flour

1/2 teaspoon salt

1/4 teaspoon cayenne pepper

1 bottle (12 ounces) stout or dark beer

1 1/2 pounds tilapia fillets, cut into 1 x 3-inch strips

3/4 pound frozen French fries

1. In a small bowl, stir together the tartar sauce and seasoning and set aside.

2. In a large pot, heat the oil over medium heat to 360°F on a deep-fry thermometer or until a cube of bread dropped into the oil takes about 40 seconds to brown.

3. In a large bowl, whisk together the flour, salt, and cayenne. Stir in the beer until a thick batter forms.

4. Drop half the tilapia strips into the batter and turn to coat. Drop the tilapia pieces, one by one, into the oil and cook, turning frequently until golden brown and the fish is cooked through, 5 to 6 minutes. Remove the fish from the oil with a slotted spoon and transfer to a paper towel–lined baking sheet. Return the oil to 360°F and repeat with the remaining tilapia.

5. Meanwhile, cook the French fries according to the package directions.

6. Line small baskets with newspaper and serve the fish and chips in the basket.

One More Notch! In addition to the tartar sauce, serve this dish accompanied by some malt vinegar and hot-pepper sauce.

BAKED TROUT WITH CUCUMBER SAUCE

SECRET INGREDIENT:

orange juice

Trout has an amazing affinity for oranges. To up the ante, we use orange juice, orange slices, and some lemon slices to flavor this easy baked fish dish. A little tarragon enhances the aromas and roasted potato wedges complete the meal. *See photograph on page 182.*

Prep Time: 30 min   **Cook Time:** 40 min   **Serves** 4

1 pound new potatoes, quartered lengthwise

Boiling water

2 teaspoons olive oil

Salt and freshly ground black pepper

4 small trout (about 2 1/2 pounds), cleaned

4 sprigs fresh tarragon

1 orange, cut into 8 slices

1 lemon, cut into 8 slices

4 tablespoons orange juice

1 large cucumber, peeled and seeded

2/3 cup plain yogurt

2 tablespoons chopped fresh mint

1 cup watercress

1. Preheat the oven to 400°F and put 2 baking sheets in the oven to heat up.

2. Place the potatoes in a large saucepan and add enough of the water to cover them. Bring to a boil, then simmer for 5 minutes. Drain and return to the pan.

3. Drizzle the oil over the potatoes and toss them quickly to coat. Spread them out

on one of the baking sheets and roast for 10 minutes. Turn the potatoes over and roast for another 10 minutes, then turn them again and roast until crisp and tender, about 5 minutes longer.

4. Meanwhile, season inside the fish and tuck in the tarragon. Cut out four squares of foil, each large enough to wrap up a fish.

5. Cut the orange and lemon slices in half. Divide half the orange and lemon slices among the foil squares, lay the fish on top, and cover with the remaining fruit slices. Sprinkle 1 tablespoon orange juice over each fish.

6. Wrap up the fish, completely enclosing it in the foil, twisting the ends to seal. Lay the parcels on the second hot baking sheet and bake until the fish is just a bit moist and filmy in the center, about 20 minutes.

7. Meanwhile, grate the cucumber, put it into a sieve, and press to squeeze out the water.

8. In a medium bowl, mix together the cucumber, yogurt, and mint, and season lightly with salt and pepper.

9. Arrange the fish, orange and lemon slices, and roasted potatoes on warm plates. Add some watercress and serve with the cucumber sauce.

One More Notch! For even more flavor, add 1 tablespoon snipped fresh chives and 1 teaspoon prepared horseradish to the sauce.

SEAFOOD

PAN-FRIED TROUT

SECRET INGREDIENT:
bacon-flavored crackers

One of the most beloved fish in the world, trout takes extremely well to pan-frying. For a touch of smoke, we coat the fillets in crushed bacon-flavored crackers mixed with cornmeal and Parmesan cheese.

Prep Time: 10 min   **Cook Time:** 10 min   **Serves** 4

1/2 cup freshly grated Parmesan cheese

1/2 cup crushed bacon-flavored crackers

1/2 cup cornmeal

1/4 to 1/2 teaspoon garlic salt

Pinch of freshly ground black pepper

2 eggs

1/2 cup milk

4 lake trout fillets (about 2 pounds),
    rinsed and patted dry

1/2 cup vegetable oil

Lemon wedges and/or snipped fresh chives
    or parsley (optional)

1. In a shallow bowl, combine the Parmesan, cracker crumbs, cornmeal, garlic salt, and pepper.

2. In another shallow bowl, beat together the eggs and milk.

3. Dip the fish in the egg mixture, then gently roll in the crumb mixture.

4. Heat the oil in a 12-inch skillet until hot. Add the fish in a single layer and fry until it flakes easily with a fork, turning once, 5 to 7 minutes. Add the lemon and/or chives or parsley, if using, before serving.

One More Notch! These fillets taste great with just a squeeze of lemon, but you can gild the lily by serving it with a quick aioli. Mix together 1/2 cup mayonnaise, 1 tablespoon fresh lemon juice, 1 tablespoon extra-virgin olive oil, and 2 minced garlic cloves.

BAKED WALLEYE

SECRET INGREDIENT:
V8 juice

Vegetable juice makes a handy simmering sauce for fish. Whether poached or baked, the fish stays moist and takes on rich flavors with no added fat. Here, we simmer a few chopped veggies in the V8 juice before baking Lake Erie's famed walleye fillets in the entire mixture.

Prep Time: 10 min   **Cook Time:** 35 min   **Serves** 4

3/4 cup chopped onion

3/4 cup seeded and chopped green bell pepper

3/4 cup chopped celery

1 tablespoon dried parsley flakes

1/2 teaspoon garlic powder

1/2 teaspoon freshly ground black pepper

1/2 teaspoon seasoned salt

1 cup V8 juice

4 walleye fillets (about 1 pound)

1. Preheat the oven to 350°F. Grease a 9 x 13-inch baking pan.

2. In a saucepan, combine the onion, green pepper, celery, parsley, garlic powder, black pepper, seasoned salt, and V8 juice. Bring to a boil. Reduce the heat, then simmer, uncovered, until the vegetables are crisp-tender, stirring occasionally, about 5 minutes.

3. Place the fish in the baking pan. Pour the vegetable mixture over the fish.

4. Cover and bake until the fish flakes easily with a fork, about 30 minutes.

Personalize It!

If you can't find walleye, use a similar fish such as pike, porgy, rockfish, red snapper, or grouper.

SEAFOOD

GRILLED CATFISH FILLETS

SECRET INGREDIENT:
Italian salad dressing

Bottled salad dressing makes a fabulous marinade. Here, it flavors Southern-style catfish that's basted with a spicy-sweet sauce made from condensed tomato soup. The entire recipe takes only 20 minutes of your time.

Prep Time: 10 min   **Cook Time:** 10 min   **Serves** 6

6 thick catfish fillets (about 3 pounds)

1 bottle (16 ounces) Italian salad dressing

1 can (10 3/4 ounces) condensed tomato soup

3/4 cup vegetable oil

3/4 cup sugar

1/3 cup vinegar

3/4 teaspoon celery seed

3/4 teaspoon salt

3/4 teaspoon freshly ground black pepper

3/4 teaspoon ground mustard

1/2 teaspoon garlic powder

1/8 to 1/4 teaspoon cayenne pepper

1. Place the fillets in a large zip-close bag or shallow glass container and cover with salad dressing. Seal the bag or cover the container, then refrigerate for 1 hour, turning occasionally. Drain and discard the marinade.

2. Preheat a grill to medium-high. Combine the soup, oil, sugar, vinegar, celery seed, salt, pepper, mustard, garlic powder, and cayenne in a medium bowl. Remove 1 cup for basting. (Refrigerate the remaining sauce for another use, such as basting chicken breasts or pork chops.)

3. Grill the fillets, covered, for 3 minutes on each side. Brush with the basting sauce. Continue grilling until the fish flakes easily with a fork, turning once and basting several times, for 5 to 6 minutes.

that's ingenious

Catfish fillets sometimes stick to the grill. To solve the problem, use a fish grilling basket, available in many hardware stores and cookware stores. Or, preheat the grill grate for at least 10 minutes then brush the grate with a paper towel dipped in oil just before adding the fillets.

extraordinary
pasta,
beans, and rice
main dishes

MACARONI AU GRATIN

SECRET INGREDIENT:
Worcestershire sauce

Macaroni and cheese purists claim that there should be little else in the dish than cooked elbow noodles and melted cheese. But a few touches really kick up the flavor. Here, ground mustard adds spark, chopped onion adds richness, and Worcestershire sauce adds just the right zing.

Prep Time: 15 min   **Cook Time:** 45 min   **Serves** 6

7 ounces elbow macaroni

1/4 cup unsalted butter or margarine

1/4 cup all-purpose flour

2 cups milk

8 ounces processed American cheese, cubed

1 tablespoon chopped onion

1/2 teaspoon Worcestershire sauce

1/2 teaspoon salt

1/4 teaspoon freshly ground black pepper

1/4 teaspoon ground mustard

2 tablespoons seasoned dried bread crumbs

1. Preheat the oven to 375°F. Grease a 2-quart baking dish.

2. Cook the macaroni according to the package directions, then drain. Place in the baking dish and set aside.

3. Meanwhile, in a medium saucepan, melt the butter or margarine over medium heat. Stir in the flour until well-blended.

4. Gradually add the milk and bring to a boil. Cook and stir until blended, 2 minutes, then reduce the heat to medium-low.

5. Add the cheese, onion, Worcestershire sauce, salt, pepper, and mustard. Stir until the cheese melts, 3 to 4 minutes.

6. Pour the cheese over the macaroni and mix well. Sprinkle with the bread crumbs.

7. Bake, uncovered, until bubbly and golden, about 30 minutes.

One More Notch! To boost the flavor, use a mixture of cheeses such as 3 ounces shredded cheddar (smoked cheddar if you like), 3 ounces shredded fontina, and 2 ounces American cheese.

GOLDEN-TOPPED MACARONI AND CHEESE CASSEROLE

SECRET INGREDIENT:
potato chips

Crushed potato chips are a great alternative to the same old bread crumb topping found on most baked macaroni and cheese casseroles. Combined with crushed cornflakes, the chips take on a delicious salty-sweet flavor. The third secret ingredient here is canned diced tomatoes. *See photograph on page 181.*

Prep Time: 20 min   **Cook Time:** 45 min   **Serves** 6

12 ounces elbow macaroni

5 tablespoons unsalted butter, divided

3 tablespoons all-purpose flour

2 cups milk

2 teaspoons paprika

1 teaspoon dry mustard

3 cups shredded sharp cheddar cheese (about 12 ounces)

1 cup shredded Colby cheese (about 4 ounces)

1/2 cup freshly grated Parmesan cheese

1 can (14 1/2 ounces) petite cut diced tomatoes, drained

1 cup crushed potato chips

1/2 cup cornflake crumbs

1. Preheat the oven to 350°F. Coat a shallow 2-quart baking dish with cooking spray.

2. Cook the macaroni according to package directions. Drain about 1 minute before the macaroni is fully cooked and rinse under cold water. Drain again and transfer to a large bowl.

3. Meanwhile, heat a medium pot over medium-high heat and melt 3 tablespoons of the butter. Stir in the flour and cook, stirring constantly with a wooden spoon, until the flour just starts to turn light tan, about 3 minutes.

4. Whisk in the milk, paprika, and mustard. Cook, whisking constantly, until the mixture thickens, about 3 minutes. Reduce the heat to low and stir in the cheddar, Colby, and Parmesan cheeses and cook, stirring, until melted, about 2 minutes.

5. Pour the cheese mixture over the macaroni and stir until combined. Stir in the tomatoes. Spread the macaroni in the baking dish.

6. In a small glass bowl, melt the remaining 2 tablespoons of butter in a microwave. Combine the potato chips and cornflakes in a medium bowl. Pour in the butter and mix until evenly moistened. Sprinkle the mixture over the macaroni and bake until bubbling and the top is golden, 25 to 30 minutes.

7. Remove from the oven and let stand 10 minutes before serving.

One More Notch! Give this dish a Tex-Mex makeover by substituting 1 1/2 cups of Pepper Jack cheese for the Parmesan and 1 cup of the cheddar and stirring in 1 1/2 cups of drained chunky salsa in place of the tomatoes.

BAKED RIGATONI RAGU

SECRET INGREDIENT:
cinnamon

Baked pasta dishes are always a hit, and they're simple to prepare. This rendition owes its complex flavor to a cinnamon stick, which is simmered in the ragu. Crushed fennel seeds lend a sweet note of licorice as well.
See photograph on page 180.

Prep Time: 15 min   **Cook Time:** 45 min   **Serves** 6

12 ounces rigatoni

1 tablespoon extra-virgin olive oil

1 pound bulk hot Italian sausage

1 cup chopped onion

4 garlic cloves, minced

1/2 teaspoon fennel seeds, crushed

1 can (28 ounces) crushed tomatoes

1 cinnamon stick

1/2 cup grated Parmesan cheese

1. Preheat the oven to 400°F and coat an 11 x 7-inch baking dish with cooking spray.

2. Bring a large pot of salted water to a boil over high heat. Add the pasta and cook according to the package directions. Drain the pasta, rinse under cold water, and drain again.

3. Heat the oil in a large nonstick skillet over medium-high heat. Add the sausage and cook, stirring occasionally with a wooden spoon to break into smaller pieces, until no longer pink, 3 to 4 minutes.

4. Stir in the onion, garlic, and fennel seeds and cook until opaque, 4 to 5 minutes.

5. Add the tomatoes and cinnamon stick and bring to a boil. Reduce the heat to medium and simmer, uncovered, until the sauce is slightly thickened, 12 to 15 minutes. Remove and discard the cinnamon stick.

6. Spread 1/2 cup of the sausage mixture over the bottom of the baking dish and top with half of the rigatoni. Spread half of the remaining sausage mixture over the rigatoni. Repeat with the remaining pasta and sausage mixture. Sprinkle the top with the Parmesan.

7. Bake until the edges of the pasta begin to brown, 18 to 20 minutes.

8. Remove from the oven and let rest for 10 minutes before serving.

that's **ingenious** !

This dish is ideal to make for company or a weeknight meal because it can be assembled ahead and refrigerated until ready to bake. Prepare the dish as directed up to the point of sprinkling with the cheese. Wrap with plastic and refrigerate up to 48 hours. Allow an extra 10 to 15 minutes of baking time to make sure the dish is heated though.

BAKED ZITI

SECRET INGREDIENT:

pepperoni

Pepperoni is usually relegated to the antipasto platter or pizza. Adding diced cubes to pasta lends a subtle spicy aroma and satisfying chew. The second secret ingredient—provolone cheese—adds a bit of sharpness to balance the milder, creamier ricotta and mozzarella cheeses.

Prep Time: 15 min   **Cook Time:** 45 min   **Serves** 4

8 ounces ziti

1 cup part-skim ricotta cheese

1 1/2 cups shredded mozzarella cheese
    (about 6 ounces), divided

1 cup shredded sharp provolone cheese
    (about 4 ounces), divided

2 ounces pepperoni, cut into 1/4-inch pieces

2 cups prepared marinara sauce

1. Preheat the oven to 350°F. Coat an 8-inch square baking pan with cooking spray. Bring a large pot of salted water to a boil over high heat. Add the pasta and cook according to the package directions. In a colander, drain the pasta 1 to 2 minutes before it is fully cooked so that it is still slightly underdone. Rinse with cold water to stop the cooking, then drain it again.

2. In a medium bowl, whisk together the ricotta, 1 cup of the mozzarella, 3/4 cup of the provolone, and the pepperoni.

3. Pour half of the ziti into the baking pan. Top with 1 cup of the marinara sauce then spread with the ricotta mixture. Top with the remaining ziti. Spread the top of the ziti with the remaining 1 cup marinara sauce. Sprinkle with the remaining 1/2 cup mozzarella and 1/4 cup provolone.

4. Bake until the ziti is bubbling and the cheese has completely melted, about 30 minutes.

5. Let stand for 10 minutes before cutting.

that's **ingenious** !

This dish is ideal for entertaining and serving at parties. Assemble it the night before, wrap in plastic, then refrigerate until about 30 minutes before you need to bake it. Then just pop it in the oven.

LASAGNA GENOVESE

sun-dried tomatoes

Most recipes call for pesto to be used as an uncooked sauce. Here, the aromatic basil paste livens up the lasagna as it bakes in the oven. A few sun-dried tomatoes also provide a jolt of flavor to the ricotta cheese, giving traditional lasagna a whole new spin.

Prep Time: 20 min   **Cook Time:** 55 min   **Serves** 8

1 container (15 ounces) part-skim ricotta cheese

1 cup shredded mozzarella cheese
  (about 4 ounces), divided

1/2 cup oil-packed sun-dried tomatoes, chopped

1 egg

1/2 teaspoon salt

1 pound bulk sweet Italian sausage

1 cup chopped onion

1 can (8 ounces) tomato sauce

12 no-boil lasagna noodles

1 cup prepared pesto sauce

1. Preheat the oven to 350°F. Coat a 9 x 13-inch baking dish with cooking spray.

2. Combine the ricotta, 1/2 cup of the mozzarella, the sun-dried tomatoes, egg, and salt in a medium bowl.

3. Heat a large nonstick skillet over medium-high heat. Add the sausage and cook, stirring with a wooden spoon and breaking into smaller pieces, until no longer pink, 2 to 3 minutes.

4. Add the onion and cook until the sausage begins to brown, 4 to 5 minutes. Pour off any fat, return the skillet to the stove, and stir in the tomato sauce. Cook for 30 seconds, then remove from the heat.

5. Spread 1 cup of the sausage mixture into the bottom of the baking dish. Top with 3 lasagna noodles. Spread 1 1/3 cups of the ricotta mixture over the pasta then top with 1/3 cup of the pesto and 3/4 cup of the sausage mixture. Repeat with 3 noodles, then the ricotta mixture and pesto but not the sausage mixture. Arrange 3 noodles over the pesto layer and spread with the remaining 1 1/3 cup ricotta cheese, 1/3 cup pesto, and the remaining sausage mixture. Top with the remaining 3 noodles and the remaining 1/2 cup mozzarella.

6. Cover with foil that has been coated with cooking spray. Bake 35 minutes. Uncover and bake until hot and bubbly, about 10 minutes longer.

7. Remove from the oven and let rest for 10 minutes before serving.

One More Notch! Do you prefer your lasagna on the spicy side? Substitute hot Italian sausage for the sweet and try adding 1/8 to 1/4 teaspoon crushed red-pepper flakes when you sauté the onions.

GRECIAN PASTA BAKE

SECRET INGREDIENT:
cinnamon

Why confine cinnamon to sweet baked goods? Take a tip from ancient Greece and add a touch of cinnamon to pasta dishes for deep, exotic flavors. Cinnamon perfectly complements the traditional lamb and feta cheese in this soul-warming dish.

Prep Time: 20 min   **Cook Time:** 55 min   **Serves** 6

1 pound ziti

1/2 cup (1 stick) unsalted butter

1/2 cup all-purpose flour

4 cups warm milk

6 ounces crumbled feta cheese

1 teaspoon salt, divided

1/2 teaspoon freshly ground black pepper, divided

3 large eggs, lightly beaten

1 pound ground lamb

2 cups chopped onion

2 garlic cloves, minced

2 cans (14 1/2 ounces) diced tomatoes

1 teaspoon ground cinnamon

1. Preheat the oven to 350°F and coat a 9 x 13-inch baking dish with cooking spray.

2. Bring a large pot of salted water to a boil over high heat. Add the pasta and cook according to the package directions. Drain, rinse under cold water, and rinse again.

3. Meanwhile, melt the butter in a medium saucepan over medium heat. After it foams, add the flour. Cook, stirring with a wooden spoon, until it just starts to brown, about 2 minutes.

4. Whisk in the milk, feta cheese, 1/2 teaspoon of the salt, and 1/4 teaspoon of the pepper. Cook until the mixture is creamy and thick, 10 to 12 minutes.

5. In a large bowl, whisk 1 cup of the milk mixture into the eggs until well-combined, then whisk the egg mixture back into the pot and cook until thickened, 1 to 2 minutes longer. Remove from the heat.

6. Heat a large nonstick skillet over medium-high heat. Add the lamb and cook, stirring often, until no longer pink, 2 to 4 minutes.

7. Stir in the onion and garlic and cook until they start to soften, 3 to 4 minutes.

8. Add the tomatoes and cinnamon and cook, stirring occasionally, until the mixture has thickened somewhat, 7 to 8 minutes.

9. Remove from the heat and stir in the remaining 1/2 teaspoon salt and the remaining 1/4 teaspoon pepper. Combine the lamb mixture and ziti in a large bowl and toss well. Pour into the baking dish and spread the milk mixture over the top in an even layer.

10. Bake until the top is puffed and golden, 40 to 45 minutes.

11. Let stand for 5 minutes, then cut into squares and serve.

Personalize It!
This dish works equally well with ground beef. Or try it with ground chicken or turkey.

CHICKEN SPAGHETTI TOSS

SECRET INGREDIENT:
lemon-pepper seasoning

Lemon-pepper is a popular seasoning that is exactly what is says: a combination of ground black pepper and dried bits of lemon peel. In this recipe, the seasoning adds surprise and spice to plain old chicken and noodles.

Prep Time: 10 min   **Cook Time:** 20 min   **Serves** 4

8 ounces uncooked thin spaghetti

5 green onions, chopped

2 garlic cloves, minced

2 tablespoons unsalted butter

2 tablespoons olive oil

1 1/2 pounds boneless, skinless chicken breasts, cubed

3 tablespoons fresh lemon juice

3 tablespoons minced fresh parsley

1 teaspoon salt

1 teaspoon lemon-pepper seasoning

1. Cook the spaghetti according to the package directions, then drain.

2. Meanwhile, in a large nonstick skillet, sauté the onions and garlic in the butter and oil until tender, about 4 minutes.

3. Stir in the chicken, lemon juice, parsley, salt, and lemon-pepper. Sauté until chicken juices run clear, 15 to 20 minutes.

4. In a large bowl, toss the spaghetti with the chicken mixture.

that's **ingenious**

If you don't have prepared lemon-pepper seasoning, simply replace it with 1/2 teaspoon grated lemon zest, 1/4 teaspoon freshly ground black pepper, and 1/8 teaspoon salt.

LINGUINE WITH NO-COOK TOMATO SAUCE

SECRET INGREDIENT:
orange zest

Basil, parsley, and mint make a fabulous herb trio for fresh tomatoes. But adding orange zest takes the combo to an entirely new level. This quick-and-easy sauce is bound to become your house favorite. It's bursting with fresh-from-the-garden flavor.

Prep Time: 15 min   **Cook Time:** 15 min   **Serves** 4

3 pounds plum tomatoes, seeded and chopped

2/3 cup chopped fresh basil

1/4 cup olive oil

1/4 cup chopped fresh flat-leaf parsley

2 tablespoons chopped fresh mint

2 teaspoons grated orange zest

3 garlic cloves, minced

1/2 teaspoon freshly ground black pepper

Salt

12 ounces linguine

1/4 cup Parmesan cheese

1. Mix the tomatoes, basil, oil, parsley, mint, orange zest, garlic, pepper, and salt, to taste, in a medium bowl. Let stand at least 30 minutes or up to 2 hours at room temperature.

2. Bring a large pot of salted water to a boil over high heat. Add the pasta and cook according to the package directions. Drain well and put into a large pasta bowl.

3. Top with the sauce and sprinkle with the Parmesan.

One More Notch! Add 1 1/2 tablespoons balsamic vinegar to the sauce for extra zip. When mixing the hot pasta with the sauce, toss in 8 ounces cubed fontina, which will soften but not completely melt from the heat of the noodles.

LINGUINE WITH WHITE CLAM SAUCE

SECRET INGREDIENT:

canned chopped clams

A white clam sauce is really hard to make from scratch, due to all the scrubbing and shucking involved. To the rescue come canned chopped clams, which not only eliminate 95 percent of the work but also add great flavor both from the clams themselves and the juice in which they're packed.

Prep Time: 10 min   **Cook Time:** 15 min   **Serves** 4

12 ounces linguine

2 tablespoons extra-virgin olive oil

6 garlic cloves, minced

1 bottle (8 ounces) clam juice

2 cans (6 1/2 ounces each) chopped clams, drained and liquid reserved

1/2 cup heavy cream

2 tablespoons fresh lemon juice

1/2 cup chopped fresh parsley

1/8 teaspoon crushed red-pepper flakes

1/2 teaspoon salt

1/4 teaspoon freshly ground black pepper

1. Bring a large pot of salted water to a boil over high heat. Add the pasta and cook according to the package directions. Drain.

2. Meanwhile, heat the oil in a medium pot over medium-high heat. Stir in the garlic and cook until lightly golden, 1 to 2 minutes.

3. Stir in the clam juice, reserved clam liquid, cream, lemon juice, parsley, pepper flakes, salt, and pepper. Bring to a boil, reduce the heat to medium-low, and simmer until very slightly thickened, 8 to 10 minutes.

4. Stir in the clams and cook until hot, about 1 minute. In a large bowl, toss the linguine and clam sauce.

that's ingenious !

For a dish that packs a little more flavor, boil the heavy cream in a small saucepan over medium heat until reduced by half before adding it to the sauce.

SWEET-AND-TANGY ANGEL HAIR

SECRET INGREDIENT:

honey

Pasta with butter and garlic is about as basic as you can get. This rendition of the Italian classic includes honey for a delightfully sweet touch.

Prep Time: 5 min   **Cook Time:** 15 min   **Serves** 8

1 pound angel hair pasta

2 to 3 garlic cloves, minced

1/2 cup unsalted butter

1/4 cup honey

1 teaspoon dried basil

1 teaspoon dried thyme

1/4 cup grated Parmesan cheese

1. Bring a large pot of salted water to a boil over high heat. Add the pasta and cook according to the package directions.

2. Meanwhile, in a large nonstick skillet, sauté the garlic in the butter, then stir in the honey, basil, and thyme.

3. Drain the pasta, add it to the garlic mixture, and toss to coat.

4. Sprinkle with Parmesan before serving.

One More Notch! To make this dish more substantial, sauté 8 ounces chicken thighs cut into strips in the butter before adding the garlic. Top with 4 ounces thinly sliced prosciutto.

CREAMY SALMON FETTUCCINE

SECRET INGREDIENT:
cream cheese

Usually served on bagels or black bread, smoked salmon becomes the star in this easy pasta dish. The subtle flavors of the salmon work wonderfully with its ubiquitous co-star—cream cheese.

Prep Time: 10 min   **Cook Time:** 15 min   **Serves** 4

12 ounces fettuccine

2 tablespoons unsalted butter

2 tablespoons extra-virgin olive oil

1 onion, finely chopped

3 ounces smoked salmon, chopped

1/2 cup cream cheese

2/3 cup heavy cream

1/4 teaspoon salt

1/8 teaspoon freshly ground black pepper

1 tablespoon chopped fresh dill

1. Bring a large pot of salted water to a boil over high heat. Add the pasta and cook according to the package directions. Drain.

2. Meanwhile, heat a large nonstick skillet over medium-high heat and add the butter and oil. Heat until the butter melts, then stir in the onion. Cook, stirring occasionally, until the onions start to soften, 2 to 3 minutes.

3. Add the salmon and cook until opaque, 1 minute. Stir in the cream cheese and cook, stirring until it melts, about 45 seconds.

4. Pour in the cream and cook until hot, 1 minute. Remove from the heat and stir in the fettuccine. Toss until well-coated. Stir in the salt, pepper, and dill and serve.

Personalize It!

To lighten up this dish, use half the amount of oil and butter, use reduced-fat cream cheese, and substitute 2% milk for the cream. Avoid boiling the sauce because the lower fat content could cause it to separate. ❄

TORTELLINI CARBONARA

SECRET INGREDIENT:
eggs

Carbonara sauce often tastes overly rich and heavy due to the gobs and gobs of added cream. This lighter version gets its rich, silky texture from a few eggs instead. The earthy flavor of mushrooms rounds out the sauce nicely. *See photograph on page 181.*

Prep Time: 15 min   **Cook Time:** 20 min   **Serves** 4

1 pound tortellini

3 eggs, lightly beaten

1/2 cup milk

3/4 cup grated Romano cheese

1/4 teaspoon salt

1/4 teaspoon freshly ground black pepper

6 slices bacon, chopped

1 cup chopped onion

2 cups sliced mushrooms

2 tablespoons dry vermouth

1. Cook the tortellini according to the package directions, then drain.

2. Meanwhile, combine the eggs, milk, Romano, salt, and pepper in a small bowl.

3. Heat a large nonstick skillet over medium-high heat and add the bacon. Cook, stirring occasionally, until the fat renders out, about 5 minutes.

4. Add the onions and cook until they begin to soften, about 2 minutes.

5. Stir in the mushrooms and cook, stirring occasionally, until the onion is slightly brown and the mushrooms release their liquid, 5 to 6 minutes.

6. Add the vermouth and cook until almost evaporated, about 1 minute.

7. Add the tortellini and stir until hot, about 30 seconds. Add the egg mixture and stir until creamy, about 30 seconds.

8. Remove from the heat and serve immediately.

Personalize It!
If you don't have tortellini on hand, use your favorite strand pasta like spaghetti, fettuccine, or linguine. ❄

PUMPKIN-NUT RAVIOLI WITH SAGE-BROWN BUTTER

SECRET INGREDIENT:
wonton wrappers

Homemade ravioli taste great but the thought of spending the time making fresh pasta can be daunting. Wonton wrappers to the rescue! They allow you to make fresh ravioli anytime in a fraction of the time. Canned pumpkin puree also shortens the prep time for this autumnal pasta dish.

Prep Time: 20 min   **Cook Time:** 10 min   **Serves** 4

1 cup canned pumpkin puree

3/4 cup part-skim ricotta cheese

1/8 teaspoon ground cinnamon

Pinch of ground nutmeg

1 teaspoon salt, divided

1/3 cup chopped pecans

36 wonton wrappers

1 large egg, lightly beaten

1/2 cup (1 stick) unsalted butter

2 tablespoons chopped sage, divided

1 tablespoon fresh lemon juice

4 tablespoons grated Parmesan cheese

1. Cover a baking sheet with wax paper and set aside.

2. In a medium bowl, whisk together the pumpkin, ricotta, cinnamon, nutmeg, and

1/2 teaspoon of the salt. Stir in the pecans until well-mixed.

3. Place 6 wonton wrappers on a work surface and cover the remaining wrappers with plastic wrap to prevent them from drying out. Place a scant 2 teaspoons of filling slightly off center on each wrapper. Lightly brush the edges of each wrapper with the egg and fold the wrappers diagonally in half over the filling to form triangles. Press the edges firmly to seal and transfer them to the baking sheet. Repeat with the remaining wrappers and filling.

4. Meanwhile, bring a large pot of salted water to a boil over high heat.

5. Heat the butter in a large nonstick skillet over medium heat. When melted and hot, add 1 tablespoon of the sage and cook until the butter begins to brown, 3 to 4 minutes. Remove from the heat and stir in the remaining sage, the lemon juice, and the remaining 1/2 teaspoon salt. Keep warm.

6. Add the ravioli to the boiling water in 3 batches, being careful not to let the water return to a boil, and cook until the ravioli float to the top, 2 to 4 minutes. Transfer the ravioli with a slotted spoon to a medium bowl with some of the pasta water in it, cover and keep warm. Repeat with the remaining ravioli.

7. Drain the cooked ravioli and divide among 4 shallow bowls. Top each with a quarter of the sage butter and sprinkle each with 1 tablespoon of the Parmesan.

Personalize It!
Not everyone loves pumpkin, so change the filling to suit your tastes. The sage-butter sauce works wonderfully well with a ricotta/mozzarella filling or a seafood filling such as crab and shrimp. ❄

PASTA AND PEAS

SECRET INGREDIENT:

tomatoes

Traditionally, pasta and peas is very simply made with garlic, olive oil, and peas dominating the sauce. This version uses cream, ham, and tomato for a richer, more complex flavor.

Prep Time: 15 min   **Cook Time:** 25 min   **Serves** 4

1 1/2 cups frozen peas

1 cup heavy cream

1/3 cup milk

1/2 cup grated Parmesan cheese

3/4 teaspoon salt, divided

12 ounces oricchiette pasta

2 tablespoons unsalted butter

1 cup chopped onion

3 garlic cloves, minced

2 ounce sliced prosciutto, chopped

1 cup chopped seeded tomato

1. In a small saucepan over medium-high heat, combine the peas and cream, then bring to a boil. Reduce the heat to medium-low and simmer until the peas are very tender, 8 to 10 minutes.

2. Remove from the heat and stir in the milk. Let the peas cool for 5 minutes, then transfer to a blender and process until smooth.

3. Return the mixture to the saucepan and stir in the Parmesan and 1/2 teaspoon of the salt. Keep the mixture warm over low heat.

4. Meanwhile, bring a large pot of salted water to a boil over high heat. Add the pasta and cook according to the package directions. Drain.

5. Heat the butter in a large nonstick skillet over medium-high heat. When melted and hot, add the onion and garlic and cook until they start to soften, 2 to 3 minutes.

6. Stir in the prosciutto and the remaining 1/4 teaspoon salt. Cook until the onions just begin to brown, 2 to 3 minutes. Stir in the pasta and toss until well-combined.

7. Divide the pasta among four shallow bowls and top each with a quarter of the sauce. Top with the tomatoes.

that's **ingenious**

A kitchen gadget that will make pureeing this sauce—or any type of creamy soup—easy is an immersion blender. It is a timesaver because you don't need to cool the sauce before pureeing, and there is less clean up in the end.

FARFALLE WITH PESTO AND BACON

SECRET INGREDIENT:

potatoes

Mixing cubes of potatoes in with the pasta makes this dish unusually satisfying. Pesto gives it a bright flavor and smoked bacon adds aroma and a salty edge. All of these flavors are brought together by mild and tangy sour cream.

Prep Time: 10 min   **Cook Time:** 20 min   **Serves** 4

1/2 pound dried farfalle or other small pasta shapes

6 ounces frozen peas

1 pound boiling potatoes, peeled and cut into 1/2-inch cubes

10 ounces smoked back bacon (rind removed), cut into 1/2-inch cubes

1 1/2 tablespoons olive oil, divided

1 onion, chopped

3 ounces pesto

1 1/4 cups sour cream or 10 ounces natural Greek yogurt

Freshly ground black pepper

Fresh basil leaves, rinsed and dried

1 tablespoon freshly grated Parmesan cheese

1. Bring a large pot of salted water to a boil over high heat. Add the pasta and cook according to the package directions. Add the peas 3 minutes before the pasta is done and cook until the pasta is tender yet slightly chewy. Drain.

2. Bring another large saucepan of salted water to a boil over high heat. Add the potatoes and cook, partially covered, over medium heat until tender, about 7 minutes. Drain and keep hot.

3. Meanwhile, fry the bacon in a skillet over medium-high heat, stirring frequently, until it is cooked, 2 to 3 minutes. Transfer to a paper towel–lined plate and set aside.

4. Add the oil to the bacon drippings in the pan, add the onion, and cook gently until soft but not brown, about 5 minutes.

5. Return the bacon to the pan and stir in the pesto and sour cream or yogurt. Season well with pepper, cover, and keep warm.

6. Drain the pasta and peas and return them to the pan. Add the potatoes and gently stir in the bacon and pesto mixture.

7. Serve sprinkled with the basil leaves and Parmesan.

that's **ingenious**

Look for smoked back bacon slices with no added water: Also known as dry-cured bacon, they taste far better than conventionally cured slices and have the added advantage of leaving no water residue in the pan after they have been cooked.

GNOCCHI WITH SEARED SHRIMP AND PESTO

SECRET INGREDIENT:

arugula

Gnocchi, little dumplings made with potatoes, are the perfect canvas for the light and aromatic flavors of pesto. Here, some of the traditional basil is replaced by peppery arugula, which perfectly complements the seared shrimp.

Prep Time: 10 min	Cook Time: 15 min	Serves 4

1 bag (16 ounces) gnocchi pasta

1/4 cup toasted walnuts

2 cup packed fresh arugula

1 cup packed fresh basil leaves

1 garlic clove

1/4 cup freshly grated Romano cheese

1 teaspoon salt, divided

1/2 cup plus 2 tablespoons extra-virgin olive oil

1 pound peeled and deveined extra-large shrimp

1/4 teaspoon freshly ground black pepper

1. Bring a large pot of salted water to a boil over high heat. Add the pasta and cook according to the package directions.

2. Combine the walnuts, arugula, basil, garlic, Romano, and 1/2 teaspoon of the salt in a food processor or blender. Pulse until the nuts, arugula, and basil are finely chopped. With the machine running, add 1/2 cup of the oil in a slow, steady stream. Process until fairly smooth but not a puree, about 1 minute.

3. Toss the shrimp with the remaining 1/2 teaspoon salt and the pepper. Heat 1 tablespoon of the remaining oil in a large nonstick skillet over medium-high heat and add half of the shrimp. Cook, turning once, until cooked through, 2 to 3 minutes per

side. Transfer to a plate and repeat with the remaining oil and shrimp.

4. Toss the gnocchi with 1/2 cup of the pesto and the shrimp. Divide among four serving bowls.

5. Serve the remaining pesto in a bowl on the side.

One More Notch! Round out the flavor by adding 1/2 cup sliced sun-dried tomatoes. The inherent sweetness of the tomatoes tempers the arugula, which can taste bitter sometimes.

NOODLE KUGEL

SECRET INGREDIENT:
cornflakes

Noodle kugel is the pasta-lover's version of bread pudding. With its perfect mix of creamy and sweet ingredients, it could very well be the ultimate comfort food. We've taken the kugel a step further by adding a crunchy top layer made from crispy cornflakes.

Prep Time: 15 min **Cook Time:** 1 hr 5 min **Serves** 6

1 pound wide egg noodles

4 tablespoons plus 3 tablespoons unsalted butter

4 eggs, lightly beaten

3/4 cup half-and-half

2/3 cup plus 3 tablespoons sugar

1 container (16 ounces) sour cream

1 container (15 ounces) part-skim ricotta cheese

1 cup golden raisins

1 teaspoon vanilla extract

1/4 teaspoon ground cinnamon

3 cups cornflakes, lightly crushed

1. Preheat the oven to 350°F. Coat a 9 x 13-inch glass baking dish with cooking spray.

2. Bring a large pot of salted water to a boil over high heat. Add the pasta and cook according to the package directions. Drain

and return to the pot, add 4 tablespoons of the butter and stir until melted.

3. Combine the eggs, half-and-half, 2/3 cup of the sugar, sour cream, ricotta, raisins, vanilla, and cinnamon in a large bowl. Add the noodles and toss well to coat. Transfer to the baking dish.

4. Melt the remaining 3 tablespoons of butter in a small microwavable bowl for 30 seconds. Combine with the cornflakes and remaining 3 tablespoons sugar in a large bowl. Sprinkle over the top of the noodle mixture.

5. Bake until the edges turn brown and the liquid has set, 50 to 55 minutes.

6. Let stand for 5 minutes before cutting.

SPAGHETTI ALFREDO

SECRET INGREDIENT:
spaghetti squash

Pasta Alfredo is a fixture on most Northern Italian restaurant menus. For a fun twist, we use spaghetti squash instead of spaghetti noodles. When the squash cooks, it separates into strands that resemble spaghetti yet have a delicious sweetness that pairs well with mild and savory Alfredo sauce.

Prep Time: 10 min **Cook Time:** 30 min **Serves** 4

1 spaghetti squash (2 3/4 to 3 pounds), halved and seeded

1/2 cup (1 stick) unsalted butter

1/2 cup heavy cream

1/2 cup grated good-quality Parmesan cheese, such as Parmigiano-Reggiano

1/2 teaspoon salt

1/4 teaspoon freshly ground black pepper

1. Preheat the oven to 400°F. Coat a large baking sheet with cooking spray.

2. Place the squash, cut side down, on the baking sheet and prick the skin all over with a fork. Bake until tender, 30 minutes. Remove from the oven and hold the skin side of the squash with an oven mitt. Scrape the inside flesh of the squash in long strokes with a fork over a medium bowl. Repeat with the second half.

3. Combine the butter and cream in a small saucepan over medium-high heat. Cook until the butter melts and is hot, 3 to 4 minutes.

4. Pour over the squash and stir in the Parmesan, salt, and pepper.

5. Serve immediately.

One More Notch! For an added level of deliciousness, sauté the squash in 2 tablespoons of the butter in a large nonstick skillet over medium-high heat for 2 to 3 minutes to help dry it out slightly and intensify the flavor.

PASTA-LESS LASAGNA

SECRET INGREDIENT:
zucchini

The best thing about lasagna is the layers of flavor from the cheese, sauce, and noodles. Here's a fun twist that replaces the layer of noodles with a layer of broiled zucchini slices. Perfect for a vegetarian main course or those looking to reduce carbohydrates.

Prep Time: 25 min   **Cook Time:** 55 min   **Serves** 4

3 zucchini (9 to 10 inches long), about 3 pounds

2 tablespoons extra-virgin olive oil

1/4 teaspoon salt

1/8 teaspoon freshly ground black pepper

1 container (15 ounces) part-skim ricotta cheese

1 1/2 cups shredded mozzarella cheese (about 6 ounces), divided

1 large egg

1/2 cup grated Parmesan cheese, divided

1 1/2 cups jarred tomato-basil sauce

1. Preheat the broiler and coat a large baking sheet with cooking spray.

2. Working one at a time, carefully cut each zucchini lengthwise into 6 slices. Brush the slices with the oil and sprinkle with salt and pepper. Arrange one-half of the slices on the baking sheet and broil 5 inches from the heat until they start to brown slightly, about 5 minutes. Turn the zucchini and broil until lightly browned, 4 to 5 minutes longer. Transfer to a plate and repeat with the remaining zucchini slices.

3. Preheat the oven to 350°F. Coat an 8-inch square baking dish with cooking spray.

4. Combine the ricotta, 1 cup of the mozzarella cheese, egg, and 1/4 cup of the Parmesan in a small bowl.

5. Spread 1/2 cup of the sauce over the bottom and top with 6 slightly overlapping slices of the zucchini. Top with one-half of the ricotta mixture and 1/2 cup of the sauce. Repeat the layering with 6 slices of zucchini and the remaining ricotta mixture and sauce. Top with the remaining 6 slices of zucchini.

6. Sprinkle the top with the remaining 1/2 cup mozzarella and the remaining 1/4 cup Parmesan. Cover with foil and bake for 35 minutes. Uncover the lasagna and bake until bubbly, about 10 minutes longer.

7. Remove from the oven and let stand 10 minutes before cutting.

Personalize It!

Don't like zucchini? Substitute slices of yellow squash or eggplant. For a little more flavor, replace the mozzarella with shredded aged provolone.

COLD SESAME NOODLES AND VEGETABLES

SECRET INGREDIENT:
peanut butter

A long-time favorite at Chinese restaurants, cold sesame noodles make a great main dish or side dish. We've replaced hard-to-find sesame paste with peanut butter and sesame oil.
See photograph on page 183.

Prep Time: 15 min   **Cook Time:** 15 min   **Serves** 4

8 ounces whole-wheat linguine

1/3 cup fresh cilantro leaves

2 tablespoons low-sodium peanut butter

2 tablespoons reduced-sodium soy sauce

2 1/2 teaspoons honey

1 tablespoon rice vinegar or apple-cider vinegar

1 tablespoon dark sesame oil

2 garlic cloves

1/4 teaspoon cayenne pepper

Salt

1/2 cup slivered carrots

1 red bell pepper, seeded and slivered

1 large stalk celery, slivered

2 scallions, slivered

1. Bring a large pot of salted water to a boil over high heat. Add the pasta and cook according to the package directions. Drain, reserving 1/2 cup of the cooking water.

2. Meanwhile, combine the cilantro, peanut butter, soy sauce, honey, vinegar, oil, garlic, cayenne, and salt, to taste, in a food processor. Puree until smooth, then transfer to large bowl and whisk in the reserved pasta cooking water. Add the linguine, carrots, bell pepper, celery, and scallions. Toss.

3. Chill at least 1 hour before serving.

One More Notch! Spice up the sauce with 1/4 teaspoon red-pepper flakes or 1/2 teaspoon prepared chili-garlic sauce. You can also make the dish more filling by sautéing 8 ounces chicken breasts, cut into strips, and 4 ounces small broccoli florets in a skillet. Toss with the sauce when you add the other ingredients.

SWEET-AND-SOUR PORK LO MEIN

SECRET INGREDIENT:
cashews

Lo mein, the popular take-out Chinese noodle dish, gets a shot of flavor with a sweet-and-sour sauce in this simple version. The trick is using canned pineapple chunks for convenience. Both the fruit and juice add flavor to the mix. Cashews round out the dish with a bit of salty crunch.

Prep Time: 15 min   **Cook Time:** 20 min   **Serves** 4

8 ounces lo mein noodles or fettuccine

1 pound pork tenderloin, cut crosswise into 1/4-inch-thick strips

2 tablespoons cornstarch, divided

1 can (8 ounces) pineapple chunks in juice, drained with juice reserved

1/4 cup rice vinegar

1/4 cup sugar

1/4 cup ketchup

1 1/2 tablespoons soy sauce

2 tablespoons canola oil, divided

2 cups sliced mushrooms

1 cup snow peas, trimmed

2 tablespoons peeled grated fresh ginger

1/2 cup chopped green onions

3/4 cup roasted salted cashews

1. Bring a large pot of salted water to a boil over high heat. Add the pasta and cook according to the package directions.

2. Combine the pork and 1 tablespoon of the cornstarch in a large bowl.

3. Combine the reserved pineapple juice, vinegar, sugar, ketchup, and soy sauce in a small bowl; mix well.

4. Heat 1 tablespoon of the oil in a large nonstick skillet over medium-high heat. Add the pork and cook until no longer pink, 3 to 4 minutes. Transfer the pork to a plate and return the skillet to the stove.

5. Heat the remaining 1 tablespoon oil and add the mushrooms, snow peas, and ginger and cook, stirring often, until crisp-tender, 4 to 5 minutes.

6. Add the pineapple cubes and green onions and cook for 30 seconds. Add the pork and cashews and cook until hot, 1 minute.

7. Add the ketchup mixture, bring to a boil, and cook until thick, 1 minute. Add the noodles and cook until hot, 1 to 2 minutes.

8. Serve immediately.

that's **ingenious**

To save a few minutes of prep time, try using 2 cups frozen vegetables cut specifically for stir-fries. Any combination will work just fine.

PAD THAI

SECRET INGREDIENT:
ketchup

Pad Thai is one of those dishes you love but never feel like you can make at home. Well we've simplified the dish and found something right in our own pantry that packs in the right flavors—ketchup! This ubiquitous condiment works perfectly as the base for a Pad Thai sauce.

Prep Time: 10 min **Cook Time:** 20 min **Serves** 4

8 ounces flat rice noodles

1/2 cup ketchup

3 tablespoons fish sauce

3 tablespoons sugar

2 tablespoons fresh lime juice

3 tablespoons peanut oil, divided

1 container (12 ounces) extra-firm tofu, drained and cut into 1/2-inch cubes

3 eggs, lightly beaten

4 green onions, cut into 1/4-inch pieces

2 tablespoons chopped fresh cilantro

1 cup bean sprouts

1/4 cup chopped salted cashews

1. Bring a large pot of salted water to a boil over high heat. Add the pasta and cook according to the package directions. Drain.

2. In a small bowl, whisk together the ketchup, fish sauce, sugar, and lime juice.

3. Heat 1 tablespoon of the oil in a large nonstick skillet over medium-high heat. Stir in the tofu and cook, stirring occasionally, until lightly browned, 5 to 7 minutes. Transfer to a medium bowl and reserve.

4. Return the skillet to the stove over medium-high heat and add 2 teaspoons of the oil. Stir in the eggs and cook, stirring occasionally, until the eggs are cooked through and in smaller pieces,

1 to 2 minutes. Transfer the eggs into the bowl with the tofu.

5. Return the skillet to the stove and heat over medium-high heat. Add the remaining 4 teaspoons oil and add the noodles. Cook, stirring, until the noodles are heated through and coated with oil.

6. Stir in the ketchup mixture, tossing until well-distributed. Add the tofu and eggs and cook until heated through, 1 to 2 minutes.

7. Remove from the heat and stir in the green onions and cilantro.

8. To serve, divide among four bowls and top each with 1/4 cup of the sprouts and 1 tablespoon of the cashews.

Personalize It!

Make this your own by adding in some of your favorite ingredients such as cooked shrimp or cubes of cooked chicken breast.

PASTA AND BEAN BAKE

SECRET INGREDIENT:
golden raisins

A layer of tangy sweet Swiss chard, enhanced with balsamic vinegar and golden raisins, transforms an average bean-and-pasta dish into a meal your family will ask for again and again.

Prep Time: 15 min   **Cook Time:** 40 min   **Serves** 4

12 ounces rotini

2 tablespoons extra-virgin olive oil

3 garlic cloves, minced

1 1/2 cups chopped onions

1 pound Swiss chard, trimmed and chopped

3/4 cup golden raisins

2 tablespoons balsamic vinegar

1 tablespoon drained capers

1/4 teaspoon salt

1/8 teaspoon freshly ground black pepper

1 can (15 ounces) cannellini beans, rinsed and drained

3 cups prepared marinara sauce

2 cups shredded mozzarella cheese (about 8 ounces)

1. Preheat the oven to 350°F. Coat an 11 x 7-inch baking dish with cooking spray.

2. Bring a large pot of salted water to a boil over high heat. Add the pasta and cook according to the package directions. Drain and rinse under cold water.

3. Heat the oil in a large nonstick skillet over medium-high heat. Add the garlic and onions and cook until they start to soften, 2 to 3 minutes.

4. Add the chard and cook, stirring often, until wilted, about 2 minutes.

5. Add the raisins and cook until the chard is tender, 3 to 4 minutes.

6. Stir in the vinegar and capers and cook until the vinegar is absorbed, about 1 minute. Remove from the heat and stir in the salt and pepper.

7. Combine the pasta, beans, and marinara sauce in a large bowl; mix well. Pour half of the pasta mixture into the pan. Top with the chard mixture and 1 cup of the mozzarella. Top with the remaining pasta mixture and sprinkle with the remaining 1 cup mozzarella. Bake until hot and the cheese has melted, 25 to 30 minutes.

8. Serve immediately.

One More Notch! Along with the chard, add 1/2 cup sliced fresh basil to the layer before you sprinkle with the mozzarella.

TAMALE PIE

corn chips

Everyone should have tamale pie in their Tex-Mex repertoire. The combination of corn and chili is a real crowd-pleaser. Pre-cooked polenta makes an easy and tasty "crust" for the pie. Corn chips are the perfect crunchy topping, but tortilla chips work as well.

Prep Time: 15 min **Cook Time:** 35 min **Serves** 6

12 ounces lean ground pork or beef

1 tablespoon chili powder

2 teaspoons ground cumin

1 teaspoon ground coriander

1/4 teaspoon ground chipotle chile pepper

2 cans (16 ounces each) refried beans

1 jar (16 ounces) mild salsa

1 can (14 1/2 ounces) diced tomatoes, drained

1 tube (1 pound) prepared polenta, cut into 1/4-inch-thick slices

3 cups corn chips

2 cups shredded Pepper Jack cheese (about 8 ounces)

1. Preheat the oven to 350°F. Coat a 9 x 12-inch baking dish with cooking spray.

2. Heat a large nonstick skillet over medium-high heat. Add the pork or beef and cook, breaking into smaller pieces with a wooden spoon, until starting to brown, 4 to 5 minutes.

3. Add the chili powder, cumin, coriander, and chipotle; cook until fragrant, about 45 seconds.

4. Add the refried beans, salsa, and tomatoes. Bring to a simmer and cook, stirring occasionally, 5 minutes.

5. Line the bottom of the baking dish with the polenta slices. Top with the pork mixture then sprinkle with the corn chips and the cheese.

6. Bake until bubbly and the cheese has melted, 25 to 30 minutes. Serve immediately.

Personalize It!

If you have a great chili recipe, make this dish your own by substituting your favorite chili for the filling given here. If pork or beef are not your favorites, you can substitute ground chicken or turkey or leave the meat out all together and add in a can of red kidney beans as a replacement.

CUBAN BEAN BURRITOS

orange zest

Cuban-style black beans taste terrific on their own but also make a fabulous filling for burritos. The creamy, earthy beans get a bright boost of flavor from grated fresh orange zest, an ingredient used in many other Cuban-style dishes.
See photograph on page 181.

Prep Time: 20 min **Cook Time:** 15 min **Serves** 4

1/2 cup long-grain white rice

2 tablespoons olive oil

1 cup chopped onion

4 garlic cloves, minced

1 1/2 cups frozen mixed bell pepper strips

3 plum tomatoes, chopped

2 tablespoons red-wine vinegar

1 teaspoon dried oregano

1 can (15 ounces) black beans, drained but not rinsed

1 tablespoon grated fresh orange zest

4 burrito-size flour tortillas (8-inch)

1/2 cup shredded sharp cheddar cheese (about 2 ounces)

1. Prepare the rice according to the package directions, omitting any fat.

2. Meanwhile, heat the oil in a large pot over medium-high heat. Add the onion, garlic, and pepper strips. Cook, stirring occasionally, until the vegetables begin to soften, about 5 minutes.

3. Stir in the tomatoes, vinegar, and oregano; cook for 2 minutes.

4. Add the beans, then reduce the heat to medium. Cover and simmer until heated through and bubbly, stirring occasionally and lightly mashing some of the beans, for 10 minutes.

5. Remove the pot from the heat and stir in the orange zest. Let stand for 3 minutes.

6. Heat the flour tortillas according to the package directions.

7. Lay the tortillas on a work surface. Spoon 1/2 cup of the rice onto each tortilla. Spoon 3/4 cup of the bean mixture onto the rice. Sprinkle each with 2 tablespoons of the cheese.

8. Fold up the bottom quarter of each tortilla and roll away from you, tucking in the sides as you go. Set on serving plates, seam side down.

Personalize It!

Kick this recipe into high gear by adding some of your favorite condiments. Try serving the burritos topped with some sour cream, prepared salsa, and guacamole. ❋

THAI SHRIMP FRIED RICE

SECRET INGREDIENT:
coconut milk

If you like Chinese fried rice, you'll love this Thai version. Coconut milk adds rich sweetness to the rice, while plum tomatoes stand in for the usual peas and carrots. After eating this, you may never go back to traditional fried rice! *See photograph on page 181.*

Prep Time: 20 min   **Cook Time:** 30 min   **Serves** 4

1 1/2 cups coconut milk

1/2 cup water

1 tablespoon sugar

1/2 teaspoon salt

1 cup long-grain white rice

3 tablespoons canola oil, divided

1 1/2 pounds peeled and deveined large shrimp

2 garlic cloves, minced

1 cup chopped onion

2 eggs, lightly beaten

3 plum tomatoes, quartered

1 1/2 tablespoons fish sauce

1/2 cup chopped green onions

1. Combine the coconut milk, water, sugar, and salt in a medium saucepan over medium-high heat and bring to a boil. Add the rice, cover, and reduce heat to medium-low and simmer until almost all of the liquid is absorbed, about 20 minutes. Remove from the heat and let stand 5 minutes. Transfer the rice to a baking sheet and spread into one layer. Let cool completely, about 15 minutes, then refrigerate at least 2 hours.

2. Heat 1 tablespoon of the oil in a large nonstick skillet over medium-high heat. Add half the shrimp and cook, turning once, until cooked through, 2 to 3 minutes per side. Transfer to a plate and repeat with the remaining shrimp.

3. Add the remaining 2 tablespoons oil to the skillet and heat. Add the garlic and onion, and cook, stirring occasionally, until they start to brown slightly, 2 to 3minutes.

4. Add the eggs and cook, stirring, for 30 seconds. Add the rice, tomatoes, and fish sauce; cook, stirring often, until hot, about 3 minutes. Add the shrimp and cook until hot, 1 minute.

5. Remove from the heat and stir in the green onions.

that's **ingenious**

Speed up this recipe by making the coconut rice up to 2 days before you need it. Refrigerate the rice in a covered bowl until you are ready to use it.

LITTLE NECK RISOTTO

SECRET INGREDIENT:

sweet Italian sausage

Good risotto requires a fair amount of stirring, so you might as well make it worth the effort by adding rich flavors. Seafood risottos tend to be on the mild side. Take them to the wild side by adding Italian sausage for meatiness and a dollop of heavy cream for a velvety finish.

Prep Time: 15 min   **Cook Time:** 45 min   **Serves** 4

2 cups water

3 dozen littleneck clams, scrubbed

3 bottles (8 ounces each) clam juice

8 ounces bulk sweet Italian sausage

1 cup finely chopped onion

4 garlic cloves, minced

1 cup Arborio rice

1/4 cup dry vermouth

1/4 cup heavy cream

2 tablespoons chopped fresh parsley

1. Bring the water to a boil in a large heavy-bottomed pot over high heat. Add the clams. Cover and cook until the clams open, 5 to 7 minutes—be sure to remove clams as they open as some will cook faster than others. Reserve 1 1/2 cups of the cooking liquid. Let the clams cool for 5 minutes, then remove them from the shells. Discard any clams that don't open.

2. Combine the clam juice with the reserved cooking liquid in a medium saucepan over medium-low heat.

3. Wipe out the pot used to cook the clams and return to the stove over medium heat. Add the sausage and cook until no longer pink, 3 to 4 minutes.

4. Stir in the onion and garlic and cook until they start to turn lightly golden, 8 to 10 minutes. Add the rice and cook for 2 minutes.

5. Pour in the vermouth and cook, stirring often, until absorbed, about 45 seconds. Ladle in 1 cup of the warm clam broth mixture and cook, stirring often, until the liquid is absorbed. Continue adding the clam juice mixture by 1/2 cupfuls until the rice is tender but still slightly firm in the center and the mixture is creamy, 20 to 25 minutes.

6. Add the clams and cook until hot, 1 minute.

7. Add the cream and cook 1 minute longer. Remove from the heat and stir in the parsley.

8. Serve immediately.

Personalize It!

Fresh clams taste best here but they do add some extra prep work. Cut your kitchen time by substituting 2 cans (6 1/2 ounces each) chopped clams. Be sure to drain and add the canning liquid to the clam juice used to make the rice. You'll most likely need an additional 1 bottle (1 cup) of clam juice or 1 cup of water to make up the difference in liquid lost from the fresh clams.

extraordinary

vegetable and side dishes

EXTRAORDINARY CHEESE & POTATO GRATIN

SECRET INGREDIENT:
evaporated milk

This beautiful gratin makes the perfect accompaniment to a Sunday roast. Evaporated milk gives it a rich texture as if you added cream, but with much fewer calories. Be sure to keep cans of evaporated milk on hand—it's a terrific pantry staple!

Prep Time: 20 min **Cook Time:** 1 hr 15 min **Serves** 6

3 tablespoons olive oil

2 Vidalia onions, thinly sliced

3/4 teaspoon salt, divided

1 garlic clove, minced

1 can (12 ounces) evaporated milk

3/4 cup chicken broth

1 1/2 pounds Yukon Gold potatoes, very thinly sliced

1 tablespoon chopped fresh thyme or 1 teaspoon dried

1/2 teaspoon freshly ground black pepper

1/2 cup grated Gruyère cheese (about 2 ounces), divided

1. Preheat the oven to 375°F. Coat a 3-quart shallow baking dish with cooking spray.

2. Heat the oil in a large nonstick skillet over medium-high heat. Add the onions and 1/2 teaspoon of the salt. Cover and cook, stirring once or twice, until soft, 5 minutes.

3. Reduce the heat to medium-low, add the garlic and cook, covered, stirring until the onions are well-browned, 5 to 8 minutes longer.

4. Bring the milk and broth to a boil over medium heat in a small saucepan.

5. Meanwhile, arrange half the potato slices in the baking dish, overlapping them slightly. Sprinkle with half of the thyme, half the black pepper, and 1/8 teaspoon of salt. Top with the onions and 1/4 cup of the cheese. Arrange the remaining potato slices on top and sprinkle with the remaining thyme, pepper, salt, and cheese. Pour the milk mixture over the top.

6. Cover with foil and bake for 30 minutes. Remove the foil and bake until almost all of the liquid is absorbed and the potatoes are tender, 30 to 35 minutes longer.

Personalize It!
If you don't have or don't like Gruyère cheese, try another Swiss-type cheese, such as Jarlsberg. Or use freshly grated Parmesan instead.

TANGY POTATO WEDGES

SECRET INGREDIENT:
limes

Tired of baked potatoes? This is a simple, fast way to make a potato side dish with a wonderfully different flavor. Lime juice and grated lime peel, coupled with other flavorful ingredients—including Romano cheese, paprika, and thyme—deliver a punch.

Prep Time: 10 min **Cook Time:** 20 min **Serves** 6

1/4 cup unsalted butter, melted

1 tablespoon fresh lime juice

1 teaspoon grated lime peel

1 teaspoon dried thyme

3 large potatoes

1/4 cup freshly grated Romano cheese

1/2 teaspoon salt

1/4 teaspoon paprika

1. Preheat the oven to 400°F. Grease a baking sheet.

2. In a large bowl, combine the butter, lime juice, lime peel, and thyme.

3. Cut each potato into 8 wedges; add to the butter-lime mixture and toss to coat. Place wedges, skin side down, on the baking sheet.

4. Combine the cheese, salt, and paprika in a small bowl. Sprinkle over the potatoes.

5. Bake until tender, 20 to 25 minutes.

One More Notch! For a little more heat and punch, add 1 teaspoon red-hot sauce to the butter-lime mixture before adding the potatoes. You can also shake a little cayenne pepper onto the wedges before baking.

CHEDDAR POTATO PUFF

SECRET INGREDIENT:
almonds

Here's a refreshing change of pace. Eggs and cream whipped into mashed potatoes lighten the texture and cause the spuds to puff up in the oven. Two forms of almond give the potatoes a nutty taste

Prep Time: 15 min   **Cook Time:** 40 min   **Serves** 6

1 1/2 pounds potatoes, peeled and quartered

1 small onion, chopped

2 tablespoons unsalted butter or margarine

2 eggs

3/4 cup whipping cream, warmed

1/2 cup ground almonds

1/2 teaspoon salt

 Dash of ground nutmeg

1/2 cup shredded cheddar cheese (about 2 ounces)

1/4 cup slivered almonds

1. Preheat the oven to 400°F. Grease a 1 1/2-quart baking dish.

2. In a large saucepan, boil the potatoes until tender, about 15 minutes. Drain and place in a large bowl.

3. In a medium nonstick skillet, sauté the onion in the butter or margarine until tender, about 4 minutes. Add to the potatoes.

4. Using an electric mixer, mash the potatoes on medium-low speed for 1 minute. Beat in the eggs, one at a time, on low speed until smooth, 1 minute longer. Beat in the cream (the mixture will be thin), then beat in the ground almonds, salt, and nutmeg.

5. Spoon the potatoes into the baking dish. Sprinkle with the cheese and slivered almonds. Bake, uncovered, until golden brown, about 20 minutes.

Personalize It!

For a sweeter side dish, replace the potatoes with sweet potatoes and replace the cheddar cheese with 2 tablespoons brown sugar.

COUNTRY-STYLE MASHED POTATOES

SECRET INGREDIENT:
bacon

To dress up mashed potatoes, mix in a little chopped fresh thyme and top the mash with beautifully browned sautéed onions. Bits of crumbled, crisply cooked bacon make it even better. *See photograph on page 184.*

Prep Time: 20 min   **Cook Time:** 20 min   **Serves** 6

3/4 teaspoon salt, divided

1 1/2 pounds russet or Eastern potatoes, peeled

1/3 cup milk, warmed

1/4 cup unsalted butter, cut into pieces

1/8 teaspoon freshly ground black pepper

2 scallions (green parts only), very thinly sliced

4 ounces bacon, coarsely chopped

1 small red onion, chopped

1 teaspoon chopped fresh thyme

1. Half-fill a medium saucepan with water; add 1/4 teaspoon salt and bring to a boil over high heat.

2. Meanwhile, cut each potato into 8 pieces. Add to the boiling water, reduce the heat to medium, and simmer until the potatoes are tender, about 10 minutes. Drain. Shake the potatoes in the pan over low heat until dry. Remove from heat, cover, and keep warm.

3. Heat the milk and butter in a small saucepan over medium heat until the butter has melted and the milk is hot and begins to bubble (do not boil), about 3 minutes. Pour over the potatoes.

4. Add the pepper and the remaining 1/2 teaspoon salt and mash to a chunky puree with a potato masher (do not use an electric mixer or food processor). Stir in the scallions, cover, and keep hot.

5. Meanwhile, sauté the bacon and onion in a medium nonstick skillet over medium-high heat until the bacon is crisp and the onions are browned, about 7 minutes. Stir in the thyme.

6. Transfer the potatoes to a serving bowl and top with the bacon-onion mixture.

Personalize It!

For a different flavor, replace the milk with buttermilk or sour cream. You can also spice up the cooking water by adding halved garlic cloves. Mash the cooked cloves right along with the potatoes.

SPANISH RICE

SECRET INGREDIENT:
V8 juice

Here's a vegetable-rich rice dish filled with bits of bell pepper, celery, mushrooms, and plum tomatoes. V8 juice and chicken broth in the simmering liquid boost the flavor of the rice itself and give it an attractive red color.

Prep Time: 20 min   **Cook Time:** 30 min   **Serves** 6

1 onion, finely chopped

1 large green bell pepper, seeded and finely chopped

1 celery stalk, finely chopped

2 garlic cloves, minced

4 ounces white mushrooms, sliced

1 cup long-grain white rice

1 1/2 cups V8 juice

1 cup chicken or vegetable broth

Salt

1/4 teaspoon freshly ground black pepper

1 bay leaf

6 plum tomatoes, halved, seeded, and diced

1. Lightly coat a deep nonstick skillet with cooking spray. Sauté the onion, green pepper, celery, and garlic until the onion is almost soft, about 3 minutes.

2. Stir in the mushrooms and rice and sauté until the rice turns golden, about 2 minutes.

3. Stir in the V8, broth, salt, to taste, black pepper, and bay leaf. Bring to a boil over medium-high heat. Cover, reduce the heat, and simmer, stirring occasionally, for 15 minutes.

4. Stir in the tomatoes. Cover and cook until the rice is tender and the liquid is absorbed, about 10 minutes longer.

5. Fluff with a fork to keep the rice from sticking together. Remove from the heat and discard the bay leaf.

To turn this into a simple shrimp paella, add a generous pinch of saffron along with the V8 juice. During the last 8 minutes of cooking, stir in 1 1/2 pounds peeled and deveined large shrimp and 2 cups peas into the rice.

GOLDEN RICE PILAF

SECRET INGREDIENT:

orange juice

Almost any liquid can be used as the cooking liquid for rice. Chicken broth, tomato juice, beer, apple juice … they all lend signature flavors. Here, we give rice the citrus treatment with orange juice in the cooking water and some grated orange zest to heighten the aromas. Serve with chicken, turkey, or fish.

Prep Time: 10 min   **Cook Time:** 15 min   **Serves** 4

1 cup diced celery

3 tablespoons chopped onion

1 tablespoon grated orange zest

1/4 cup unsalted butter or margarine

1/2 teaspoon salt

3 tablespoons fresh orange juice

1 1/3 cups water

1 1/2 cups uncooked instant rice

1. In a 3-quart saucepan, sauté the celery, onion, and orange zest in the butter or margarine until tender but not brown, about 5 minutes. Add the salt.

2. Combine the orange juice and water in a measuring cup and add to the celery mixture. Bring to a boil.

3. Stir in the rice. Remove from the heat; cover and let stand for 10 minutes. Fluff with a fork.

One More Notch! To add a mildly spicy aroma, toss a cinnamon stick and a knob of peeled ginger into the cooking water. Remove both before serving.

SUNNY RISOTTO

SECRET INGREDIENT:

carrot juice

The moment you take a bite of this rich-tasting, aromatic risotto, you'll forget how healthy it is. The secret to its ultra creamy texture is constant stirring and the rich carrot juice, which also gives it a gorgeous golden color.

Prep Time: 15 min   **Cook Time:** 35 min   **Serves** 4

2 teaspoons olive oil

1 small onion, finely chopped

2 large carrots, cut into 1/4-inch pieces

1 cup arborio rice

1/2 cup dry white wine

1 can (14 1/2 ounces) reduced-sodium chicken or vegetable broth

1 cup carrot juice

1/2 cup water

Salt

1/4 cup grated Parmesan cheese

1/4 teaspoon freshly ground black pepper

1. In a medium nonstick saucepan, heat the oil over medium heat. Add the onion and sauté until tender, about 5 minutes.

2. Add the carrots and sauté until crisp-tender, about 4 minutes.

3. Add the rice, stirring to coat.

4. Add the wine and cook, stirring occasionally, until evaporated by half, about 2 minutes.

5. In a medium bowl, combine the broth, carrot juice, water, and salt, to taste. Add to the rice, 1/2 cup at a time, and cook, stirring, until absorbed, before adding the next 1/2 cup (total time will be about 20 minutes.)

6. Remove from the heat. Stir in the Parmesan and pepper before serving.

One More Notch! To add some crunch to the creaminess, add 1/4 cup chopped blanched almonds along with the rice.

QUINOA PILAF

SECRET INGREDIENT:
dried cherries

Grainlike quinoa (pronounced KEEN-wah) is not a grain at all, but the nutritious seed of a plant related to Swiss chard. It cooks up like rice and takes well to a variety of flavors. Here, it's made into an aromatic pilaf with thyme, walnuts, and a generous amount of dried cherries for chewy sweetness. Serve with pork or poultry.
See photograph on page 185.

Prep Time: 10 min   **Cook Time:** 30 min   **Serves** 12

2 teaspoons olive oil

1 large onion, finely chopped

2 cups quinoa, rinsed until the water runs clear

2 cups boiling water

Salt

1 teaspoon freshly ground black pepper

1/2 teaspoon thyme

1 cup dried cherries

1/2 cup toasted and coarsely chopped walnuts

1. Heat the oil in a large saucepan over medium heat. Add the onion and cook, stirring frequently, until golden brown, about 7 minutes.

2. Meanwhile, place the quinoa in a large skillet over medium heat and cook, stirring often, until lightly toasted, about 5 minutes.

3. Add the quinoa to the onions. Stir in the water, salt, to taste, pepper, and thyme. Return to a boil, cover, and gently boil for 10 minutes. Uncover and cook, stirring occasionally, until the liquid has been absorbed and the quinoa is tender, 10 to 12 minutes.

4. Remove from the heat and stir in the cherries and walnuts. Serve hot, at room temperature, or chilled.

SNEAKY FRIES WITH CHIPOTLE KETCHUP

SECRET INGREDIENT:
prepared polenta

Homemade fries taste great but they're an awful lot of work. Sneaky fries use logs of store-bought prepared polenta that fry up crisp and take half the work! Try them with burgers, hot dogs, or just alone as a great snack.
See photograph on page 185.

Prep Time: 15 min   **Cook Time:** 15 min   **Serves** 4

1/2 cup ketchup

1/8 teaspoon ground chipotle chile pepper

1 pound tube pre-cooked polenta, halved crosswise then cut lengthwise into 1/4-inch-thick wedges

1 tablespoon all-purpose flour

1 tablespoon grated Parmesan cheese

1/2 cup canola oil

1/2 teaspoon salt

1. Preheat the oven to 325°F.

2. Combine the ketchup and chile pepper in a small bowl and mix well.

3. Place the polenta sticks in a large bowl and add the flour and Parmesan. Toss well.

4. Heat the oil in a large skillet over medium-high heat until hot. Fry the polenta in 2 to 3 batches, turning occasionally, until lightly golden, 4 to 5 minutes.

5. Transfer to a paper towel–lined baking sheet, sprinkle lightly with salt, and keep warm in the oven. Repeat with the remaining polenta sticks.

6. Serve with the ketchup.

One More Notch! Add another layer of flavor to the fries by starting with flavored polenta. Look for mushroom, sun-dried tomato and garlic, basil, or a host of other flavors in the refrigerated produce section.

VEGETABLE AND SIDE DISHES

POLENTA WITH SMOKED CHEESE

SECRET INGREDIENT:
olives

Smoked cheese lends fantastic aroma to nutty-tasting polenta. This easy-to-make side dish also gets a shot of salty chewiness with bits of chopped olives.

Prep Time: 10 min   **Cook Time:** 20 min   **Serves** 4

2 cups instant polenta

3 1/2 cups water

Small bunch of sage, oregano, basil, or parsley

1/2 pound smoked mature cheese such as smoked cheddar or smoked fontina, shredded or diced (about 2 cups)

1 1/2 teaspoons black or mixed peppercorns, crushed

8 pitted black olives (preferably oil-cured), finely chopped

1. Combine the polenta and water in a large saucepan. Bring it to a boil over high heat, then reduce the heat and let simmer until it becomes thick and starts to stiffen, stirring the polenta frequently with a large wooden spoon or paddle to remove any lumps, about 10 minutes.

2. Meanwhile, strip the leaves from the herb stalks and chop them finely.

3. Stir in the herbs, cheese, peppercorns, and olives. Beat vigorously until the cheese is incorporated and the mixture begins to leave the sides of the saucepan when stirred.

4. Serve immediately or let stand to stiffen further, 5 to 10 minutes. It will remain hot.

Personalize It!
If you like a more stylish presentation, when the completed polenta is stiff, mold it into egg shapes, using two large metal spoons. Serve on plates. ❄

KICKED-UP CHEESE GRITS

SECRET INGREDIENT:
chile peppers

Grits have a mild and chewy taste that everyone seems to love. Here's a version for the adults, spiked with green chiles.

Prep Time: 10 min   **Cook Time:** 50 min   **Serves** 6

3 cups water

1 teaspoon salt

1 garlic clove, minced

1 cup quick-cooking grits

1/2 cup unsalted butter or margarine

1 1/2 cups shredded cheddar cheese (about 6 ounces), divided

3 tablespoons canned chopped green chile or jalapeño peppers

2 eggs

1/2 cup milk

1. Preheat the oven to 350°F. Grease a 2-quart baking dish.

2. In a saucepan, bring the water, salt and garlic to a boil; slowly stir in the grits. Reduce the heat; and stir until thickened, 3 to 5 minutes. Remove from the heat.

3. Add the butter or margarine, 1 cup of the cheese, and the chiles; stir until blended.

4. Beat the eggs and milk in a small bowl. Add to the grits and mix well.

5. Pour the grits into the baking dish. Bake, uncovered, until just set and a toothpick inserted in the center comes out moist but not wet, about 45 minutes. Sprinkle with the remaining cheese.

One More Notch! Make a more substantial casserole by sautéing 4 ounces sweet or hot sausage cut into coins. Add the sautéed sausage coins to the grits along with 1/2 teaspoon dried thyme before pouring into the baking dish.

VEGETABLE AND SIDE DISHES

SESAME GREENS AND BEAN SPROUTS

SECRET INGREDIENT:
oyster sauce

With a little inspiration and the easy availability of international ingredients, even the most humble vegetables can be elevated to new heights. This succulent stir-fried side dish is full of flavor and crunch. Oyster sauce gives it a bold and briny edge. Try it with fish, poultry, pork, or beef.

Prep Time: 5 min   **Cook Time:** 10 min   **Serves** 6

1 tablespoon sesame seeds

2 teaspoons canola oil

1 onion, chopped

2 garlic cloves, chopped

1 small Savoy cabbage, finely shredded

1 small head bok choy, finely shredded

1 cup bean sprouts

1/4 cup oyster sauce

2 tablespoons water

Salt and freshly ground black pepper

1. Heat a wok or large nonstick skillet and dry-roast the sesame seeds over medium heat, shaking the pan frequently, until they are just beginning to brown, 2 to 3 minutes. Turn the seeds out into a small bowl and set aside.

2. Heat the oil in the pan. Add the onion and garlic, and stir-fry until softened slightly, 2 to 3 minutes.

3. Raise the heat to high, then add the cabbage and bok choy and stir-fry until the vegetables are just beginning to soften, 2 to 3 minutes.

4. Add the bean sprouts and continue cooking for a few seconds.

5. Make a well in the center of the pan. Add the oyster sauce and water in the well and stir until hot. Toss the vegetables into the sauce. Add salt, if necessary (this will depend on the saltiness of the oyster sauce), and pepper, to taste.

6. Serve immediately, sprinkled with the sesame seeds.

that's ingenious !

> Look for oyster sauce in the Asian section of your grocery store. If you can't find it, replace it with 2 1/2 tablespoons soy sauce or teriyaki sauce mixed with 4 teaspoons of the liquid from canned oysters and a generous pinch of sugar.

SAUTÉED BRUSSELS SPROUTS

SECRET INGREDIENT:
orange zest

Golden fried Brussels sprouts mingle with crisp morsels of bacon and crunchy water chestnuts in this simple side dish. The grated zest of an orange and a smidgen of coarse mustard give the flavors a refreshing lift. *See photograph on page 175.*

Prep Time: 10 min   **Cook Time:** 15 min   **Serves** 4

1 tablespoon vegetable oil

5 slices smoked bacon, diced

1 tablespoon grated orange zest

3 tablespoons unsalted butter

2 teaspoons coarse mustard

1 pound fresh Brussels sprouts, rinsed, trimmed, and halved

1 can (4 ounces) whole water chestnuts, drained and chopped

Salt and freshly ground black pepper

1. Heat the oil in a nonstick skillet, then add the bacon and fry it until it turns golden brown, 2 to 3 minutes.

VEGETABLE AND SIDE DISHES

2. Add the orange zest, butter, mustard, and Brussels sprouts. Cook over medium heat, stirring, until the Brussels sprouts are crisp-tender, about 5 minutes.

3. Stir in the water chestnuts and cook until the Brussels sprouts are golden and the chestnuts are heated through, 3 to 4 minutes.

4. Add salt and pepper, to taste, and serve.

Personalize It!

For a delightfully different flavor, replace the mustard with good-quality balsamic vinegar.

MOLASSES GLAZED ONIONS

SECRET INGREDIENT:

soy sauce

Enrobed in a rich glaze of molasses, mustard, and rosemary, these onions make the perfect partner for grilled or roast pork, beef, or venison. A spoonful of soy sauce in the glaze gives it salty spark.

Prep Time: 20 min	**Cook Time:** 20 min	**Serves** 4

1 pound button or pickling onions

Boiling water

1/2 teaspoon dried rosemary

1 1/2 tablespoons unsalted butter

1 tablespoon dark molasses

2 teaspoons Dijon mustard

1 tablespoon soy sauce

1. Put the onions in a large saucepan, cover with the water, and cook over medium heat until they start to soften, about 5 minutes. Place them in a colander and cool under running water. When they are cool enough to handle, drain thoroughly and peel the skins.

2. Crush the rosemary as finely as possible, using a pestle and mortar or the end of a rolling pin.

3. Melt the butter gently in a skillet over medium heat, then add the rosemary, molasses, mustard, and soy sauce. Mix well to make an emulsion.

4. Stir in the onions and cook gently, stirring and basting with the sauce, until the glaze thickens and the onions are tender and golden brown, 10 to 15 minutes. Watch them continuously as it is important not to allow the glaze to burn.

One More Notch! Create a more complex flavor by using 1 1/2 teaspoons molasses plus 1 1/2 teaspoons maple syrup and adding 1/2 teaspoon ground ginger or Chinese five-spice powder.

SPICED RED BEETS AND CABBAGE

SECRET INGREDIENT:

cranberry sauce

There's more you can do with canned cranberry sauce than slice it and serve it at Thanksgiving. Here, it sweetens and deepens the color of sautéed red beets and cabbage, a time-honored side dish for pork. *See photograph on page 185.*

Prep Time: 15 min	**Cook Time:** 15 min	**Serves** 4

2 tablespoons olive oil

1 1/2 cups coarsely shredded red cabbage

1 1/2 cups peeled, coarsely shredded cooked fresh or canned whole baby beets

1/3 cup canned whole-berry cranberry sauce

1 tablespoon balsamic vinegar

1 teaspoon salt

1/4 teaspoon freshly ground black pepper

1/8 teaspoon ground allspice

1/8 teaspoon ground cloves

1. In a 10-inch nonstick skillet or Dutch oven over medium heat, heat the oil for 1 minute. Add the cabbage and sauté, stirring occasionally, until it begins to soften, about 5 minutes.

2. Stir in the beets, cranberry sauce, vinegar, salt, pepper, allspice, and cloves. Cook, covered, until tender, about 10 minutes.

One More Notch! Give the sauté some crunch by serving it with toasted sliced almonds.

ROASTED CAULIFLOWER WITH PARMESAN AND ALMONDS

SECRET INGREDIENT:
raisins

If you've never been a fan of cauliflower, this recipe may change your mind. Coated with a crunchy almond-Parmesan breading and roasted until golden brown, cauliflower florets take on a whole new identity. A handful of raisins in the breading provides a touch of sweetness. *See photograph on page 185.*

Prep Time: 10 min   **Cook Time:** 30 min   **Serves** 4

1 large head cauliflower (about 1 1/2 pounds), cut into florets

1/2 cup raisins

1/3 cup plain dried bread crumbs

2 tablespoons grated Parmesan cheese

1 tablespoon sliced almonds

2 teaspoons olive oil

2 tablespoons fresh lemon juice

1. Preheat the oven to 400°F. Cover a large roasting pan with foil and spray the foil with cooking spray.

2. Cook the cauliflower in a steamer set over a pan of boiling water until crisp-tender, about 5 minutes. Transfer the cauliflower to the roasting pan.

3. Stir together the raisins, bread crumbs, Parmesan, almonds, and oil in a medium bowl.

4. Sprinkle over the cauliflower. Roast until the crumbs are toasted, about 20 minutes.

5. Drizzle the lemon juice over the top and roast until the liquid evaporates, about 5 minutes longer. Serve hot or at room temperature.

One More Notch! To take this dish over the top, serve it with an anchovy dipping sauce. Mix together 2 tablespoons mayonnaise, 1 tablespoon anchovy paste, 1 tablespoon extra-virgin olive oil, 2 teaspoons lemon juice, and 1/4 teaspoon minced garlic.

PORTOBELLO MUSHROOM FANS

SECRET INGREDIENT:
maple syrup

Portobello mushrooms have a wonderfully meaty texture that's amplified when the mushrooms are grilled or broiled. In this elegant dish, maple syrup and soy sauce enhance the rich mushroom flavor. You can also use whole button mushrooms on skewers for this recipe.

Prep Time: 10 min   **Cook Time:** 10 min   **Serves** 4

2 tablespoons olive oil

2 tablespoons soy sauce

2 tablespoons chopped fresh thyme

3 garlic cloves, minced

2 teaspoons toasted sesame oil

2 teaspoons pure maple syrup

1/4 teaspoon salt

1/4 teaspoon freshly ground black pepper

4 portobello mushroom caps, stems removed

1. In a large zip-close bag, combine the olive oil, soy sauce, thyme, garlic, sesame oil, syrup, salt, and pepper.

2. Add the mushrooms, then press out the air and seal the bag. Gently massage the marinade into the mushrooms and let rest at room temperature for at least 1 hour or up to 6 hours.

3. Preheat a grill to medium or turn on the broiler. Remove the mushrooms from the marinade and grill or broil 4 to 6 inches from the heat. Cook until tender when poked in the center, about 5 minutes per side, brushing or pouring the marinade over the mushrooms on each side.

4. Remove the mushrooms to a platter or plates and thinly slice them on the diagonal, fanning out the slices.

One More Notch! For more flavor, serve the mushrooms with a simple-flavored mayonnaise. Stir 1 teaspoon crab boil seasoning and 2 teaspoons chopped fresh parsley into 1/4 cup mayonnaise. Add a dollop to each mushroom.

APPLE, WALNUT, AND PRUNE STUFFING

SECRET INGREDIENT:
port wine

Stuffings are akin to salads but are made with bread instead of greens. They welcome all kinds of additions from fruit to nuts. In this hearty stuffing, full-bodied port wine deepens the flavor of apples, walnuts, and prunes.

Prep Time: 20 min **Cook Time:** 45 min **Makes** 8 cups

1/2 cup pitted prunes, cut into small pieces

1/4 cup port wine

2 tablespoons unsalted butter

2 large red baking apples, such as Rome Beauty or Cortland, peeled, cored, and cut into bite-size pieces

3 large celery stalks, coarsely chopped

1 extra-large onion, chopped

8 cups day-old bread cubes (16 slices)

1 cup coarsely chopped toasted walnuts

1/4 cup chopped fresh parsley

1/4 cup chopped fresh sage

1 teaspoon poultry seasoning

1 teaspoon freshly ground black pepper

1 cup low-sodium chicken broth

1 large egg, beaten

1. Place the prunes in a small saucepan, add the port wine, and bring to a simmer over medium heat. The fruit will become plump and absorb the liquid. Transfer to a large bowl.

2. In a large nonstick skillet, melt the butter over medium-high heat. Add the apples, celery, and onion and sauté until crisp-tender, about 5 minutes. Transfer to the bowl with the prunes.

3. Add the bread and mix well, then stir in the walnuts, parsley, sage, poultry seasoning, and pepper. Gently stir in the broth and egg just until the ingredients are moistened (do not overmix as this may make the stuffing tough).

4. Spoon the mixture into a 9 x 13-inch pan, cover with foil, and bake until heated through and steamy, about 25 minutes. Uncover and bake until lightly browned, about 10 minutes longer.

Personalize It!

If you prefer stuffing in the bird, simply stuff the mixture into the neck and body cavities of a chicken or turkey. Shape any leftover stuffing into 2-inch balls. Refrigerate the balls, then bake on a buttered baking sheet in the same oven with the bird (at 325°F or 350°F) during the last 25 minutes of roasting. The stuffing is done at 165°F; the turkey, at 180°F.

SAUSAGE-CORNBREAD STUFFING

SECRET INGREDIENT:
apricots

Crumbled cornbread flecked with meaty sausage and flavored with onions and garlic makes a terrific stuffing. It's a staple in the kitchens of Southern cooks. To give ours a bit more chew and some sweetness, we add chopped dried apricots.

Prep Time: 15 min   **Cook Time:** 40 min   **Serves** 12

1 cup dried apricot halves

1 cup boiling water

6 ounces sweet Italian sausage, casings removed, if necessary

1 onion, finely chopped

2 garlic cloves, minced

1/2 teaspoon dried sage

1/4 teaspoon salt

7 cups crumbled cornbread (1 1/2 pounds)

1 can (10 ounces) water-packed chestnuts, drained and chopped

2 cups chicken broth

1 tablespoon unsalted butter or margarine, melted

1. Preheat the oven to 450°F.

2. In a small heat-proof bowl, combine the apricots and water; set aside.

3. Meanwhile, crumble the sausage into a large nonstick skillet and cook over medium heat until it has browned and rendered its fat, about 5 minutes. Add the onion, garlic, sage, and salt and sauté until the onion is soft, 5 minutes. Transfer to a large bowl.

4. Drain the apricots and coarsely chop. Add the apricots, cornbread, and chestnuts to the bowl. Drizzle with the broth and butter or margarine, tossing to coat.

5. Spoon into a 9 x 13-inch pan, cover with foil, and bake until heated through and steamy, about 20 minutes. Uncover and bake until lightly browned on top, about 10 minutes longer.

Personalize It!
Don't like apricots? Try dried apples or prunes.

WILD RICE AND PECAN STUFFING

SECRET INGREDIENT:
water chestnuts

Take a break from the usual bread stuffing with this savory wild rice stuffing. It gets delicious crunch from pecans and the old stir-fry favorite, water chestnuts. Use it to stuff chicken or Cornish hens, or serve it on the side.

Prep Time: 10 min   **Cook Time:** 1 hr   **Serves** 6

2 teaspoons vegetable oil

1 large onion, finely chopped

3 garlic cloves, minced

1 carrot, halved lengthwise and thinly sliced

1 celery stalk, halved lengthwise and thinly sliced

1 cup wild rice

1 cup chicken broth

2 cups water

3/4 teaspoon salt

1/2 teaspoon crumbled dried rosemary

1/2 teaspoon freshly ground black pepper

1 cup canned sliced water chestnuts, drained

1/3 cup chopped pecans

1. Preheat the oven to 350°F.

2. In a Dutch oven or flame-proof casserole, heat the oil over medium heat. Add the onion and garlic and sauté until soft, about 5 minutes.

3. Add the carrot and celery and sauté until the carrot is crisp-tender, about 4 minutes.

VEGETABLE AND SIDE DISHES

4. Stir in the rice, broth, water, salt, rosemary, and pepper. Bring to a boil. Cover, transfer to the oven, and bake until the rice is tender, about 50 minutes.

5. Stir in the water chestnuts and pecans before serving.

Personalize It!

Instead of dried rosemary, use 1/2 teaspoon poultry seasoning, or try a mix of dried thyme, sage, and marjoram. ❄

CRANBERRY RELISH

SECRET INGREDIENT:

oranges

Cranberries are sometimes flavored with orange juice, as in this relish, but the real surprise here is using whole oranges for serving. The oranges are cut in half with a zigzag edge and the pulp is removed to make decorative bowls. Filled with the crimson relish, the orange bowls make an impressive presentation.

Prep Time: 15 min   **Cook Time:** 10 min   **Serves** 6

3 oranges

1/2 cup firmly packed light brown sugar

1/2 cup fresh orange juice

1/4 cup water

1 tablespoon finely chopped crystallized ginger

1/4 teaspoon ground ginger

Dash of ground cloves

2 cups fresh cranberries

1. Cut the oranges in half, making a zigzag edge. Remove the pulp. Cover and store the orange shells in the refrigerator (will keep for 1 day).

2. In a large saucepan, stir together the brown sugar, orange juice, water, crystallized ginger, ground ginger, and cloves. Bring the mixture to a boil over high heat, stirring until the sugar is dissolved, about 2 minutes. Lower the heat to medium-high and cook, uncovered, for 3 minutes, stirring occasionally.

3. Add the cranberries. Return to a boil over high heat. Lower the heat to medium-high and cook until the skins pop, stirring occasionally, 2 to 3 minutes.

4. Transfer to a covered container and refrigerate for at least 1 hour before serving. Store in the refrigerator (will keep for 1 week).

5. To serve, spoon into the orange shells.

One More Notch! Flavor up the relish by adding 1 can (8 ounces) crushed pineapple, drained, and 1 1/2 teaspoons vanilla extract along with the cranberries.

ZUCCHINI AND GOAT CHEESE SOUFFLÉS

SECRET INGREDIENT:

ham

Puffed and golden, these individual soufflés make a pretty first course. Sliced ham arranged over each soufflé adds a salty edge to the mild and pleasing combination of goat cheese and zucchini.

Prep Time: 20 min   **Cook Time:** 45 min   **Serves** 6

2 tablespoons olive oil

2 zucchini, roughly chopped

2 tablespoons unsalted butter

3 tablespoons all-purpose flour

1 cup milk, warmed

7 ounces crumbled fresh goat cheese, divided

1 tablespoon chopped fresh thyme

3 large eggs, separated

Freshly ground black pepper

6 tablespoons crème fraîche

6 thin slices of dry-cure ham, such as Virginia ham

1. Preheat the oven to 350°F. Lightly grease six ramekin dishes.

2. Heat the oil in a large nonstick skillet over medium heat. Add the zucchini and cook, covered, until just tender, about 5 minutes. Transfer to a sieve and let drain for a few minutes. Transfer to a blender or food processor and puree until finely chopped.

3. Melt the butter in a large saucepan over medium heat, add the flour and cook, stirring, until the flour is lightly toasted, about 1 minute.

4. Whisk in the milk, then stir until the mixture boils and thickens.

5. Remove from the heat and mix in 6 ounces of the goat cheese, the thyme, zucchini, egg yolks, and pepper, to taste.

6. In a small bowl, beat the egg whites until soft peaks form. Using a large metal spoon, lightly fold the egg whites into the cheese mixture until well-combined, then spoon into the ramekins.

7. Place the ramekins in a baking pan and add enough hot water to come halfway up the sides of the ramekins. Bake until puffed and set, about 20 minutes. Remove from the oven and set aside to cool.

8. To serve, run a sharp knife around the sides of the soufflés and invert onto a deep serving dish. Spoon a tablespoon of crème fraîche over each soufflé, then top with a slice of ham and the remaining goat cheese. Return to the oven and bake until puffed and golden, 15 minutes.

that's **ingenious**

If you don't have crème fraîche, replace it with a mixture of equal parts sour cream and regular cream. Or simply use sour cream or yogurt.

CHEDDAR-ASPARAGUS QUICHE WITH POTATO CRUST

SECRET INGREDIENT:
evaporated milk

How do you get the rich taste of a classic quiche with a fraction of the fat? Three techniques: first, make the crust with thinly sliced potatoes instead of fatty pastry. Second, use a combination of eggs and egg substitute. And finally, use evaporated milk instead of cream for richness without adding extra calories.

Prep Time: 20 min   **Cook Time:** 45 min   **Serves** 6

1 tablespoon plain dry bread crumbs

8 ounces small all-purpose potatoes, peeled and very thinly sliced

1 pound asparagus, trimmed

3/4 teaspoon salt, divided

3/4 cup shredded reduced-fat sharp cheddar cheese, divided

3 scallions, sliced

1 can (12 ounces) evaporated fat-free milk

1/2 cup fat-free egg substitute

1 large egg

2 teaspoons margarine, melted

1 teaspoon dry mustard

1/4 teaspoon freshly ground black pepper

1. Preheat the oven to 400°F. Coat a 9-inch pie plate with cooking spray.

2. Sprinkle the pie plate with bread crumbs. Beginning in the center, arrange the potato slices in slightly overlapping circles up to the rim. Lightly coat with cooking spray and press down gently. Bake until the surface is dry, about 10 minutes.

3. Set 8 to 12 asparagus spears aside. Cut the remaining spears into 1-inch pieces.

4. Sprinkle the crust with 1/4 teaspoon of the salt and 1/4 cup of the cheese. Cover

with the asparagus pieces, then sprinkle with the scallions and another 1/4 cup of the cheese. Arrange the whole asparagus spears on top.

5. In a medium bowl, beat the evaporated milk, egg substitute, egg, margarine, mustard, pepper, and the remaining 1/2 teaspoon salt. Pour into the pie plate and sprinkle with the remaining 1/4 cup cheese.

6. Bake until a knife inserted in the center comes out clean, about 35 minutes.

Personalize It!

Give the quiche a different flavor by replacing the asparagus with broccoli florets and by using low-fat Swiss or provolone instead of cheddar cheese.

LEEK AND CHEDDAR CHEESE TART

SECRET INGREDIENT:
mustard

Ready-made puff pastry lets you turn a simple combination of leeks and cheese into a dish that looks as pretty as a picture. A thin layer of mustard on the leeks sharpens their flavor. *See photograph on page 185.*

Prep Time: 20 min   **Cook Time:** 25 min   **Serves** 4

7 to 8 slim leeks (about 2 pounds)

Salt and freshly ground black pepper

1/2 pound frozen puff pastry sheets, thawed

1 tablespoon Dijon mustard

1 egg

3/4 cup shredded cheddar cheese
  (about 3 ounces)

1. Preheat the oven to 450°F. Put a kettle of water on to boil.

2. Trim the leeks to a length of about 7 inches and rinse them. Arrange them in a single layer in a wide saucepan or skillet, cover with boiling water from the kettle, and add a pinch of salt. Return to a boil, reduce the heat, and simmer, covered, until crisp-tender, 6 to 8 minutes.

3. Meanwhile, roll out the puff pastry on a lightly floured surface to form a 10-inch square. Cut a 1/2-inch strip of pastry from each of the four sides. Transfer the pastry square onto a baking sheet and dampen the edges with water. Lay the four pastry strips on the dampened edges, trimming as needed, so that it looks like a picture frame. Press them lightly into place.

4. Drain the leeks and cool them under cold running water. Drain again, then wrap them in a folded tea towel and press them gently to remove any remaining moisture. Arrange the leeks inside the pastry square and brush them with the mustard.

5. Break the egg into a small bowl and beat it lightly. Brush the border of the tart with the egg, and spread the remainder evenly over the leeks. Sprinkle with the cheese.

6. Bake on the top rack of the oven until the pastry is risen and golden and the cheese has melted and is bubbling, about 15 minutes.

7. Remove the tart from the oven and cut it into quarters with a serrated knife. Serve hot or warm.

that's **ingenious**

Sometimes food manufacturers get it right. Homemade puff pastry is time-consuming and a bit tricky to make. Pepperidge Farm has made good-quality puff pastry readily available to home cooks. Look for puff pastry sheets and shells in the frozen bread section of your grocery store. These convenience products allow you to create sophisti-cated dishes in a fraction of the time it would take to make from scratch.

STUFFED PEPPERS WITH CHEESE

SECRET INGREDIENT:
linguine

Traditionally, stuffed peppers are prepared with rice. In this unique recipe, noodles are used and baked in the pepper shells with a cheesy custard dotted with fresh tomatoes and herbs.

Prep Time: 40 min   **Cook Time:** 25 min   **Serves** 4

2 large red, orange, or yellow bell peppers

2 ounces linguine

2 eggs, beaten

2/3 cup shredded cheddar cheese

1 teaspoon dry mustard

3 tablespoons milk

3 tablespoons chopped fresh chives

1/2 teaspoon dried marjoram or oregano

2 tomatoes, peeled, seeded, and diced

Salt and freshly ground black pepper

1. Preheat the oven to 350°F. Halve the peppers lengthways, carefully cutting through the stem. Remove the membrane and seeds. Cook the pepper shells in boiling water until tender, 6 to 8 minutes. Drain thoroughly and place on a paper towel.

2. Cook the linguine in boiling water for 10 minutes, or according to the package instructions, until al dente. Drain well and set aside.

3. Beat the eggs with the cheese, mustard, milk, chives, and marjoram or oregano. Stir in the tomatoes and season lightly with salt and pepper.

4. Place the peppers in a shallow ovenproof dish or roasting pan, supporting them with pieces of crumpled foil, if necessary, to ensure that they are level (otherwise the filling will spill out). Fill each pepper halfway full with linguine, then spoon the egg and cheese mixture over the pasta.

5. Bake until the filling is set and beginning to turn golden, 20 to 25 minutes. Serve garnished with whole chives.

One More Notch! Stir 4 pitted green olives, finely chopped, into the egg mixture for a more complex flavor.

extraordinary
sauces, dips,
and spreads

EXTRA-BOLD BARBECUE SAUCE

SECRET INGREDIENT:
coffee

Most barbecue sauces start with ketchup, vinegar, and sugar then get a flavor boost from herbs and spices. This rendition features strong brewed coffee in the base for an extra-rich, dark taste. It's perfect for beef and pork. *See photograph on page 173.*

Prep Time: 10 min **Cook Time:** 20 min **Makes** 2 1/2 cups

2 tablespoons hot dry mustard

1/2 cup brewed espresso or strong, dark coffee

1 cup ketchup

1/2 cup cider vinegar

1/2 cup firmly packed light brown sugar

1 cup finely chopped onion

2 garlic cloves, crushed

1 tablespoon Louisiana red-hot sauce

2 tablespoons Worcestershire sauce

2 tablespoons ground cumin

2 tablespoons chili powder

1. Mix the mustard, espresso or coffee, ketchup, vinegar, brown sugar, onion, garlic, red-hot sauce, Worcestershire sauce, cumin and chili powder in a medium saucepan. Bring to a simmer over medium-high heat. Lower the heat so the mixture is just simmering and let simmer for 20 minutes.

2. Remove the pan from the heat, let the mixture cool, then puree it in a blender or food processor fitted with the steel blade.

3. Use immediately or refrigerate and reheat before serving.

One More Notch! Like your barbecue spicy? Add 2 to 3 seeded and minced fresh chile peppers, such as jalapeño (wear gloves when handling). Add 1/2 teaspoon freshly ground black pepper to give bite to the sauce.

ALL-PURPOSE SOUTHWEST TOMATO SAUCE

SECRET INGREDIENT:
salsa

A two-ingredient sauce is a thing of beauty. This one combines prepared salsa and butter for a seamless sauce that guests will think you slaved over. Use this 5-minute sauce with beef, pork, poultry, or fish.

Prep Time: 2 min **Cook Time:** 8 min **Makes** 1 cup

1 3/4 cups jarred salsa

1/3 cup unsalted butter, cut in pieces

1. Bring the salsa to a boil in a small saucepan over medium-high heat. Boil until most of the liquid is gone, stirring occasionally, about 5 minutes.

2. Remove from the heat and stir in the butter until the sauce is smooth. Serve immediately or refrigerate and reheat before serving.

that's ingenious !

Everyone knows that fresh is best. But you might not know that fresh salsa is available in most supermarkets. Look for fresh salsa in the refrigerated produce section of your store. It's sold in tubs and beats the jarred stuff by a mile.

MOROCCAN RED WINE SAUCE

SECRET INGREDIENT:
red currant jelly

Here's a great pan sauce with Moroccan spices, great for pork, lamb, or venison. A few spoonfuls of red currant jelly gives it body and a delicious sweetness. Consider this the last step in a meal of pan-fried meat.

Prep Time: 2 min **Cook Time:** 8 min **Makes** 3/4 cup

2 teaspoons cumin seeds

1/2 teaspoon paprika

1/2 teaspoon ground cinnamon

1/2 teaspoon ground coriander

1 1/4 cups red wine

2 to 3 teaspoons red currant jelly

Salt and freshly ground black pepper

1. Remove fried meat from the pan. Pour off all but about 1 tablespoon of fat or oil from the pan, being careful to leave all the browned bits behind.

2. Place the pan over medium-high heat and stir in the cumin seeds, paprika, cinnamon, coriander, and wine. Swirl and stir, scraping up the browned bits, until the wine comes to a boil.

3. Add the currant jelly, stirring until melted. Continue cooking, stirring frequently, until the liquid is reduced by almost half, 5 minutes. Season with salt and pepper, to taste, and pour over the meat.

One More Notch! Add 1/4 teaspoon ground ginger and a few pinches of chopped fresh cilantro or parsley to the sauce.

BRANDY CREAM SAUCE

SECRET INGREDIENT:
balsamic vinegar

Here's another fabulous pan sauce to serve with beef, pork, lamb, or venison. Make this the last step in the recipe after pan-frying or roasting the meat. Balsamic vinegar gives it a dark, rich tanginess. The recipe only calls for a tablespoon, so use the best-quality balsamic you have.

Prep Time: 5 min **Cook Time:** 5 min **Makes** 3/4 cup

4 tablespoons brandy

1 tablespoon chopped fresh thyme or
    1 teaspoon dried

1 tablespoon tomato puree

1 tablespoon balsamic vinegar

1/2 cup heavy cream

Salt and freshly ground black pepper

1. Remove fried meat from the pan. Pour off all but about 1 tablespoon of fat or oil from the pan, being careful to leave all the browned bits behind.

2. Place the pan over medium heat and add the brandy. Allow it to bubble gently for 1 to 2 minutes, stirring and scraping up the bits from the bottom of the pan.

3. Add the thyme, tomato puree, and vinegar and simmer, stirring, until smooth, about 1 minute.

4. Stir in the cream and bring to a boil. Add the salt and pepper, to taste, and spoon over the meat.

Personalize It!

If you prefer, use chopped fresh tarragon, rosemary, or parsley instead of the thyme.

RED GINGER SAUCE

SECRET INGREDIENT:
cherry pie filling

If pork is on the menu, consider this vibrantly colored sauce. It goes with pork roast, pork chops, pork tenderloin, and stir-fried pork. Cherries and ginger are a classic combination, and this recipe gives you a jump on things by starting with a can of cherry pie filling.

Prep Time: 2 min **Cook Time:** 3 min **Makes** 2 1/4 cups

1 can (21 ounces) cherry pie filling

1/4 cup fresh lemon juice

1 tablespoon brown sugar

1/2 teaspoon ground ginger

1/4 teaspoon seasoned salt, such as Lawry's

1/4 teaspoon vinegar

1. Combine the pie filling, lemon juice, brown sugar, ginger, salt, and vinegar in a small saucepan. Bring to a boil over medium heat, stirring constantly, Boil for 1 minute, then remove from the heat.

2. Use immediately or refrigerate and reheat before serving.

Personalize It!
Don't like cherries? Use a can of apple pie filling instead and serve with pork or chicken.

HORSERADISH CREAM SAUCE

SECRET INGREDIENT:
apple

A true classic, horseradish sauce is at home on beef, pork, and smoked fish to name a few. Stirring in some diced fresh apple gives the sauce a welcome crunch and hint of sweetness. You might never want to serve this sauce without the crunch again!

Prep Time: 5 min **Cook Time:** 1 hr **Makes** 1 1/4 cups

1/2 cup sour cream

1/2 cup finely chopped peeled Granny smith apple

3 tablespoons mayonnaise

2 tablespoons well-drained prepared horseradish

1 teaspoon cider vinegar

1/2 teaspoon sugar

1/4 teaspoon salt

1/8 teaspoon freshly ground black pepper

1. Combine the sour cream, apple, mayonnaise, horseradish, vinegar, sugar, salt, and pepper in a medium bowl.

2. Serve immediately or refrigerate for up to 4 days before serving.

Personalize It!
Not a fan of apple? Like heat? Want more tang? Try adding pear or jicama instead of apple. Use hot horseradish instead of regular and up the vinegar to 2 teaspoons. This recipe is very forgiving and can be easily adjusted to your preferences.

MOROCCAN CARROT DIP

SECRET INGREDIENT:
honey

Put a bowl of this dip out with crackers or pita chips and it will disappear in minutes. The sweetness of cooked and pureed carrots makes a perfect backdrop for cinnamon, ginger, cumin, and paprika. A spoonful of honey adds just the right enhancement.
See photograph on page 187.

Prep Time: 15 min **Cook Time:** 20 min **Makes** 1 3/4 cups

1 pound carrots, thickly sliced

1 teaspoon ground cinnamon

1 teaspoon ground cumin

2 garlic cloves, crushed

1 teaspoon ground ginger

1 tablespoon honey

1 tablespoon olive oil

1 teaspoon paprika

3 tablespoons vinegar or lemon juice

Salt and freshly ground black pepper

1. Place the carrots in a large saucepan, cover with water, and bring to a boil. Reduce the heat and simmer until they are very soft, 20 to 25 minutes.

2. Rinse the carrots in a colander under cold running water, then drain thoroughly. Put them in a medium bowl and mash with a potato masher until mostly smooth.

3. Stir in the cinnamon, cumin, garlic, ginger, honey, oil, paprika, and vinegar or lemon juice. Blend well and season with salt and pepper, to taste.

that's **ingenious**!

> For a pretty presentation, drizzle the honey over the top of the dip rather than mixing it in.

SOPHISTICATED ONION DIP

SECRET INGREDIENT:
blue cheese

Plain old onion dip, the soup-mix kind, seems to be on every party buffet and on the menu for the Sunday game. But this homemade version is far better; it's made with freshly caramelized onions and the secret addition of some crumbled blue cheese for a grown-up twist.

Prep Time: 15 min **Cook Time:** 15 min **Makes** 1 2/3 cups

1 tablespoon olive oil

1 pound onions, chopped

2 tablespoons sugar

3/4 cup sour cream

1/4 cup mayonnaise

1/3 cup crumbled blue cheese

1/4 teaspoon salt

1/8 teaspoon cayenne pepper

1. Heat the oil in a medium nonstick skillet over medium heat. Add the onions and sugar and cook, stirring occasionally, until lightly golden, 14 to 16 minutes. Transfer to a medium bowl and cool completely, about 20 minutes.

2. Stir in the sour cream, mayonnaise, blue cheese, salt, and cayenne.

3. Serve immediately or refrigerate for up to 2 days before serving.

One More Notch! For super flavorful results, be sure to make this recipe the day before you need it. Chilling the dip overnight allows the flavors to blend and develop.

WARM AND CREAMY ARTICHOKE DIP

SECRET INGREDIENT:
bacon

There are as many artichoke dip recipes as cooks who make them. So feel free to experiment. We added crisped bacon for smoky crunch and shiitake mushrooms to enhance the earthiness of the chokes. It tastes especially good with pita chips.

Prep Time: 15 min **Cook Time:** 40 min **Makes** 3 1/2 cups

4 ounces smoked bacon, chopped

4 ounce shiitake mushrooms, stems removed and thinly sliced

2 garlic cloves, minced

12 ounces cream cheese, softened

1/2 cup mayonnaise

1/3 cup sour cream

2 teaspoons fresh lemon juice

1 1/2 teaspoons Worcestershire sauce

2 packages (9 ounces each) frozen artichoke hearts, thawed and chopped

3/4 cup shredded Parmesan cheese, divided

1. Preheat the oven to 400°F. Coat an 11 x 7-inch glass baking dish with cooking spray.

2. Heat a medium nonstick skillet over medium-high heat. Add the bacon and cook, stirring often, until crisp, 5 to 6 minutes. Transfer the bacon with a slotted spoon to a paper towel–lined plate to drain. Add the mushrooms to the skillet and cook, stirring occasionally, until beginning to brown, 5 to 6 minutes. Add the garlic and cook until light brown, about 1 minute longer. Remove from the heat and cool 5 minutes.

3. In a large bowl, beat the cream cheese, mayonnaise, sour cream, lemon juice, and Worcestershire sauce together. Add the bacon, shiitake mixture, artichokes, and 1/2 cup of the Parmesan.

4. Transfer to the baking dish and sprinkle with the remaining 1/4 cup Parmesan. Bake until browned and bubbly, about 30 minutes. Serve warm.

that's **ingenious** !

Make this dip ahead by assembling it up to the point that you would bake it. Wrap in plastic and refrigerate the dip for up to 2 days. If baking straight from the refrigerator, allow an extra 8 to 10 minutes cooking time.

GULF COAST HOT CRAB DIP

SECRET INGREDIENT:
Worcestershire sauce

All along the Gulf Coast, crab is gobbled up with bowls of melted butter for dipping. Skip the butter and enjoy this favorite seafood in a hot and creamy dip with chunks of crab in every bite. Serve piping hot with crackers or bagel chips. *See photograph on page 187.*

Prep Time: 15 min **Cook Time:** 20 min **Makes** 3 cups

12 ounces fresh lump crabmeat or 2 cans (6 ounces each) lump crabmeat, drained

1 package (8 ounces) cream cheese, softened

1 cup sour cream

1 small onion, finely chopped

1 tablespoon prepared horseradish

2 teaspoons Worcestershire sauce

1/4 teaspoon hot red-pepper sauce

3 tablespoons plain dry bread crumbs

1/2 teaspoon paprika

1. Preheat the oven to 350°F. Coat a gratin dish or deep-dish pie plate with oil or cooking spray.

2. Pick through the crabmeat, discarding any shells and cartilage. Rinse the crabmeat and drain.

3. Stir the cream cheese in a medium bowl until smooth. Blend in the sour cream, onion, horseradish, Worcestershire sauce, and red-pepper sauce. Gently fold in the crabmeat. Spoon into the baking dish and smooth out top.

4. Combine the bread crumbs and paprika in a cup and sprinkle evenly over the crabmeat mixture. Bake until bubbly, about 20 minutes.

Personalize It!

If you can't get good crabmeat or don't like it, make this dip with canned tuna or salmon. In that case, add 2 tablespoons grated Parmesan cheese to the dip for extra flavor.

GUACAMOLE WITH A KICK

SECRET INGREDIENT:

yogurt

Chunks of onion, tomato, and jalapeño peppers add so much zing to this zesty dip, your mouth will sing! Yogurt and sour cream stretch two avocados to feed a horde of hungry tortilla chip dunkers. *See photograph on page 186.*

Prep Time: 20 min **Cook Time:** 0 min **Makes** 3 cups

1/2 cup plain yogurt

2 small jalapeño peppers, seeded and minced (wear gloves when handling)

2 plum tomatoes, finely chopped

1 small white onion, finely chopped

2 tablespoons minced cilantro

1/2 teaspoon salt

1/2 cup sour cream

2 large Haas avocados, peeled, halved, and pitted

2 tablespoons fresh lime juice

1. Line the bottom of a strainer with cheese-cloth, a coffee filter, or paper towels and set over a medium bowl (strainer should not touch the bottom of the bowl). Spoon in the yogurt, cover, and refrigerate 8 hours or overnight, until yogurt "cheese" is thick and creamy.

2. Mix the jalapeños, tomatoes, onion, cilantro, and salt in large bowl. Fold in the yogurt cheese and sour cream.

3. In a large bowl, mash the avocados with a potato masher until mashed but not completely smooth. Sprinkle with the lime juice and quickly fold into the tomato mixture.

4. Serve immediately or press plastic wrap against the surface and refrigerate for up to 4 hours before serving.

One More Notch! For an even greater kick, add 1 small diced serrano pepper instead of the jalapeño. Add a peeled, diced mango to crown the top of the guacamole for a festive look.

MUSHROOM MOUSSE

SECRET INGREDIENT:

cream cheese

Mousses tend to be high in fat from heavy cream. This lightened version uses whipped reduced-fat cream cheese to slash calories without sacrificing taste. Serve as a side dish for chicken or beef. Or, serve as a spread with crackers.

Prep Time: 15 min **Cook Time:** 10 min **Makes** 1 1/2 cups

1 tablespoon unsalted butter

3 shallots, finely chopped (about 1/3 cup)

8 ounces mushrooms, chopped

1 garlic clove

1/4 teaspoon salt

1/4 teaspoon freshly ground black pepper

4 ounces Neufchâtel cream cheese, softened

2 tablespoons minced fresh parsley (optional)

1 hard-cooked egg, finely chopped (optional)

1. In a 10-inch nonstick skillet, melt the butter over medium heat. Add the shallots and cook, stirring, until they begin to soften, for 1 minute.

2. Add the mushrooms, garlic, salt, and pepper and cook, stirring occasionally, until the mushrooms have released their juices, about 5 minutes. Raise the heat to high and cook until the mixture is almost dry, 3 to 5 minutes longer. Remove from the heat and let cool.

3. In a food processor or blender, whirl the mushroom mixture with the cream cheese until smooth, 30 seconds.

4. Transfer the mousse to a serving dish and sprinkle with the parsley and egg, if using.

5. Cover and chill for 2 hours.

One More Notch! Mix 1/2 teaspoon lemon zest into the mousse and use it as a filling for breaded chicken breasts. Cut a pocket in the chicken breasts, stuff with the mousse, then coat with breading. Pan-fry or bake until the juices run clear when the chicken is pierced with a knife, 10 to 15 minutes.

SALMON PÂTÉ

SECRET INGREDIENT:

horseradish

An elegant appetizer for a dinner party, this rich-hued pâté gets a flavor lift from lemon zest and chives, and a bit of bite from horseradish.

Prep Time: 15 min **Cook Time:** 5 min **Makes** 4 cups

1 packet unflavored gelatin

1/2 cup cold water

1 can (14 3/4 ounces) salmon, drained, skin removed

3/4 cup plain yogurt

2/3 cup sour cream

2 tablespoons drained prepared horseradish

2 tablespoons grated onion

2 1/2 teaspoons grated lemon zest

1 tablespoon fresh lemon juice

3/4 teaspoon salt

1/3 cup minced chives

1. Sprinkle the gelatin over the water in a heat-proof glass measuring cup. Let stand 5 minutes to soften. Set the measuring cup in a small saucepan of simmering water and heat until the gelatin has melted, about 2 minutes. Set aside to cool slightly.

2. Place the salmon in a food processor and pulse until smooth. Add the yogurt, sour cream, horseradish, onion, lemon zest, lemon juice, and salt and pulse until the mixture is blended.

3. Add the chives and gelatin mixture and pulse until combined.

4. Transfer to a 4-cup bowl, crock, or decorative mold. Cover and refrigerate until set, at least 3 hours.

5. Serve directly from the bowl or crock. Or, if using a decorative mold, unmold onto a serving plate.

that's **ingenious**!

Canned salmon works fine in this recipe, but if you have freshly cooked salmon, use that. When making your next salmon meal, cook an extra pound of salmon, let cool, then use in the recipe. It will keep in the refrigerator for about a week.

CHEESY PESTO SPREAD

SECRET INGREDIENT:
cream cheese

Refrigerated prepared pesto from the supermarket is a great timesaver. The quality is good and the sauce versatile. Here, the sauce becomes a delicious spread by adding cream cheese, sun-dried tomatoes, and mozzarella. *See photograph on page 187.*

Prep Time: 5 min   **Cook Time:** 0 min   **Makes** 1 cup

1/2 cup soft light tub-style cream cheese

1/3 cup prepared pesto sauce

1/4 cup shredded mozzarella cheese

4 oil-packed sun-dried tomatoes, finely chopped

1. Combine the cream cheese, pesto, mozzarella, and tomatoes together in a small bowl and mix until well-combined.

2. Serve immediately or refrigerate for up to 4 days before serving.

Personalize It!

We suggest serving this spread on focaccia bread or slather it on a toasted bagel or use it as a pizza topping. You could even toss with some hot tortellini as a sauce.

LEMON BUTTER SPREAD

SECRET INGREDIENT:
eggs

Tea time in England often includes jams, jellies, and spreads to accompany sweet tea breads. Keep this refreshing spread on hand to slather over toast, muffins, pound cake, or scones. You could even use this spread as a cake filling. Eggs give it a rich texture closer to lemon curd. *See photograph on page 187.*

Prep Time: 5 min   **Cook Time:** 1 hr   **Makes** 3 cups

1 cup (2 sticks) unsalted butter

2 cups sugar

3 eggs, lightly beaten

1/2 cup fresh lemon juice

1 tablespoon grated lemon zest

1. In the top of a double boiler over boiling water, melt the butter. Stir in the sugar, eggs, lemon juice, and lemon zest. Reduce the heat and cook over simmering water until thickened, stirring occasionally, about 55 minutes.

2. Pour into shallow containers. Store in the refrigerator for up to 2 weeks.

One More Notch! Add a cinnamon stick and a vanilla bean to the mixture as it simmers. Remove before pouring into shallow containers.

ORCHARD SPREAD

SECRET INGREDIENT:
allspice

Two things make this fruit spread particularly delicious. First, it uses dried fruit rather than fresh for more intense flavor and texture. Second, allspice—typically used in pies and baking—is added for a more complex, well-rounded flavor.

Prep Time: 30 min **Cook Time:** 35 min **Makes** 4 cup

1 pound tart cooking apples
   (such as Jonathan), peeled, cored,
   and coarsely chopped (about 3 cups)

1 1/2 cups dried pears

1 1/2 cups dried peaches

1 1/2 cups apple juice

1 1/2 cups water

1 teaspoon ground allspice

1 1/2 to 2 teaspoons fresh lemon juice

1. Place the apples, pears, peaches, apple juice, water, and allspice in a large, heavy saucepan. Bring the fruit mixture to a boil over high heat, stirring occasionally.

2. Reduce the heat to low and simmer, uncovered, until the mixture is reduced to a pulp and no liquid is visible on the surface, about 30 minutes. Stir frequently to prevent the mixture from sticking to the bottom of the pan.

3. Remove the pan from the heat and let the mixture cool slightly. Stir in the lemon juice, then taste and add a little more lemon juice if the mixture is too sweet.

4. Transfer to a food processor or blender and process until a thick puree forms. Let the spread cool at room temperature for about 1 hour before serving. Refrigerate the spread in a covered jar for up to a week.

Personalize It!

If you like berries, try a mixed fruit spread instead. Substitute 3 cups dried mixed fruits, such as blueberries, cranberries, pineapple, and golden raisins, for the dried pears and peaches. Substitute fresh orange juice for the apple juice and 1/2 teaspoon ground ginger for the allspice. ❄

extraordinary **beverages**

BLUEBERRY-BANANA SMOOTHIE

SECRET INGREDIENT:
apple juice

Smoothies are generally a mix of pureed fresh fruit and ice cubes. This one uses frozen fruit instead of ice cubes to avoid diluting the flavor of the smoothie. Apple juice stands in for the liquid content of the ice cubes and boosts the fruit flavor.

Prep Time: 5 min **Cook Time:** 0 min **Serves** 1

1 frozen banana

3/4 cup frozen blueberries

1 1/4 cups apple juice

2 teaspoons honey

Pinch of ground cinnamon

Pinch of salt

1. Puree the banana, blueberries, apple juice, honey, cinnamon, and salt in a blender or small food processor until smooth.

2. Serve in a tall glass.

MANGO SURPRISE SMOOTHIE

SECRET INGREDIENT:
avocado

Smoothies have become a great way to get extra fruits into our diets. This one uses avocado, which, aside from the great nutritional benefits, lends a rich and creamy mouth feel. *See photograph on page 162.*

Prep Time: 15 min **Cook Time:** 0 min **Serves** 1

1 cup chopped ripe mango

1/4 Haas avocado, peeled, pitted, and chopped

1/2 cup mango sorbet

1/4 cup skim milk

2 tablespoons honey

2 teaspoons lime juice

1/4 cup crushed ice

2 mango slices, 1/2-inch thick

1 lime slice

1. In a blender, combine the chopped mango, avocado, sorbet, milk, honey, lime juice, and ice. Blend on high until smooth.

2. Pour into a tall glass. Slit the sliced mango and the sliced lime halfway through to the centers. Attach them to the rim of the glass before serving.

STRAWBERRY-YOGURT SMOOTHIES

SECRET INGREDIENT:
orange juice

When summer arrives and strawberries are in season, this is the perfect way to enjoy them. Whirl up the berries with yogurt for a creamy, refreshing snack. Orange juice adds a sweet tang. *See photograph on page 189.*

Prep Time: 15 min **Cook Time:** 0 min **Serves** 4

1 quart (4 cups) ripe strawberries

1 cup plain yogurt

1/2 cup fresh orange juice

1 tablespoon sugar

4 thin orange slices (optional)

1. Hull all but 4 of the strawberries. Add the hulled strawberries to a food processor or blender. Add the yogurt, orange juice, and sugar. Process on the highest speed until a well-blended puree forms, about 15 seconds, stopping to scrape down the sides of the container once or twice. Taste the mixture and sweeten with more sugar, if you wish.

2. Pour into tall glasses. Slit the 4 whole strawberries and the orange slices halfway through to the centers. Attach 1 strawberry

BEVERAGES

and 1 orange slice, if using, to the rim of each glass before serving.

Personalize It!

For an ultra-smooth beverage, strain the mixture, using a wooden spoon to push the drink through a mesh strainer. Discard the strawberry seeds. ❄

that's **ingenious**

Have fruit on hand to make your smoothies in a jiffy. Peel, pit, and cube ripe mango and store it in zip-close plastic freezer bags and freeze until ready to use. This way, you can grab a cupful the next time you want to make a smoothie with a lot less cleanup.

CREAMSICLE SHAKES

SECRET INGREDIENT:

orange-tangerine juice

The combination of orange and vanilla is a classic. This shake uses orange-tangerine juice to put a fun twist on the tried-and-true. Look for orange-tangerine juice near the plain orange juice in the refrigerated section. *See photograph on page 189.*

Prep Time: 5 min **Cook Time:** 0 min **Serves** 2

1 cup orange-tangerine juice

1 cup vanilla ice cream

1 cup orange sherbet

1/2 teaspoon vanilla extract

1. Combine the juice, ice cream, sherbet, and vanilla in a blender and puree until smooth.

2. Pour into tall glasses and serve.

One More Notch! Take this shake over the top by adding a ripe banana and a few strawberries, or sprinkle with fresh blueberries.

MOCHA MALTEDS

SECRET INGREDIENT:

chocolate-covered malt balls

For many kids, malted milk is a sweet treat. This grown-up version features malted milk balls to provide a light touch of chocolate, and espresso powder for sophistication and depth. Look for instant espresso powder near the instant coffee in a well-stocked supermarket.

Prep Time: 15 min **Cook Time:** 0 min **Serves** 2

1 cup milk

14 large chocolate-covered malted milk balls, divided

1 tablespoon chocolate syrup

1/2 teaspoon instant espresso powder

1 1/2 cups vanilla ice cream

Sweetened whipped cream

1. In a blender, combine the milk, 12 of the malted milk balls, the chocolate syrup, and espresso powder and puree. Pour the mixture through a wire mesh strainer to remove the chocolate that does not puree.

2. Return the strained milk mixture to the blender, add the ice cream, and blend until creamy.

3. Pour into two tall glasses and top each with a dollop of whipped cream and a malted milk ball.

Personalize It!

If chocolate is your absolute favorite, substitute chocolate ice cream instead of vanilla and up the espresso powder to 3/4 teaspoon. ❄

NEW-FASHIONED EGG CREAM

SECRET INGREDIENT:
flavored seltzer

The key to a great New York–style egg cream is to get a good "head" on the beverage, similar to the foam on a perfectly poured beer. By using heavy cream, you get both a richer drink and better foam. Flavored seltzer lends a twist on the traditional version, and vanilla syrup adds sweet aromas. Look for vanilla syrup, such as Torani, in the store beverage aisle.

Prep Time: 5 min **Cook Time:** 0 min **Serves** 1

2 tablespoons vanilla syrup, preferably chilled

1/4 cup heavy cream

3/4 cup cold raspberry-flavored seltzer

1. Combine the syrup and cream in a tall glass and stir with a long spoon.

2. Slowly pour in the seltzer while stirring rapidly with the spoon to create a foamy head. Serve immediately.

Personalize It!

Not a fan of raspberry? Use orange-flavored seltzer to get a beverage with a creamsicle taste. Or, if you prefer chocolate, just substitute chocolate syrup for the vanilla.

NOT-YOUR-AVERAGE-ROOT-BEER FLOAT

SECRET INGREDIENT:
heavy cream

Almond extract gives this classic root beer float a delightful hint of cherry while heavy cream adds richness—and just as important, helps create three layers of color in the glass. *See photograph on page 189.*

Prep Time: 10 min **Cook Time:** 0 min **Serves** 1

1 1/2 cups cold root beer

1/4 teaspoon almond extract

1/2 cup vanilla ice cream

2 tablespoons heavy cream

1 maraschino cherry

1. Pour the root beer into a tall glass. Gently stir in the almond extract.

2. Slowly and carefully scoop the ice cream into the root beer. Pour the cream over the ice cream and top with the cherry.

PIÑA COLADARITA

SECRET INGREDIENT:
lime juice

This drink takes two popular tropical cocktails—piña coladas and margaritas—and combines them into something even better. The sweet richness of coconut is still here, but lime juice and tequila help to lighten the drink, adding the right touch of tartness.

Prep Time: 10 min **Cook Time:** 0 min **Makes** 1

6 tablespoons (3 ounces) pineapple juice

1/4 cup (2 ounces) cream of coconut

1 tablespoon lime juice

3 tablespoons (1 1/2 ounces) tequila

2 tablespoons (1 ounce) triple sec

1 cup crushed ice

1. In a blender, combine the pineapple juice, cream of coconut, lime juice, tequila, triple sec, and ice. Blend until smooth.

2. Pour into either a tall glass or a margarita glass.

that's **ingenious**

> This drink is great for a summer party or anytime. Just make a large batch, leaving out the ice, and then blend with the ice when ready to serve.

CUBAN SUMMER SIPPERS

SECRET INGREDIENT:
beer

This light and refreshing summer beverage has a taste reminiscent of really good limeade. Beer kicks it up in flavor, making it a treat for grown-ups. *See photographs on pages 166 and 189.*

Prep Time: 5 min   **Cook Time:** 0 min   **Serves** 2

1/4 cup sugar

1/4 cup water

3 tablespoons lime juice

Crushed ice

1/2 cup lemon-lime soda

1 bottle (8 ounces) cold beer

Lime slices (optional)

1. In a small saucepan, heat the sugar and water over high heat, stirring, until the sugar dissolves. Transfer the mixture to a heat-proof pitcher or bowl with a spout and let cool for 15 minutes. Transfer to the refrigerator and chill until cold, about 30 minutes.

2. Remove the sugar mixture from the refrigerator and stir in the lime juice.

3. Fill two tall glasses with ice and divide the sugar mixture between them. Pour 1/4 cup

of the soda into each, then top off each glass with half of the beer. Add lime slices, if using.

One More Notch! If you'd like to make this more of a cocktail than a light beverage, add 1 ounce light rum to each glass before adding the sugar mixture.

ICED TEA ADE

SECRET INGREDIENT:
frozen lemonade concentrate

When the weather is hot, some folks cool off with iced tea, others with lemonade. Here, both favorites are combined into one fabulous summer drink. *See photograph on page 168.*

Prep Time: 10 min   **Cook Time:** 20 min   **Serves** 8

8 orange pekoe tea bags

8 cups simmering water

1 can (12 ounces) frozen lemonade concentrate, thawed

Lemon wedges (optional)

1. Combine the tea bags and water in a large heat-proof pitcher or bowl with a spout and let stand 20 minutes. Discard the tea bags and stir in the lemonade. Transfer to the refrigerator and chill 1 1/2 hours.

2. Pour into eight glasses over ice to serve. Add lemon wedges, if using.

that's **ingenious**

> Make a quick recipe even less work. Combine the tea bags, cold water, and unthawed lemonade concentrate in a large pitcher and put it in the refrigerator. Let it steep at least 4 hours. Discard the tea bags, give it a stir, and serve.

BEVERAGES

FLAMING CAFÉ BRÛLOT

SECRET INGREDIENT:
triple sec

Make this post-meal drink at your next dinner party and your guests will rave. Brandy and triple-sec are set ablaze to flavor spice-infused hot coffee.

Prep Time: 15 min   **Cook Time:** 5 min   **Serves** 8

4 whole allspice berries

4 whole cloves

1 cinnamon stick (3 inches), broken

Zest from 2 large oranges, slivered, divided

Zest from 1/2 large lemon, slivered

8 teaspoons sugar

4 cups hot, strong coffee, divided

1/2 cup brandy

1/4 cup triple sec, Grand Marnier, or other orange-flavored liqueur

1. Make a spice bag by placing the allspice, cloves, and cinnamon pieces in the center of a small piece of cheesecloth or a clean coffee filter. Bring up the edges and tie securely with cotton string. Set aside 8 slivers of the orange zest.

2. In a medium saucepan, combine the remaining orange zest with the lemon zest, sugar, and spice bag. Stir in 1 cup of the coffee, plus the brandy and orange liqueur.

3. Simmer, uncovered, over medium-low heat for 5 minutes, stirring and mashing the zest and sugar until the sugar dissolves and the mixture is hot. Using a slotted spoon, remove and discard the spice bag and zest. Light a wooden match, then standing with your body away from the coffee mixture, carefully ignite. Pour the remaining 3 cups of coffee into the ignited mixture.

4. Ladle into demitasse cups, and add the reserved orange zest.

One More Notch! Scrape the seeds from a vanilla bean and add to the spice bag. You can also add 3 ounces bittersweet chocolate for a mocha flavor. Add the chocolate along with the brandy and stir until melted.

WARM PINEAPPLE-GINGER PUNCH

SECRET INGREDIENT:
black peppercorns

Mulled cider always turns up on holiday menus. Why not mull a different fruit juice? Pineapple juice makes a fantastic warm punch, especially when spiced with fresh ginger and a few black peppercorns for extra zing. *See photograph on page 188.*

Prep Time: 5 min   **Cook Time:** 45 min   **Serves** 4

1 cup sliced fresh ginger

1 cinnamon stick (3 inches), broken in half

8 whole cloves

8 black peppercorns

1 quart pineapple juice

1 tablespoon honey

1. Make a spice bag by placing the ginger, cinnamon pieces, cloves, and peppercorns in the center of a small piece of cheesecloth or a clean coffee filter. Bring up the edges and tie securely with cotton string.

2. Combine the pineapple juice and honey in a medium saucepan and add the spice bag. Bring to a boil. Reduce to a gentle simmer and cook for 45 minutes. Remove and discard the spice bag. Serve warm ladled into mugs.

One More Notch! Add a seeded, deveined, sliced jalapeño pepper (wear gloves when handling) to the spice bag.

BEVERAGES

SOUTH-OF-THE-BORDER HOT CHOCOLATE

SECRET INGREDIENT:
ancho chile pepper

We've become so accustomed to just-add-water packets of hot chocolate that we forget how good this drink can really be. Take a cue from the Mexican version. A few pinches of ground ancho chile pepper give the drink more spunk and a faint hint of earthiness.
See photograph on page 189.

Prep Time: 10 min   **Cook Time:** 0 min   **Serves** 4

3 cups half-and-half

1 cup skim milk

1/2 cup firmly packed dark brown sugar

1/4 cup cocoa powder

1/2 teaspoon ground ancho chile pepper

1/4 teaspoon ground cinnamon

3 ounces semi-sweet chocolate

1 teaspoon vanilla extract

1/3 cup heavy cream

1/4 cup confectioners' sugar

1. In a medium saucepan over medium heat, whisk together the half-and-half, milk, brown sugar, cocoa powder, chile pepper, and cinnamon. Bring to a simmer and cook, stirring, 1 minute.

2. Remove from the heat and stir in the chocolate and vanilla until the chocolate has melted. Keep warm over low heat.

3. In a medium bowl, whisk together the heavy cream and confectioners' sugar. Beat until the cream has stiff peaks.

4. Pour the hot chocolate into four coffee mugs and top each with a generous dollop of whipped cream.

MULLED CITRUS CIDER

SECRET INGREDIENT:
cranberry juice

Here's a warm drink with an edge. In addition to the usual sweet spices—cinnamon, allspice, and cloves—this mulled cider includes cranberry juice for a tart counterpoint to the sweet cider.

Prep Time: 5 min   **Cook Time:** 55 min   **Serves** 12

1 quart apple cider

2 cups cranberry juice

1 cup orange juice

3/4 cup lemon juice

1/2 cup sugar

1 teaspoon whole allspice

1 teaspoon whole cloves

3 cinnamon sticks (3 inches long)

1. Pour the apple cider, cranberry juice, orange juice, and lemon juice into a large saucepan; then stir in the sugar.

2. Make a spice bag by placing the allspice, cloves, and cinnamon pieces in the center of a small piece of cheesecloth or a clean coffee filter. Bring up the edges and tie securely with cotton string. Add the spice bag to the juice mixture. Cover and simmer for 55 minutes. Remove and discard the spice bag. Serve warm ladled into mugs.

One More Notch! For a more pronounced orange flavor to complement the cranberry juice, add the zest of 1 orange removed in one continuous strip. Remove from the cider before serving.

MULLED WINE

lemon spice tea bags

Mulled wine is great to serve in the winter after a long day in the cold. To avoid the same old flavors, we've spiced ours with lemon spice tea bags. The tea perfectly complements the rich wine flavor and adds a layer of complexity to the brew.

Prep Time: 5 min   **Cook Time:** 15 min   **Serves** 4

1 bottle (750ml) dry red wine, such as Syrah

10 black peppercorns

2 cinnamon sticks

10 whole allspice berries

3 whole cloves

1 lemon, sliced

Pinch of ground nutmeg

1/2 cup sugar

1 cup water

1 lemon spice tea bag

1. Combine the wine, peppercorns, cinnamon, allspice berries, cloves, lemon slices, and nutmeg in a large saucepan over medium heat. Heat until the mixture is hot but not boiling. Stir in the sugar and water, stirring until the sugar dissolves. Continue heating 2 minutes longer.

2. Remove from the heat and add the tea bag; let stand 4 minutes.

3. Strain the mixture and serve warm ladled into mugs.

One More Notch! Take this one to the jolly ol' England of Charles Dickens by adding 2 cups ruby port after straining out the spices. The resulting drink packs quite a punch.

EGGNOG PUNCH

orange juice

If you need a last-minute beverage for a holiday party, look no further. Orange juice gives eggnog a welcome burst of citrus flavor and ginger ale adds a festive effervescence.

Prep Time: 5 min   **Cook Time:** 0 min   **Serves** 8

1 quart eggnog

1 can (12 ounces) frozen orange juice concentrate, thawed

1 can (12 ounces) ginger ale, chilled

1. In a pitcher, stir the eggnog and orange juice concentrate until well-mixed. Pour in the ginger ale and stir gently.

2. Serve in tall glasses.

Personalize It!

To celebrate in style, add 1/2 cup rum to the punch. You could also use lemon-lime soda in place of the ginger ale.

extraordinary
cookies
and bars

OAT-RAGEOUS CHOCOLATE CHIP COOKIES

SECRET INGREDIENT:
peanut butter

Some people like oatmeal cookies. Some like chocolate chip cookies. Yet others prefer peanut butter cookies. This recipe combines all three! The peanut butter in the dough makes them extra rich and delicious.

Prep Time: 15 min **Cook Time:** 10 min **Makes** 3 doz

1/2 cup (1 stick) unsalted butter or margarine, softened

1/2 cup creamy peanut butter

1/2 cup sugar

1/3 cup firmly packed brown sugar

1 egg

1/2 teaspoon vanilla extract

1 cup all-purpose flour

1/2 cup quick-cooking oats

1 teaspoon baking soda

1/4 teaspoon salt

1 cup (6 ounces) semi-sweet chocolate chips

1. Preheat the oven to 350°F.

2. In a large bowl, cream the butter or margarine, peanut butter, sugar, and brown sugar. Beat in the egg and vanilla.

3. In a small bowl, combine the flour, oats, baking soda, and salt.

4. Add the dry ingredients into the creamed mixture and stir until well-combined. Stir in the chocolate chips.

5. Drop by rounded teaspoonfuls onto an ungreased baking sheet. Bake until lightly browned, 10 to 12 minutes.

TRIPLE CHOCOLATE COOKIES

SECRET INGREDIENT:
sour cream

Chocolate chips, chocolate sprinkles, and cocoa powder create a triple shot of chocolate flavor. Sour cream gives the cookies an irresistibly soft and tender crumb.
See photograph on page 172.

Prep Time: 30 min **Cook Time:** 10 min **Makes** 5 1/2 doz

1 1/4 cups (2 1/2 sticks) unsalted butter or margarine, softened

2 1/4 cups confectioners' sugar

1/3 cup cocoa powder

1/4 cup sour cream

1 tablespoon vanilla extract

2 1/4 cups all-purpose flour

2 cups (12 ounces) semi-sweet chocolate chips

1/4 cup chocolate sprinkles

1. In a large bowl, cream the butter or margarine, confectioners' sugar, and cocoa powder until light and fluffy.

2. Beat in the sour cream and vanilla. Stir in half the flour and mix well. Add the remaining flour, then stir in the chocolate chips and refrigerate for 1 hour.

3. Preheat the oven to 325°F.

4. Remove from the refrigerator and roll the dough into 1-inch balls. Dip one side of the cookie balls in the sprinkles. Place, sprinkle side up, 2 inches apart on an ungreased baking sheet.

5. Bake until set, about 10 minutes. Cool for 5 minutes then remove to a wire rack to cool completely.

One More Notch! Give the cookies a mocha flavor by mixing 3 tablespoons finely ground espresso coffee right in with the flour.

GINGERSNAPS

SECRET INGREDIENT:

dried cranberries

Some commercial gingersnap cookies taste like just about every baking spice *except* ginger. To make up for that, we use both ground and fresh ginger here. Dried cranberries make a terrific stir-in that adds a sweet, chewy contrast.

Prep Time: 30 min **Cook Time:** 30 min **Makes** 5 doz

2 1/2 cups all-purpose flour

1 teaspoon baking soda

1 teaspoon ground ginger

1/2 teaspoon ground cinnamon

1 cup firmly packed dark brown sugar

3/4 cup (1 1/2 sticks) unsalted butter or margarine, softened

1 egg

2 tablespoons peeled grated fresh ginger

1/4 cup molasses

1/2 cup dried cranberries

1/4 cup sugar

1. Preheat the oven to 350°F. Line a baking sheet with parchment paper.

2. Combine the flour, baking soda, ground ginger, and cinnamon in a medium bowl.

3. In the bowl of an electric mixer beat together the brown sugar and butter on high speed until light and fluffy, about 2 minutes. Beat in the egg, grated ginger, and molasses, stopping to scrape down the sides of the bowl. Reduce the speed to low and mix in the flour until a dough forms. Mix in the cranberries.

4. Pour the sugar in a small bowl. Roll level tablespoons of the dough into balls, then roll the balls in the sugar to evenly coat.

5. Arrange the cookie balls about 1 1/2 inches apart on the baking sheet. Bake on the center rack of the oven until the cookies flatten and darken slightly, about 14 minutes. Transfer the cookies to a wire rack to cool completely. Allow the baking sheet to cool before adding another batch of cookie balls, or use multiple baking sheets and alternate the pans with each batch.

One More Notch! These cookies taste delicious right out of the oven, but to maximize their flavor, store them in an airtight container and let the gingery aromas bloom overnight.

NO-BAKE PEANUT BUTTER COOKIES

SECRET INGREDIENT:

cornflakes

This amazingly simple four-ingredient recipe makes a delicious cookie that is both gooey and crunchy. Store-bought cornflakes provide the crunch.

Prep Time: 10 min **Cook Time:** 5 min **Makes** 8 doz

1 cup sugar

1 cup light corn syrup

2 cups peanut butter

4 cups cornflakes

1. Place the sugar and corn syrup in a deep saucepan. Bring to a boil, then continue boiling for 1 minute, stirring constantly.

2. Add the peanut butter and stir until melted. Stir in the cereal.

3. Drop by rounded teaspoonfuls onto wax paper. Let set.

AUSTRIAN ALMOND COOKIES

SECRET INGREDIENT:
raspberry jam

These traditional sandwich cookies feature chopped almonds in the dough and slivered almonds on top of the cookie to create an extra nutty taste. Raspberry jam makes a super simple filling for sandwiching between the cookies.

Prep Time: 30 min   **Cook Time:** 10 min   **Makes** 20

COOKIES

1 cup all-purpose flour

2/3 cup finely chopped almonds

1/3 cup sugar

1/2 cup (1 stick) cold unsalted butter

1/2 cup raspberry jam

FROSTING

1 square (1 ounce) unsweetened chocolate

2 tablespoons unsalted butter
   or margarine

1/3 cup confectioners' sugar

Slivered almonds

1. Preheat the oven to 375°F.

2. For cookies, combine the flour, almonds, and sugar in a medium bowl. Cut in the butter until the mixture resembles coarse crumbs.

3. Form into a ball; then cover and refrigerate for 1 hour.

4. Remove from the refrigerator and roll the ball of dough on a floured surface to 1/8-inch thickness. Cut with a 2-inch round cutter and place 1 inch apart on greased baking sheets.

5. Bake until the edges are lightly browned, 7 to 10 minutes. Remove to wire racks to cool completely.

6. Spread 1/2 teaspoon jam on half of the cookies; top each with another cookie.

7. For frosting, combine the chocolate and butter or margarine in a medium microwavable bowl. Microwave on medium until the chocolate and butter or margarine are melted, about 3 minutes, stopping to stir every minute.

8. Stir in the confectioners' sugar and let cool slightly. Spread on top of cookies. Decorate with the slivered almonds.

FRENCH CHRISTMAS COOKIES

SECRET INGREDIENT:
graham crackers

Graham crackers have a sweet, nutty taste that makes a fabulous flour for cookies when crushed into crumbs. Chopped walnuts enhance the nutty flavor even more. With a simple chocolate topping, these moist treats will have everyone reaching for seconds.

Prep Time: 15 min   **Cook Time:** 15 min   **Makes** 9 doz

1 cup firmly packed brown sugar

1/2 cup (1 stick) unsalted butter or
   margarine, softened

2 3/4 cups graham cracker crumbs

2 cups finely chopped walnuts

3 1/4 cups (20 ounces) milk chocolate chips,
   divided

1 cup milk

1. Preheat the oven to 375°F.

2. In a large bowl, cream the sugar and butter or margarine. Add the cracker crumbs, walnuts, 2 cups of the chocolate chips, and the milk. Mix well.

3. Fill miniature paper baking cups three-quarters full. Place the cups 1 inch apart on baking sheets. Bake until the surfaces look dry, 10 to 12 minutes. Cool on wire racks.

4. Melt the remaining 1 1/4 cups chocolate chips in a microwavable bowl on medium heat for 3 minutes, stopping to stir every minute. Top each cookie with 1/4 teaspoon melted chocolate. Store in the refrigerator for up to 1 week.

COCONUTTY MACAROONS

SECRET INGREDIENT:

sesame seeds

These sweet golden cookies make a great treat after dinner, at tea time, or anytime. Toasted sesame seeds give them a delicate crunch and a nutty aroma. The sesame seeds blend in nicely but add just enough interest in each and every bite.

Prep Time: 20 min **Cook Time:** 22 min **Makes** 3 doz

1 bag (14 ounces) sweetened coconut flakes

1/2 cup plus 2 tablespoons sugar

3 tablespoons toasted sesame seeds

1/3 cup all-purpose flour

3 large egg whites

1/4 teaspoon salt

1 teaspoon vanilla extract

1/4 teaspoon coconut extract

1. Preheat the oven to 325°F. Place one oven rack in the upper third and one in the lower third of the oven. Cover two large baking sheets with parchment paper.

2. Combine the coconut, 1/2 cup of the sugar, sesame seeds, and flour in a large bowl; mix well.

3. Beat the egg whites in a medium bowl with an electric mixer on high speed until soft peaks begin to form. With the mixer running, beat in the remaining 2 tablespoons of sugar until stiff peaks form. Beat in the vanilla and coconut extract.

4. Stir 1/4 of the egg whites into the coconut mixture to lighten. Gently fold in the remaining whites.

5. Drop tablespoonfuls 1 1/2 inches apart on each baking sheet and bake until golden, 22 to 25 minutes. Transfer the cookies to a wire rack and cool completely.

One More Notch! Take these cookies over the top by drizzling them with 1 ounce of melted semi-sweet chocolate after they cool.

ESPRESSO BISCOTTI

SECRET INGREDIENT:

ground coffee

Coffee-flavored desserts are all the rage. Here, instead of adding brewed coffee, we found that you get more bang for the buck by baking ground coffee right into the cookies. A touch of cocoa powder and cinnamon will have you dreaming of a frothy cappuccino.
See photograph on page 173.

Prep Time: 20 min **Cook Time:** 40 min **Makes** 5 doz

1 3/4 cup all-purpose flour

2/3 cup sugar

1/4 cup cocoa powder

3 tablespoons ground coffee

1 teaspoon baking powder

1/4 teaspoon ground cinnamon

1/4 teaspoon salt

6 tablespoons cold unsalted butter, diced

3/4 cup walnuts

2 eggs, lightly beaten

1 teaspoon vanilla extract

1. Preheat the oven to 350°F. Coat a baking sheet with cooking spray.

2. In a medium bowl with an electric mixer, combine the flour, sugar, cocoa powder, coffee, baking powder, cinnamon, and salt.

3. Add the butter and mix until the mixture resembles coarse meal. Add the walnuts, eggs, and vanilla and mix until a fairly dry dough forms. Divide the dough in two. On a lightly floured surface, use your palms to shape each half of the dough into a 14 x 1 3/4 x 1-inch cylinder. Transfer to the baking sheet and pat the tops of each cylinder to 3/4 inch high.

4. Bake until the logs are firm to the touch and a toothpick inserted into the dough comes out clean, 20 to 25 minutes. Transfer logs to a cutting board and let cool for 10 minutes. Using a serrated knife, cut the logs crosswise into 1/4-inch-thick slices.

5. Arrange the cookie slices in a single layer on the baking sheet. Lower the oven temperature to 300°F. Bake the cookies for 20 minutes, turning once. Transfer the cookies from the baking sheet to a wire rack and cool completely. The biscotti will crisp as they cool.

ROCKY ROAD BROWNIES

SECRET INGREDIENT:
mini marshmallows

Brownies are great to have around for a quick dessert or snack. They're always a hit, and adding mini marshmallows makes them a little more fun and a lot more tasty.
See photograph on page 191.

Prep Time: 15 min	**Cook Time:** 45 min	**Makes** 24

4 ounces unsweetened chocolate

1 cup (2 sticks) unsalted butter

1 1/2 cups sugar

4 eggs

2 teaspoons vanilla extract

3/4 cup all-purpose flour

1 cup coarsely chopped walnuts

1 1/2 cups mini marshmallows, divided

1/4 teaspoon baking powder

1/4 teaspoon salt

1. Preheat the oven to 325°F. Coat a 9 x 13-inch baking pan with cooking spray and dust with a little flour.

2. Bring a medium saucepan of water to a simmer over medium heat. Place the chocolate and butter in a medium heat-proof bowl and set over the water. Stir occasionally until melted. Remove from the heat and cool for 5 minutes.

3. Meanwhile, combine the sugar, eggs, and vanilla in a medium bowl and mix well.

4. Combine the flour, walnuts, 3/4 cup of the marshmallows, baking powder, and salt in a large bowl.

5. Whisk the egg mixture into the chocolate mixture until well-combined. Stir in the flour mixture until combined. Pour into the pan and spread to an even thickness.

6. Bake for 30 minutes then top with the remaining 3/4 cup mini marshmallows and bake until a toothpick inserted near the center comes out nearly clean, about 2 minutes longer. Cool in the pan for 30 minutes before cutting.

Personalize It!

If you like your brownies more fudgey, cook them 3 to 4 minutes less than the recipe directs. For a real treat, sandwich a scoop of your favorite ice cream between two brownies and indulge!

CHOCOLATE PEANUT BUTTER TREATS

SECRET INGREDIENT:
marshmallows

If you like crispy rice treats, you'll love chocolate peanut butter treats. Marshmallows are the key to their light and fluffy texture, but creamy peanut butter, butterscotch chips, and semi-sweet chocolate chips make a richer and more satisfying treat.

Prep Time: 10 min   **Cook Time:** 10 min   **Makes** 12

1/4 cup (1/2 stick) unsalted butter
   or margarine

1 package (10 ounces) marshmallows

3/4 cup creamy peanut butter

5 cups crispy rice cereal

1 cup (6 ounces) butterscotch chips

1 cup (6 ounces) semi-sweet chocolate chips

1. In a large saucepan or microwavable bowl, melt the butter or margarine and marshmallows. Remove from the heat; then stir in peanut butter. Gradually add the cereal and mix until well-coated.

2. Spread and press into a greased 9 x 13-inch pan; set aside.

3. In a small microwavable bowl or the top of a double-boiler over simmering water, melt the butterscotch chips and chocolate chips. Spread over the cereal mixture.

4. Cover and freeze until the chocolate is set, 15 to 20 minutes.

One More Notch! Add another layer of flavor by stirring 1/2 teaspoon ground cinnamon in with the peanut butter.

LEMON BAR SURPRISE

SECRET INGREDIENT:
zucchini

Lemon bars make a refreshing afternoon pick-me-up with tea. With zucchini stirred right into the lemon mixture, the snack becomes truly extraordinary.

Prep Time: 20 min   **Cook Time:** 1 hr 5 min   **Makes** 16

CRUST

4 cups all-purpose flour

2 cups sugar

1/2 teaspoon ground cinnamon

1/2 teaspoon salt

1 1/2 cups (3 sticks) cold unsalted butter
   or margarine

FILLING

8 to 10 cups (4 to 5 pounds) peeled,
   seeded, and cubed zucchini

2/3 cup lemon juice

1 cup sugar

1 teaspoon ground cinnamon

1/2 teaspoon ground nutmeg

1. Preheat the oven to 375°F.

2. For crust, combine the flour, sugar, cinnamon, and salt in a large bowl. Cut in the butter or margarine until crumbly. Reserve 3 cups.

3. Pat the remaining crumb mixture into the bottom of a greased 9 x 13-inch baking pan. Bake until lightly browned, about 12 minutes.

4. For filling, place the zucchini and lemon juice in a large saucepan and bring to a boil. Reduce the heat, cover, and cook until the zucchini is crisp-tender, 6 to 8 minutes.

5. Stir in the sugar, cinnamon, and nutmeg, then cover and simmer for 5 minutes (mixture will be thin). Spoon over the crust, then sprinkle with the reserved

crumb mixture. Bake until golden, 40 to 45 minutes.

One More Notch! For extra-lemony bars, add the finely grated zest of 1 lemon to the lemon juice and zucchini.

APPLE SNACK SQUARES

SECRET INGREDIENT:
butterscotch chips

Kids love these snack bars after school, after dinner, or anytime. Butterscotch chips give them an old-time flavor that adults love, too!

Prep Time: 10 min **Cook Time:** 35 min **Makes** 2 doz

2 cups sugar

2 eggs

3/4 cup vegetable oil

2 1/2 cups self-rising flour

1 teaspoon ground cinnamon

3 cups peeled diced tart apples

1 cup chopped walnuts

3/4 cup butterscotch chips

1. Preheat the oven to 350°F.

2. In a large bowl, combine the sugar, eggs, and oil. Mix well. Stir in the flour and cinnamon (batter will be thick).

3. Stir in the apples and walnuts. Spread into a greased 9 x 13-inch baking pan. Sprinkle with the butterscotch chips.

4. Bake until golden and a toothpick inserted near the center comes out clean, 35 to 40 minutes. Cool before cutting.

that's **ingenious**

> If you don't have walnuts, use pecans or almonds. If you don't have butterscotch chips, try cinnamon chips or chocolate chips.

CHEESECAKE SQUARES

SECRET INGREDIENT:
ricotta cheese

There are thousands of recipes for cheesecake, but the best ones usually include more than one type of cheese. Combining cream cheese with ricotta cheese gives the cheesecake more body and a more interesting flavor. A little sour cream doesn't hurt either.

Prep Time: 10 min **Cook Time:** 1 hr **Makes** 20

2 packages (8 ounces each) cream cheese, softened

1 cup ricotta cheese

1 1/2 cups sugar

4 eggs

1/4 cup (1/2 stick) unsalted butter or margarine, melted and cooled

3 tablespoons cornstarch

3 tablespoons all-purpose flour

1 tablespoon vanilla extract

2 cups (16 ounces) sour cream

Seasonal fresh fruit (optional)

1. Preheat the oven to 325°F.

2. In a medium bowl, beat the cream cheese, ricotta, and sugar until smooth.

3. Add the eggs, one at a time, mixing well after each addition. Add the butter or margarine, cornstarch, flour, and vanilla. Beat until smooth. Fold in the sour cream.

4. Pour into a greased 9 x 13-inch baking pan. Bake, uncovered, for 1 hour. Turn the oven off but do not open the oven door. Let the cheesecake stand in the closed oven for 2 hours. Cool completely on a wire rack.

5. Chill several hours or overnight. Cut into squares and serve with the fruit, if using.

One More Notch! Instead of fresh fruit, top the cooled cheesecake with fruit sauce before cutting into squares. For a strawberry sauce, melt 2 tablespoons strawberry preserves over medium heat. Add 2 tablespoons brandy, a pinch of salt, and 1 pint sliced strawberries. Cook until the berries fall apart and the liquid begins to thicken. Cool.

BLACK-AND-WHITE CHEESECAKE BARS

SECRET INGREDIENT:
sweetened condensed milk

Cheesecake bars with two layers can be time-consuming to make. But thanks to the convenience of sweetened condensed milk, these bars take only 15 minutes of kitchen time. When a dessert is this easy—and this good—you know you'll make it often.

Prep Time: 15 min **Cook Time:** 30 min **Makes** 4 doz

2 cups (12 ounces) semi-sweet chocolate chips

1/2 cup (1 stick) unsalted butter or margarine

2 cups graham cracker crumbs, divided

1 package (8 ounces) cream cheese, softened

1 can (14 ounces) sweetened condensed milk

1 egg

1 teaspoon vanilla extract

1. In a double-boiler or microwave, melt the chocolate chips and butter or margarine, stirring occasionally.

2. Set aside 1/4 cup of the cracker crumbs. Stir the remaining cracker crumbs into the chocolate mixture.

3. Press the chocolate mixture into an ungreased 9 x 13-inch baking pan.

4. Preheat the oven to 325°F. In a medium bowl, beat the cream cheese until smooth. Gradually beat in the milk, egg, and vanilla.

Pour over the crust and sprinkle with the reserved crumbs.

5. Bake until lightly browned, 25 to 30 minutes. Cool.

6. Refrigerate until completely chilled, about 3 hours. Cut into bars and store in the refrigerator.

Personalize It!

For a lower-calorie dessert, use reduced-fat cream cheese (Neufchâtel cheese) and fat-free sweetened condensed milk.

MIXED NUT BARS

SECRET INGREDIENT:
butterscotch chips

Here's a way to take that can of mixed nuts in your cupboard to new heights of flavor. Mix them with melted butterscotch chips and bake them on a sweet pastry crust. These addictive salty-sweet bars will become your new favorite afternoon snack!

Prep Time: 15 min **Cook Time:** 25 min **Makes** 3 1/2 doz

CRUST

1 1/2 cups all-purpose flour

3/4 cup firmly packed brown sugar

1/4 teaspoon salt

1/2 cup (1 stick) cold unsalted butter or margarine

TOPPING

1 can (11 1/2 ounces) mixed nuts

1 cup butterscotch chips

1/2 cup light corn syrup

2 tablespoons unsalted butter or margarine

1. Preheat the oven to 350°F.

2. For the crust, combine the flour, brown sugar, and salt in a medium bowl. Cut in the butter or margarine until the mixture resembles coarse crumbs.

3. Press into a greased 9 x 13-inch baking pan and bake for 10 minutes.

4. For topping, sprinkle the baked crust with the nuts. Melt the butterscotch chips in a small microwavable bowl on medium power for 3 minutes, stopping to stir every minute. Add the corn syrup and butter or margarine and mix well. Pour over the nuts.

5. Bake for 10 minutes longer. Cool.

Personalize It!

Use your favorite salted nuts, such as cashews, peanuts, almonds, and walnuts. If you can, avoid mixes that include very large nuts such as Brazil nuts. These are harder to cut into bars once baked into this dessert.

CHERRY-NUT RUGELACH

SECRET INGREDIENT:
cherry preserves

Rugelach is a decadent treat, and the best ones are almost always homemade. Typically they are filled with raisins, chocolate, or cinnamon and sugar, but this version goes in another direction and takes full advantage of the tangy-sweet flavor of cherry preserves.

Prep Time: 45 min **Cook Time:** 20 min **Makes** 4 doz

1 cup (2 sticks) unsalted butter, softened

8 ounces cream cheese, at room temperature

1/2 cup sugar

3 cups all-purpose flour

1/2 teaspoon salt

3/4 cup cherry preserves

1 cup very finely chopped walnuts

1. Combine the butter and cream cheese in a medium bowl. With an electric mixer, beat on high speed until light, 1 to 2 minutes.

2. Add the sugar and beat on medium,

stopping to scrape down the bowl, until combined, 1 to 2 minutes. Stop the mixer and add the flour and salt and mix on low speed until a rough dough forms, about 2 minutes.

3. Turn the dough out onto a lightly floured surface and knead until smooth, 4 or 5 times.

4. Divide the dough into 8 pieces and form into balls. Flatten each ball into a 3-inch disk and wrap in plastic. Chill at least 3 hours or overnight.

5. Preheat the oven to 350°F.

6. Remove from the refrigerator and, working a disk at a time, roll the dough between pieces of floured wax paper to a 7-inch-diameter circle. Remove the wax paper and spread each disk with 4 teaspoons of the preserves and 2 tablespoons of the nuts.

7. Cut each circle into six wedges. Starting at the outside edge, roll each wedge up tightly jellyroll–style. Place rolls, tip pointing down, on an ungreased baking sheet and form into crescent shapes.

8. Bake until lightly browned, 20 to 22 minutes. Remove from the oven and allow to cool on the baking sheet for 10 minutes. Loosen the cookies with a small spatula, if necessary. Store in an airtight container until ready to serve.

that's **ingenious**

Need cookies on hand for the holidays? Make a batch or two of these rugelach. Cool completely, then freeze in zip-close freezer bags for up to 3 months. Thaw before serving.

extraordinary cakes and pies

RED VELVET DEVIL'S CAKE

SECRET INGREDIENT:

tomato juice

Think of this as a red velvet cake crossed with a rich devil's food cake. The secret to the cake's moist crumb is nothing other than tomato juice. The acidity of the tomato balances the deep flavor of the chocolate. *See photograph on page 190.*

Prep Time: 25 min **Cook Time:** 22 min **Serves** 12

CAKE

1 1/2 cups cake flour

1/2 cup cocoa powder

1 teaspoon baking powder

1/2 teaspoon baking soda

1/4 teaspoon salt

3/4 cup (1 1/2 sticks) unsalted butter, softened

1 1/2 cups sugar

3 large eggs

1 1/2 teaspoons vanilla extract

1 teaspoon red food coloring

1 cup tomato juice

FROSTING

3/4 cup (1 1/2 sticks) unsalted butter, softened

12 ounces cream cheese, at room temperature

2 teaspoons vanilla extract

3 cups confectioners' sugar

1. Preheat the oven to 350°F. Coat two round 9-inch cake pans with cooking spray then lightly dust with some flour.

2. For cake, sift together, twice, the flour, cocoa powder, baking powder, baking soda, and salt in a large bowl.

3. In a large bowl with an electric mixer, beat the butter and sugar on high speed until light and fluffy, 2 to 3 minutes. Beat in the eggs, one at time, scraping down the bowl in between. Beat in the vanilla and food coloring until well-combined.

4. With the mixer on low speed, beat in the flour mixture and the tomato juice in three alternating additions until well-combined. Divide the batter between the two baking pans.

5. Bake on the center rack of the oven until a toothpick inserted into the center comes out clean, 22 to 25 minutes. Cool the cakes in the pans on a wire rack for 10 minutes. Turn the cakes out onto the wire rack and cool completely, about 1 hour.

6. Meanwhile, for frosting, combine the butter and cream cheese in a medium bowl. With an electric mixer, beat on high speed until smooth, 1 to 2 minutes. Reduce the speed to low and beat in the vanilla and the confectioners' sugar until smooth.

7. To assemble, place one cake layer, flat side up, on a platter. Spread 1 cup of the frosting over the top of the cake. Top with the second cake layer, flat side down. Spread the remaining frosting over the top and sides of the cake. Cut into 12 wedges and serve.

that's **ingenious**

This easy cake can be made up to 2 days before serving if wrapped with plastic and stored in the refrigerator. To keep the frosting from sticking, use a few toothpicks inserted into the top and sides of the cake to keep the plastic wrap away from the cake. Let the cake stand for 1 hour to come to room temperature before serving.

PEANUT BUTTER CHOCOLATE CAKE

SECRET INGREDIENT:
coffee

This chocolate sheet cake won't last long in your house. A combination of cream cheese and peanut butter gives it a finger-licking-good frosting. And strong brewed coffee deepens the dark flavor of the chocolate cake.

Prep Time: 15 min   **Cook Time:** 35 min   **Serves** 12

CAKE

2 cups all-purpose flour

2 cups sugar

2/3 cup cocoa powder

2 teaspoons baking soda

1 teaspoon baking powder

1/2 teaspoon salt

2 eggs

1 cup milk

2/3 cup vegetable oil

1 teaspoon vanilla extract

1 cup strong brewed coffee,
   room temperature

FROSTING

1 package (3 ounces) cream cheese, softened

1/4 cup creamy peanut butter

2 cups confectioners' sugar

2 tablespoons milk

1/2 teaspoon vanilla extract

1. Preheat the oven to 350°F.

2. For cake, combine the flour, sugar, cocoa powder, baking soda, baking powder, and salt in a large bowl. Add the eggs, milk, oil, and vanilla, then beat for 2 minutes. Stir in the coffee (batter will be thin).

3. Pour into a greased 9 x 13-inch baking pan. Bake until a wooden pick inserted near the center comes out clean, 35 to 40 minutes. Cool completely on a wire rack.

4. For frosting, beat the cream cheese and peanut butter in a medium bowl until smooth. Beat in the confectioners' sugar, milk, and vanilla. Spread over the cake. Cut into 12 squares and serve.

One More Notch! To dress up the cake, sprinkle it with miniature chocolate chips or a mixture of chocolate chips and finely chopped peanuts.

ORANGE BLOSSOM CAKE

SECRET INGREDIENT:
applesauce

Here's a sunny-tasting cake made rich with buttermilk, chopped nuts, dates, and orange zest. Applesauce makes the cake extra moist and tender, and an orange glaze adds an uplifting citrus flavor.

Prep Time: 20 min   **Cook Time:** 1 hr   **Serves** 10

CAKE

1/2 cup (1 stick) unsalted butter
   or margarine, softened

1 cup sugar

1/2 cup applesauce

2 eggs

1 tablespoon grated orange zest

2 1/2 cups all-purpose flour

1 teaspoon baking powder

1 teaspoon baking soda

1/4 teaspoon salt

1 cup buttermilk

1 cup chopped dates

1 cup chopped almonds, walnuts,
   or pecans

GLAZE

1 cup sugar

1/2 cup orange juice

1. Preheat the oven to 350°F.

2. For cake, cream the butter or margarine and sugar in a large bowl. Add the applesauce, eggs, and orange zest. Mix well.

3. In a medium bowl, combine the flour, baking powder, baking soda, and salt. Add to the creamed mixture alternately with buttermilk and mix well. Fold in the dates and nuts.

4. Pour into a greased 9-inch springform pan. Bake until a toothpick inserted near the center comes out clean, 55 to 60 minutes.

5. For glaze, combine the sugar and orange juice in a small saucepan. Bring to a boil, then pour over the cake while they are both hot. Cool completely in the pan. Cut into 10 slices and serve.

RICH AND MOIST CHOCOLATE BUNDT CAKE

SECRET INGREDIENT:
sour cream

Everyone has their favorite chocolate cake, and most folks claim that their recipe is the best. You be the judge of this one. Sour cream keeps it incredibly rich and moist.

Prep Time: 15 min   **Cook Time:** 40 min   **Serves** 12

Dry bread crumbs

2 1/4 cups all-purpose flour

1/2 cup cocoa powder

1 teaspoon baking powder

1/2 teaspoon baking soda

1/2 teaspoon salt

1/2 cup (1 stick) unsalted butter, softened

1 1/2 cups firmly packed dark brown sugar

4 large eggs

3/4 cup sour cream

2 teaspoons vanilla extract

1. Preheat the oven to 350°F. Coat a 12-cup tube or Bundt pan with cooking spray.

2. Add enough bread crumbs to coat the pan, swirling them around until they adhere.

3. In a medium bowl, whisk together the flour, cocoa, baking powder, baking soda, and salt.

4 In a large bowl, beat the butter and brown sugar with an electric mixer on medium speed until well-blended, about 5 minutes. Beat in the eggs one at a time, making sure to incorporate each well.

5. Decrease the mixer speed to low and beat in the flour mixture alternately with the sour cream in three additions. Beat in the vanilla.

6. Scrape into the baking pan and bake until a toothpick inserted into the center comes out with only a few moist crumbs, 40 to 50 minutes.

7. Cool in the pan on a wire rack for 10 minutes, then turn out onto the rack to cool completely. Cut into 12 slices and serve.

that's **ingenious**

Cakes are usually reserved for special occasions. There's always so much to do to prepare for the occasion that store-bought cake sometimes takes the place of homemade. Get a jump on things by making this cake up to 1 month ahead. Cool the cake completely then wrap it in plastic and foil and store in the freezer. Bring to room temperature before serving.

ORANGE-ROSEMARY BUNDT CAKE

SECRET INGREDIENT:
olive oil

Remarkably easy to make, this aromatic cake can be served for dessert or brunch. Olive oil makes it moist and rich, though you never actually taste it.

Prep Time: 20 min   **Cook Time:** 40 min   **Serves** 12

3 cups all-purpose flour

2 cups sugar

2 tablespoons finely chopped fresh rosemary

2 1/2 teaspoons baking powder

1/2 teaspoon baking soda

1/2 teaspoon salt

4 large eggs

1 cup olive oil

1/2 cup milk

1/3 cup plus 4 1/2 teaspoons orange juice

1 tablespoon grated orange zest

1 cup confectioners' sugar

1. Preheat the oven to 350°F. Coat a 10-inch Bundt or tube pan with cooking spray and dust with a little flour.

2. Combine the sugar, rosemary, baking powder, baking soda, and salt in a medium bowl. With an electric mixer on low speed, beat in the eggs, oil, milk, 1/3 cup of the orange juice, and orange zest until well-combined. Pour into the pan.

3. Bake on the center rack of the oven until a toothpick inserted into the center of the cake comes out clean, 40 to 45 minutes. Cool in the pan on a wire rack for 15 minutes, then remove from the pan and cool on the wire rack for 30 minutes.

4. Stir together the confectioners' sugar and the remaining 4 1/2 teaspoons of orange juice in a small bowl. With a spoon, drizzle the glaze over the top of the cake and let stand for 5 minutes. Cut into 12 slices and serve.

One More Notch! For a more intense citrus flavor, substitute 2 tablespoons lemon juice for 2 tablespoons of the orange juice and add 1 tablespoon lemon zest to the batter.

RED CHOCOLATE BUNDT CAKE

SECRET INGREDIENT:
beets

Beets are so sweet that they are often processed into granulated sugar. It may sound odd, but pureed cooked beets perfectly complement the bittersweet taste of chocolate and give chocolate cakes an attractive red hue.

Prep Time: 15 min   **Cook Time:** 50 min   **Serves** 16

1 cup (2 sticks) unsalted butter or margarine, softened, divided

1 1/2 cups firmly packed dark brown sugar

3 eggs

4 squares (1 ounce each) semi-sweet chocolate

2 cups pureed cooked beets

1 teaspoon vanilla extract

2 cups all-purpose flour

2 teaspoons baking soda

1/4 teaspoon salt

Confectioners' sugar

1. Preheat the oven to 375°F.

2. In a medium bowl, cream 3/4 cup of the butter or margarine and the brown sugar. Add the eggs and mix well.

3. Melt the chocolate with the remaining butter or margarine in a small microwavable bowl on medium power for 3 minutes, stopping to stir every minute until smooth. Cool slightly. Blend the chocolate mixture, beets, and vanilla into the creamed mixture (mixture will appear separated).

4. Combine the flour, baking soda, and salt. Add to the creamed mixture and mix well.

5. Pour into a greased and floured 10-inch fluted tube or Bundt pan. Bake until a toothpick inserted near the center comes out clean, 45 to 55 minutes.

6. Cool in the pan for 10 minutes before removing to a wire rack. Cool completely. Dust with confectioners' sugar. Cut into 16 slices and serve.

One More Notch! For a richer chocolate flavor, use bittersweet chocolate instead of semi-sweet and add 1/3 cup cocoa powder along with the flour.

SEATTLE CHIFFON CAKE

SECRET INGREDIENT:
coffee

Chiffon cakes tend to feature delicate aromas such as lemon. This cake takes a different route to flavor with rich-tasting cocoa powder, cinnamon, and brewed espresso. Walnut oil gives the cake a delightfully nutty quality, but you could also use extra-light olive oil or canola oil. *See photograph on page 173.*

Prep Time: 15 min	**Cook Time:** 45 min	**Serves** 16

2 1/4 cups cake flour

1 1/2 cups sugar

1 tablespoon baking powder

3/4 teaspoon ground cinnamon

1/2 teaspoon salt

1/2 cup walnut oil, extra-light olive oil, or canola oil

2 large eggs, separated, plus 4 large egg whites

3/4 cup brewed espresso or other dark-roast coffee, at room temperature

2 tablespoons unsweetened cocoa powder

1 teaspoon vanilla extract

1/2 teaspoon cream of tartar

Confectioners' sugar

1. Preheat the oven to 325°F.

2. Stir together the flour, sugar, baking powder, cinnamon, and salt in a medium bowl.

3. Whisk the walnut, olive, or canola oil with the egg yolks, espresso or coffee, cocoa powder, and vanilla together in a large bowl until smooth. Fold the flour mixture into the egg mixture until well-combined.

4. Beat the 6 egg whites until frothy in a small bowl. Beat in the cream of tartar and continue beating until stiff peaks form. Gently fold egg whites into the batter.

5. Spoon the batter into an ungreased 10-inch tube or Bundt pan. Bake until a toothpick inserted in the center comes out clean, about 45 minutes.

6. Invert the pan to cool. Once cooled, run a metal spatula around the inner and outer edges of the cake and invert it onto a serving plate. Dust the cake with confectioners' sugar. Cut into 16 slices and serve.

One More Notch! To enhance the chocolate and coffee flavors, top the cake with a mocha glaze instead of dusting with confectioners' sugar. Combine 2 cups confectioners' sugar with 2 tablespoons brewed espresso or strong coffee and 1/2 teaspoon vanilla extract. Add additional espresso by the teaspoonful, if necessary, until the glaze can be drizzled over the cake.

FOOLPROOF POUND CAKE

SECRET INGREDIENT:
cream cheese

With only six ingredients and no special baking talent required, this cake is truly foolproof. Cream cheese and butter combine to make a tender cake with a velvety, tight crumb. Serve at tea time, for dessert, or toast thick slices and spread with jam as a snack.

Prep Time: 15 min **Cook Time:** 1 hr 30 min **Serves** 12

1 1/2 cups (3 sticks) unsalted butter (no substitutes), softened

1 package (8 ounces) cream cheese, at room temperature

2 1/3 cups sugar

6 eggs, at room temperature

3 cups all-purpose flour

1 teaspoon vanilla extract

1. Preheat the oven to 300°F.

2. In a large bowl, cream the butter and cream cheese. Gradually add the sugar, beating until light and fluffy, 5 to 7 minutes.

3. Add the eggs, one at a time, beating well after each addition.

4. Gradually add the flour and beat just until blended. Stir in the vanilla.

5. Pour into a greased and floured 10-inch tube or Bundt pan. Bake until a toothpick inserted into the center comes out with only moist crumbs, about 1 1/2 hours.

6. Cool in the pan for 15 minutes before removing to a wire rack to cool completely. Cut into 12 slices and serve.

Personalize It!

To make lemon-poppy seed pound cake, add 2 tablespoons grated lemon zest and 6 tablespoons poppy seeds to the batter along with the vanilla.

PUMPKIN-PECAN CAKE

SECRET INGREDIENT:
vanilla wafers

If you need a three-layer cake that's not the same old chocolate or vanilla variety, give this one a try. Each layer has a surprisingly nutty-tasting crust made with pecans and vanilla wafer cookies.

Prep Time: 30 min **Cook Time:** 30 min **Serves** 16

CRUST

2 cups crushed vanilla wafers (about 50)

1 cup chopped pecans

3/4 cup (1 1/2 sticks) unsalted butter or margarine, softened

CAKE

1 box (18 1/4 ounces) spice cake mix

1 can (16 ounces) solid-pack pumpkin

1/4 cup (1/2 stick) unsalted butter or margarine, softened

4 eggs

FILLING

2/3 cup unsalted butter or margarine, softened

1 package (3 ounces) cream cheese, softened

3 cups confectioners' sugar

2 teaspoons vanilla extract

1/2 cup caramel ice cream topping

1. Preheat the oven to 350°F.

2. For crust, beat the cookies, pecans, and butter or margarine in a medium bowl with an electric mixer on medium speed until crumbly, about 1 minute. Press into 3 greased and floured 9-inch round cake pans.

3. For cake, beat the cake mix, pumpkin, butter or margarine, and eggs in a medium bowl until well-blended, 3 minutes. Spread over the crust in each pan.

4. Bake until a wooden pick inserted near the center comes out clean, about

30 minutes. Cool in the pans for 10 minutes, then invert the cakes to remove from the pans then invert again and cool completely on the wire racks.

5. For filling, combine the butter or margarine and cream cheese in a small bowl. Add the sugar and vanilla, then beat on medium speed until light and fluffy, about 3 minutes.

6. Stack the cake layers, crumb-side down, on a cake plate, thinly spreading the filling between each layer. Spread the remaining filling over the sides of cake. Spread the caramel topping over the top of the cake, allowing some to drip down the sides. Cut into 16 slices and serve. Store in the refrigerator.

One More Notch! To enhance the autumnal flavors, replace 1 cup of the confectioner's sugar in the filling with 1/2 cup pure maple syrup. Mix a little maple syrup into the caramel topping before drizzling it over the cake, too.

CINNAMON-NUT STREUSEL COFFEECAKE

SECRET INGREDIENT:
ripe bananas

Why throw out bananas that are riper than you like? They make a great flavor addition to this coffeecake.

Prep Time: 20 min   **Cook Time:** 1 hr   **Serves** 12

1 3/4 cups firmly packed light brown sugar, divided

1 cup chopped pecans

2 teaspoons ground cinnamon

2 cups all-purpose flour

2 teaspoons baking powder

1/2 teaspoon baking soda

1/4 teaspoon salt

10 tablespoons unsalted butter or margarine, softened

2 large eggs

4 ripe bananas, mashed (about 1 cup)

2/3 cup buttermilk

1/2 cup white chocolate morsels

1. Preheat the oven to 350°F. Coat an 8-inch square baking dish with cooking spray and dust lightly with flour.

2. Combine 3/4 cup of the brown sugar, the pecans, and cinnamon in a small bowl. Mix well and set aside.

3. Combine the flour, baking powder, baking soda, and salt in a large bowl.

4. Combine the remaining 1 cup brown sugar and butter or margarine in a medium bowl. With an electric mixer, beat on medium speed until light and fluffy. Beat in the eggs, stopping to scrape down the sides of the bowl.

5. Add the bananas and buttermilk. Mix until well-combined. With the mixer on low speed, add the flour mixture and mix until well-combined, 1 to 2 minutes.

6. Spread half the batter in the baking dish and sprinkle with half the pecan mixture and the white chocolate morsels. Top with the remaining batter then sprinkle the top with the remaining pecan mixture.

7. Bake the coffeecake until a toothpick inserted into the center comes out clean, 60 to 65 minutes. Transfer to a wire rack and cool for 30 minutes. Cut into 12 slices and serve.

Personalize It!

If you don't care for white chocolate morsels, substitute an equal amount of semi-sweet or bittersweet chocolate chips. For extra chocolatyness, sprinkle the top with 1/2 cup chocolate morsels about 5 minutes before removing the coffeecake from the oven.

CAKES AND PIES

HONEY PECAN CHEESECAKE

maple extract

If you're a fan of pecans, you'll love them in the crust and the filling of this sweetly aromatic cheesecake. Maple extract combined with vanilla extract gives the filling an extra blast of aroma.

Prep Time: 25 min   **Cook Time:** 55 min   **Serves** 12

CRUST

1 cup vanilla wafer crumbs

5 tablespoons unsalted butter or margarine, melted

2 tablespoons sugar

1/4 cup ground pecans

FILLING

3 packages (8 ounces each) cream cheese, softened

1 cup firmly packed dark brown sugar

3 eggs

2 tablespoons all-purpose flour

1 tablespoon maple extract

1 teaspoon vanilla extract

1/2 cup chopped pecans

TOPPING

1/4 cup honey

1 tablespoon unsalted butter or margarine

1 tablespoon water

1/2 cup chopped pecans

1. Preheat the oven to 350°F.

2. For crust, combine the cookie crumbs, butter or margarine, sugar, and pecans in a medium bowl. Press onto the bottom only of a greased 9-inch springform pan. Refrigerate until the filling is ready.

3. For filling, beat the cream cheese and brown sugar in a medium bowl. Add the eggs and beat until smooth. Add the flour, maple extract, and vanilla and mix well. Stir in the pecans.

4. Pour into the crust. Bake until the center is nearly set, 50 to 55 minutes. Turn off the oven, open the door, and let stand in the oven for 1 hour.

5. Remove from the oven and cool completely. Refrigerate for several hours or overnight.

6. For topping, combine the honey, butter or margarine, and water in a small saucepan. Cook and stir over medium heat for 2 minutes. Add the pecans and cook 2 minutes longer (mixture will be thin).

7. Spoon the topping over the cheesecake. Carefully remove the sides of the pan before serving. Refrigerate leftovers.

Personalize It!
To make maple pecan cheesecake, replace the honey with pure maple syrup and omit the water. ✳

MOCHA CUPCAKES

mayonnaise

There are plenty of reasons to bake up a batch up chocolate cupcakes. Mix some instant coffee into the frosting and—shazaam!—you have mocha cupcakes. But the real surprise here is the ultra-tender crumb achieved by using mayonnaise in place of eggs and butter.

Prep Time: 20 min   **Cook Time:** 20 min   **Makes** 18

CUPCAKES

1 cup boiling water

1 cup regular mayonnaise (no substitutes)

1 teaspoon vanilla extract

2 cups all-purpose flour

1 cup sugar

1/2 cup cocoa powder

2 teaspoons baking soda

3/4 cup confectioners' sugar

1/4 cup cocoa powder

1/2 to 1 teaspoon instant coffee granules

Pinch of salt

1 1/2 cups whipping cream

1. Preheat the oven to 350°F.

2. For cupcakes, combine the water, mayonnaise, and vanilla in a large bowl.

3. In a medium bowl, combine the flour, sugar, cocoa, and baking soda. Add to the mayonnaise mixture and beat until mixed.

4. Fill greased or paper-lined muffin cups two-thirds full. Bake until a wooden pick inserted near the center of a muffin comes out clean, 20 to 25 minutes. Cool in the tins for 10 minutes, then remove to wire racks and cool completely.

5. For frosting, combine the sugar, cocoa, coffee, and salt, to taste, in a medium bowl. Stir in the cream, then cover and chill with the beaters of an electric mixer for 30 minutes (cold beaters help the cream whip up faster).

6. Beat the frosting until stiff peaks form. Frost the cupcakes.

Personalize It!

To make mocha cake instead of cupcakes, use two greased 8-inch round cake pans instead of the muffin cups. Frost between the layers and on the sides and top of the cake. Prepared this way, the dessert yields 12 servings instead of 18. ❄

CHOCOLATE TOFFEE CUPCAKES

SECRET INGREDIENT:

Hershey's SKOR candy

Toffee is a traditional British candy made by cooking sugar and butter with some water until the sugar caramelizes and browns. To skip the hassle of making toffee candy from scratch, this recipe uses Hershey's SKOR candy toffee bits. The delightfully crunchy bits add flavor to the cupcakes and frosting, and serve as a decorative topping.

Prep Time: 25 min   **Cook Time:** 20 min   **Makes** 18

CUPCAKES

1 1/2 cups all-purpose flour

1 cup sugar

1/4 cup cocoa powder

1 teaspoon baking soda

1 cup water

1/4 cup vegetable oil

1 tablespoon vinegar

1 teaspoon vanilla extract

1/2 cup Hershey's SKOR toffee bits

FROSTING

1 1/2 cups confectioners' sugar

1/3 cup cocoa powder

1/3 cup unsalted butter or margarine, softened

3 tablespoons milk

3/4 teaspoon vanilla extract

3/4 cup Hershey's SKOR toffee bits, divided

1. Preheat the oven to 350°F.

2. For cupcakes, in a large bowl, combine the flour, sugar, cocoa powder, and baking soda. Stir in the water, oil, vinegar, and vanilla until smooth. Add the toffee bits.

3. Fill paper-lined muffin cups two-thirds full. Bake until a toothpick inserted in the center comes out clean, 20 to 25 minutes. Remove to wire racks to cool completely.

4. For frosting, combine confectioners' sugar and cocoa powder in a medium bowl and set aside.

5. In a medium bowl, beat the butter or margarine and 1/2 cup of the cocoa mixture. Add the milk, vanilla, and the remaining cocoa mixture, and beat until the desired spreading consistency is reached. Stir in 1/2 cup of the toffee bits. Frost cupcakes.

6. Cover and refrigerate. Top with the remaining toffee bits before serving

BANANA CREAM PIE WITH HONEY-WAFER CRUST

SECRET INGREDIENT:

orange juice

A low-cholesterol cream pie? Is it possible? Absolutely! This one has all the flavor of a traditional custard pie but with less fat and cholesterol. There are plenty of luscious, healthy bananas in every bite, and a splash of orange juice gives the fruit a refreshing lift! *See photograph on page 182.*

Prep Time: 30 min	**Cook Time:** 5 min	**Serves** 8

CRUST

48 reduced-fat vanilla wafers
    (about 8 ounces)

2 tablespoons honey

2 tablespoons water

FILLING

1/2 cup sugar

1/3 cup all-purpose flour

Salt

3 cups reduced-fat (2%) milk

1/2 cup fat-free egg substitute

1 tablespoon unsalted butter or margarine

1 tablespoon vanilla extract

6 large bananas

1/4 cup orange juice

3 tablespoons apricot preserves, melted

1. Preheat the oven to 350°F. Lightly coat a 9-inch pie plate with nonstick cooking spray.

2. For crust, pulse the cookies, honey, and 2 tablespoons water in a food processor until fine crumbs form.

3. Press into the pie plate to shape the crust. Bake until set, about 10 minutes. Cool on a wire rack.

4. Meanwhile, for filling, whisk the sugar, flour, and salt in medium saucepan until blended. Slowly whisk in the milk and bring to a simmer over medium heat.

5. Measure the egg substitute in a 2-cup measure and whisk in about 1 cup of the hot milk mixture, then return the mixture to pan (this avoids curdling). Cook, whisking, until the mixture comes to a full boil and thickens.

6. Remove from the heat. Whisk in the butter or margarine and vanilla. Let cool for 15 minutes.

7. Slice the bananas and toss with the orange juice. Line the crust with one-third of the bananas and top with one-half of the filling. Repeat.

8. Arrange the remaining bananas on top in a spiral design, with the slices overlapping. Brush the preserves over the bananas. Cool for 30 minutes at room temperature, and then chill at least 4 hours, or overnight. Cut into 8 slices and serve.

One More Notch! Make a chocolate crust using reduced-fat chocolate wafers instead of vanilla wafers. Use strawberry jam in place of the apricot preserves.

TRIPLE PUMPKIN PIE

SECRET INGREDIENT:
pumpkin seeds

Some people just can't get enough pumpkin pie. If that's you, here's a pie with three forms of pumpkin to satisfy your craving. In addition to pureed pumpkin in the filling, the crust also includes pumpkin seed oil and ground pumpkin seeds.

Prep Time: 15 min   **Cook Time:** 55 min   **Serves** 10

CRUST

32 individual squares graham crackers (about 8 ounces), broken into pieces

1/4 cup hulled pumpkin seeds

2 tablespoons sugar

1/4 teaspoon salt

1 1/2 tablespoons pumpkin seed oil

3 tablespoons water

FILLING

1/4 teaspoon salt

1 can (15 ounces) solid-pack pumpkin

3/4 cup firmly packed light brown sugar

1 1/4 cups low-fat milk

2 large eggs

2 tablespoons bourbon or rum

2 teaspoons pumpkin pie spice

1. Preheat the oven to 375°F.

2. For crust, in a food processor, process the graham cracker pieces, pumpkin seeds, sugar, and salt until finely ground. Add the oil and water and process until thoroughly moistened.

3. Spray a 9-inch deep-dish glass or ceramic pie plate with nonstick cooking spray.

4. Press the crumb mixture into the bottom and up the sides of the pie plate. Bake until crisp and set, about 10 minutes. Cool on a wire rack.

5. For filling, combine the salt, pumpkin, brown sugar, milk, eggs, bourbon or rum, and pumpkin pie spice in a large bowl. Stir until well-combined.

6. Pour the pumpkin filling into the crust and bake until a knife inserted between the center and the edge of the pie comes out clean, 45 to 50 minutes.

7. Let the pie cool to room temperature, then refrigerate for at least 2 hours. Cut into 10 slices and serve.

Personalize It!

If you don't have pumpkin seed oil, use walnut oil, almond oil, avocado oil, or canola oil. ❄

GINGER-PEAR PIE

SECRET INGREDIENT:
Chinese five-spice powder

Ginger and pears are a natural combination that makes this pie a winner all on its own. The addition of Chinese five-spice powder— a combination of cinnamon, cloves, fennel seed, star anise, and Szechuan pepper—gives it yet another dimension of interest.

Prep Time: 20 min   **Cook Time:** 50 min   **Serves** 8

1 box (15 ounces) refrigerated pie crusts

3 pounds pears, peeled, cored, and cut into 1/4-inch-thick slices

3/4 cup sugar

3 tablespoons all-purpose flour

3 tablespoons chopped crystallized ginger

1 teaspoon vanilla extract

1/2 teaspoon Chinese five-spice powder

1. Preheat the oven to 400°F. Coat a 9-inch pie plate with cooking spray.

2. Line the pie plate with 1 of the pie crusts and set aside.

3. Combine the pears, sugar, flour, ginger, vanilla, and Chinese five-spice in a large bowl and toss well. Transfer into the crust.

4. Top with the remaining pie crust and crimp the edges to seal. Pierce the top of the pie a few times with the tip of a knife to vent. Bake until the crust is golden and the pie is bubbling, 50 to 55 minutes. Let cool for 30 minutes. Cut into 8 slices and serve.

Personalize It!

If you don't like pears, you can substitute apples. In the summertime, use ripe peaches or nectarines. Cranberry fans can also stir in 1/2 cup dried cranberries.

DOUBLE PEANUT PIE

SECRET INGREDIENT:
corn syrup

Peanut butter and roasted peanuts combine to create an extra-rich, salty-sweet peanut pie. This quick-to-fix dessert also includes two types of corn syrup that create a wonderfully gooey texture and deep, sweet flavor.

Prep Time: 10 min   **Cook Time:** 30 min   **Serves** 6

2 eggs

1/3 cup creamy peanut butter

1/3 cup sugar

1/3 cup light corn syrup

1/3 cup dark corn syrup

1/3 cup unsalted butter or margarine, melted

1 teaspoon vanilla extract

1 cup salted peanuts

1 unbaked pastry shell (9-inch)

1. Preheat the oven to 375°F.

2. In a large bowl, beat the eggs. Gradually add the peanut butter, sugar, light and dark corn syrup, butter or margarine, and vanilla. Mix well. Fold in the peanuts.

3. Pour into the crust. Bake until set, 30 to 35 minutes. Cool. Cut into 6 slices and serve.

GLAZED APPLE TART

SECRET INGREDIENT:
granola with raisins

With a rich butter crust and plenty of juicy apples, this tart is about as classic and comforting a dessert as you can get. What's different in this version is that the apples are crowned with an extra-crunchy almond topping made with store-bought granola cereal.
See photograph on page 161.

Prep Time: 20 min   **Cook Time:** 1 hr 5 min   **Serves** 16

3/4 cup (1 1/2 sticks) unsalted butter or margarine

2 cups all-purpose flour

1/2 cup sugar, divided

1 egg yolk, lightly beaten

3 tablespoons cold water

6 baking apples, peeled, seeded, and chopped

1 1/2 cups granola cereal with raisins

1/2 cup slivered almonds

1 cup confectioners' sugar

2 tablespoons lemon juice

1. Preheat the oven to 350°F.

2. In a large bowl, cut the butter into the flour and 1/4 cup of the sugar until the mixture resembles coarse crumbs.

3. Combine the egg yolk and water in a cup. Stir into the flour mixture and mix lightly.

4. Form the dough into a ball, press onto the bottom and sides of an ungreased 10 x 15-inch baking pan. Bake until lightly browned, about 15 minutes.

5. Sprinkle the apples over the crust. Combine the granola, almonds, and remaining sugar in a medium bowl. Sprinkle over the apples.

6. Bake until the apples are tender, about 50 minutes. Cool on a wire rack.

7. Combine the confectioners' sugar and lemon juice in a cup until smooth, then drizzle over the top. Cut into 16 slices and serve.

One More Notch! Serve the tart with scoops of vanilla ice cream and drizzles of caramel sauce to take it over the top.

BLUEBERRY-ORANGE TART

SECRET INGREDIENT:
black pepper

Oranges and blueberries make a winning combination, but the sweet acidity of both fruits always seems to need a little something. Black pepper, believe it or not, balances the flavors with just the right amount of spice.
See photograph on page 191.

Prep Time: 30 min   **Cook Time:** 40 min   **Serves** 8

CRUST

1 1/2 cups all-purpose flour

1/3 cup confectioners' sugar

2 teaspoons grated orange zest

1/2 teaspoon baking powder

1/2 teaspoon salt

1/4 cup plus 3 tablespoons olive oil

2 tablespoons fresh orange juice

FILLING

2 bags (12 ounces each) frozen unsweetened blueberries

1/4 cup fresh orange juice

1/2 cup sugar, divided

1/2 teaspoon freshly ground black pepper

1/8 teaspoon nutmeg

3 tablespoons cornstarch

1. For crust, in a large bowl, stir together the flour, confectioners' sugar, orange zest, baking powder, and salt. Add the oil and orange juice and stir until the mixture comes together into a soft dough.

2. Transfer the dough to a lightly floured work surface and knead until the dough forms a ball, about 10 times. Flatten into a disk, wrap in plastic, and let stand for 30 minutes at room temperature.

3. Preheat the oven to 350°F.

4. With your fingertips, gently press the dough onto the bottom and sides of a 9-inch tart pan with a removable bottom. Prick the bottom of the shell with a fork and line the pan with foil. Fill the foil with pie weights or dried beans, and bake the shell for 15 minutes. Remove the foil and weights, and bake the shell until golden brown, about 10 minutes more. Cool on a wire rack.

5. Meanwhile, for filling, in a medium saucepan, combine the blueberries, orange juice, 6 tablespoons of the sugar, the pepper, and nutmeg. Bring to a boil. Reduce to a simmer and cook for 5 minutes.

6. In a small bowl, stir together the remaining 2 tablespoons sugar and the cornstarch. Stir into the berries and cook until the berry mixture is thick, about 2 minutes. Remove from the heat and let cool to room temperature.

7. Spoon the blueberries into the shell, then chill the tart for 1 hour. Cut into 8 slices and serve.

One More Notch! Intensify the flavor of the tart by using a mixture of blueberries and raspberries.

extraordinary
frozen treats
and sweet surprises

CHOCOLATE ALMOND ICE CREAM WEDGES

SECRET INGREDIENT:
Amaretti cookies

Here's a fuss-free treat that looks impressive but takes only 15 minutes of your time. And it's fun to make—mostly, you roll balls of ice cream in crushed cookies! The Amaretti cookies add a wonderful almond flavor and delicious crunch.

Prep Time: 15 min   **Cook Time:** 0 min   **Serves** 4

1 cup crushed Amaretti cookies

1 pint chocolate ice cream

4 tablespoons prepared chocolate fudge topping

4 tablespoons whipped cream

Maraschino cherries

1. Place the cookies on a sheet of wax paper. Scoop the ice cream into 4 balls and roll the balls in the cookie crumbs. Place balls on a plate and refreeze until firm.

2. Spread a thin layer of the chocolate topping on four small plates. Cut each ball into 4 wedges. Arrange the wedges on each plate. Add a dollop of whipped cream and a maraschino cherry.

that's **ingenious**

Amaretti are small Italian almond cookies available in many grocery stores. If you can't find them, use crushed almond biscotti or Chinese almond cookies. Or change up the flavor by using crushed graham crackers.

CHOCOLATE ICE CREAM CAKE

SECRET INGREDIENT:
peanut butter

If you like to have desserts on hand for unexpected company or impromptu special occasions, try this one. It's easy, but people will think that you slaved for hours to make it. *See photograph on page 183.*

Prep Time: 25 min   **Cook Time:** 0 min   **Serves** 10

CRUST

1 cup vanilla wafer cookie crumbs

1/2 cup finely chopped peanuts

1/4 cup (1/2 stick) unsalted butter or margarine, melted

2 tablespoons confectioners' sugar

FILLING

6 cups chocolate ice cream, softened

1 package (3 ounces) cream cheese, softened

1/3 cup crunchy peanut butter

3/4 cup confectioners' sugar

1/4 cup milk

1/2 cup whipping cream, whipped

1. Line the bottom and sides of a 9 x 5-inch loaf pan with heavy-duty foil.

2. For crust, in a medium bowl, combine the cookie crumbs, peanuts, butter or margarine, and confectioner's sugar. Press half of the mixture into the bottom of the pan. Freeze for 15 minutes.

3. For filling, remove the pan from the freezer and spread half of the ice cream over the crust. Freeze until firm, about 1 hour.

4. Meanwhile, beat the cream cheese and peanut butter in a medium bowl. Add the sugar and milk; mix well. Fold in the whipped cream. Spread over the ice cream and freeze until firm, about 1 hour.

5. Spread with the remaining ice cream (pan will be very full). Press the remaining crumb mixture on the top. Cover and freeze for several hours or overnight.

6. Remove from the freezer 10 minutes before serving. Lifting by the foil, remove the loaf from the pan, then remove and discard the foil. Cut into slices using a serrated knife.

One More Notch! Drizzle the top crust alternately with chocolate sauce and caramel sauce to create a decorative pattern.

HOMEMADE ICE CREAM SANDWICHES

SECRET INGREDIENT:
chocolate cake mix

These corner-store favorites are easy to make at home. A box of chocolate cake mix can be quickly transformed into rectangles of soft cakelike cookies for sandwiching the ice cream. Just cut a rectangular box of ice cream into thick slices and you're ready to assemble. *See photograph on page 192.*

Prep Time: 50 min	Cook Time: 10 min	Makes 16

1 package (18 1/4 ounces) chocolate cake mix

1/4 cup shortening

1/4 cup (1/2 stick) unsalted butter or
   margarine, softened

1 egg

1 tablespoon water

1 teaspoon vanilla extract

1/2 gallon ice cream, any flavor
   (rectangular box)

1. Preheat the oven to 350°F.

2. In a large bowl, combine the cake mix, shortening, butter or margarine, egg, water,

and vanilla. Beat until well-blended. Divide into 4 equal parts.

3. Between wax paper, roll 1 part into a 6 x 10-inch rectangle. Remove the top piece of wax paper and flip the dough onto an ungreased baking sheet. Score the dough into 8 pieces, each 3 x 2 1/2 inches. Repeat with the remaining dough.

4. Bake until puffed, 8 to 10 minutes. Immediately cut along the scored lines and prick holes in each piece with a fork. Cool on the baking sheets.

5. Cut the ice cream into 16 slices, each 3 x 2 1/2 x 1 inch. Place the ice cream between 2 chocolate cookies and wrap in plastic. Freeze on a baking sheet overnight. Store in an airtight container.

that's **ingenious**

Make a double batch of these grab-and-go treats to keep in the freezer. Wrap each sandwich in plastic then store in an airtight plastic tub in the freezer for up to 2 months.

CARAMEL FRIED ICE CREAM

cornflakes

Fried ice cream is always a hit. The cool ice cream contrasted with the crunchy-fried coating never fails to excite the senses. Crushed cornflakes make the perfect sweet coating for these treats. We mix the cornflakes with coconut and cinnamon for extra flavor.

Prep Time: 30 min   **Cook Time:** 15 min   **Serves** 8

ICE CREAM BALLS

1 quart vanilla ice cream

1/4 cup whipping cream

2 teaspoons vanilla extract

2 cups flaked coconut, finely chopped

2 cups finely crushed cornflakes

1/2 teaspoon ground cinnamon

SAUCE

1 cup sugar

1/2 cup (1 stick) unsalted butter
   or margarine

1/2 cup evaporated milk

Oil for deep-fat frying

1. For ice cream balls, scoop the ice cream into 8 equal balls and place on a baking sheet. Cover and freeze until firm, about 2 hours.

2. In a medium bowl, combine the whipping cream and vanilla. In a large bowl, combine the coconut, cornflakes, and cinnamon.

3. Remove the ice cream from the freezer and, wearing plastic gloves, shape the ice cream into balls. Dip the balls into the cream mixture, then roll in the coconut mixture, making sure to coat entire surface.

Place the coated balls on a baking sheet. Cover and freeze until firm, at least 3 hours.

4. For sauce, heat the sugar in a heavy saucepan over medium heat until partially melted and golden, stirring occasionally. Add the butter or margarine. Gradually add the milk, stirring constantly. Cook and stir until the sauce is thick and golden, about 8 minutes. Keep warm.

5. Heat the oil in an electric skillet or deep-fat fryer to 375°F. Fry the ice cream balls until golden, about 30 seconds.

6. Drain on paper towels. Serve immediately with the caramel sauce.

Personalize It!

Vanilla isn't the only flavor in town. Use chocolate, strawberry, or your favorite flavor for these ice cream balls. Butter pecan is particularly good. ✻

BROWNIE BOMBE

SECRET INGREDIENT:

strawberry preserves

Some desserts are truly showstopping, and this is one of them. A dome of decoratively piped whipped cream encases rounded layers of fudgy walnut brownies, strawberry ice cream, and strawberry preserves. Bet you never thought that jar of jam in your cupboard could be used to make something so lavish!

Prep Time: 45 min **Cook Time:** 30 min **Serves** 16

1 package (21 1/2 ounces) fudge brownie mix

1/2 cup chopped walnuts

1/2 cup strawberry preserves

1 quart strawberry ice cream, softened

2 cups heavy cream

3 drops red food coloring (optional)

1/4 cup confectioners' sugar

Fresh strawberries and mint (optional)

1. Preheat the oven to 350°F. Grease two 8-inch round baking pans, then line with parchment paper. Grease the paper.

2. Prepare the brownie mix according to package directions for cakelike brownies. Stir in the walnuts. Pour the batter into the pans and bake until a toothpick inserted near the center comes out clean, about 30 minutes. Cool completely in pans.

3. Line a 1 1/2-quart metal bowl with foil. Cut and fit one brownie layer to evenly line the inside of the bowl (brownie may crack). Spread the preserves over the brownie layer and freeze for 15 minutes.

4. Remove the bowl from the freezer and add the ice cream, smoothing the top. Cover and freeze until the ice cream is firm, about 3 hours.

5. Place the remaining brownie layer on a serving plate. Remove the bowl from the freezer. Uncover and invert onto the plate, then remove the bowl and foil. Return to the freezer.

6. In a medium bowl, beat the cream and food coloring, if using, until soft peaks form, 3 to 4 minutes. Add the sugar and beat until stiff peaks form; set aside 1 1/2 cups.

7. Spread the remaining whipped cream over the top and sides of the bombe. Cut a small hole in the corner of a pastry bag or heavy-duty zip-close bag and insert a star pastry tip #8B or #20. Fill with the reserved whipped cream, then pipe a border along the base of the bombe. Holding the bag straight up and down, form stars on top. (If you don't have a pastry tip, you can still pipe the whipped cream through the hole in the bag, but it won't be as decorative.)

8. Add the strawberries and mint, if using, before serving.

One More Notch! For a nice touch, dip the strawberries in melted chocolate before decorating the dessert. Melt 1 cup chocolate chips in a small microwavable bowl on medium for 3 minutes, stopping to stir every minute. Dip in the strawberries and let cool on wax paper or upside-down in an empty egg carton to keep the chocolate in tact while drying. To make this dessert ahead, cover and store the unfrosted bombe in the freezer for up to 3 days. Spread and pipe with whipped cream 1 hour before serving.

FROZEN TREATS AND SWEET SURPRISES

SUNSHINE SHERBET

SECRET INGREDIENT:
canned evaporated milk

When milk is canned, it is heated to evaporate excess moisture, a process that partially cooks the milk and creates a wonderfully toasty, caramelized aroma. That's the secret behind the rich flavor of this simple lemon-orange sherbet.

Prep Time: 5 min   **Cook Time:** 10 min   **Makes** 2 qts

2 cups sugar

1 1/2 cups water

2 cups milk

2 cups heavy cream

1 1/2 cups orange juice

1 can (12 ounces) evaporated milk

1/3 cup fresh lemon juice

2 teaspoons grated orange peel

8 drops red food coloring (optional)

1/2 teaspoon yellow food coloring (optional)

1. In a large saucepan over medium heat, bring the sugar and water to a boil, then boil for 5 minutes. Remove from the heat and cool completely.

2. Add the milk, cream, orange juice, evaporated milk, lemon juice, orange peel, and food coloring, if using. Mix well.

3. Pour the sherbet into the cylinder of an ice cream freezer and freeze according to the manufacturer's directions. Remove from the freezer 10 minutes before serving.

One More Notch! To enhance the tropical flavors, add 1/2 teaspoon almond extract to the sugar and water just before removing from the heat.

that's ingenious !

If you don't have an ice cream maker, you can still make this sorbet, but it won't be quite as smooth. Transfer the mixture to an 11 x 7-inch glass baking dish and freeze until fairly firm, about 3 hours. Transfer to a food processor and pulse the mixture until smooth and serve immediately.

LIME SORBET

SECRET INGREDIENT:
tequila

With a splash of tequila, this grown-up version of lime sorbet becomes a frozen margarita. You might just want to salt your spoon between bites.

Prep Time: 10 min   **Cook Time:** 5 min   **Serves** 8

2 cups water

1 cup sugar

3/4 cup fresh lime juice

1/2 cup tequila

1/3 cup orange juice

1 teaspoon grated fresh lime zest

1. Combine the water and sugar in a medium saucepan over high heat. Bring to a boil, stirring until the sugar dissolves, and cook 2 minutes.

2. Remove from the heat and stir in the lime juice, tequila, orange juice, and lime zest. Cool completely.

3. Pour the sorbet into the cylinder of an ice cream freezer and freeze according to the manufacturer's directions.

FROZEN TREATS AND SWEET SURPRISES

PEAR GRANITA

SECRET INGREDIENT:
fennel seeds

Granitas are easy-to-make granular ice desserts that are great for dinner parties. The combination of pear and crushed fennel seeds gives this one a complex flavor that will have your guests raving. Make them guess your secret!

Prep Time: 15 min   **Cook Time:** 5 min   **Serves** 6

1/2 cup sugar

1/3 cup water

1 teaspoon fennel seeds, lightly crushed

2 cups pear nectar

1. Combine the sugar, water, and fennel seeds in a small saucepan over high heat. Bring to a boil, stirring until the sugar dissolves. Reduce the heat to medium and simmer 2 minutes. Remove from the heat and cool for 10 minutes. Transfer the syrup to a medium bowl and chill for 30 minutes.

2. Strain the syrup into a large glass measure. Add the pear nectar, mixing well. Pour into an 8-inch square glass baking dish and freeze for 30 minutes. Remove from the freezer and, with a fork, scrape any ice that has formed on the sides of the dish to the center. Return the pan to the freezer and repeat the process every 30 minutes until the mixture is icy and granular, 2 1/2 to 3 hours longer.

that's ingenious

To speed up the process, chill the syrup by setting the bowl in a larger bowl filled with ice water. Stir the syrup with a clean spoon every few minutes. Pear nectar is available in most grocery stores in the international or Mexican section.

APPLE STRUDEL

SECRET INGREDIENT:
sour cream

The filling in apple strudel is similar to that in apple pie. What makes strudel special is its tender, flaky dough made up of several paper-thin layers. A little acidity in the dough keeps it from becoming too tough. Sour cream adds just the right amount, along with satisfying richness.

Prep Time: 35 min   **Cook Time:** 55 min   **Makes** 3

STRUDEL

1 cup (2 sticks) cold unsalted butter or margarine

2 cups all-purpose flour

1 cup (8 ounces) sour cream

1/4 teaspoon salt

FILLING

2 cups dry bread crumbs

1/4 cup (1/2 stick) unsalted butter or margarine, melted

4 baking apples, peeled, seeded, and chopped

2 cups sugar

1 cup golden raisins

1/2 cup chopped pecans

2 teaspoons ground cinnamon

Confectioners' sugar (optional)

1. Preheat the oven to 350°F.

2. For strudel, cut the butter or margarine into the flour in a medium bowl until the mixture resembles coarse crumbs. Add the sour cream and salt; mix well. Shape into a ball, cover, and refrigerate at least 6 hours.

3. For filling, in a large bowl, combine the bread crumbs and butter or margarine. Add the apples, sugar, raisins, pecans, and cinnamon. Mix well and set aside.

4. Remove the dough from the refrigerator, divide it into thirds, and turn onto a floured board. Roll each third into a 12 x 15-inch rectangle.

5. Spoon the filling evenly onto the dough, spreading to within 1 inch of the edges. Roll up from one long side and pinch the seams and the ends to seal.

6. Carefully place the strudel, seam side down, on an ungreased baking sheet. Bake until light brown, 55 to 60 minutes. Cool completely on wire racks. Dust with confectioners' sugar, if using.

Personalize It!

To make pear strudel, replace the apples with pears and the pecans with almonds. ❄

BANANA BREAD PUDDING WITH BOURBON GLAZE

SECRET INGREDIENT:

cinnamon raisin bread

Among the umpteen variations, everyone has a favorite style of bread pudding. This one may soon become yours. Using cinnamon raisin bread cuts down on prep time and gives the pudding built-in flavor.

Prep Time: 15 min   **Cook Time:** 55 min   **Serves** 6

PUDDING

12 slices cinnamon raisin bread, cut into 1-inch squares

3 bananas, cut in half then halved lengthwise

1 cup heavy cream

4 eggs

1/3 cup sugar

1 teaspoon vanilla extract

GLAZE

2 tablespoons unsalted butter or margarine

1/2 cup heavy cream

1/4 cup sugar

1/3 cup maple syrup

1 tablespoon bourbon

1. Preheat the oven to 350°F. Coat an 8-inch square baking dish with cooking spray.

2. For pudding, arrange half of the bread in a layer in the bottom of the baking dish then arrange the bananas, cut side down, in a single layer over the bread. Top with the remaining bread.

3. Combine the cream, eggs, sugar, and vanilla in a small bowl and mix well. Pour over the bread and let stand 20 minutes.

4. Bake on the center rack in the oven until puffed, lightly browned, and the eggs are set, about 45 minutes. Remove from the oven and let cool for 10 minutes before cutting.

5. Meanwhile, for glaze, melt the butter or margarine in a small saucepan over medium-high heat. Add the cream, sugar, and maple syrup and bring to a boil, then continue boiling for 4 minutes. Remove from the heat and stir in the bourbon. Return to the stove, bring to a boil, then continue boiling for 1 minute.

6. To serve, place a square of bread pudding on a serving plate and spoon 2 tablespoons of the glaze on top.

One More Notch! Like nuts? Scatter 1/4 cup toasted chopped walnuts over the bananas. Take the recipe to another level by sautéing the bananas in a tablespoon of butter before layering them in the baking dish.

BLACKBERRY COBBLER

SECRET INGREDIENT:
raspberry juice

What's the difference between fruit crisp and fruit cobbler? Crisp has a crumbly topping and cobbler has a sweet biscuit topping. While there are many fruit choices—and combinations—that work well in either, we like blackberries, especially when enhanced with a little raspberry juice.

Prep Time: 15 min   **Cook Time:** 45 min   **Serves** 6

1/4 cup (1/2 stick) unsalted butter or margarine, softened

1/2 cup sugar

1 cup all-purpose flour

2 teaspoons baking powder

1/2 cup milk

2 cups fresh or frozen blackberries

3/4 cup raspberry juice

Ice cream or whipped cream (optional)

1. Preheat the oven to 350°F.

2. In a medium bowl, cream the butter and sugar.

3. In a small bowl, combine the flour and baking powder. Add to the creamed mixture alternately with the milk. Stir until just moistened.

4. Pour into a greased 1 1/2-quart baking pan. Sprinkle with blackberries. Pour raspberry juice over all.

5. Bake until golden brown, about 45 to 50 minutes.

6. Serve warm, topping with ice cream or whipped cream, if using.

that's **ingenious**

If you don't have raspberry juice, use cran-raspberry juice or apple juice.

BAKED ALMOND-STUFFED PEACHES

SECRET INGREDIENT:
Amaretti cookies

Try this recipe the next time peaches are in season. Stuffed with dried apricots, toasted almonds, and crushed Amaretti cookies to bind the filling together, peaches make a fabulous warm dessert. Vanilla ice cream is a natural go-with; ginger ice cream is even better. *See photograph on page 191.*

Prep Time: 30 min   **Cook Time:** 40 min   **Serves** 8

5 large ripe but firm peaches, divided

10 dried apricot halves, finely chopped

6 Amaretti cookies, crumbled

2 teaspoons almond extract

1 tablespoon brandy

1 large egg white

1/3 cup chopped, blanched almonds

1/4 cup firmly packed light brown sugar

Vanilla ice cream (optional)

1. Preheat the oven to 350°F.

2. Half-fill a large saucepan with water and bring to a boil over high heat. Cut 4 of the peaches in half (do not peel) and remove the pits. Slide the peaches into the boiling water and cook until they just begin to soften, about 2 minutes.

3. Using a slotted spoon, transfer the peaches onto paper towels to drain. Place the peaches, cut side up, in a 9 x 13-inch baking dish.

4. Peel, pit, and finely chop the remaining peach into a medium bowl. Add the apricots, cookie crumbs, almond extract, brandy, and egg white. Stir until thoroughly mixed.

5. Heat a small nonstick skillet over high heat for 1 minute, then add the almonds. Turn and toss them until golden and lightly

toasted, 2 to 3 minutes. Add the almonds to the fruit mixture and toss.

6. Spoon the mixture into the cavities of each peach half, heaping it up and pressing it together gently. Sprinkle with the brown sugar. Cover the baking dish with foil.

7. Bake until tender, about 25 minutes. Remove the foil, increase the oven temperature to 400°F, and bake until the topping is golden brown, 5 minutes longer.

8. Serve warm with ice cream, if using.

Personalize It!

To make raisin-stuffed apples, substitute red-skinned baking apples (such as Cortland, Jonathan, or Rome Beauty) for the peaches and 1/2 cup golden raisins for the apricots. Use 1 cup coconut macaroon crumbs instead of the Amaretti cookie crumbs, 1 teaspoon vanilla extract in place of almond extract, and light rum instead of brandy. Add 1 teaspoon ground cinnamon.

RASPBERRY AND VANILLA RISOTTO

SECRET INGREDIENT:
lemon zest

Think of this dessert as upscale rice pudding. Ultra-creamy Arborio is the rice, and it's flavored with a heady perfume of vanilla, raspberries, and lemon. Heavy cream drizzled over the top is the crowning touch.
See photograph on page 191.

Prep Time: 30 min **Cook Time:** 20 min **Serves** 6

3 1/2 cups milk

1 vanilla bean, split lengthwise

5 ounces Arborio rice

1 strip lemon zest

3 tablespoons light brown sugar

6 tablespoons slivered almonds

7 ounces fresh raspberries, divided

6 tablespoons heavy cream

Vanilla beans (optional)

1. Pour the milk into a heavy saucepan and add the vanilla bean. Sprinkle in the rice, stirring constantly. Bring to a boil over medium heat, stirring, then reduce the heat to simmer. Add the lemon zest and brown sugar. Cook, stirring frequently, until the rice is tender and the liquid is thick and creamy, 15 to 18 minutes.

2. Meanwhile, put the almonds in a small nonstick skillet and toast over low heat until lightly browned, 4 to 5 minutes. Set aside.

3. When the risotto has finished cooking, remove the vanilla bean and lemon zest. Stir in half of the raspberries. Remove from the heat and continue stirring until the fruit softens and begins to turn the risotto pink, 1 to 2 minutes.

4. Warm 6 small microwavable bowls in the microwave for 30 seconds. Spoon the raspberry risotto into the bowls and drizzle 1 tablespoon cream over each. Sprinkle the almonds over the top and add the remaining raspberries.

5. Decorate with vanilla beans, if using, and serve at once—the risotto thickens as it cools.

that's **ingenious**

If you don't have a vanilla bean, stir 2 to 3 teaspoons vanilla extract into the rice mixture along with the raspberries.

CHESTNUT BRANDY MOUSSE

SECRET INGREDIENT:
chocolate

Chestnut puree is always available during the holidays, and here's a fabulous way to use it. Whip it with heavy cream, sugar, and brandy to make a lusciously creamy cold dessert. Grated dark chocolate intensifies the flavors. *See photograph on page 192.*

Prep Time: 20 min   **Cook Time:** 0 min   Serves 4

1 can (9 ounces) unsweetened chestnut puree

2 tablespoons brandy

2 tablespoons confectioners' sugar

1 cup heavy cream

1 3/4 ounces dark, bitter chocolate, grated

1. In a large bowl, combine the chestnut puree, brandy, and confectioners' sugar. Beat together thoroughly, until the mixture is smooth, using either an electric beater or a handheld balloon whisk.

2. In a bowl, whip the cream until it holds soft peaks, then fold it into the chestnut mixture. Add half the chocolate to the mixture.

3. Spoon the cream into four glasses, sprinkle with the rest of the chocolate, and chill for 15 minutes before serving.

that's **ingenious**

Look for chestnut puree in the baking or nut aisle of your grocery store. Most markets carry it around the holidays. If you can't find it, make it at home. Put 1 cup shelled and peeled chestnuts (can use canned or jarred) in a small saucepan and cover with milk. Simmer over low heat until very tender, about 1 hour. Add more milk, as necessary, to keep the chestnuts covered. Puree in a small food processor or blender and press through a sieve.

ANISE PANNA COTTA

SECRET INGREDIENT:
tarragon

This silky smooth unbaked custard is the perfect way to end a sumptuous meal. Think of it as uptown pudding. Fresh tarragon and anise seeds lend the custard a subtle licorice flavor with very little effort.

Prep Time: 20 min   **Cook Time:** 5 min   **Serves** 8

2 cups heavy cream

1 cup milk

1/2 cup fresh tarragon, crushed

1/2 teaspoon anise seeds

1 envelope unflavored gelatin

1/4 cup water

1/2 cup sugar

1. Combine the cream and milk in a small saucepan over medium-high heat and bring to a simmer. Remove from the heat and stir in the tarragon and anise seeds; let stand for 15 minutes. Strain out the tarragon and anise seeds then return the milk mixture to the saucepan.

2. Sprinkle the gelatin over the water in a small bowl and let stand for 3 minutes.

3. Heat the milk mixture over medium heat and add the sugar, stirring, until dissolved. Remove from the heat and stir in the gelatin until dissolved. Divide the mixture among eight (6-ounce) custard cups. Cool to room temperature, about 30 minutes, then transfer to the refrigerator and chill until set, about 4 hours.

4. To serve, run the tip of a knife around the edge of each custard cup and dip the bottom into hot water for 15 seconds. Invert a plate

FROZEN TREATS AND SWEET SURPRISES

over the custard cup then flip over to allow the custard to fall onto the plate.

One More Notch! Gild the lily here with a simple raspberry fruit sauce. Stir 2 teaspoons fresh lime juice into 3/4 cup seedless raspberry jam and microwave briefly to help soften the jam. Spoon the warm sauce around the cool panna cotta.

CARAMEL CORN

SECRET INGREDIENT:

molasses

Molasses is one of those ingredients that most people have in the pantry but rarely use. Pull it out for this easy-to-make caramel corn. It's an addictive treat that owes its deep, dark flavor to molasses and dark brown sugar.

Prep Time: 15 min **Cook Time:** 1 hr 10 min **Serves** 6

3 tablespoons canola oil

1/2 cup popcorn kernels

1 cup firmly packed dark brown sugar

1/2 cup light corn syrup

1/2 cup (1 stick) unsalted butter

2 tablespoons molasses

1 1/2 teaspoons vanilla extract

1/2 teaspoon baking soda

1/2 teaspoon salt

1. Preheat the oven to 250°F and coat a large baking sheet with cooking spray.

2. Combine the oil and popcorn kernels in a large pot over medium-high heat and cook, shaking the pot often, until the kernels pop, 5 to 7 minutes. Transfer the popcorn to a large bowl.

3. Combine the brown sugar, corn syrup, butter, and molasses in a medium saucepan over medium heat and bring to a boil; stir once and continue boiling for 5 minutes.

Remove from the heat and stir in the vanilla, baking soda, and salt. Pour over the popcorn in a steady stream while stirring to evenly coat.

4. Transfer the popcorn to the baking sheet and bake on the center rack of the oven until the surfaces are dry, stirring every 15 minutes, about 1 hour. Remove from the oven and stir the popcorn to break up any large clumps. Cool for 15 minutes and serve, or cool completely and store in zip-close plastic bags.

that's **ingenious** !

To make the recipe even easier, use 12 cups store-bought unsalted popcorn instead of popping your own. Or use the same amount of microwave popcorn.

KICKIN' KETTLE CORN

SECRET INGREDIENT:

curry powder

Who says popcorn seasonings have to stop at butter and salt? Some people know that cayenne pepper is great on popcorn, but try curry powder, too! These spices mixed with the sweetness of sugar create out-of-this-world flavor. Make a double batch, and this kettle corn will disappear faster than you can fill another bowl. *See photograph on page 189.*

Prep Time: 5 min **Cook Time:** 5 min **Serves** 8

2/3 cup popcorn kernels

1/3 cup sugar

1/4 cup canola oil

1 teaspoon curry powder

1 teaspoon salt

1/8 teaspoon cayenne pepper

Combine the popcorn kernels, sugar, oil, curry powder, salt, and cayenne in a large pot over medium-high heat and cook, shaking the pot often, until the kernels pop, 5 to 7 minutes. Transfer to a large bowl. Cool for 2 minutes before serving.

Personalize It!

Swap cumin and coriander for the curry and cayenne. For a sweeter version, try using cinnamon and allspice. Vary the spices to suit your tastes. ❉

MIXED NUT BRITTLE

SECRET INGREDIENT:

cracked black pepper

Take ordinary nut brittle up a notch—or three!—with the surprising addition of cracked black pepper. Most snackers can't resist the combination of sweet, peppery, and salty.

Prep Time: 10 min   **Cook Time:** 20 min   **Serves** 24

2 cups sugar

1 cup water

1 cup light corn syrup

1/2 teaspoon salt

3 cups salted mixed nuts

2 tablespoons unsalted butter

2 teaspoons baking soda

2 teaspoons vanilla extract

1 teaspoon hot red-pepper sauce

1 teaspoon cracked black pepper

1/4 teaspoon crushed red-pepper flakes

1. Coat a large baking sheet with cooking spray.

2. Combine the sugar, water, and corn syrup in a medium saucepan over medium-high heat. Bring the mixture to a boil and cook until the sugar has dissolved and the temperature has reached 270°F on a candy thermometer, about 15 minutes.

3. Stir in the salt and nuts and cook, stirring, until the temperature reaches 300°F, 5 to 6 minutes longer.

4. Remove the pan from the heat and stir in the butter, baking soda, vanilla, red-pepper sauce, black pepper, and red-pepper flakes. Pour onto the baking sheet and spread with a spatula into as thin a layer as possible.

5. Let cool completely, about 1 hour, then break into smaller pieces to serve.

that's ingenious !

Make the nut brittle ahead of time to keep on hand for parties, snacking, or giving as gifts. Store in an airtight container in a cool place for up to 2 weeks.

{ extraordinary }
uses for everyday
pantry items

Be warned: Once you start reading this next section, you'll never stop! Here are more than 550 ingenious ways to use everyday pantry items in your cooking, organized A-to-Z by item. From applesauce to strawberry jam, peanut butter to potato chips, you'll discover that, with a little creativity, your cooking can be transformed merely by opening up your pantry doors.

❋Anchovies

To add a savory flavor to tomato sauce, add 1/4 teaspoon anchovy paste or mashed anchovies per cup of sauce. Don't stop at tomato sauces. Anchovies are the secret behind the savoriness of many sauces such as those in braised meats and vegetables.

For a one-of-a-kind twist on roasted chicken, slip a few anchovies under the skin before roasting. Or spread anchovy paste under the skin. The briny taste of the anchovies seasons the meat as it cooks, lending an incredible flavor boost.

To kick up the taste of tuna salad, stir in 1 to 2 teaspoons anchovy paste. A squeeze of lemon juice also blends well with anchovy paste and balances the saltiness with acidity.

For more complex tasting vinaigrettes, whisk 1/2 teaspoon mashed anchovy into the dressing. Taste the dressing before adding salt, as anchovies pack their own punch of sodium. You can even add anchovy to store-bought bottled dressing. Just pour the needed amount into a small bowl and whisk in the mashed anchovy.

For an Italian-style chicken salad sandwich, combine the following ingredients: 1 cup finely chopped cooked chicken breast, 4 finely chopped hard-cooked eggs, 1/3 cup mayonnaise, 1 can (2 ounces) drained and chopped anchovy fillets, 1 small grated onion, 1/4 teaspoon freshly ground black pepper, and a pinch of salt. Spread butter over your favorite sandwich bread and top with the chicken filling.

To give plain old couscous a more aromatic flavor, prepare a box (10 ounces) instant couscous according to the package directions. Drain 1 jar (6 ounces) roasted red peppers and cut into strips. Add to the couscous along with 3 tablespoons chopped fresh basil, 3 tablespoons grated Parmesan cheese, 8 chopped anchovy fillets, the juice of 1/2 lemon, 2 tablespoons extra-virgin olive oil, 1 minced garlic clove, 1/8 teaspoon salt, and 1/8 teaspoon freshly ground black pepper.

To make a Mediterranean-style sauce for pan-fried fish, remove the fish fillets after frying and transfer to a platter to keep warm. Add 1 tablespoon butter and 1 tablespoon olive oil to the skillet, and cook until the butter melts. Stir in 1 1/2 tablespoons tiny, well-drained capers, 3 chopped anchovy fillets, 2 tablespoons chopped fresh parsley, and 2 tablespoons fresh lemon juice. Cook for 1 minute over medium heat, then pour over pan-fried fish fillets. The anchovy, while not a dominant taste, adds an irreplaceable depth of flavor to the sauce.

✳Apple Cider

For an autumnal twist on steamed broccoli, use apple cider to make the sauce. Sauté 1/2 chopped onion in 1 tablespoon vegetable oil along with 1 teaspoon crumbled, fresh rosemary leaves until soft. Add 1/2 cup apple cider and boil until the liquid is reduced to a syrup that is about 2 tablespoons in volume. Add the steamed broccoli and toss until heated through. Drizzle with 1 teaspoon fresh lemon juice.

To mix up a sweet glaze for roasted pork chops, stir together 1/2 cup apple cider, 2 tablespoons dark rum, 2 tablespoons packed brown sugar, 1 teaspoon ground ginger, and 1/4 teaspoon ground allspice. Pour over four boneless pork chops and roast at 400°F for about 30 minutes. For more flavor, add a few sliced apples and some dried thyme.

For a wintertime sauce to accompany roasted chicken, sauté 2 thinly sliced apples in 2 teaspoons butter until the apples are soft, about 3 minutes. Add 1/2 cup apple cider and 1/2 cup chicken broth. Cook until slightly reduced in volume, about 3 minutes. Stir in 1/4 cup sliced scallions and cook 1 minute more. Serve with the chicken.

To make apple pot roast, use apple cider as the base liquid. Combine 1 1/3 cups apple cider, 3/4 cup dry white wine, and 1/3 cup fresh orange juice to use as the liquid instead of the broth, wine, or other liquid in your favorite recipe. Add 4 large minced garlic cloves, 1 cinnamon stick (3 inches long), and 1 teaspoon dried thyme for more flavor. Serve the pot roast with roasted potatoes, turnips, parsnips, and carrots.

To make a marinade and sauce for pork tenderloin, mix together:

1 cup apple cider	1 tablespoon Dijon mustard
6 ounces beer	1 teaspoon poultry seasoning
1/2 cup chopped onion	1/2 teaspoon salt
1/2 cup chopped fresh apple	1/4 teaspoon freshly ground
2 tablespoons vegetable oil	black pepper

Add 2 pounds of pork tenderloin and marinate in the refrigerator for 4 to 8 hours. Grill or broil the pork. Meanwhile, boil the marinade for 5 minutes, adding a little sauerkraut, if you like. The apples will fall apart and thicken the sauce. Serve with the pork.

To make a quick Asian-inspired sauce for chicken, fish, pork, or beef, combine 1 cup apple cider, 1/3 cup hoisin sauce, 2 teaspoons toasted sesame oil, and 1/8 teaspoon freshly ground black pepper in a small saucepan. Heat over medium heat until the liquid simmers.

❊Apples

To make richer-tasting pureed squash soup, add a cut-up apple to the soup and puree along with the other ingredients. Almost invariably, ingredients that grow in the same season make perfect partners in the kitchen. Apples and squash are an excellent example.

To make broccoli soup with a touch of sweetness, add apples, especially if you're making the soup in the fall. In a medium saucepan, cook 1 small, finely chopped onion in 2 tablespoons unsalted butter over medium heat until soft, about 5 minutes. Add 2 boxes (10 ounces each) frozen broccoli pieces, 2 finely chopped, peeled, and cored large apples, and 4 cups chicken broth. Cook until the apples and broccoli are soft, about 10 minutes. Season with 1/4 teaspoon salt and 1/8 teaspoon ground white or black pepper. Puree in a food processor or blender, then stir in 1/4 cup sour cream. This soup can be served hot or cold.

To spruce up a chicken salad sandwich, add 2 tablespoons finely chopped apples and 2 tablespoons chopped toasted pecans to 3/4 cup of your favorite chicken salad.

To give grilled cheese sandwiches a new twist, add a few thin slices of apple to each sandwich before toasting on the griddle.

To lend a sweet kiss to horseradish sauce, add some diced apple. Mix together mayonnaise, sour cream, prepared horseradish, and a generous handful of finely chopped tart apples, such as Granny Smith.

To salvage hardened brown sugar, put a slice of fresh apple in the bag and seal for 2 days.

To make better-tasting cranberry sauce for the Thanksgiving feast, add an apple. Combine the following ingredients in a medium saucepan: 1 bag (12 ounces) fresh cranberries, 3/4 cup sugar, 1/2 cup water, and 1 cinnamon stick (3 inches long). Bring to a boil over medium heat, then reduce the heat to low and simmer, uncovered, until most of the cranberries pop, about 8 minutes. Peel, core, and finely chop 1 McIntosh apple and add to the sauce.

Simmer until the apple is tender, about 5 minutes longer. Taste the sauce and add more sugar, if needed. Turn into a medium bowl, cool slightly, then cover and refrigerate until cold. Keeps for up to 1 week in the refrigerator.

Tidbit With more than 7,000 varieties, apples are one of the most diversified fruits on the planet. Growers are constantly developing new crossbreeds of apples in the search for better taste, color, and resiliency. As a result, many apple varieties are protected by patents. There is also a patent for French fries made from apples.

To put a sweet twist on fennel salad, mix in a couple chopped apples. Almost any salad will benefit from the gentle sweetness of apples. Combine 1 thinly sliced fennel bulb, 2 chopped apples, and 1/2 cup walnut pieces in a large bowl. Toss with a mixture of 1/3 cup olive oil, 1/3 cup apple juice, 1 tablespoon fresh lemon juice, 1 teaspoon ground fennel seed, 1/4 teaspoon salt, and 1/8 teaspoon freshly ground black pepper.

For the perfect autumn appetizer, make apple-cheddar pizza. Sprinkle a pizza pan with 1 tablespoon cornmeal and pat a prepared pizza dough (homemade or purchased) into the pan. Bake at 500°F on the lowest rack of the oven until lightly browned, about 5 minutes. Arrange 2 cored and thinly sliced apples over the dough and top with 4 thinly sliced large shallots (or substitute one thinly sliced small, mild onion). Sprinkle on 1/2 cup shredded cheddar cheese (2 ounces) and 1/2 cup shredded mozzarella cheese (2 ounces). Bake until the cheese is melted and the crust is golden brown, about 8 minutes longer. Cut into wedges and serve.

For a couscous dish that will warm you up in winter, top the cooked grain with apples and roasted vegetables. Heat 1 tablespoon olive oil in a Dutch oven over medium heat. Add 1 red onion cut into 8 wedges and cook for 5 minutes. Stir in:

3 cups cubed butternut squash (1 1/2 pounds)	3 garlic cloves, chopped
1 1/2 cups chopped rutabaga (about 1 1/4 pounds)	2 teaspoons ground cumin
3 carrots, sliced	2 teaspoons ground coriander
2 Granny Smith apples, peeled, cored, and cubed	1 can (15 ounces) chickpeas, rinsed and drained
	1 can (14 ounces) vegetable broth

Bring to a simmer. Cover and roast at 400°F until the vegetables are tender, about 45 minutes. Stir in 2 cups sliced Swiss chard and 1/8 teaspoon hot-pepper sauce. Bake for 5 minutes longer. Serve over 4 cups cooked couscous and top each serving with 1 tablespoon plain yogurt.

✳Applesauce

To balance the spiciness of a curry sauce, add applesauce for sweetness. About 1/2 cup of applesauce for each cup of curry sauce will do the trick.

To make a turkey salad with Creole panache, add some applesauce to the base. Combine in a medium bowl:

1/4 cup applesauce

1/2 cup mayonnaise

3 tablespoons ketchup

1 tablespoon hot-pepper sauce

1 tablespoon sugar

1 tablespoon distilled white vinegar

1/2 teaspoon salt

1/4 teaspoon freshly ground black pepper

Add 4 cups finely chopped roasted turkey meat, 2 finely chopped celery stalks, and 1/2 cup finely chopped red onion. Toss to mix.

For a juicier meatball, use applesauce. Grandmothers have used this trick for decades. Here's a simple recipe: Combine 1 1/2 pounds ground beef, 2 slightly beaten eggs, 1 cup bread crumbs, 1 cup applesauce, 1 teaspoon salt, and freshly ground black pepper, to taste. Shape into balls and roll in flour. Brown them in a skillet and then add to your favorite spaghetti sauce and simmer until cooked through. Or, after browning, put them in a casserole, top with your favorite sauce or gravy, and bake until cooked through.

For a healthy alternative to butter in baked goods, replace 1/2 cup of the butter with 1/4 cup well-drained unsweetened applesauce and 1/4 cup buttermilk. As a fat replacement, applesauce works best with lighter-colored batters and spice batters. The applesauce will create a slightly chewier texture in the final baked good. To lighten the texture, use pastry flour or cake flour. Upping the sugar a bit will also give you more crispness on the surface, especially in muffins.

To round out the flavor of sweet potato or squash soup, stir in 2 tablespoons unsweetened applesauce per cup of soup.

✳Artichoke Hearts

For a lightning-quick Greek-style sauce for pasta, chop 1 jar (6 ounces) marinated artichoke hearts and toss the artichokes with 3/4 pound cooked pasta, along with the artichoke marinade from the jar, 1/4 cup olive oil, and 1 cup crumbled feta cheese.

For a flavored bread that guests can't resist, make a filling with chopped marinated artichoke hearts. First, sauté 2 finely chopped leeks (white parts only) and 1 minced garlic clove in 1 tablespoon olive oil until soft, about 4 minutes. Add 1/2 package (5 ounces) frozen chopped spinach, and cook until almost dry. Season with 1/2 teaspoon salt, 1/8 teaspoon freshly ground black pepper, and a pinch of nutmeg. Remove from the heat and add 1/4 cup drained, chopped marinated artichoke hearts. Spoon this mixture over 1/2 pound thawed frozen white bread dough patted into a 6 x 8-inch rectangle. Roll up like a jelly roll, starting at a wide side. Pinch the ends closed and place the bread, seam side down, on a greased baking sheet. Cover with a damp towel and let rise in a warm place (85°F) free from drafts until the dough has doubled in bulk, about 1 1/2 hours. Preheat the oven to 400°F, then slash the top of the loaf and brush with ice water. Bake until crisp and golden, about 40 minutes. Cool on a rack for 15 minutes before slicing and serving.

To give rice salad a distinctly Mediterranean twist, add artichokes. Bring 8 cups water to a boil in a large saucepan. Add 1 cup white rice, reduce the heat to medium, and simmer until the rice is tender, 15 to 20 minutes. During the last 5 minutes of cooking, stir 2 halved and sliced zucchini into the rice. Drain the cooked rice in a colander. In a large bowl, whisk together 1/3 cup V8 juice, 3 tablespoons fresh lemon juice, 1 tablespoon olive oil, and 1/2 teaspoon salt. Stir in 2 large chopped tomatoes, 1 can (15 ounces) drained and chopped artichoke hearts, 1/4 cup chopped, pitted, oil-cured black olives, 1/4 cup crumbled feta cheese, and 3 tablespoons chopped fresh parsley. Add the drained rice mixture and toss to coat. Serve immediately. Or to make ahead, mix together the dressing and salad mixture separately, then combine them right before serving.

Tidbit Eating artichokes creates a chemical reaction in your mouth that makes other foods taste sweeter. The effect is due to a compound called cynarine, which stimulates the sweetness receptors on your tongue. To offset the effect, it's best to pair artichokes with neutral-tasting foods like pasta. Note that eating artichokes with wine can make the wine taste sweeter.

For a quick and irresistible dip, blend the following ingredients in a food processor or blender:

1 can (14 ounces) water-packed artichoke hearts, drained	3 tablespoons water
	2 teaspoons fresh lemon juice
1 can (9 ounces) sour cream onion dip	1/4 teaspoon dried dill
	1/4 teaspoon salt
2 garlic cloves	1/4 teaspoon freshly ground black pepper
3 tablespoons olive oil	

To dress pork chops, lamb, fish, or chicken with an innovative salsa, finely chop the contents of 1 jar (6 1/2 ounces) marinated artichoke hearts, saving the marinade. Toss the artichokes and their marinade with 1 small minced garlic clove, the juice of 1/2 large lemon, and 1/3 cup pine nuts. Serve over the meat.

For hot sandwiches with a bit more zip, add chopped marinated artichoke hearts. For instance, arrange 3 or 4 thin slices of mozzarella cheese over 2 large slices of country-style bread such as sourdough. Add 1/4 cup drained and finely chopped marinated artichoke hearts and a pinch of freshly ground black pepper. Assemble the sandwich and toast in butter on a griddle.

To make a pizza that vegetarians will love, spread a pizza crust with pesto, then layer with drained and chopped artichoke hearts, chopped jarred roasted red peppers, and a few spoonfuls of drained canned diced tomatoes. Top with 1 to 2 cups shredded fontina or mozzarella cheese and bake at 450°F until the cheese melts and the crust is crisp, 8 to 10 minutes.

✳Bacon

To keep grilled fish from drying out, wrap whole fish or fillets in strips of smoked bacon. The bacon also enhances the smoky aromas of grilled fish.

To give your favorite tomato sauce recipe a little something special, cook chopped bacon until crisp, then remove with a slotted spoon and use the bacon fat to sauté the onions and other ingredients in your recipe.

For an unexpected-yet-welcome flavor in pancakes, add cooked crumbled bacon. Use the bacon drippings to cook the pancakes. You'll be amazed at how well the bacon goes with the maple syrup poured over the pancakes!

To make bacon cornbread, fry 8 slices of bacon until crisp, then use the drippings to replace part of the fat in the recipe. Crumble the bacon and add to the batter.

For out-of-this-world roasted pork, rub the roast (tenderloin or sirloin) with your favorite spice rub. Then wrap the roast in slices of bacon and brush with some maple syrup. Roast and serve sliced. The bacon will baste the meat, adding moisture and flavor as the roast cooks.

For a delicious savory pie crust, fry 6 to 8 slices of bacon until crisp, then drain, finely chop, and add to the pie dough. Chill and roll the dough as usual. This makes an incredible crust for quiche, potpie, and other savory pies.

To add flavor and moisture to meat loaf, wrap strips of bacon around the shaped loaf before baking. If you like, mix some crumbled cooked bacon into the meat loaf mixture as well.

To reduce the fat in cooked bacon, bake it at 375°F on a rack set over a rimmed baking sheet. The fat will drip into the baking sheet. Bonus: baked bacon stays flat instead of curling up.

For mashed potatoes you won't soon forget, mix in crumbled cooked bacon. A little sour cream in the mash complements the bacon really well.

To enliven creamy dips, stir in crumbled crispy bacon. For even more flavor, also add sautéed shiitake mushrooms.

Jidbit It is believed that the phrase "bring home the bacon" first arose in the Middle Ages in Dunmow, England. Young married couples living there were rewarded with a chunk of back bacon if they were able to prove that they survived their first year of marriage without any arguments.

To give lentil salads a smoky kiss, add some chopped cooked bacon. Here's a basic recipe: Put 1 cup (about 1/2 pound) sorted and rinsed brown lentils in a saucepan and add cold water to cover by 1 1/2 inches. Bring to a boil over high heat, then reduce the heat to low and simmer, uncovered, until the lentils are tender yet firm, 15 to 20 minutes. Watch the lentils carefully, as they easily fall apart when overcooked. Drain the lentils and cool. Toast 1/2 cup chopped walnuts in a skillet over medium-low heat until fragrant, about 5 minutes. Cut 5 or 6 slices meaty bacon into small squares and cook in the same skillet over medium heat until crisp. Drain on a paper towel–lined plate and let cool. To serve, divide 4 cups (about 1/4 pound) mesclun greens or baby spinach and 2 peeled and thinly sliced carrots among four salad plates. Squeeze 1/4 cup fresh lemon juice into a medium bowl and slowly whisk in 1/2 cup olive oil in a thin stream. Add the lentils, 2 tablespoons chopped fresh basil or oregano, and 1 teaspoon salt. Mix well then spoon over the greens and sprinkle with the bacon and walnuts. Top with plenty of freshly cracked black pepper.

To enhance the flavor of poultry stuffing, cook bacon until crisp, then use the bacon fat to sauté the onions, celery, and other stuffing ingredients. Crumble the bacon and add to the stuffing.

To give popcorn a new twist, cook 4 strips of bacon in a large, heavy pot. Remove and drain on a paper towel–lined plate, then chop very finely. Add enough oil to the bacon drippings to make about 3 tablespoons oil in the pan. Heat over high heat until very hot. Add 1 cup popping corn, cover and shake until the popping sounds stop, about 2 minutes, venting the pan lid occasionally. Remove from the heat and toss the popped corn with the minced cooked bacon, 1/2 teaspoon onion powder, and 1/2 teaspoon salt.

For a white seafood pizza with panache, add some crispy bacon to the toppings. For instance, top a prepared pizza crust (such as Boboli) with ricotta cheese, mozzarella cheese, fresh chopped garlic, extra-virgin olive oil, crumbled crisp bacon, dried oregano, and canned chopped clams. Bake at 450°F until the cheese melts and the crust is golden brown, 8 to 10 minutes.

BACON

✳Bananas

To use overripe bananas, store them whole in the freezer to make smoothies later. When ready, peel off the skins from the frozen bananas with a paring knife. Slice into a blender and add berries, milk or yogurt, and fresh orange juice. Blend until smooth.

For a tropical ice cream that will cool you down in the summertime, peel 2 bananas, wrap them in plastic, and freeze until solid. Then place in a food processor with:

1/2 cup heavy cream	1/2 cup fresh or frozen blueberries
1/2 cup canned coconut milk	or strawberries
1/2 teaspoon vanilla extract	1/2 teaspoon ground cinnamon

Blend to the desired smoothness (or chunkiness). Pour into a shallow metal pan, cover, and freeze until firm. Scrape out servings with a spoon. Keeps frozen for up to 2 months.

For complex-tasting blueberry muffins with less fat, replace the butter in your favorite recipe with a mixture of mashed bananas and vegetable oil.

To give the kids a more nutritious frozen treat, make chocolate-covered frozen bananas on a stick. Peel whole bananas and skewer each one with a wooden craft stick or chopstick, then freeze until solid. Dip each banana into 1/4 cup melted chocolate (melted chocolate chips work fine). If you like, quickly roll in chopped nuts or sprinkles before the chocolate firms ups. Place on wax paper and return the chocolate-covered bananas to the freezer for 15 minutes.

Tidbit Adding a banana to a bag of peaches will help ripen the fruit faster. Ethylene gas emitted by the banana speeds the ripening process.

✳Barbecue Sauce

To give meat loaf a whole new taste, replace the tomato sauce or ketchup in your favorite recipe with bottled barbecue sauce. The smoky taste of the barbecue sauce will add a new dimension of flavor to your old recipe.

For a smoky hamburger spread, stir together 1 tablespoon barbecue sauce and 2 tablespoons mayonnaise. Use on hamburgers or in salads.

To mix up a quick steaming liquid for clams, put 3 dozen scrubbed littleneck clams on a very large sheet of heavy-duty foil and drizzle with 1/2 cup spicy barbecue sauce and the juice of 1 lemon. Fold the foil over the clams, leaving ample space for the clams to open, and crimp the edges to seal. Bake at 375°F or put the foil bag on the grill and cook until the liquid in the foil is bubbling and the clams open, 10 to 12 minutes. Slit open the foil and serve the clams with the sauce. Discard any unopened clams.

Tidbit Generally speaking, barbecuing differs from grilling in that barbecued food is traditionally cooked "low and slow" while grilled food is cooked "high and fast." That is to say, barbecued food cooks over low heat for a long period of time (2 hours to 2 days) with plenty of wood smoke. Grilled food cooks over high heat for a relatively short period of time (less than 30 minutes) with little or no wood smoke.

For moist and marvelous hamburgers, mix 1/4 cup barbecue sauce into 1 to 1 1/2 pounds ground beef. Shape into 4 patties and grill, broil, or pan-fry over medium heat. Cooked to about 160°F on an instant-read thermometer and the meat is no longer pink, about 4 to 6 minutes per side, basting the burgers with additional barbecue sauce as they cook.

To make delicious baked turkey tenderloins, split 2 turkey tenderloins lengthwise in half and remove the vein. Place the tenderloins in a foil-lined baking dish. Mix together 1/2 cup barbecue sauce, 1/4 cup finely chopped onion, 1/2 teaspoon dry mustard, and 1/4 teaspoon chipotle chile powder. Spoon or brush over the turkey until completely covered. Bake at 350°F until a thermometer inserted into the center of the thickest portion registers 165°F and the juices run clear, 15 to 20 minutes. Let stand for 10 minutes before slicing and serving.

For hot roast beef sandwiches with just the right flavor, bring 1/4 cup bottled barbecue sauce to a simmer in a saucepan. Add 1/4 pound sliced deli roast beef and heat through for 5 minutes. Put on a roll with some prepared horseradish.

✳Bean Dip

For spicy black bean soup in an instant, bring 4 cups chicken or vegetable broth to a boil in a medium saucepan. Stir in 1 box (7 ounces) instant black bean dip, 1 drained can (15 ounces) black beans, and 1 cup chunky salsa. Simmer for 5 minutes, then season with 1/4 teaspoon salt and 1/8 teaspoon freshly ground black pepper.

To make a fast vinaigrette for Southwestern-style salads, mix together:

1/2 cup jarred black bean dip	1 garlic clove, minced
1/2 cup mild salsa	1/4 teaspoon salt
1 1/2 tablespoons red-wine vinegar	1/8 teaspoon freshly ground black pepper

Beer

For a more complex tasting dinner bread, replace the water in a basic egg-bread recipe with beer (but not light beer—you'll need the full-calorie version!). Use these proportions as a starting point: 4 cups flour, 1/4 cup sugar, 2 tablespoons baking powder, 1 bottle (12 ounces) beer, 2 teaspoons salt, 2 beaten eggs.

For tastier corned beef and cabbage, add half a bottle of brown beer to the pot in which the food is simmering.

To make a quick marinade for pork tenderloin, mix together dark beer, molasses, herbs, onion, garlic, and freshly ground black pepper.

To make Wisconsin's favorite tailgating dish, grill your favorite bratwurst until well browned all over. Mix together 1 bottle (12 ounces) beer, 1 thinly sliced onion, 1 seeded and thinly sliced green bell pepper, and 1 drained can (14 ounces) sauerkraut in a large disposable aluminum pan. Sink the browned brats into the stew in the pan and put the pan on the grill. Cover the grill and simmer on low for 30 minutes or up to 3 hours. Serve the brats on buns with some kraut, onions, peppers, and a squirt of mustard.

For Belgian-style steamed mussels, simmer the mussels in a covered pot with beer (lager or ale is best but avoid dark beers), clam broth, chopped tomatoes, garlic, onions, and fresh basil or parsley.

Tidbit The first can of beer was sold in Richmond, Virginia, on January 24, 1935. Ever since, the battle of cans versus bottles has raged. In 2005, the state that most preferred canned beer was Arkansas, according to the Beer Institute. The state in which beer drinkers will most likely ask if you have a bottle opener is Nebraska.

To make a marinade for steak fajitas, combine 6 ounces of beer, 1 drained can of seeded, deveined, and sliced jalapeño peppers (wear gloves when handling), and 2 tablespoons Worcestershire sauce. Drop in a thinly sliced flank steak (1 1/2 pounds) and marinate for 4 to 8 hours. Grill or pan-fry the steak slices and serve with grilled or pan-fried sliced onions and peppers.

For a delicious corn side dish, simmer corn kernels in beer for 2 minutes, then drain and stir in butter and seasonings.

For a new spin on lemonade, use beer instead of water. Mix together beer, lemon-lime soda, fresh lemon or lime juice, and sugar.

To give battered and fried fish a shot of flavor, add beer. For instance, mix together 1 1/2 cups all-purpose flour, 1/2 teaspoon salt, 1/4 teaspoon cayenne pepper, and 1 bottle stout or dark beer.

For Southwestern chicken fajitas, mix together 6 ounces beer and 1 can (15 ounces) red enchilada sauce. Add 1 1/2 pounds boneless, skinless chicken breasts or thighs and marinate in the refrigerator for 4 to 8 hours. Grill or broil the chicken along with chunks of onions and seeded bell peppers. Slice the chicken and veggies and serve in warm tortillas with salsa and sour cream.

To deepen the flavor of stews and chilis, stir in 6 ounces beer along with the broth in your favorite recipes.

To doctor up store-bought barbecue sauce, stir in 1/4 cup dark beer per cup of sauce.

For a fun twist on boiled shrimp, use beer as the simmering liquid. Combine 6 ounces beer, 1 tablespoon fresh lemon juice, 4 minced garlic cloves, 3 tablespoons unsalted butter, 3 tablespoons chopped fresh parsley, and 1/2 teaspoon lemon-pepper seasoning in a deep, 12-inch-wide skillet. Add 1 pound peeled and deveined shrimp, then cover and simmer until the shrimp are pink and cooked through, for 5 minutes. Dust the shrimp with paprika before serving.

To keep a whole grilled chicken moist, make Beer Can Chicken. The steam from the open can of beer keeps the bird incredibly moist and gently flavors the meat. To make it, season a 3 1/2- to 4-pound chicken inside and out with your favorite seasonings. Set a half-full beer can in a grill that is set up for indirect grilling (on a 3-burner gas grill, light the outside burners and set the can in the center over the unlit burner; on a 2-burner gas grill, light one of the burners and set the can over the unlit burner; on a charcoal grill, spread the coals to opposite sides and put the can over the unheated middle part of the grill). Hold the chicken upright and lower the chicken over the beer can, easing the can into the bird cavity. Pull the chicken legs forward to make a tripod so it sits steadily on the grill. Cover and grill over indirect heat for about 1 hour 15 minutes. Using tongs and oven mitts, pull the chicken off the beer can and set on a platter. Let rest for 5 minutes before carving.

For drunken pulled pork, simmer the pork in beer. Cut boneless pork butt or shoulder into cubes and put in a Dutch oven with beer, onions, chili powder, cumin, salt, and freshly ground black pepper. Bring to a boil, then reduce to low heat, cover, and simmer until the pork is fork-tender. Shred the pork with 2 forks and stir in the bottled barbecue sauce, simmering until heated through.

To make a spicy marinade for spareribs, combine 6 ounces beer, 1 1/4 cups barbecue sauce, 1 drained can sliced jalapeños, 2 teaspoons Worcestershire sauce, and 1 teaspoon hot-pepper sauce.

❊Berries

For a better-tasting pancake syrup, mix together 1/2 cup maple syrup, 1/2 cup fresh blueberries, and 1/2 teaspoon grated orange zest in a microwavable bowl. Microwave on high power until warm, 30 seconds to 1 minute. Use to top waffles, pancakes, or French toast.

Tidbit Blueberry muffins often become discolored gray-green due to a chemical reaction between blueberries and baking soda. If your favorite recipe includes baking soda, omit the baking soda and replace any acidic liquid in the recipe (such as buttermilk or yogurt) with plain milk. If baking soda is the only leavener, replace it with 1 tablespoon baking powder for every 2 cups flour.

To make a simple syrup for cake or ice cream, put 1 1/2 pints cleaned berries, 2 tablespoons unsalted butter, and 2 tablespoons sugar in a medium sauce-pan. Cook over medium-low heat until the berries are heated through and glossy, 5 to 8 minutes. Remove from the heat and deglaze the pan with 2 tablespoons brandy or dark rum.

❊Black Pepper

For more complex tasting gingerbread, add freshly ground black pepper. Here's a simple recipe. Preheat the oven to 375°F. In a large, heavy saucepan, melt 1/2 cup (1 stick) unsalted butter over medium heat. Remove from the heat and add 1/2 cup sugar, 1 cup dark molasses, 1 teaspoon brown mustard, 2 tablespoons instant coffee granules, and 2 eggs, beating with a whisk until smooth. Add 1 tablespoon ground ginger, 1 teaspoon freshly ground black pepper, 1 teaspoon ground cinnamon, 1/2 teaspoon ground allspice, and 2 teaspoons baking soda. Stir until well-blended. Mix in 2 1/3 cups flour, and beat for 30 seconds. Mix in 1 cup boiling water then scrape the batter into a greased 9-inch square baking pan. Bake until the gingerbread is springy and a tooth-pick inserted in the center comes out with just a few crumbs clinging to it, 40 to 45 minutes. Cool in the pan on a rack for 10 minutes. Invert and remove from the pan. Invert again and cool right side up. Serve warm or completely cooled with ice cream or whipped cream.

To make fruit punch taste livelier, add a few grindings of fresh black pepper.

For homemade nut brittle with a bit of zip, stir cracked black pepper into the mixture before it hardens.

For the simplest of toppings on fresh sliced strawberries, add sweetened whipped cream, then a few grindings of fresh black pepper. The pepper blends perfectly with the cream.

To make fruit tarts stand out from the crowd, toss the fruit with sugar and a grinding of fresh black pepper.

✳Bread

To thicken pureed soups, sauces, dips, and spreads, use stale bread. Slices of stale bread contain starch that can be easily pureed with liquids and used as a thickener. Gazpacho, a quickly made Spanish soup, is traditionally thickened with leftover bread that is soaked in liquid.

To make stiff brown sugar soft again, put a slice of bread in the bag and seal for up to 48 hours.

For an extra-crispy pizza crust, use pita bread. Split a pita in half horizontally to make 2 rounds. Place, inside up, on a greased rimmed baking sheet. Brush each half with olive oil and top with 2 tablespoons pizza sauce, 1/2 ounce shredded or chopped mozzarella cheese, and any other toppings you like. Bake at 350°F until the cheese is melted and the edges of the bread are browned, 8 to 10 minutes.

To turn stale bread into a delicious new meal, make a bread salad. Tear 8 ounces stale Italian bread into bite-size pieces and combine with 4 seeded and chopped tomatoes, 1 peeled, seeded, and chopped cucumber, 1 chopped red onion, and 1/2 cup torn basil leaves. Toss with 3/4 cup red-wine vinaigrette and let stand for 20 minutes.

Tidbit To prolong the moistness of cookies, store them in an airtight container with a slice of bread. This trick works great with chewy and moist drop cookies such as chewy chocolate chip cookies.

For a quick snack, make seasoned pita chips. Split 2 pitas in half horizontally to make 2 rounds. Cut each round into 12 wedges. Arrange in a single layer on an oiled rimmed baking sheet and spray with cooking spray. Bake at 375°F until crisp, 5 to 8 minutes. Remove from the oven and immediately season with 1/8 teaspoon garlic salt and 2 tablespoons grated Parmesan cheese.

For better-tasting bread pudding, use cinnamon-raisin bread instead of plain old white bread. It also helps to use cream or half-and-half instead of regular milk.

✳Brownie Mix

To make a no-fuss chocolate torte, mix and bake the brownie mix according to the package directions but use a round springform pan. Top the torte with chocolate sauce and chopped nuts, then cut into wedges.

For a super-easy chocolate soufflé, combine brownie mix with egg yolks and whipped egg whites, then bake in a soufflé dish.

✳Buttermilk

To make more tender cakes, use buttermilk instead of whole milk. Add 1/2 teaspoon baking soda for each cup of buttermilk. The acidity of buttermilk tenderizes the cake better than plain milk can, and the baking soda balances out that acidity.

For a quick, creamy sauce for cooked fish or chicken, combine 1/4 cup buttermilk with 1/2 cup bottled blue cheese salad dressing.

Tidbit Buttermilk was originally the liquid left over after churning milk into butter. Nowadays, most buttermilk sold to consumers is made by thickening plain milk with special bacteria.

To create a thick, rich texture in cold soups, sauces, and salad dressing without adding too much fat, use buttermilk in place of some or all of the cream or oil used in your favorite recipe. A spoonful of low-fat sour cream further enriches the texture.

To make a luscious pumpkin pie, mix together 1 1/2 cups canned pumpkin, 2/3 cup buttermilk, 3 egg yolks, 1 cup firmly packed light brown sugar, 1 teaspoon ground cinnamon, and 1/2 teaspoon ground ginger. Beat 3 egg whites with 1/4 teaspoon salt in a small bowl until soft peaks form, 2 to 3 minutes. Fold into the pumpkin mixture. Pour into an unbaked 9-inch pie shell and bake at 375°F until set, about 1 hour.

For quickbreads with a lighter crumb, use a combination of buttermilk and whole milk. Buttermilk works especially well in pancakes, cornbread, and banana bread.

To make fluffier, richer-tasting mashed potatoes, use buttermilk instead of plain milk.

✳Candy Bars

To breathe new life into your old cheesecake recipe, use chocolate wafer crumbs instead of graham crackers in the crust. Before pouring the batter into the crust, coarsely chop 2 Heath candy bars (1.4 ounces each) and sprinkle the pieces across the bottom of the crust. After adding the batter, grate some bittersweet chocolate over the top.

For cookie bars your kids will love, press prepared sugar-cookie dough (homemade or store-bought) into the bottom of a 9 x 13-inch baking dish. Chop your kids' favorite candy bars into small pieces and scatter over the top. Bake as directed, cool completely, and cut into squares before serving.

Spark your brownies with candy-bar chunks. Prepare the brownie mix according to the package directions, but add chopped candy bars to the mix prior to pouring it into the baking pan. Two or three candy bars is enough for a standard-size package of brownie mix. Bars to consider include Baby Ruth, Almond Joy, Butterfinger, Milky Way, Snickers, even Reese's Peanut Butter Cups.

✳Canned Beans

To do something different with chickpeas, roast them as a snack. Drain 1 can (15 ounces) chickpeas and toss with 2 teaspoons olive oil and 1 1/2 teaspoons Cajun seasoning. Bake at 375°F until dry and golden, 35 to 40 minutes. Let cool completely so they get crisp. For a Mexican flavor, replace the Cajun seasoning with 1 teaspoon chili powder, 1/2 teaspoon ground cumin, and 1/8 teaspoon cayenne pepper.

For beef burritos with a little more oomph, use a combination of browned ground beef and refried beans. Brown 1/2 pound ground beef in a skillet then add 1 can (16 ounces) refried beans. Cook for 3 to 4 minutes then stir in 3/4 teaspoon ground cumin, 3/4 teaspoon dried oregano, and 1/4 cup salsa. Bring to a simmer, then add 1 cup shredded sharp cheddar cheese. Stir to melt. Fill four flour tortillas to make burritos. Or serve warm as a dip.

To fill out a Mediterranean-style pasta dish, add white beans. For instance, boil 1 pound oricchiette or other small pasta until just slightly firm. While the pasta cooks, sauté 2 tablespoons finely chopped onion in 1/4 cup olive oil for 2 minutes, then add 1 minced garlic clove and 1 teaspoon crumbled dried rosemary. Cook for another 30 seconds. Add 1 undrained can (6 ounces) oil-packed tuna and mix well. Cook for another minute. Add 1 cup drained canned cannellini beans and season with 1 tablespoon chopped fresh parsley, 1/4 teaspoon salt, and 1/8 teaspoon freshly ground black pepper. Heat through and toss with the hot pasta.

To build quesadillas into a more satisfying snack, add black beans. Mix together 1 drained can (15 ounces) black beans, 1/2 cup salsa, 1 teaspoon chili powder, and a squirt of lime juice, mashing half of the beans. Spread onto cheddar cheese–topped tortillas in a skillet, cook until browned on the bottom, and fold over before serving.

To stir up a snappy island-style salsa, combine 1 drained can (15 ounces) black beans, 1 can (8 ounces) crushed pineapple, 1/2 cup seeded, chopped red bell pepper, 1 teaspoon Jerk seasoning, and a squirt of lime juice.

To make a tabbouleh salad more substantial, stir in some chickpeas along with the cooked bulgur, fresh lemon juice, olive oil, tomatoes, garlic, and parsley.

For a new take on tuna melts, combine 2 drained cans (6 ounces each) tuna, 1 drained can (14 ounces) small white beans, 1/3 cup low-fat creamy Italian vinaigrette, 2 tablespoons sliced black olives, 2 sliced scallions, and 2 tablespoons chopped fresh parsley. Sandwich the filling between bread slices and provolone cheese before toasting on a buttered griddle.

❋Canned Cheese Dip

For beef kebabs like you've never had them, toss cubed sirloin or top round beef with steak seasoning and chopped fresh parsley. Thread onto skewers with canned whole new potatoes. Mix together canned cheese dip and Worcestershire sauce in a microwavable bowl and microwave on high power until hot. Grill the kebabs and brush with the cheese sauce during the last 5 minutes of cooking. Yum!

To make easy cheddar cheese soup, use canned cheese dip as the base. Sauté the onions, carrots, and celery, then add canned cheddar cheese dip, shredded sharp cheddar cheese, and chicken broth. A touch of Worcestershire sauce and dry mustard will round out the cheese flavor nicely.

For a quick cheese sauce for sautéed chicken, combine 1 can (9 ounces) cheddar cheese dip and 1 can (10 ounces) chicken gravy. Simmer in the pan along with the chicken.

To simplify the ingredients for corn pudding, start with canned cheese dip. Combine 1 can (9 ounces) cheddar cheese dip, 2 1/2 cups corn kernels, 1/2 cup shredded sharp cheddar cheese, 1/2 cup chopped onion, and 2 beaten eggs in a 2-quart baking dish. Bake at 350°F until set, about 45 minutes.

For a new surprise in meat loaf, mix 1/2 cup canned cheddar cheese dip into the meat loaf mixture. Bake as usual and drizzle with more warmed cheese dip before serving.

To make creamy and rich-tasting mashed potatoes, stir in some canned cheddar cheese dip once the spuds are mashed.

❋Canned Fruit

For the simplest fruit sorbet, combine 1 undrained can (16 ounces) fruit packed in juice, 1/3 cup white grape juice concentrate, and 3 tablespoons honey in a food processor. Puree until smooth. Freeze in an ice cream maker or in a shallow metal pan, stirring occasionally.

To make baked chicken more special around the holidays, combine 1 can (16 ounces) whole-berry cranberry sauce and 1/2 cup bottled Italian dressing. Pour a layer of the mixture into the bottom of a large baking dish. Add 4 pounds bone-in chicken pieces and top with the remaining sauce. Bake at 400°F until the juices run clear when the chicken is pierced with a fork, about 40 minutes, turning occasionally.

For a summertime granita to cool you off, freeze 1 unopened can (8 ounces) pineapple in heavy or light syrup until solid. Open the can and dig out the contents. Chop in a food processor along with 1/4 teaspoon vanilla extract until the mixture is finely chopped but still lightly icy. Spoon into dessert cups and serve. Keep a can of pineapple in the freezer so you're always ready to make this on a hot summer day.

For fruit salsa in a jiffy, make your favorite fresh salsa recipe (or use store-bought salsa) then stir in 1 drained can (15 ounces) mandarin oranges in syrup. Try other canned fruits, too, like sliced peaches for peach salsa or pineapple chunks for pineapple salsa. Once you try the combination of fruit and tomatoes in salsa, you'll be hooked!

❋Canned Tuna

To make a more substantial pizza without adding a lot of fat, drop a few tablespoonfuls of drained canned tuna over the tomato sauce before topping with the cheese.

To turn couscous from a side dish into a main dish, add canned tuna. For example, prepare 1 box (10 ounces) instant couscous according to the package directions. Toss with 1 undrained can (6 ounces) olive oil–packed tuna, 1/2 cup chopped toasted hazelnuts, 2 minced garlic cloves, 2 tablespoons chopped fresh dill, 1/4 teaspoon salt, and 1/8 teaspoon freshly ground black pepper.

Make potato salad, Mediterranean-style. An extremely easy version is to boil a pound of your favorite potatoes (cleaned but with skin on), until tender, about 15 minutes. Cut into bite-size chunks, then put in a large bowl. Add 1 can (6 ounces) tuna packed in olive oil and 1 red onion, cut into bite-size pieces. Add salt, freshly ground black pepper, fresh lemon juice, and extra olive oil, to taste. Toss and serve warm or at room temperature.

*Carrots

To sneak some veggies into your kids' burgers, add finely shredded carrots to the meat mixture. Carrots go especially well with burgers made from ground lamb or a mixture of ground beef and pork.

To get a jump-start on making a vegetable soup, use carrot juice as the base along with chicken or vegetable broth.

For golden-colored risotto or steamed rice, use a mixture of carrot juice and vegetable broth as the cooking liquid.

To prevent oil from blackening when deep-frying, add a wedge of carrot to the oil. It will act like a magnet, attract the black flecks created by deep-frying, and keep your fried food pristine.

To give buns and rolls a sunny color, dissolve the yeast for the dough in carrot juice instead of in water. Carrot juice adds a kiss of sweetness, too. For flecks of orange in the bread, add some shredded carrots to the dough. For an extra touch of sunny flavor, add orange zest as well.

For low-fat salad dressings with tons of flavor, replace one-fourth of the oil with carrot juice.

Tidbit "Baby-cut" carrots sold in bags in supermarkets are not actually small, baby carrots. They are mature carrots that have been machine cut for convenience.

*Cereal

To make bran muffins, replace 1 1/2 cups flour with 1 1/2 cups bran cereal or raisin bran cereal in your favorite basic muffin recipe that makes 12 muffins. Mix the cereal into the wet ingredients and let sit 5 minutes before stirring in the remaining dry ingredients.

For an extra-crunchy topping on crisps and crumbles, use granola or Grape-Nuts cereal instead of or in addition to old-fashioned rolled oats.

To give cookies or spice cakes a bit more crunch, add crisped rice or another crisp cereal to the dough.

For quickbreads with a crisp surprise, add 1/2 cup Grape-Nuts cereal to the batter.

For the easiest peanut butter balls on the planet, melt 1 cup sugar and 1 cup corn syrup in a saucepan. Stir in 2 cups peanut butter and 4 cups cornflakes. Drop bite-size balls onto wax paper and let set.

For a crunchy coating on sautéed chicken breasts or fish fillets, used crushed cornflakes instead of cornmeal or flour.

For yummy pudding squares, try Cheerios. Butter a 9-inch square baking pan. In a large saucepan, combine 1 package (4 ounces) chocolate, butterscotch, or vanilla pudding with 1/2 cup corn syrup, and bring to a boil over medium heat, stirring constantly. Remove from the heat after a minute of boiling and blend in 1/3 cup peanut butter. Stir in 4 cups Cheerios until evenly coated. Spread the mixture evenly in the pan with the back of a spoon. Cool until firm, about 30 minutes. Cut into squares and serve.

To achieve the crunchiness of nuts in baked goods without adding extra fat and calories, use Grape-Nuts cereal instead.

For a new shade of crispy rice treats, use Fruity Pebbles cereal or Fruit Loops in place of the traditional crispy rice cereal.

To make the perfect breading for fried ice cream, finely crush cornflakes and mix with ground cinnamon. Coat ice cream balls with the cereal mixture, then deep-fry just until browned and crisp.

To put a new spin on your grandmother's noodle kugel, scatter cornflakes over the noodle mixture to make a crispy topping.

To make a wake-me-up breakfast parfait, sauté some sliced bananas in a little unsalted butter with some brown sugar and rum. Layer the bananas in a parfait glass with crunchy granola cereal, yogurt, and a few drizzlings of honey.

For a wonderful batter for fried fish, mix together the following ingredients, adding just enough beer to give the mix a batterlike texture:

2 cups flour	1 teaspoon onion salt
2 tablespoons fresh lemon juice	1 tablespoon chopped fresh parsley
1 finely chopped onion	2 big handfuls cornflakes, crushed
	1 to 2 cans beer

Coat the fish in the batter and fry in oil until golden brown.

To give breakfast casseroles extra crunch, use cornflakes as the topping. Cereal flakes add the perfect golden color and just the right touch of sweetness to bread puddings and other custardy breakfast casseroles.

To make garlic sticks like you've never had them, start with a can of refrigerator biscuits. Cut each biscuit in half and roll into sticks 5 to 6 inches long. Dip each stick into a wide bowl holding about 1/4 cup milk, then roll in crushed cornflakes. Finally, sprinkle each stick with garlic salt. Place the sticks 1 inch apart on a buttered baking sheet and bake at 450°F degrees until crisp and brown, 8 to 10 minutes.

CEREAL

For a new take on peaches and cream, top it off with cornflakes. Preheat the oven to 375°F. Drain 1 can (28 ounces) peaches, keeping 1/2 cup of the liquid. Arrange the peaches, cut side up, in an 8-inch square baking dish, then pour the reserved peach liquid over the top. Combine a little sugar and cinnamon, sprinkle over the peaches, then top each peach piece with a dot of butter and 1 tablespoon cornflakes. Bake for 15 minutes. Serve warm with ice cream.

✳Cheddar Cheese

For richer, tastier mashed potatoes, grate a few ounces of cheddar cheese into the mash and stir in until melted.

To make hamburgers with a surprise inside, form two thin patties out of the meat mixture and sandwich a chunk of cheddar cheese between them. Blue cheese and feta cheese work well, too!

For super-yummy squash soups, stir in a little shredded sharp cheddar cheese.

To take plain hot dogs up to the next level, stuff them with cheddar cheese and wrap them in bacon. First preheat the grill or griddle. Cut the hot dogs lengthwise through the side, almost all the way through but not quite. Stuff with thin strips of cheddar cheese then wrap 1 slice of bacon around each hot dog in a spiral, securing the ends with toothpicks. Grill over medium heat or fry on a hot griddle until the bacon is cooked through, the hot dogs are browned, and the cheese is melted.

✳Chili Powder

For livelier string beans, melt 2 tablespoons unsalted butter and mix in 1/2 teaspoon salt, 1/2 teaspoon chili powder, and 1/8 teaspoon garlic powder. Steam a pound of string beans, drain, and then toss with the butter mixture.

To make brownies from hell, add 1/2 teaspoon pure chile powder (such as ancho or chipotle chile powder) to a 9 x 11-inch pan of chocolate brownies. A few pinches of cinnamon add to the flavor, too. If you like the combination of spicy and sweet, you'll die for these brownies!

For kicked up corn-on-the-cob, shuck fresh sweet corn and then wrap each ear with 1 or 2 strips of bacon. Place each ear on a piece of heavy-duty foil and sprinkle lightly with chili powder. Wrap securely, twisting the ends of the foil to make handles for turning. Grill over medium-high heat until the corn is tender and the bacon is cooked, turning once, about 20 minutes.

To mix up a spicy butter for cooked fish fillets, chicken, or potatoes, combine 1/2 cup (1 stick) softened butter, 1 teaspoon chipotle chile powder, and 1/4 teaspoon salt. Wrap in plastic and store in the refrigerator for up to 2 weeks.

To perk up plain old burgers, add 2 tablespoons chili powder per pound of ground meat.

If you like your cornbread hot and spicy, add chipotle chile powder to the batter. Chipotle chiles are dried smoked jalapeño peppers, so they add a nice touch of smoke aroma as well. Look for chipotle chile powder on the gourmet spice rack at your supermarket.

Tidbit People often argue about the spelling of chili. Is it chili with an "I" or chile with an "E"? The answer: it's both. Chile with an "E" refers to the spicy pepper pods that are used to make the popular stew known as chili with an "I."

For hot chocolate with a kick, add ground ancho chile powder, ground cinnamon, and almond extract to the mix.

When you don't want to settle for plain old popcorn again, make it spicy with some ground red pepper. First cook popping corn in a heavy pot in hot oil. When it's popped, toss the popcorn with a little curry powder, ground red pepper, sugar, and salt.

❈Chocolate Syrup

To give poached pears a final flourish, drizzle chocolate syrup over them just before serving. The combination of chocolate and pears is irresistible. Plus, the chocolate syrup is fat-free.

For an effortless chocolate trifle, arrange layers of ladyfingers, vanilla pudding, and chocolate syrup in a dessert bowl.

To mix up a quick dip for fresh fruit, combine 1/3 cup chocolate syrup and 1 package (8 ounces) cream cheese in a food processor. Blend until smooth. Serve with strawberries, bananas, kiwifruits, oranges, pears, and other favorite fruits.

When you want homemade hot chocolate, mix together 2 tablespoons chocolate syrup, 1 cup half-and-half, 1/4 teaspoon vanilla extract, and 2 drops of almond extract in a microwavable mug. Microwave on high power until hot, 1 to 2 minutes. Top with a squirt of whipped cream and a dash of cinnamon.

When your angel-food cake screams for chocolate, make a devilishly easy chocolate glaze. Stir together 3 tablespoons chocolate syrup and 2/3 cup confectioners' sugar until smooth. Spoon over the top of the angel-food cake, letting it run slowly down the sides.

For ridiculously easy chocolate-cherry sorbet, freeze 1 unopened can (16 ounces) sweet cherries in syrup, then dig out the contents and put in a food processor. Add 1 cup chocolate syrup, 1 tablespoon brandy or rum, and 1/2 teaspoon vanilla extract. Process until smooth, then pour into a shallow metal pan and freeze until solid. Scrape off servings with a spoon.

To make easy chocolate bread pudding, mix together:

1/2 cup chocolate syrup	1/4 cup firmly packed brown sugar
2 cups milk	1/2 teaspoon vanilla extract
3 eggs, beaten	1/4 teaspoon ground cinnamon

Cut 6 slices of bread into bite-size cubes, then put into an 8-inch square baking dish and pour the chocolate mixture over the top, coating the bread evenly. Bake at 350°F until the pudding is set, 20 to 30 minutes.

✴Cinnamon

To perk up chocolate chip cookies, add 1/2 teaspoon cinnamon along with the flour. Try adding 1/2 teaspoon almond extract, too.

To flavor up a pot roast, add a cinnamon stick to the braising liquid.

For hot chocolate with a spicy aroma, stir in a pinch of ground cinnamon.

To make rice pilaf with more flavor, add a cinnamon stick to the simmering liquid. This trick is perfect for rice that will accompany Indian or Mexican dishes.

For grain salads with a Moroccan flair, add cinnamon and almonds. This tip works well for rice, couscous, barley, and other grain salads, especially if the dressing includes lemon juice and olive oil.

Tidbit True cinnamon is often labeled as "Ceylon cinnamon" or "Seychelles Islands cinnamon." However, most of the cinnamon sold in Western countries is actually cassia, a similar spice with a less complex yet more pronounced flavor.

To make spiced coffee, brew 4 cups of strong coffee, adding 1 tablespoon ground cinnamon to the coffee grounds (this trick works well in a drip-style coffee maker).

For a new twist on baked rigatoni, make the tomato sauce with sausage, onion, garlic, and cinnamon.

To enhance the flavor of brownies, stir 1/2 teaspoon ground cinnamon into the flour for an 8-inch square pan of brownies.

To boost the taste of your favorite pie crust, add 1/2 teaspoon ground cinnamon to the dough for a 2-crust pie.

❄ Cocoa Powder

To give Southwestern soups and stews a new depth of flavor, stir in 1 tablespoon unsweetened cocoa powder. Chocolate goes especially well with chile peppers and forms the basis of flavor in traditional Mexican mole sauce.

To make 3-minute hot-fudge sauce, combine 1/2 cup unsweetened Dutch-process cocoa powder, 3/4 cup sugar, and 1/8 teaspoon salt in a small saucepan. Add 1/2 cup water (or brewed coffee for more flavor) and stir to mix. Bring to a boil over medium-high heat, stirring constantly. Remove from the heat and stir in 1 tablespoon unsalted butter and 1/4 teaspoon vanilla extract, until the butter is melted. Use while still warm.

Tidbit Natural or "nonalkalized" cocoa powder includes the natural acidity of the cocoa beans from which it is made. Dutch-process cocoa has an alkali added to neutralize the acidity, mellowing the flavor. Use natural cocoa for a stronger chocolate flavor, especially in baked goods or when the cocoa needs to stand up to other strong-flavored ingredients. Choose Dutch-process cocoa when there are only a few ingredients in the recipe or when the acidity of natural cocoa may taste too harsh, as when cocoa powder is dusted over the surface of chocolate truffles.

❄ Coffee

To jazz up a spice rub, add ground coffee. For an especially good combination, mix together ground espresso or other coffee, paprika, chili powder (or pure ancho chile powder), cumin, salt, and freshly ground black pepper. Add a touch of sugar to balance the bitterness of the coffee. This spice rub is especially good with grilled beef and pork.

For onion soup with that *je ne sais quois*, stir in 1/4 teaspoon instant espresso powder per 1 cup broth.

To supercharge bottled barbecue sauce, stir in a few tablespoons of strong-brewed coffee or espresso.

To create a mocha flavor in chocolate desserts, dissolve 1 to 2 teaspoons instant espresso powder in 1 to 2 tablespoons hot water (or other warm liquid from your recipe). Add to the ingredients for an 8-inch square pan of brownies. Try it in other chocolates desserts, too, like chocolate pudding, fondue, mousses, and chocolate sauce.

To perk up the taste of a spicy gelatin dessert, dissolve the gelatin in brewed coffee instead of in water.

For a blast of flavor in homemade biscotti, add freshly ground coffee to the batter.

For a simple glaze for cupcakes or muffins, mix together strong-brewed coffee and enough confectioners' sugar to make the mixture spreadable.

To make ham steak with red-eye gravy, stir 1 cup brewed coffee into the skillet used to fry the ham, scraping the pan bottom to loosen any browned bits. Stir in 1/2 cup heavy cream or half-and-half and simmer over medium-low heat until the gravy thickens up a bit, 8 to 10 minutes. Season with salt and freshly ground black pepper, then pour over the ham steak. Some say the name "red-eye" in this classic Southern sauce comes from the slightly red tinge the sauce gets from the smoked ham being cooked in the same skillet. Others say the name refers to the red-eyed early risers who often make this dish in the morning to help wake them up.

To make a novel marinade for turkey, improvise a combination of brewed coffee, cider vinegar, garlic, Worcestershire sauce, freshly ground black pepper, sugar, and ground cinnamon. Use to marinate boneless, skinless turkey breast before grilling or broiling.

Tidbit Coffee is the second largest traded commodity in the world. Oil is the first.

✳Coleslaw Mix

To make a quick Asian chicken wrap, toss 2 cups finely chopped cooked chicken along with 3 tablespoons bottled teriyaki sauce and 1 teaspoon grated fresh ginger. Separately, toss together the following:

1 bag (16 ounces) coleslaw mix	1 teaspoon sesame oil
3 tablespoons white-wine vinegar	1 teaspoon olive oil
2 teaspoons bottled teriyaki sauce	1 teaspoon grated fresh ginger
	1/4 teaspoon hot-pepper sauce

Spoon the chicken and slaw onto four 10-inch flour tortillas. Top each with 1 tablespoon chopped fresh cilantro. Fold in the sides and roll up tightly. Cut in half and serve.

To sneak some veggies into your favorite meat loaf, sauté 2 cups coleslaw mix and 1 chopped onion in 2 tablespoons olive oil over medium heat until browned, about 15 minutes. Let cool, then stir into 1 1/2 pounds of meat loaf mixture along with your favorite seasonings.

For a super-easy stir-fry, sauté 1 pound of meat in a wok or skillet then remove and keep warm. Sauté 1 tablespoon chopped fresh ginger and 1 minced garlic clove in 1 tablespoon oil in the wok or skillet. Add 2 cups coleslaw mix and stir-fry for 2 minutes. Return the meat to the pan and pour in some bottled stir-fry sauce.

✳Cookies

To make extra-special s'mores, use shortbread cookies instead of graham crackers. You can also use chocolate hazelnut spread such as Nutella in place of the traditional Hershey bars. The fire-toasted marshmallows, however, are impossible to replace!

For a quick stuffing for baked apples or peaches, mix together crushed amaretti cookies or biscotti, brown sugar, cinnamon, and pine nuts.

For easy no-bake cookies, use vanilla wafer cookies. First mix 1/2 cup rum or bourbon with 3 tablespoons corn syrup in a large bowl. Stir in:

1 1/4 cups confectioners' sugar	3 tablespoons unsweetened cocoa powder
3/4 cup toasted chopped pecans	1/4 teaspoon salt
1/2 teaspoon ground cinnamon	

Crush 1 package (12 ounces) vanilla wafer cookies in a food processor and add to the bowl (the mixture will be stiff). Let sit for 10 minutes to soften, then roll into 1-inch balls between your palms. Finally, roll the cookie balls in confectioners' sugar to coat. Store in an airtight container at room temperature for up to 2 weeks.

To switch up the breading for fried fish and seafood, use crushed amaretti cookies, graham crackers, or gingersnaps. Crushed cookies work especially well as a breading for shellfish like shrimp.

For homemade ice-cream sandwiches that kids and adults will love, make your favorite cookie recipe, using 2 tablespoons cookie dough to make 3-inch-diameter cookies. Spoon 1/2 cup to 2/3 cup of your favorite ice cream (slightly softened) onto a cookie and flatten gently until the ice cream reaches the edges of the cookie. Top with another cookie, wrap in plastic, and freeze for at least 4 hours.

To keep the crust in fruit pies from getting soggy, crush amaretti cookies or biscotti into fine crumbs and scatter over the crust before adding the fruit filling. The cookies add tremendous flavor as well.

❊ Corn

To give soups a rich, creamy texture without adding fat, use pureed corn. The corn adds a welcome touch of sweetness, too. Try it in butternut squash soup, cheese soup, and other creamy soups.

For richer-tasting cornbread, replace half of the milk with creamed corn.

To liven up store-bought salsa, mix in 1/2 cup corn kernels, 1/2 finely chopped, seeded red bell peppers, a dash of chili powder, and a squirt of lime juice. Half a can of black beans makes a nice addition, too.

To give beef chili more color and flavor, stir in corn kernels.

For creamier casseroles without additional calories, mix some pureed corn into the filling. Pureed corn extends the creaminess of cheese in casseroles allowing you to use less of the cheese (a great substitution of you are trying to cut calories). Try it in enchilada and lasagna fillings.

❊ Cornmeal

To add crunch and color to plain old pancakes and waffles, use cornmeal to replace up to one-fourth of the flour in the batter.

For thicker chili and stews, stir in a few tablespoons of cornmeal. The corn lends a slightly sweet, nutty flavor and a wonderfully chewy texture.

❊ Corn Syrup

For smoother frozen desserts, such as sherbets or sorbets, replace 3 to 4 tablespoons of the sugar with corn syrup.

To make cookies more crisp, replace 2 tablespoons of the sugar in your favorite recipe with 1 tablespoon corn syrup. When making low-fat cookies, avoid a gummy texture by replacing 1/4 cup of the sugar with 2 tablespoons corn syrup.

For brownies with less fat, replace 1/4 cup of the butter or oil with corn syrup.

❊ Crackers

For an incredibly savory crust on pan-fried fish, use crushed bacon-flavored crackers in the breading.

For a better topping on potpie, toss crushed saltine crackers with melted unsalted butter and scatter over the top.

CORN

To give breaded chicken a bold new flavor, use cheese crackers such as Cheez-Its in the breading. First soak the chicken in evaporated milk and fresh lemon juice for 2 to 4 hours, then dip in seasoned flour, beaten egg, and finally the crushed cheese crackers. Pan-fry or bake as usual and serve with cheese sauce or chicken gravy.

To give crab cakes a flavor lift, use crushed saltines or Ritz crackers as the binder in place of plain bread crumbs. Ritz crackers are especially rich and buttery, making exceptional seafood cakes.

❋Cream Cheese

For cream pie fillings with less fat, replace the cream in your favorite recipe with a mixture of reduced-fat cream cheese and half-and-half. This combination provides the velvety texture and rich flavor of cream pies without all the fat.

To make a reduced-fat pie crust, replace up to one-fourth of the butter or shortening with reduced-fat cream cheese. Add 1 tablespoon sugar and 1/2 teaspoon baking powder to the dough for tenderness and a lighter, flakier texture.

When you hanker for ultra-rich scrambled eggs, melt butter and cream cheese in a skillet before adding the beaten egg mixture. Cook over medium-low heat until the eggs are just firm yet moist.

To make instant creamy pasta sauce, stir vegetable-flavored cream cheese into your favorite tomato sauce until melted.

For a creamy salmon sauce, sauté onions in unsalted butter then stir in diced smoked salmon and cream cheese until melted. Finish with a little heavy cream and chopped fresh dill.

Tidbit American cream cheese was an attempt to replicate the style of French neufchâtel cheese as it was made in the 1800s. Cream cheese was first made in 1872 in New York State by dairyman William A. Lawrence. Eight years later, the enterprising cheese distributor A. L. Reynolds packaged the cheese in foil wrappers and called it Philadelphia Brand because the public associated the City of Brotherly Love with high-quality food products. To this day, Philadelphia cream cheese has a monopoly on the cream cheese market.

For super-easy stuffed chicken breasts, spread scallion cream cheese over pounded chicken breasts, then roll up and sauté.

To make richer-tasting pesto, stir in cream cheese that has been melted in a saucepan or microwavable bowl.

To make super-moist roasted chicken, spread herbed cream cheese underneath the skin of the bird before roasting.

For an easy cheese-log appetizer, mix together cream cheese and goat cheese, form into a log using plastic wrap, then roll in herbs.

To make a low-fat dip for fresh fruit, blend together 3 ounces softened reduced-fat cream cheese, 1/2 cup marshmallow creme, and 1/2 teaspoon vanilla extract. Serve with cut-up fruit wedges.

To whip up an easy cake frosting, combine 1 package (8 ounces) cream cheese, 5 tablespoons unsalted butter, 2 teaspoons vanilla extract, and 2 cups confectioners' sugar in a food processor. Puree until smooth. For more flavor, add grated lemon or orange zest, and rum, Kahlua, or another liqueur. For a chocolate frosting, stir in 1 cup semi-sweet or bittersweet chocolate that has been melted in a microwavable bowl.

✳Eggnog

To make ultra-rich holiday French toast, replace the milk with a mixture of eggnog and heavy cream or half-and-half. Eggnog gives the bread a decadently creamy texture and most commercial eggnogs contain just the right combination of spices for French toast.

For a wonderful holiday punch, mix together eggnog, fresh orange juice, and mint or basil leaves. A splash of rum or bourbon makes it even better.

When holiday breads need a brand-new twist, use eggnog in place of the cream or milk in the recipe. This trick does wonders for cinnamon rolls, coffee cakes, and other quickbreads.

Tidbit Traditionally, eggnog contains rum or another liqueur along with the eggs, cream, and sugar. However, the festive drink was originally made with ale. The word "nog" is an archaic English word referring to strong ale.

❋Eggplant

To make richer-tasting mashed potatoes, add mashed roasted eggplant. Pierce the skin of an eggplant all over with a fork (so it won't explode). Roast it on a baking sheet at 425°F until the skin wrinkles all over and the flesh becomes tender, about 45 minutes. Or to char, cook the whole eggplant on a grill over direct heat until blackened all over and the flesh is soft. Cool the eggplant, then halve lengthwise and scoop the flesh from skin. Puree or mash the flesh with 1 minced garlic clove and 2 tablespoons extra-virgin olive oil. Meanwhile, boil 3 pounds russet or golden potatoes in plenty of lightly salted water until tender, 30 to 40 minutes. Drain, peel, and chop. Mash in the pot with a potato masher and mix in the pureed eggplant, 1/3 cup plain yogurt, 1/2 teaspoon salt, and 1/4 teaspoon freshly ground black pepper.

❋Energy Drink

To give marinated chicken a lemon-lime flavor, use an energy drink such as Gatorade as the base for the marinade. Add herbs, olive oil, and/or garlic for more flavor.

Tidbit In 1965, a coach for the Florida Gators college football team and one of the university's kidney specialists came up with a concoction of water, salt, sugar, and lemon juice to keep the school's football players hydrated and energized while playing football under the hot Southern sun. Two years later, Gatorade was marketed nationally and has since netted the University of Florida more than $90 million in revenues.

To make a simple lemon-lime sorbet, blend the following ingredients in a food processor:

- 1 cup energy drink, such as Gatorade
- 1 can (11 ounces) mandarin oranges, drained
- 1 can (5 ounces) crushed pineapples, undrained
- 1 container (6 ounces) piña colada or coconut yogurt
- 1/2 cup orange sherbet
- 3 ounces cream cheese

Pour into a metal pan, cover, and freeze until firm. Scrape out servings with a spoon. Keeps frozen for up to 1 month.

Evaporated Milk

For a creamy marinade for chicken or fish, use evaporated milk. The milk subtly flavors the food without breaking down its delicate fibers. It is especially good paired with spicy sauces or seasonings.

To doctor up gravy for leftover turkey sandwiches, combine 1 can (5 ounces) evaporated milk, 1 can (15 ounces) turkey gravy, and 1/2 teaspoon poultry seasoning in a small saucepan. Simmer over medium heat for 5 minutes. Arrange the turkey over toast and pour the gravy over the top.

For quick-and-easy pumpkin pie filling, mix evaporated milk with canned pumpkin, brown sugar, eggs, and pumpkin pie spice.

For a healthy alternative to whipped cream, chill a can of evaporated milk, then whip just like heavy whipping cream. Use to top your favorite desserts.

To make creamy sauces and soups with less fat, use evaporated milk instead of cream. Enrich the texture with a tablespoon or two of sour cream after removing the sauce or soup from the heat. This trick is especially good with cheese soups.

To stir up a quick pasta sauce, mix together evaporated milk, cream cheese, and blue cheese.

To make richer-tasting mashed potatoes, replace 1/2 cup of the regular milk with evaporated milk.

For better-tasting meat loaf, soak 2 bread slices in 1 can (5 ounces) evaporated milk until saturated. Break up the bread and use in place of breadcrumbs in your favorite recipe.

For a healthy alternative to sour cream, mix together 1 cup fat-free evaporated milk and 1 tablespoon fresh lemon juice.

To give sherbets and ice creams a smooth, rich texture, use evaporated milk in place of the cream.

For rich-tasting gratins and quiches without excess fat, use evaporated milk instead of cream or whole milk.

Gelatin

To enhance soups and stews with a silkier texture, stir in 1 envelope (1/4 ounce) unflavored gelatin per 4 quarts of soup or stew. This is the secret to the silky soups of many professional chefs and crafty home cooks. This technique also makes store-bought broth taste richer. Here's how it works: When you simmer animal bones to make traditional stock, the bones release gelatin and collagen, which gives the stock a velvety texture. Packaged gelatin produces the same mouthfeel in soups and stocks without the bones. Of course, if you combine stock made from bones with additional gelatin, the texture will be even richer.

For ultra-velvety chicken soup, remove the meat from half a roasted chicken. Remove and discard the skin, then cut the meat into 1/2-inch pieces and set aside. In a large pot, boil the chicken bones in 1 cup white wine for 3 minutes, then add:

2 quarts chicken broth	1 tablespoon ground coriander
2 carrots, sliced	1 tablespoon finely chopped lemon zest
2 celery stalks, sliced	
3 tablespoons chopped fresh parsley	1 teaspoon ground cumin
	1/2 teaspoon red-pepper flakes

Soften 1 envelope (1/4 ounce) unflavored gelatin in 2 tablespoons water and add to the pot. Bring to a simmer, stirring often, then add 1/3 cup uncooked rice and simmer for 30 minutes. Remove and discard the bones, then stir in the juice of 1 1/2 lemons, 1/3 cup chopped fresh cilantro, and the reserved chicken meat. Simmer for 2 minutes more to heat through.

Tidbit Years ago, gelatin was made from beef bones or cartilage. Today, commercial gelatin is usually a by-product of pig skin.

❋Half-and-Half

To shave calories without sacrificing flavor, use half-and-half in place of cream in sauces and soups. Heavy whipping cream contains 30 to 35 percent butterfat, but half-and-half contains only 10 to 12 percent butterfat.

For a luscious oyster stew, combine 1 quart half-and-half and 2 dozen shucked oysters with their liquids in a soup pot. Heat very slowly over low heat until the oysters plump and curl at their edges, about 10 minutes, stirring occasionally. Be sure not to boil the mixture. Add 1/4 teaspoon salt (or more to taste), a pinch of cayenne pepper, 1 tablespoon paprika, and 2 to 4 tablespoons unsalted butter. Heat until the butter melts. Serve with oyster crackers.

To give hot chocolate a lusciously rich texture, use half-and-half instead of milk.

❋Ham

For a smoky aroma in cooked greens, simmer 2 smoked ham hocks in water for 3 hours. Strain the liquid and discard the ham hocks. Let the broth cool, then chill, so that the fat solidifies on top. Remove and discard the fat. Cook greens such as collards in the liquid until very tender, about 1 hour. Add a pinch of cayenne pepper to kick it up a bit.

To make a delicious broth for pea or bean soups, put 1 meaty ham bone in a large pot and add cold water to generously cover (about 3 quarts). Add 12 whole cloves and bring to a boil. Partly cover and simmer gently until the joint falls apart and the meat is very tender, 3 to 4 hours. Place a colander over a large bowl and strain the broth into the bowl. When the bone is cool enough to handle, remove the meat and discard the bone. Let the broth cool, then chill, so that the fat solidifies on top. Remove and discard the fat. Freeze the broth for up to 6 months and use as the base for soup.

To give potatoes, beans, or rice dishes a shot of smoky flavor, add chopped smoked ham.

For a healthier alternative to bacon, use smoked ham.

To enrich a lentil soup, add chopped ham. First sauté 1 cup chopped onion, 1 chopped carrot, and 1 chopped celery stalk in 2 tablespoons olive oil until tender. Add to a pot along with:

1 cup chopped skinless smoked ham	1/2 teaspoon dried rosemary
6 cups chicken or vegetable broth	1/4 teaspoon dried thyme
1 1/8 cups (1/2 pound) sorted and rinsed lentils	1 bay leaf

Simmer until the lentils are tender, about 25 minutes. Stir in 1 chopped roasted red pepper, 1 tablespoon tomato paste, 1/2 teaspoon salt, and 1/8 teaspoon freshly ground black pepper. Remove the bay leaf before serving.

To pull together a succotash salad from pantry ingredients, combine 2 cups corn kernels, 2 cups lima beans, 2 cups chopped ham, and 1/4 cup chopped sweet pickles. Dress with a mixture of 1/3 cup olive oil, 1/4 cup apple-cider vinegar, 3 tablespoons honey, 2 teaspoons Dijon mustard, 1/2 teaspoon salt, and 1/4 teaspoon freshly ground black pepper.

✳Hoisin Sauce

To make Chinese ketchup, mix together 1 cup ketchup, 2 tablespoons hoisin sauce, and 1/8 teaspoon garlic salt. Use as a condiment, marinade, or glaze.

To stir up an Asian pan sauce for sautéed chicken breasts or pork chops, remove the sautéed meat from the pan and add 1 small minced garlic clove, 1 teaspoon finely chopped fresh ginger, and a pinch of red-pepper flakes to the pan. Cook for 1 minute, then add 3 tablespoons hoisin sauce and 2/3 cup chicken broth. Heat until the mixture simmers, stirring often, 2 to 3 minutes. Serve over the chicken or meat.

For a quick glaze on grilled or broiled fish steaks, mix together hoisin sauce, chili sauce, ginger, garlic, and lemon juice. Brush over grilled fish during the last 5 minutes of grilling. This glaze tastes especially good when the fish has been marinated in soy sauce, ginger, and garlic.

✳Honey

For an amazing spread for bread, particularly cornbread, combine 1/2 cup softened butter with 2 tablespoons honey.

To make pumpkin pie without sugar, combine 1 can (16 ounces) pureed pumpkin, 1 cup evaporated milk, 2/3 cup honey, 3 eggs, 1 teaspoon ground cinnamon, 1/4 teaspoon ground ginger, and 1/4 teaspoon ground allspice until smooth. Pour into an unbaked 9-inch deep-dish pie shell and bake at 400°F until a knife comes out clean, about 45 minutes.

For a touch of sweetness in homemade spaghetti sauce, stir in 1 to 2 teaspoons honey. This trick works especially well when the tomatoes are not at the peak of ripeness.

Tidbit Bees were first domesticated in artificial hives in 2400, B.C., by the Egyptians.

✳Horseradish

To give potato salad more pizzazz, stir in a few teaspoons of prepared horseradish.

To liven up creamy salad dressings, stir in a teaspoon of prepared horseradish. This technique is perfect for creamy Italian, ranch, blue cheese, or other dressings with a base of sour cream or buttermilk.

For a delicious bacon dip, bring 2 cups sour cream to room temperature. Cook 8 to 10 slices of hickory-smoked bacon until crisp and golden, about 5 minutes. Drain and chop the bacon. In a small bowl, combine the sour cream, the bacon, 2 tablespoons drained prepared horseradish, 1/2 teaspoon Worcestershire sauce, 1/2 teaspoon salt, and 1/4 teaspoon freshly ground black pepper. Cover and chill for 24 hours. Stir and transfer to a serving dish. Garnish with additional crumbled bacon, if you like.

To make zestier deviled eggs, hard cook 6 eggs. Halve the eggs lengthwise and cut a slice from the bottom of each half so that the eggs sit flat. Remove the yolks and mash them with:

1 tablespoon mayonnaise	1/4 teaspoon salt
1 tablespoon prepared horse-radish	1/8 teaspoon freshly ground black pepper
1/2 garlic clove, minced	

Mound into the egg white halves and dust with paprika.

To give fish stews and soups a lift, prepared horseradish is the answer. It blends in perfectly and adds a sharp counterpoint to the mild-tasting fish. A dash of hot-pepper sauce doesn't hurt either.

To whip up classic cocktail sauce for shrimp or other seafood, combine 2/3 cup bottled chili sauce, 1 tablespoon prepared horseradish, 1 tablespoon fresh lemon juice, and 1/4 teaspoon hot-pepper sauce.

For an even easier cocktail sauce, mix together equal parts horseradish and ketchup. If that's too strong, add more ketchup to taste.

For a no-fail sauce for roast beef, prime rib, and filet mignon, whip 1/2 cup cold heavy cream in a chilled bowl until almost stiff. Fold in 3 tablespoons drained prepared horseradish or 1 1/2 tablespoons peeled and grated fresh horseradish, 1 teaspoon fresh lemon juice, 1/2 teaspoon grated lemon zest, and 1/2 teaspoon salt.

✳Hot-Pepper Sauce

To perk up scrambled eggs, use 1/2 teaspoon hot-pepper sauce for every 8 eggs.

For a novel topping for corn muffins, mix together 1 cup honey and 3 tablespoons hot-pepper sauce. Store at room temperature. Try it on grilled shrimp, too.

To make a spicy yogurt marinade, combine 1 cup plain yogurt, 1/4 cup fresh lemon juice, 2 tablespoons hot-pepper sauce, and 2 teaspoons cayenne pepper. Use to marinate 3 to 4 pounds of chicken parts for 1 hour. The chicken will be spicy but not unbearably hot.

For mahi-mahi tacos with a kick, simmer mahi-mahi fillets in picante sauce, then add lime juice and cilantro. Serve in warm flour tortillas or crispy corn tortillas with sour cream, cheddar cheese, shredded lettuce, chopped onions, and lime wedges for squeezing over the top.

To make nut brittle that will surprise your guests, mix a little hot-pepper sauce into the sugar mixture before spreading the mixture on a baking sheet.

To make a simple sauce for Buffalo-style chicken wings, merely combine equal parts melted unsalted butter and hot-pepper sauce. You can dip the entire wing into the sauce, or use it as a separate dipping sauce for fried or grilled chicken. Better yet, use as a baste on grilled chicken. Some people add ketchup to the butter and hot-sauce combo to reduce the heat and strong vinegar flavor.

Tidbit Hot-pepper sauces contain a potent blend of chile peppers, vinegar, and salt. While we people often love the flavor, most animals run from these ingredients. For that reason, hot-pepper sauce makes an effective organic pesticide. Put some hot-pepper sauce in a spray bottle (diluted with some extra vinegar and water, if necessary) and spray it on your garden plants to keep bugs and other critters away. The spray is effective for 3 to 5 days.

❋Hummus

To thicken and flavor soups, mix in some plain or flavored store-bought hummus. This technique works especially well with vegetable soups.

To bind fish or crab cakes, use plain hummus instead of eggs or bread crumbs. Just a bit of hummus binds the ingredients together and adds an unexpectedly pleasant flavor.

For an outstanding hot dip that will keep guests noshing, combine hummus and cream cheese or another flavorful semisoft cheese (such as Brie or Camembert) and microwave just until the cheese melts. Serve with crackers, bread, or cut-up vegetables.

To stir up a quick sauce for poultry, thin out plain or flavored hummus with chicken broth.

When you're out of mayonnaise and need a tasty sandwich spread, use hummus. It works especially well with wrap sandwiches that include vegetables and chicken or turkey.

✳Jams and Jellies

To spruce up store-bought coleslaw, stir in some orange marmalade and toasted chopped almonds.

To balance the flavor of tomato sauce, stir in 1/4 cup grape jelly for every 4 cups homemade sauce. The sweetness of the jelly helps to balance the acidity of less-than-perfect tomatoes.

To make muffins with a surprise inside, spoon 2 tablespoons muffin batter into each muffin cup. Make an indentation in the muffin batter with the back of a spoon and ladle in 1 teaspoon jam, marmalade, or preserves. Spoon the remaining batter over the jam in each muffin cup. Bake as directed in the recipe.

To make overnight stuffed French toast, cut 1 loaf Italian bread crosswise into 8 to 10 slices that are each about 1 1/2 inches thick. Cut a slit through the top crust of each slice to form a deep pocket. In a medium bowl, mix together 1 package (8 ounces) cream cheese, 2 tablespoons confectioners' sugar, and 1/2 teaspoon almond extract. Spread the cream cheese mixture equally inside the bread pockets, then spread 1/2 to 3/4 cup strawberry, raspberry or cherry preserves equally inside the pockets, opposite the cream cheese. Lay the stuffed bread in a single layer in a shallow 4-quart baking dish (roughly 15 x 10 inches). In a medium bowl, combine 5 eggs, 1 1/2 cups light cream or half-and-half, 1 teaspoon vanilla extract, 1 tablespoon confectioners' sugar, and a pinch of salt. Pour evenly over the bread, tilting the pan and swirling the egg mixture to completely saturate the bread. Cover and chill in the refrigerator overnight. In the morning, bring the bread to room temperature, then cook in unsalted butter or oil on a griddle until golden brown on both sides, 3 to 5 minutes per side. Serve with maple syrup.

To make a quick glaze for baked or grilled chicken, mix together cherry preserves and fresh orange juice. Brush onto the chicken before baking or during the last 5 minutes of grilling to create a glaze.

For a quick carrot slaw with a twist, combine 3 cups pre-shredded carrots, 1/2 chopped red onion, 1/4 cup golden raisins, 1 tablespoon orange marmalade, 1/4 cup olive oil, 3 tablespoons capers, 3 tablespoons red-wine vinegar, 1/4 teaspoon salt, and 1/4 teaspoon freshly ground black pepper.

For sweet and savory slow-cooked brisket, put a 3-pound brisket in a slow cooker, in one or two pieces. In a medium bowl, combine 1 cup ketchup, 1/4 cup grape jam, 1 envelope onion soup mix, and 1/2 teaspoon freshly ground black pepper. Add the mixture to the slow cooker, making sure the meat is well-coated. Cover and cook on low until the meat is tender, 8 to 10 hours.

To thicken a vinaigrette, whisk in a few teaspoons of orange marmalade, apricot jam, or raspberry preserves.

For a quick filling for thumbprint cookies or nut rolls, mix together raspberry jam and almond extract.

To pull together a fresh strawberry dessert sauce, melt 2 tablespoons strawberry preserves over medium heat. Add 2 tablespoons brandy, a pinch of salt, and 1 pint sliced strawberries. Cook until the berries begin to fall apart. Cool, then serve the sauce over cake or ice cream.

For an easy cherry marinade for grilled chicken, combine:

1/4 cup cherry preserves	2 tablespoons olive oil
6 ounces black cherry soda	1/2 teaspoon salt
2 tablespoons fresh lemon juice	1/4 teaspoon ground cinnamon

Add to the mixture 2 pounds of boneless, skinless chicken breasts or thighs and marinate in the refrigerator for 4 to 8 hours. Grill or broil the chicken, then bring the marinade to a boil in a saucepan. Add another 6 ounces of black cherry soda, a drained can of dark sweet Bing cherries, and boil for 5 minutes. Dissolve 1 tablespoon cornstarch in 1 tablespoon cold water and stir into the marinade until thickened. Serve with the chicken. Some grated orange zest makes a nice touch.

For a wonderful sauce for salmon or chicken, mix 1 part blueberry or raspberry jam into 2 parts barbecue sauce. Spoon a layer of the sauce over the salmon or chicken and broil until finished. Spoon a little more sauce over the salmon or chicken before serving.

For a simply outstanding glaze for roasted or grilled leg of lamb, use red currant jelly mixed with fresh orange juice.

To stir up a quick glaze for barbecued ribs, combine 2/3 cup apricot preserves, 2 tablespoons Dijon mustard, 1 tablespoon toasted sesame oil, and 1/4 teaspoon cayenne pepper in a saucepan. Simmer over low heat for 5 minutes, then brush onto the barbecued ribs during the last 10 minutes of cooking.

For an easy apple glaze for pork, combine 1/4 cup apple jelly, 2 tablespoons fresh lemon juice, 1/2 teaspoon ground cinnamon, and 1/4 teaspoon ground allspice. Place 1 pork tenderloin in a small roasting pan and brush with half of the apple-jelly mixture. Roast in a 375°F oven until the center registers 155°F on an instant-read thermometer and the juices run clear, about 25 minutes. Let stand for 10 minutes. Meanwhile, on a broiler pan, arrange 2 cored and thinly sliced red apples and brush with the remaining apple-jelly mixture. Broil 5 inches from the heat until the apple slices are tender, about 5 minutes. Serve with the sliced tenderloin.

To make an easy orange sauce for fruit desserts or cheesecake, boil 3 cups fresh orange juice until reduced to 1 1/2 cups, then stir in 1/2 cup orange marmalade and 1/4 cup firmly packed brown sugar. Thicken with a mixture of 1 tablespoon cornstarch dissolved in 1 tablespoon fresh lemon juice.

To make upside-down muffins, spoon 1 1/2 teaspoons of your favorite jam or preserves into the bottom of each greased muffin cup in the pan. Top with your favorite muffin batter and bake as directed in the recipe. Run a knife around the sides and invert the muffins onto a rack to cool.

To thicken and extend a fruit pie or cobbler filling, mix some jam or preserves in with the fresh fruit. For example, stir together:

1/2 cup blackberry jam	1 tablespoon sugar
1/4 cup blackberry brandy	1 tablespoon fresh lemon juice
2 tablespoons cornstarch	1 teaspoon grated lemon zest

Add 2 pints fresh blackberries and/or blueberries to the mixture and toss gently. Turn into a greased 8 x 12-inch baking dish. To make a topping, in a large bowl, stir together:

1 1/2 cups all-purpose flour	1/4 teaspoon baking soda
1/3 cup sugar	Pinch of salt
2 teaspoons baking powder	

Make a well in the center of the dry mix. Pour in 2/3 cup milk, 3 tablespoons melted unsalted butter, 1 tablespoon fresh lemon juice, and 2 teaspoons vanilla extract. Stir quickly, just to blend. Spoon the batter over the top of the cobbler without smoothing it. Sprinkle with 1 tablespoon sugar. Bake at 400°F until golden brown and bubbly, 25 to 30 minutes. Let stand for 20 minutes before serving. Serve warm with whipped cream or ice cream.

To make a glaze for Brie cheese, stir together 1/2 cup strawberry or cherry preserves, 1/2 teaspoon grated lemon zest, and 1/4 teaspoon almond extract. Spread over the wheel of Brie and bake at 350°F until the cheese just begins to melt, 12 to 15 minutes.

For a jump-start on cold strawberry soup, combine strawberry preserves and buttermilk as the base.

For a dessert of strawberries with warm rhubarb sauce, cook 1 pound frozen, cut-up rhubarb and 1/2 cup sugar in a saucepan over medium heat until the rhubarb is softened, about 10 minutes. Stir in 1 cup strawberry preserves. Serve warm over 1 1/2 pints sliced strawberries. Garnish with sour cream or whipped cream, if you like.

To doctor up plain yogurt, stir in strawberry, raspberry, or blueberry jam. It's both cheaper and healthier than buying yogurt cups that are premixed with "fruit at the bottom."

For an easy cake filling, mix 1/2 cup of your favorite jam, jelly, or preserves with 1 tablespoon brandy or liqueur and microwave until the mixture can be stirred smooth.

To quickly glaze a fruit tart or cheesecake and give it a pretty sheen, melt some red currant jelly in a microwavable bowl. Brush the melted jelly over the top of the fruit tart or cheesecake.

❊Ketchup

To make real Russian dressing, whisk together 1/4 cup mayonnaise, 1/4 cup sour cream, 2 tablespoons ketchup, and 3 tablespoons fresh lemon juice. Then, to be truly authentic, fold in 2 tablespoons red or black caviar (remember— salmon eggs are very reasonably priced if you don't want to splurge on the serious stuff).

For a basic sweet-and-sour stir-fry sauce, dissolve 1 teaspoon cornstarch in 1 tablespoon cold water in the bottom of a medium bowl. Stir in:

1/3 cup rice vinegar	1/2 teaspoon finely chopped fresh ginger
3 tablespoons ketchup	
2 1/2 to 3 tablespoons dark brown sugar	1/2 garlic clove, minced
	1 tablespoon rice wine or dry sherry

Add the sauce to the hot wok or skillet at the end of stir-frying and cook until thickened, about 1 minute. This sauce tastes great with chicken, pork, and seafood.

To make an easy braising liquid for beef brisket, mix 2 1/2 cups ketchup with 2 1/2 cups beef broth. Scatter 1/2 teaspoon salt and 1/4 teaspoon freshly ground black pepper over 2 to 3 pounds of beef brisket. Brown the brisket in a Dutch oven in 1 tablespoon vegetable oil. Remove the brisket and sauté 2 large chopped onions in the pan. Add the ketchup mixture and simmer for 2 minutes. Add the brisket, cover, and simmer until the meat is fork-tender, about 2 hours. Skim the fat from the gravy, then slice the meat and serve with the gravy.

For a sweet-and-sour Creole vinaigrette, combine:

1/3 cup ketchup	2 tablespoons apple-cider vinegar
2 tablespoons spicy brown mustard	1 tablespoon prepared horseradish
2 tablespoons sugar	1 garlic clove, minced
	1/2 teaspoon hot-pepper sauce

Whisk in 1 cup vegetable oil in a slow, steady stream until the dressing is thick. Add 1/4 teaspoon salt and 1/8 teaspoon freshly ground black pepper.

Lemons and Limes

To freshen up mayonnaise, stir 1 teaspoon fresh lemon juice and 1 teaspoon extra-virgin olive oil into each 1/4 cup mayonnaise.

For fluffier rice, add fresh lemon juice while the rice is cooking.

To make better roasted chicken, take a tip from the popular Italian cooking teacher Marcella Hazan, who made this technique famous. First, rinse a 3- to 4-pound chicken inside and out. Pat the chicken dry with paper towels. Roll 2 small lemons on a hard surface, pressing firmly to soften them. Using a paring knife, prick each lemon about 15 times to pierce all over. Place one lemon and 1 large fresh tarragon or rosemary sprig (or 1 teaspoon dried tarragon or rosemary) in the chicken body cavity. Push in the second lemon and secure the opening with toothpicks. Rub 1 tablespoon olive oil all over the bird and sprinkle with 1/2 teaspoon salt and 1/4 teaspoon freshly ground black pepper. If you like, tie together the drumsticks with string so that the chicken will hold its shape. Place the chicken, breast side up, in a shallow roasting pan and roast at 450°F for about 20 minutes. Reduce the oven temperature to 325°F and roast until the breast meat registers 180°F on a meat thermometer and the juices run clear, 40 to 60 minutes longer. Remove from the oven, turn the chicken breast side down, and let rest in the pan for 15 to 20 minutes before carving. After carving, open the chicken cavity and pour the juices all over the chicken meat.

To give any quickbread a refreshing aroma, add 1 tablespoon grated lemon zest. Try it in pancakes, waffles, muffins, and coffee cakes, especially if the quickbread includes fruit such as blueberries.

To make aromatic olive oil, heat 1/2 cup olive oil in a saucepan over medium heat for 5 minutes. Remove from the heat and add 1/4 cup grated lemon or lime zest. Cool to room temperature, then refrigerate the flavored oil in a sealed container for up to 1 week. If the oil solidifies, let it come to room temperature and become liquid again. Use the citrus-flavored oil on chicken and fish and in salads.

To give poached white fish fillets an especially bright white color, add a tablespoon of fresh lemon juice to the poaching liquid. You get a nice flavor bonus, too!

For an island-style marinade for roast pork, mix together:

Juice and zest of 1 lime

1/2 cup pineapple juice

1/4 cup cream of coconut or coconut milk

2 tablespoons dark rum

1 tablespoon chopped fresh ginger

1 tablespoon chopped garlic

1/2 teaspoon salt

Marinate a 2-pound pork roast in the mixture in the refrigerator for 8 to 10 hours. Roast the pork until cooked through, then boil the marinade for 5 minutes. Dissolve 1 teaspoon cornstarch in 1/4 cup cold chicken broth and stir into the marinade to thicken it. Serve with the pork.

To add a sweet citrus aroma to Brussels sprouts without discoloring the vegetable, toss the sprouts with grated lemon zest after cooking. The acidity of lemon juice can discolor green vegetables such as Brussels sprouts and broccoli, but the zest contains only the flavorful lemon oil and none of the acid that can cause discoloration.

To rescue cake frosting that has become granular from sugar, add a squeeze of fresh lemon juice and mix until smooth.

Tidbit California and Arizona produce about 95 percent of America's lemons.

For a lively pan sauce for sautéed chicken breasts, veal scalloppine, or fish fillets, remove the chicken, veal, or fish from the pan then add 3 tablespoons unsalted butter, 1 tablespoon finely chopped onion or shallot, and 1 minced garlic clove. Sauté for 1 minute, then stir in the juice of 1 lemon and 1 tablespoon chopped fresh parsley. Heat until the mixture simmers. Serve over the chicken, veal, or fish.

To add zip to spaghetti, boil the pasta without salt and instead squeeze the juice from 1/2 lemon into the water.

❋Maple Syrup

To make a quick sweet-and-sour sauce for pork, mix together:

2 tablespoons balsamic vinegar

1 tablespoon maple syrup

1 tablespoon olive oil

1 tablespoon water

2 teaspoons Dijon mustard

4 drops hot-pepper sauce

For a better-tasting honey mustard, mix together 1/2 cup Dijon mustard, 2 tablespoons honey, and 1 tablespoon maple syrup. This sauce is excellent with breaded and fried chicken tenders.

For a fabulous marinade for portobello mushrooms, mix together:

2 tablespoons olive oil

2 tablespoons soy sauce

2 tablespoons chopped fresh rosemary

3 garlic cloves, minced

2 teaspoons toasted sesame oil

2 teaspoons maple syrup

1/4 teaspoon salt

1/4 teaspoon freshly ground black pepper

Add 4 portobello mushroom caps, refrigerate for 1 to 6 hours, then grill or broil until tender.

To deepen the flavor of store-bought barbecue sauce, stir 2 tablespoons pure maple syrup into 1 cup bottled barbecue sauce.

For moist and flavorful pork tenderloin, rub pork tenderloin with store-bought seasoning blend, then wrap the roast in slices of bacon. Brush all over with maple syrup before roasting and slicing.'

Tidbit Maple tree sap is about 98 percent water and only 2 percent sugar. Maple syrup is made by boiling off most of that water; it takes 40 gallons of sap to make 1 gallon of maple syrup. No wonder pure maple syrup is so expensive!

To make a wonderful turkey salad using leftover turkey meat, mix together:

1/2 cup mayonnaise

3 tablespoons maple syrup

2 tablespoons sweet orange marmalade

2 tablespoons apple-cider vinegar

1 tablespoon hot-pepper sauce

1/4 teaspoon salt

1/8 teaspoon freshly ground black pepper

Add to the mixture 4 cups (about 1 1/3 pounds) chopped boneless roasted turkey meat, 1/2 cup finely chopped red onion, the halved sections of 3 oranges, and 2 chopped celery stalks. Toss to mix.

To make better-than-usual applesauce, put 2 pounds peeled, cored, and coarsely chopped apples (preferably McIntosh) in a saucepan. Add 1 pound sliced rhubarb (fresh or frozen) and 1/4 cup water. Cover and cook over medium heat until all of the fruit is soft, about 10 minutes, stirring occasionally. Stir in 6 tablespoons pure maple syrup. Serve with vanilla ice cream or frozen yogurt.

For an instant, homemade granola with a sweet surprise, improvise a mix of oatmeal with maple syrup, honey, nuts, sunflower seeds, and mixed chopped dried fruit such as dried cranberries and/or cherries.

For a delicious fruit dessert, arrange 12 fresh pineapple slices in a single layer on a foil-lined baking sheet. In a small bowl, combine 3 tablespoons maple syrup, 2 tablespoons brown sugar, and 2 teaspoons rum. Brush over the pineapple slices. Roast in a 400°F oven for 10 minutes. Turn on the broiler and place the baking sheet under the broiler until the pineapple is golden brown, about 1 minute.

To make a Cobb salad something special, use maple syrup in the dressing. Arrange chopped lettuce, avocado, hard-cooked egg, cooked and crumbled bacon, and blue cheese on plates. For the dressing, mix together the drippings from the cooked bacon, olive oil, vinegar, mustard, and maple syrup.

To deepen the flavor of chicken wings, use maple syrup instead of sugar or honey in the glaze. Pure maple syrup and hot sauce make an irresistible sweet-and-sour combination.

To give whipped cream an autumnal flavor, sweeten it with maple syrup instead of sugar. Whip 1 cup chilled heavy cream in a chilled bowl using chilled beaters. When the cream just holds a shape, add 1/4 cup pure maple syrup. Beat until the cream holds soft peaks when the beaters are lifted. Serve chilled.

To make an easy glaze for roast pork or poultry, mix 1/2 cup pure maple syrup, 1 tablespoon Worcestershire sauce, and 1 tablespoon olive oil. Brush onto the meat during the last 30 minutes of roasting.

✳Mayonnaise

To make a lightning fast anchovy sauce, mix together 2 tablespoons mayonnaise, 1 tablespoon anchovy paste, 1 tablespoon extra-virgin olive oil, 2 teaspoons fresh lemon juice, and 1/4 teaspoon minced garlic. Use to top cooked fish fillets.

For ultra-rich omelets and scrambled eggs, whip in 1 tablespoon mayonnaise per egg until the mayonnaise is fully incorporated and no flecks of white remain.

To create a crisp, golden skin on roasted chicken, slather mayonnaise all over the bird before roasting.

To make extra-creamy spinach-artichoke dip, sauté 1/2 cup finely chopped red onion and 1 minced garlic clove in 2 teaspoons oil in a saucepan. Stir in:

1 cup sour cream	1 cup drained and chopped canned or thawed artichoke hearts
1/2 cup mayonnaise	
3/4 cup freshly grated Parmesan cheese	5 cups baby spinach leaves

Cook until the spinach wilts. Serve warm in a hollowed-out loaf of pumpernickel bread with the removed bread cut into cubes. You'll need another loaf of bread to have enough for dipping.

To doctor up store-bought mayonnaise, just stir in your favorite ingredients. Here are some easy-flavored mayonnaise ideas. Start with 1/4 cup mayonnaise, then flavor away!

Sesame: 1 teaspoon toasted sesame oil and 1/2 teaspoon fresh lemon juice, fresh lime juice, or rice vinegar.

Mediterranean caper: 1 tablespoon coarsely chopped drained capers, 1 teaspoon olive oil, and 1 teaspoon fresh lemon juice.

Anchovy: 2 to 3 teaspoons anchovy paste, 1 teaspoon olive oil, and 1 teaspoon lemon juice.

Olive: 3 tablespoons finely minced pitted black olives (such as kalamata or other brine-cured olives).

Cilantro: 3 tablespoons chopped fresh cilantro, 1 teaspoon olive oil, 1 teaspoon fresh lemon or lime juice, 1/8 teaspoon ground cumin, and a grinding of fresh black pepper.

Curry: 1 teaspoon toasted curry powder and 1/2 teaspoon honey.

Aioli: 1 mashed garlic clove and 1/4 teaspoon salt.

For a quick, creamy Italian dressing, whisk together 1/2 cup Italian-style or garlic vinaigrette salad dressing and 2 tablespoons mayonnaise.

To make broiled fish fillets super-moist, coat them with plain or flavored mayonnaise. Dijon mustard, chopped parsley, and lemon zest make nice additions for fish. Broil until the fish is just a bit filmy and moist in the center when tested.

To make ultra-rich and velvety chocolate cake, replace one-third of the butter with mayonnaise. Be sure to blend the mayonnaise thoroughly into the batter until no lumps or white flecks are visible.

❋Molasses

To deepen the flavor of cornbread, add 2 tablespoons molasses to the batter for a 10-inch round pan of cornbread.

For incredible homemade caramel corn, mix together 1/2 cup firmly packed brown sugar, 1/4 cup corn syrup, 1/4 cup unsalted butter, and 1 1/2 tablespoons molasses in a medium saucepan. Bring to a boil over medium heat and boil for 5 minutes. Remove from the heat and stir in 3/4 teaspoon vanilla extract, 1/4 teaspoon baking soda, and 1/4 teaspoon salt. Pour over 6 cups unsalted purchased or homemade popcorn, stirring constantly to evenly coat the popcorn. Spread onto a greased baking sheet and bake at 250°F for about an hour, stirring often. Remove from the oven and break up any clumps of popcorn. Cool completely before serving.

When your homemade barbecue sauce needs more oomph, stir in 2 to 4 tablespoons molasses per 3 cups of sauce. A shot or two of Worcestershire also does wonders.

To enrich beef and pork stews, add 1 to 2 tablespoons molasses to the broth before simmering the meat.

Tidbit Unsulfured molasses has a lighter, cleaner taste than sulfured molasses, which is processed with sulfur dioxide as a preservative. Most supermarkets now sell unsulfured molasses.

❋Mozzarella Cheese

For a fun twist on fried rice, add mozzarella cheese. Most Chinese recipes call for beaten uncooked eggs to be drizzled over the fried rice right at the end of the cooking to help hold the rice and other ingredients together. Try adding a cup or so of shredded mozzarella at the end instead. It will have the same effect but with a fresh and different taste and texture!

To give frittatas an irresistible topping, sprinkle shredded mozzarella cheese over the top, then broil until lightly browned.

❄Mustard

To add spark to egg-based dishes, like soufflés, quiches, and savory custards, add a teaspoon of Dijon mustard.

For a crispy catfish po'boy, coat catfish fillets with mustard then dip them in cornmeal. Sauté the catfish in oil and serve on a baguette or French bread with lettuce, tomato, thinly sliced onion, and a sauce made from mayonnaise, mustard, Tabasco sauce, parsley, and pickle relish.

To perk up grilled cheese sandwiches, spread a thin layer of mustard on the bread before assembling and grilling the sandwich.

To make a special sauce for burgers, mix together 1 tablespoon ketchup, 1 tablespoon mayonnaise, and 1 teaspoon spicy brown mustard. A burger chain popularized this secret sauce, which is easily replicated at home.

To thicken and liven up a pan sauce for sautéed meats, use Dijon mustard. After pan-searing chicken, pork, or beef, swirl in some red wine, port, or sherry and a few tablespoons of unsalted butter to deglaze the pan, then reduce the liquid to half its volume. Stir in a teaspoon of Dijon mustard for kick.

For quick-and-easy homemade barbecue sauce, combine in a saucepan:

1 cup ketchup
1 tablespoon soy sauce
1 teaspoon chili powder
1 garlic clove, minced

1/4 cup white or red wine
2 tablespoons red-wine vinegar
  or apple-cider vinegar

Simmer over medium heat for 5 to 10 minutes to blend the flavors and reduce the volume slightly. Finally, stir in 1 teaspoon prepared mustard.

When you need a fast sweet-and-sour dip or sauce, whisk together 1/2 cup currant jelly and 5 tablespoons Dijon mustard. Let stand for 5 minutes and whisk again until smooth. Use as a dip for crudités or a sauce for broiled shrimp, pork, or chicken skewers.

For a brown-sugar glaze for ham, combine 3/4 cup firmly packed light brown sugar, 1/4 cup spicy brown mustard or Dijon mustard, and 2 tablespoons apple-cider vinegar. Pat over the top of a baked ham 45 minutes before it is done.

To doctor up store-bought barbecue sauce, stir in 1 tablespoon prepared mustard per cup of sauce.

✳Nuts

To add another dimension of flavor to a green salad, mix in some toasted nuts such as pecans, walnuts, or pine nuts. Toast the nuts in a dry skillet over medium heat until they smell fragrant, shaking the pan often.

For hamburgers with a deliciously crunchy crust, sprinkle 1/2 to 3/4 cup chopped, unsalted peanuts on a sheet of wax paper. Press one side of each burger into the chopped nuts and broil, grill, or pan-fry the burgers.

To give frittatas and omelets interesting crunch, add chopped nuts such as cashews or almonds to the egg mixture.

For a pie crust that's amazingly tasty and healthy, use ground nuts and oil in place of shortening or butter. In a food processor, combine 1/2 cup toasted slivered almonds, 1/3 cup sugar, and 1/4 teaspoon salt until finely ground. Add 1 cup plain dried bread crumbs and pulse until mixed. Drizzle in 1 beaten egg white and 2 tablespoons olive oil. Pulse until just combined. Press into a 9-inch springform pan or pie plate. Pre-bake the crust on a baking sheet for 10 minutes before adding the filling.

To give sauces rich body, add finely ground nuts. For instance, ground walnuts, blue cheese, and half-and-half make a fabulous sauce for pasta. Finely ground pine nuts lend flavor and body to pesto sauce. Pureed chestnuts make a rich base for sauces and soups.

For a tropical crust on fish fillets, add ground macadamia nuts to the breading. Or coat the fillets in flour, then beaten eggs, then chopped macadamia nuts. Sauté and serve topped with a simple pineapple salsa of cubed pineapple, chopped cilantro, red onion, and fresh lime juice.

> *Tidbit* Cashews are members of the same plant family as poison ivy. The shell of cashew nuts contains an oil that irritates the skin and causes some people to get blisters. That's why cashews are never sold in the shell. The nut itself has none of these affects.

To make stuffing taste better, stir about 1 cup toasted and chopped pecans into 6 to 8 cups of your favorite poultry stuffing.

If you overcooked your stir-fry, add crunch with crushed peanuts or cashews.

For a new twist on breaded chicken, stir finely ground nuts into the bread crumb mixture. Pecans, walnuts, almonds, cashews, and peanuts all work well.

For an effortless muffin topping, sprinkle chopped nuts onto the muffin batter in each muffin cup before baking.

To make delicious walnut popcorn, cook popping corn in hot oil in a heavy saucepan. Meanwhile, finely chop 2/3 cup walnut pieces in a food processor until finely ground and oily but not a smooth paste. Toss the popped corn with the ground walnuts, 1/2 teaspoon salt, and 1/2 teaspoon sugar.

To make more substantial rice pilafs, add chopped nuts such as pistachios, macadamias, or almonds.

To liven up egg salad or chicken salad sandwiches, add 1/2 cup toasted and chopped pecans, walnuts, almonds, or cashews to every 2 to 3 cups of salad.

❊Oats

For a low-calorie alternative baked good topping, use rolled oats instead of nuts.

To add a novel flavor to soups and stews, use old-fashioned oatmeal instead of rice or barley. Stir in 1/3 cup old-fashioned oatmeal per 4 cups of liquid. Let simmer until the oatmeal is tender but not mushy. Old-fashioned oats add a wonderfully chewy texture.

For heartier, more nutritious pancakes, add old-fashioned rolled oats to the batter. Pecans and sesame seeds add even more crunch.

❊Olive Oil

To make cakes with less saturated fat, replace half of the butter with olive oil. Fruity green olive oil with a low acid content lends a rich, fruity flavor to cakes.

For aromatic mashed potatoes with a rich taste, use olive oil instead of butter. Step up the flavor by also adding a small amount of your best-quality extra-virgin olive oil.

Tidbit Olive oil is so useful that Homer called it liquid gold. Use it as a skin moisturizer, an alternative to traditional shave cream, a lubricant to unstick a stuck zipper or silence squeaky doors, a furniture polish, and a makeup remover.

To make desserts with a blend of savory and sweet flavors, use olive oil as the fat instead of shortening or butter. Pastries, cakes, and even ice cream made with olive oil, sugar, fruit, and herbs, achieve a tantalizing blend of sweet and savory tastes.

To reduce the amount of butter in your diet, do as many fine restaurants do and serve olive oil as a flavoring for bread, rather than butter. Place small bowls of olive oil on the table so that people can dunk chunks of bread.

For a nearly instant topping for a pound of pasta, heat 4 ounces olive oil in a small pan, then add 4 thinly sliced garlic cloves. Sauté until the garlic is golden. Add a few tablespoons of freshly chopped parsley to the oil, plus salt and freshly ground black pepper, and pour over the cooked pasta. Toss and serve with Parmesan cheese on the side.

*Olives

For an exquisite dip for crackers or bread, combine in a food processor:

1 cup pitted Kalamata olives	1 tablespoon olive oil
2 cups fresh parsley leaves	1 tablespoon fresh lemon juice
2 tablespoons drained capers	1/2 teaspoon dried thyme
1 garlic clove	1/4 teaspoon freshly ground black pepper
1 cup pine nuts	

Process until finely minced but not quite smooth.

To make hamburgers with an edge, mix 1/2 cup sliced pimiento-stuffed green olives into 1 to 1 1/2 pounds ground beef. Shape into 4 patties and grill, broil, or pan-fry over medium heat until the center registers 160°F on an instant-read thermometer and the meat is no longer pink, 4 to 6 minutes per side.

To give polenta more texture and a rich Mediterranean flavor, stir in a few pitted and halved or chopped oil-cured or brine-cured olives.

To give tomato sauces a deeper flavor, stir in several pitted and chopped oil-cured olives.

To give bread-machine white breads an Italian twist, add in chopped black olives, preferably oil-cured or brined-cured varieties. Also use olive oil in place of butter in the recipe.

To add Mediterranean flavors to rice, cook the rice as you normally would, but add such ingredients as chopped oil-cured olives, diced roasted red peppers, a squeeze of lemon, and a pinch of thyme, oregano, or basil.

✳Orange Juice

For a deliciously healthy breakfast treat, slice a banana into a bowl and top it with fresh orange juice. The juice adds sweetness, tang, and moisture to the banana—it's a perfect flavor and texture combination.

For instant "pickles", mix orange juice with Asian-style ingredients. In a small bowl, combine:

4 parts fresh orange juice

2 parts vegetable oil

2 parts rice vinegar

2 parts soy sauce

1 part sesame oil

Mix well and pour over sliced cucumbers to cover. Serve immediately, or let the cucumber slices soak in the refrigerator for up to 24 hours to absorb more flavor.

To stir up a fast and fabulous vinaigrette, whisk together 1/4 cup fresh orange juice, 1 teaspoon grated orange zest, 1 tablespoon fresh lemon juice, 1/2 teaspoon Dijon mustard, and 1/2 teaspoon salt. Gradually whisk in 1/2 cup fruity olive oil. Excellent on spinach salads.

For an herb-scented Bundt cake, add chopped fresh rosemary, fresh orange juice, and grated orange zest to the batter. Replacing half of the recipe's butter with olive oil also adds to the fruity flavor.

For an easy mango sorbet, mix 1/2 cup orange juice, 1/2 cup sugar, 1 package (about 5 ounces) frozen mango chunks, and 1 teaspoon vanilla extract in a food processor. Process until smooth and thick, using 4- to 5-second pulses. Scrape into a shallow metal pan and freeze for up to 2 hours. Scrape out servings with a spoon. If you freeze longer, return the mixture to the food processor and pulse to revive its creamy texture.

For an aromatic marinade for pork tenderloin, mix together:

1 can (6 ounces) thawed orange juice concentrate

1/4 cup chicken broth

2 tablespoons chopped fresh rosemary

3 garlic cloves, minced

2 tablespoons olive oil

2 tablespoons rum

1/2 teaspoon salt

1/2 teaspoon freshly ground black pepper

Marinate 2 pounds pork tenderloin in the mixture for 4 to 8 hours. Grill or broil the pork, then boil the marinade for 5 minutes. Dissolve 1 teaspoon cornstarch in 1/4 cup cold chicken broth, then stir into the marinade to thicken. Serve with the pork.

To make a tasty glaze for carrots, peel and cut 1 pound carrots, then simmer for 4 minutes in a covered saucepan along with:

1/2 cup water	1 tablespoon unsalted butter
1/2 cup fresh orange juice	1 tablespoon chopped
3 tablespoons honey	crystallized ginger
2 teaspoons grated orange zest	1/2 teaspoon salt

Uncover and boil until the most of the liquid evaporates and the carrots are glazed.

When you can't think of what to do with chicken yet again, mix up this quick and surprising marinade. Grate the zest and squeeze the juice from 1 lime and 1 lemon into a large zip-close bag. Stir in 1 can (6 ounces) thawed orange juice concentrate, 1/2 cup tomato sauce, 2 minced garlic cloves, 1 teaspoon dried Italian seasoning, and 1/2 teaspoon hot-pepper sauce. Drop in 2 pounds boneless chicken parts and marinate in the refrigerator for 4 to 8 hours. Grill or broil the chicken and serve with prepared salsa.

To make a refreshing brine for fish, combine 2 cups fresh orange juice, 2 tablespoons fennel seeds, 2 tablespoons sugar, 3 tablespoons kosher salt, and 1/2 teaspoon freshly ground black pepper. Add thick fish steaks or fillets and refrigerate for up to 2 hours. Remove from the brine and grill, broil, or pan-fry the fish.

To breathe new life into creamy squash or red-pepper soups, stir in 1/4 cup fresh orange juice.

For a new twist on tapioca pudding, combine 2 cups fresh orange juice, 1/3 cup sugar, 3 tablespoons quick-cooking tapioca, and a pinch of salt in a saucepan. Let stand for 5 minutes. Bring to a boil over medium heat, stirring constantly. Remove from the heat and cool for 20 minutes. The pudding will thicken as it cools. Stir until smooth and serve warm or chilled.

To freshen up spaghetti sauce, squeeze in the juice from 1 to 2 oranges.

For a lively teriyaki marinade, mix together:

1/2 cup fresh orange juice	1 teaspoon grated orange zest
1/4 cup soy sauce	2 garlic cloves, minced
2 tablespoons honey	1 tablespoon toasted
1 tablespoon grated fresh ginger	sesame oil

Use to marinate beef, pork, or chicken.

For a quick creamy orange smoothie, combine orange-tangerine juice, vanilla ice cream, vanilla extract, and orange sherbet in blender. Process until smooth.

To give steamed rice an uplifting aroma, add 1/4 cup fresh orange juice to the cooking water.

✳Parmesan Cheese

To enrich the breading for pan-fried or baked chicken, add 1/4 to 1/3 cup grated Parmesan cheese to each cup of bread crumbs.

For a fun new taste in muffins, add Parmesan cheese. Preheat the oven to 350°F and line 12 muffin cups with paper liners. Sauté 4 shallots and 3 garlic cloves in 1 tablespoon olive oil then set aside to cool. Whisk together 2 cups flour, 2 teaspoons baking powder, 2 teaspoons crumbled dried rosemary (or Italian herb seasoning) and 1/2 teaspoon salt in a large bowl. In a small bowl, whisk 1/3 cup olive oil, the cooled shallot mixture, 1 cup milk, 1 egg, and 1/3 cup grated Parmesan cheese. Stir into the dry ingredients until just moistened. Spoon the batter into the muffin cups and sprinkle with another 2 tablespoons grated Parmesan. Bake until a toothpick inserted in the center comes out almost clean, about 15 minutes.

For nifty Parmesan cheese baskets, heat a 10-inch nonstick skillet over medium-high heat. Sprinkle about 3 tablespoons shredded (not grated) best-quality Parmesan cheese over the bottom of the pan, sprinkling more in the center for stability and less around the edges for a delicate, lacy look. When the Parmesan disk is melted and golden brown on the bottom, 2 to 3 minutes, use a spatula and your fingers to carefully lift it out of the pan. Quickly flip and drape the disk over the bottom of an inverted drinking glass (the golden side of the disk should be on top). Gently press in the sides in a few spots to create folds and the look of an upside-down basket. Let cool until firm, about 5 minutes. When cool, invert and fill with cold chicken salad, tuna salad, green salad, or another cold food. Avoid hot foods as these will melt the cheese again and cause the basket to collapse. The baskets will keep at room temperature for several hours or covered and refrigerated for up to 1 day.

To make Parmesan butter, combine:

1/2 cup (1 stick) softened unsalted butter	1/2 teaspoon dried oregano
1/4 cup grated Parmesan cheese (preferably Parmigiano-Reggiano)	1/4 teaspoon salt
	1/4 teaspoon freshly ground black pepper

Use on crusty bread or melted over broiled chicken, pork, beef, or shrimp.

To add flavor, color, and aroma to a gratin or other casserole, top with a sprinkling of freshly grated Parmesan cheese.

❋Peanut Butter

For a yummy glaze on ham steaks, combine 3 tablespoons orange marmalade, 2 tablespoons peanut butter, and 1 tablespoon water. Broil the ham steaks and when they are nearly done, add the glaze to one side and broil until the glaze is lightly browned, about 1 minute.

For a simple, fun appetizer, spread peanut butter into the grooves of celery sticks. Then for sweetness, place a few raisins on top and drizzle with honey.

To make a novel wrap out of grilled shrimp, combine peanut butter, olive oil, fresh lemon juice, and parsley until smooth. Grill some shrimp and serve in a tortilla wrap with shredded lettuce, chopped tomato, chopped onions, chopped cucumbers, and the peanut sauce.

For a mid-afternoon snack, spread 1 slice of raisin bread with 3 tablespoons peanut butter, then top with 2 tablespoons raisins and 1 tablespoon honey. Add a dash of ground cinnamon if you like. Top with another slice of raisin bread. Cook the sandwich in a buttered griddle until browned on both sides.

To give creamy potato soups or vegetable soups an Afro-Caribbean flavor, stir in a few tablespoons of peanut butter.

To make an Asian-style dipping sauce for beef, shrimp, or chicken, whisk together 3 tablespoons peanut butter, 1 tablespoon soy sauce, 1 tablespoon apple-cider vinegar, 1 tablespoon peanut oil or vegetable oil, 1 teaspoon sugar, and 1 teaspoon sesame oil. Blend until smooth.

For banana muffins with a twist, replace half of the butter or shortening in the recipe with peanut butter. Top the muffin batter with a sprinkling of shredded coconut before baking.

To breathe new life into chocolate chip cookies, replace half of the butter with peanut butter in your favorite recipe.

Tidbit Americans eat roughly 700 million pounds of peanut butter every year. That's enough to coat the entire floor of the Grand Canyon.

PEANUT BUTTER

❄Peas

If your freezer is full of frozen peas that you want to use up, make sweet pea puree. In a large saucepan, combine 3 packages (10 ounces each) frozen peas and 2 1/2 cups water. Bring to a boil, reduce the heat to medium-low, and simmer until tender, about 2 minutes. Drain the peas, then return them to the pot, and shake for 15 seconds to dry. Let cool for about 10 minutes, then transfer the peas to a food processor. Add 1/4 cup heavy cream, 3 tablespoons unsalted butter, 3/4 teaspoon salt, and 1/8 teaspoon freshly ground black pepper. Puree until smooth. For an ultra-silky puree, force the mixture through a sieve. Reheat the puree in a small saucepan over low heat before serving, or keep it hot in the top of a double boiler.

For a novel pasta sauce, puree cooked peas with heavy cream and Parmesan cheese. Serve over bowtie pasta and top with crumbled cooked bacon, caramelized onions, and chopped sun-dried tomatoes.

To make low-fat guacamole, puree peas and use them to replace some or all of the avocados in your favorite guacamole recipe.

❄Pesto Sauce

To get out of the mayonnaise and mustard rut, use pesto as a sandwich spread. Pesto lends terrific flavor to chicken sandwiches and Italian subs.

For basil mashed potatoes, stir in 1 to 2 tablespoons pesto along with the other ingredients in the mash.

To bring Dr. Seuss to the breakfast table, make green eggs and ham by stirring 1 to 2 tablespoons pesto into scrambled eggs before cooking. Serve with Canadian bacon.

To add bright flavor to lasagna or stuffed pastas, like ravioli and manicotti, stir pesto into the ricotta cheese in the filling. Try adding other high-flavor ingredients, too, like sun-dried tomatoes, sausage, prosciutto, and oil-cured olives.

To give brothy soups such as chicken noodle an extra shot of flavor, stir in a little pesto at the end of the cooking time. Pesto also works in almost any vegetable soup for a last-minute flavor boost (the French call a vegetable soup with pesto added at the end a Pistou Soup).

For an aromatic and rich-tasting roast turkey, rub prepared pesto under the skin and in the cavity of a whole turkey. Stuff the turkey cavity with cut-up lemons and onions. Rub the outside of the turkey with some butter, and roast. Make a pan gravy out the drippings, adding a little pesto to the gravy as well.

When you want roasted potatoes to taste bolder, stir in 1 to 2 tablespoons pesto into the spuds right after they come out of the oven.

For a no-fuss crust on roasted lamb, pork, or beef, slather prepared pesto over the surface before roasting. The oil in pesto bastes the meat as it cooks, keeping the meat moist, and the garlic, basil, and Parmesan cheese add fantastic flavor.

✳Pickles

To liven up a salad, add a mixture of sweet and dill pickles. The sweet-and-sour taste does wonders for potato, tuna, and chicken salads. Use about 1/4 cup chopped sweet pickles and 1/4 cup chopped dill pickles for each 4 cups of salad.

For curried egg salad with a twist, combine chopped hard-cooked eggs, mayonnaise, curry powder, chopped red onion, chopped cilantro, golden raisins, and chopped sweet gherkins.

To make last-minute party pinwheels, mix chopped sweet pickles, seeded and chopped bell peppers, chopped pimientos, and a little chili powder into cream cheese. Spread on tortilla wraps, then roll up and slice crosswise.

To give stir-fries a sweet-and-sour flavor, chop some bread and butter pickles and add to the stir-fry during the last minute of cooking.

✳Pie Filling

To make a unique cookie bar, press a tube of prepared sugar or chocolate chip cookie dough into the bottom of a 9 x 13-inch baking pan. Bake at 350°F for 15 minutes. Top with a can of cherry, raspberry, or strawberry pie filling, leaving a 1/4-inch border around the edge. Bake for 10 to 15 minutes more, then cool completely in the pan before cutting into squares.

For quick-and-easy mini fruit pies, add a teaspoon or so of pie filling to the center of a wonton wrapper, wet the edges, then fold over and pinch closed. Drop into boiling water and cook until the "pies" float. Remove, dry, and pan-fry in a nonstick skillet coated with cooking spray until golden brown, about 5 minutes Sprinkle with confectioners' sugar and serve at room temperature.

✳Potato Chips

For a rich and crunchy breading on pan-fried chicken or fish, finely crush 1 can (5 ounces) sour cream and onion potato chips or Pringles and mix with 2 teaspoons lemon-pepper seasoning, 1 teaspoon paprika, and 1/8 to 1/4 teaspoon cayenne pepper. Soak 1 1/2 pounds white fish fillets (catfish, cod, or grouper) or chicken breast cutlets in 1 cup evaporated milk for 30 minutes, then roll in the crushed chip mixture. Pan-fry until golden brown and the fish just begins to flake when tested in the center or the chicken juices run clear when the chicken is pierced with a fork.

To make the best baked macaroni and cheese ever, top the macaroni and cheese with buttered crushed potato chip and cornflake crumbs before baking. Grease a shallow 2-quart baking dish or 9-inch pan. Boil 8 ounces elbow macaroni until just tender. Drain. Melt 1/4 cup (1/2 stick) unsalted butter in a large saucepan over medium heat. Stir in 1/2 cup all-purpose flour and cook for 1 to 2 minutes. The mixture will be dry. Add 1 cup hot milk and whisk until the mixture begins to thicken. Add another 2 cups hot milk, 3/4 teaspoon salt, 1/4 teaspoon grated nutmeg, and 1/4 teaspoon freshly ground black pepper. Stir constantly until the sauce thickens and comes to a boil. Simmer for 2 minutes, stirring often. Add 1 1/2 cups chopped or grated sharp cheddar cheese and 1 1/2 cups chopped or grated American cheese. Stir until smooth and melted. Remove from the heat, add the macaroni and toss. Turn into the pan. Crush enough potato chips and cornflakes to make about 3/4 cup. Melt 1/4 cup butter in a saucepan and toss with the chips and cornflakes in a medium bowl. Sprinkle the buttered crumbs over the macaroni, then bake at 375°F until golden brown and bubbly, 25 to 30 minutes.

Tidbit In 1853, a customer at Moon Lake Lodge in Saratoga Springs, New York, kept sending French fries back to the kitchen because the customer complained that they were too thick. Chef George Crum is said to have sliced the potatoes thinner and thinner for the customer, finally giving birth to our modern-day potato chips.

*Potato Flakes

To add flavor to fish and crab cakes, use reconstituted potato flakes as the binder. Reconstitute potato flakes in buttermilk and combine with fresh cod or crab, chopped scallions, an egg, and seasonings. Fry in oil then serve on hamburger buns with sliced onion, tomato, lettuce, and spicy mayonnaise.

For focaccia with an extra-tender texture, add mashed potato flakes. To the mixture of flour, water, yeast, extra-virgin olive oil, sugar, and salt, add instant mashed potato flakes. After pressing out the dough, top the focaccia with roasted garlic paste, chopped fresh rosemary, sun-dried tomatoes, and grated Parmesan cheese before baking.

For better flavor and texture in meat loaf, add instant potato flakes rather than bread crumbs to your mix.

To keep chocolate cakes moist and rich tasting, add instant mashed potato flakes reconstituted with enough buttermilk to create a consistency similar to thick pancake batter. Add the potato mixture to the creamed butter and sugar in your recipe in two additions alternately with the dry ingredients. Works great in devil's food cakes without replacing or reducing any of the other ingredients.

✳Pretzels

For a super-simple-yet-wonderful kids treat, melt several ounces of semi-sweet chocolate in a wide dish in the microwave. Roll pretzel sticks in the chocolate until thoroughly coated, then place on a tray covered with wax paper. Place the tray in the refrigerator until the chocolate cools and hardens.

To give homemade chocolate ice cream a new spin, mix in some crushed pretzels.

For chicken cutlets with an extra-crispy coating, use pretzel nuggets or regular pretzels. Dip the chicken cutlets in flour, beaten egg, and then crushed pretzel nuggets. Sauté in a little unsalted butter or olive oil, then remove from the pan. Make a quick pan sauce with shallots, raspberry vinegar, raspberry preserves, and unsalted butter.

✳Pumpkin Puree

For a Halloween breakfast treat, make pumpkin pancakes. In a large bowl, combine:

2 cups flour	1/2 teaspoon ground cinnamon
1 tablespoon baking powder	1/4 teaspoon ground ginger
1/2 teaspoon salt	1/4 teaspoon ground nutmeg

Make a well in the center and add 1 1/2 cups milk or buttermilk, 1 cup canned pumpkin puree, 3 egg whites, 2 tablespoons melted unsalted butter, and 2 tablespoons brown sugar. Briefly stir the liquids in the well to combine them. Stir the dry ingredients into the liquid ingredients until just combined. Drop by 1/4 cupfuls onto a buttered heated griddle. Cook until golden brown, 1 to 2 minutes per side.

To make pumpkin ravioli, mix together canned pumpkin puree, toasted chopped pecans, grated Parmesan cheese, an egg, some melted butter, chopped fresh sage, lemon juice, and lemon zest. Use to fill wonton wrappers. Moisten the wrapper edges with water then fold over the filling and pinch the edges to seal. Cook the ravioli in salted boiling water until tender, 3 to 5 minutes. Serve with Alfredo sauce.

✳Ramen

To make frittatas and omelets more filling, crush a bag of ramen and cook according to the package directions, omitting the seasoning packet. Drain and stir into the egg mixture for your frittata or omelet, then cook as usual.

For a no-cook Asian noodle salad, crush a bag of ramen into small pieces and discard the seasoning packet. Mix the ramen with 1/2 cup bottled sesame ginger salad dressing and let stand at room temperature until the liquid is mostly absorbed, about 1 hour. Stir in vegetables such as sliced snow peas, shredded carrots, and sliced water chestnuts. Serve cold or at room temperature. Don't worry: The ramen noodles taste terrific, despite not being cooked!

For a 10-minute beef casserole for one, cook ramen according to the package directions. In a separate pan, brown about 1/4 pound ground beef with some chopped onions and seeded green bell peppers. Drain the fat, then toss with the cooked ramen noodles. Mix in a few tablespoons of your favorite barbecue sauce or other savory dressing and voilà, an instant meal!

Tidbit Each 3-ounce package of ramen contains about 79 noodles, each of which is more than 2 feet long. That's nearly 160 feet of ramen per bag!

✳Ricotta Cheese

To give an old cheesecake recipe new life, replace half of the cream cheese with ricotta cheese.

For pancakes with a light and fluffy texture, combine egg yolks, sugar, flour, ricotta cheese, and lemon zest. Whip the egg whites and fold into the batter. Cook the pancakes and serve topped with yogurt sweetened with honey.

To make a quick dessert mousse, whip 1 cup ricotta cheese with 2 tablespoons confectioners' sugar until creamy, then stir in 1 teaspoon fresh orange juice, 1/2 teaspoon vanilla extract, 1/3 cup chopped almonds, and 1/3 cup semi-sweet chocolate chips. Fold in 1 1/2 cups whipped cream and serve.

To make a no-cook ricotta sauce for pasta, combine:

1 cup ricotta cheese	1/3 cup chopped fresh basil
2 tablespoons extra-virgin olive oil	7 tablespoons freshly grated Parmesan and/or Romano cheese
2 garlic cloves, minced	1/4 teaspoon salt
3 red bell peppers, seeded, roasted, and chopped	1/8 teaspoon freshly ground black pepper

Toss with 3/4 pound pasta cooked according to the package directions.

For a new spin on creamed spinach, sauté 2 tablespoons finely chopped onion and 1 minced garlic clove in 2 tablespoons unsalted butter until tender, 2 minutes. Add 20 ounces trimmed and cleaned spinach. Cook, tossing once or twice, until just wilted, about 1 minute. Stir in 1/4 cup ricotta cheese, 1/2 teaspoon salt, and 1/4 teaspoon freshly ground black pepper (or more to taste).

For an easy overnight cream pie, beat together 1 1/2 cups ricotta cheese, 1 1/2 cups cream cheese, 3/4 cup sugar, 3 tablespoons brandy or rum, 1 tablespoon vanilla extract, and 3 eggs. Pour into a prepared graham cracker crust and bake at 200°F overnight (6 to 8 hours). Cool completely on a rack then refrigerate for 1 hour before serving.

✳Salad Dressing

To easily marinate chicken breasts, use bottled Italian salad dressing. It contains a combination of oil, vinegar, and salt that is similar to many poultry marinades. Caesar salad dressing is particularly good.

For Creole-style boiled shrimp, combine bottled Caesar salad dressing, Worcestershire sauce, unsalted butter, paprika, and thyme in a saucepan. Bring to a boil then add shrimp. Cook the shrimp until pink and cooked through, then serve hot over white rice.

For easy turkey "London broil," pour 1 cup bottled Italian salad dressing into a zip-close bag. Add a 2-pound boneless butterflied whole turkey breast (turkey London broil) and marinate in the refrigerator for 4 to 8 hours. Preheat a grill to medium. Meanwhile, remove the turkey from the marinade and let stand at room temperature for 15 minutes. Grill the turkey until the thickest section of meat feels firm when pressed and registers 170°F on an instant-read thermometer, 8 to 10 minutes per side. Let rest for 2 minutes before slicing. Cut into 1/4-inch-thick slices.

To lend robust flavor to a creamy soup, stir in some bottled blue cheese salad dressing toward the end of the cooking time.

To make a quick filling for a sandwich wrap, mix together 2 drained cans of oil-packed tuna, 1 drained and rinsed can (15 ounces) small white beans, 1/3 cup bottled Italian vinaigrette, 2 sliced scallions, and 1 tablespoon chopped fresh parsley. Roll up in large tortilla wraps and cut each in half crosswise before serving.

For a quick blue cheese baste and sauce for grilled poultry, mix together 1 cup bottled blue cheese salad dressing and 1/4 cup bottled Italian salad dressing. Divide the dressing mixture between two bowls. Brush 1 pound poultry cutlets (each about 1/4 inch thick) with the dressing mixture from one bowl. Grill or broil the poultry on an oiled grill grate or broiler pan 4 inches from a hot fire or heating element until firm and the juices run clear when the meat is pierced with a fork, 2 to 3 minutes per side. Serve with the dressing mixture in the other bowl.

To give roast beef or corned beef sandwiches a flavor lift, spread bottled Russian salad dressing on rye bread and top with some prepared horseradish before adding the beef.

For an easy sweet-and-sour glaze, melt 6 tablespoons apricot jelly in a small saucepan over low heat, stirring often. Mix in 1 cup bottled French salad dressing and 1 package (1 ounce) dry onion soup mix. Use as a glaze for baked chicken, roast turkey, roast pork, ham, baked pork chops, spareribs, beef ribs, or meatballs.

To make extra-crispy oven-fried chicken that is low in fat and high in flavor, toss 4 pounds skinless bone-in chicken parts with 1 cup bottled reduced-fat French salad dressing. Cover and marinate in the refrigerator for at least 1 hour or overnight. Pulverize 3 cups unsweetened cereal flakes (such as cornflakes) until finely ground and place into a 1-gallon zip-close freezer bag. Lift the chicken from the marinade and toss in the bag until well-coated with the crushed cereal. Place the coated chicken in a nonstick glass or ceramic baking pan. Bake at 450°F until the thickest portion registers 170°F on an instant-read thermometer and the juices run clear when the chicken is pierced with a fork, 45 to 50 minutes.

For an alternative to garlic bread, combine 2 cups shredded Monterey Jack cheese and 3/4 cup bottled ranch salad dressing in a medium bowl. Cut a 1-pound loaf of French bread in half lengthwise, brush with melted unsalted butter, and broil 4 inches from the heat until golden brown. Spread the cheese mixture onto the bread and bake at 350°F until the cheese is melted, 10 to 15 minutes. Sprinkle with minced fresh parsley, cut into 1 1/2-inch slices and serve.

To make a quick salad from leftover salmon, combine:

1 1/2 cups cooked salmon

1 can (15 ounces) white beans, drained

3 scallions, thinly sliced

1/2 cup finely chopped red onion

2 tablespoons chopped flat-leaf parsley

1 garlic clove, minced

1/3 cup bottled Italian salad dressing

Garnish the salad with 12 pitted and chopped oil-cured black olives. Chill well and serve on romaine lettuce leaves or in pita bread.

Tidbit Ranch dressing really was invented on a ranch! Fifty years ago, visitors at the Hidden Valley dude ranch in California began clamoring to take home the tasty salad dressing that the owners made. Soon the ranchers had an international condiment business ... which was probably easier to handle than teaching city folk to herd cattle.

✳Salsa

To get a jump on making a spicy rice dish, sauté tomato salsa in a skillet, then add rice and water, cover and simmer.

For instant gazpacho, mix 1/4 to 1/2 cup of your favorite salsa into a can of tomato soup.

To make a Southwestern version of gumbo, make a gumbo with a roux, garlic, onions, bell pepper strips, celery, okra (frozen is fine), shrimp, and kielbasa. Add salsa instead of tomatoes. Serve over rice.

For super-easy black bean soup, mix together 2 cans (15 ounces each) chicken broth, 1 rinsed and drained can (15 ounces) black beans, 1 box (7 ounces) instant black beans, and 1 cup chunky salsa in a saucepan. Bring to a boil and simmer for 5 minutes. Add more broth if you like a thinner soup. Sour cream and chopped scallions make nice garnishes.

To make salsa ketchup, mix together 1 cup ketchup and 1 cup spicy salsa. Use as a condiment whenever you would use salsa or ketchup alone.

For more lively spaghetti sauce, add 1 to 2 tablespoons salsa. Most salsas contain lots of tomatoes and onions, plus subtle amounts of minced peppers, oregano, and cilantro, all of which blend perfectly with tomato-based spaghetti sauces.

To whip up quick Mexican-style tuna, toss 2 drained cans (6 ounces each) white water-packed tuna with 1 cup salsa and 1 tablespoon olive oil. Use as a sandwich spread, a filling for tacos, or a dip for tortilla chips.

For Mexican-style pan-fried fish, use salsa. Add 1/2 teaspoon ground cumin and 1/2 teaspoon dried oregano to the flour. Dredge the fish in the seasoned flour, then in beaten eggs, then in cornmeal and pan-fry in olive oil. Remove the fish to a platter and keep warm. Add 1 tablespoon olive oil to the skillet, and sauté 1 minced garlic clove and 3 sliced scallions for 30 seconds. Add 3/4 cup salsa and bring to a simmer. Remove from the heat and stir in 3 to 4 tablespoons chopped fresh cilantro. Pour the sauce over the fried fish fillets.

To make salsa vinaigrette, blend 1 cup salsa, 3 tablespoons olive oil, and 2 tablespoons fresh lime juice in a blender. Use as a dressing for bean salads, rice salad, or to top grilled or broiled fish or chicken.

For the fastest chili on earth, cook 1 pound ground beef in a nonstick skillet over medium heat until no longer pink, about 5 minutes, stirring often and breaking up the meat with a spoon. Drain off any fat and add 1 can (16 ounces) seasoned chili beans and 1/2 cup of your favorite salsa. Simmer for 2 minutes. Serve topped with sour cream or shredded cheddar cheese and chopped scallions.

For a rich-tasting but lightning-fast sauce for pork or poultry, boil 1 1/2 cups salsa in a saucepan until almost all of the liquid evaporates. Remove from the heat and stir in 3 tablespoons unsalted butter until melted.

To give meat loaf a Southwestern flavor profile, use salsa instead of ketchup in your favorite recipe.

✳Sloppy Joe Sauce

To pull together a quick sauce for sweet-and-sour meatballs, combine the following ingredients in a saucepan and heat over medium heat:

1 can (15 ounces) sloppy Joe sauce	1/2 cup seeded and finely chopped green bell peppers
1 can (8 ounces) crushed pineapple, drained	2 tablespoons brown sugar
2 tablespoons teriyaki sauce	1 tablespoon spicy brown mustard

Add already-cooked meatballs and simmer in the sauce until heated through, 15 to 20 minutes.

To punch up the flavor of meat loaf, replace the ketchup with sloppy Joe sauce in your favorite recipe. Mix about half a 15-ounce can of sloppy Joe sauce into the meat mixture and pour the rest over the top of the meat loaf. A little sloppy Joe sauce in hamburgers also adds moisture and tons of flavor. It's perfect for lean ground beef that needs moisture to keep the meat from becoming dry when cooked.

For a homemade peach-flavored barbecue sauce, blend the following ingredients in a food processor:

1 can (15 ounces) bold-flavored sloppy Joe sauce

1 can (15 ounces) sliced peaches, drained

2 teaspoons Worcestershire sauce

1/4 cup firmly packed brown sugar

1/2 teaspoon hot-pepper sauce

1/2 teaspoon ground ginger

Brush the sauce over barbecued pork such as ribs or chops during the last 10 minutes of cooking.

✳Soda

To give marinated chicken, turkey, or pork a refreshing sweet flavor, use lemon-lime soda in the marinade. Ginger ale works great, too.

For a brand-new spin on baked beans, combine:

1 can (12 ounces) black cherry soda

1/2 cup ketchup

2 tablespoons prepared mustard

2 teaspoons apple-cider vinegar

1/8 teaspoon freshly ground black pepper

Stir in 3 drained cans (15 ounces each) of your favorite beans, such as pinto or white beans and bake in a 2-quart baking dish at 350°F until bubbly, 30 to 45 minutes. Add a little chopped bacon or ham to make these taste even better.

To make an Asian marinade for flank steak, combine:

6 ounces ginger ale

1 can (6 ounces) thawed orange juice concentrate

1/4 cup teriyaki sauce

1/2 teaspoon toasted sesame oil

3 garlic cloves, minced

Add a flank steak (1 1/2 pounds) and marinate for 4 to 8 hours before grilling or broiling.

For zesty glazed ribs, use root beer as a base for a glaze. First, rub pork spareribs with a spice rub of paprika, dry mustard, brown sugar, salt, and freshly ground black pepper. Grill the ribs over indirect heat until the meat is shrunken back from the bones and very tender. Meanwhile, combine root beer, sugar, orange zest, lemon juice, bourbon, and hot-pepper sauce in a saucepan. Boil until the mixture is reduced in volume and syrupy in consistency. Brush the glaze all over the ribs during the last 10 minutes of cooking.

To make a simple marinade for steak, combine 1 can (12 ounces) cola, 3 tablespoons Worcestershire sauce, 3 minced garlic cloves, 1 sliced onion, and 1 table-spoon steak seasoning. Marinate your favorite steaks in the mixture in the refrigerator for 2 to 4 hours.

For Asian-inspired pork stew, brown cubes of pork shoulder in a heavy pot, then add onions, carrots, ginger, garlic, soy sauce, and cola to the pot. Simmer over low heat until the pork is fork-tender. Serve over udon or other Asian noodles (spaghetti will do in a pinch).

To doctor up bottled barbecue sauce, combine 1 cup ginger ale and 1 cup barbecue sauce in a small saucepan. Bring to a boil over medium heat. Reduce the heat to medium-low and simmer until thickened and reduced to about 1 1/2 cups in volume, 15 to 20 minutes. Excellent with spicy seasoned pork.

To make an Indian-inspired marinade for bone-in chicken parts or pork chops, mix together:

6 ounces ginger ale	1 tablespoon chopped fresh garlic
1/2 cup chopped onion	
1 tablespoon curry powder	1/2 teaspoon salt
1 tablespoon chopped fresh ginger	1/8 to 1/4 teaspoon cayenne pepper

Use to marinate 1 1/2 pounds bone-in chicken parts or pork chops for 4 to 8 hours.

For moist and delicious pork chops, mix together 1 cup ketchup and 1 cup cola. Pour the mixture over 6 to 8 lightly breaded pork chops in a baking dish. Sprinkle with a little brown sugar and bake at 350°F until cooked through, about 1 hour.

Tidbit Recycling soda cans wasn't always a way of life. Before 1970, cans and bottles were tossed in the trash with everything else. Then, Earth Day and environmental entrepreneurs turned aluminum-can recycling alone into a billion-dollar business. About 65 billion aluminum cans (mostly from canned soda) are recycled each year. It takes only 60 days for old aluminum cans to be collected, recycled, and returned to supermarket shelves as new cans made with more than 50 percent recycled material.

For a surprisingly fun and yummy dessert, dissolve 1 package (3 ounces) cherry Jell-O in 1 cup boiling water. Then add 1 cup cola, mix thoroughly, and pour equal amounts of the Jell-O mix into four small glasses. Chill until set, about 2 hours. Serve with whipped topping and maraschino cherries, if desired.

*Sour Cream

For a sweet and surprising maple sauce, combine 1/2 cup low-fat cottage cheese, 1/4 cup sour cream, 1/4 cup maple syrup, and 1 tablespoon honey in a mini food processor or blender (you could also use a hand blender and combine the mixture in a tall glass). Puree until smooth. Chill the sauce for at least 30 minutes before using. Can be used on desserts, as a vegetable dip, or however you wish.

To whip up a super-fast chocolate frosting for cakes and cupcakes, melt 1 cup semi-sweet chocolate chips in a microwavable bowl. Stir in 1/2 cup sour cream until smooth. Spread over your favorite cakes and cupcakes and refrigerate until ready to serve.

To give chocolate cookies and cakes a luscious texture, replace half of the butter in your favorite recipe with sour cream. The acidity of the sour cream helps to tenderize the cookie dough or cake batter.

To make a homemade, low-fat version of crème fraîche, mix together 1/2 cup reduced-fat sour cream, 1/2 cup 1% milk, and 1/4 teaspoon sugar. Cover and let stand in a warm place overnight to thicken. Refrigerate for at least 4 hours before using. Keeps refrigerated for up to 2 weeks.

To enrich deviled eggs, mix a little sour cream into the filling.

For extra-creamy guacamole, add a few tablespoons of sour cream into the mixture.

To enrich bottled spaghetti sauce or prepared pesto sauce, stir in 1/4 cup sour cream per 2 cups of sauce. Cook over low heat until the sour cream just blends into the sauce. Keep the sauce warm over low heat, but don't allow it to boil or the sour cream may curdle.

To give black bean dip a super-creamy texture, add sour cream. Drain 1 can (16 ounces) black beans and place them in a food processor or blender. Add:

1/4 cup sour cream	1/2 teaspoon ground cumin
1/4 cup chicken broth	1/2 teaspoon dried oregano
1 scallion, sliced	1/2 teaspoon salt
1 small garlic clove, minced	1/2 teaspoon hot-pepper sauce
2 tablespoons dry sherry	1/4 teaspoon freshly ground black pepper
1 tablespoon fresh lemon juice	

Puree until the texture is smooth. Remove from the processor or blender and store in the refrigerator. Bring to room temperature before serving. This recipe doubles easily and tastes great with corn chips.

For sweetened creamy polenta, make polenta with yellow cornmeal, milk, honey, and butter. Finish the polenta by stirring in sour cream. Top with fresh berries or strawberry, cherry, or raspberry jam.

✳Sour Cream Onion Dip

To simplify the sauce for smothered chicken, mix together 1 can (9 ounces) sour cream onion dip, 2 teaspoons Worcestershire sauce, and 1/4 cup chicken broth.

For smoked oyster dip in a jiffy, combine 1 can (9 ounces) sour cream onion dip, 1 tablespoon chopped fresh parsley, 1 teaspoon Worcestershire sauce, and 1/4 teaspoon hot-pepper sauce in a microwavable bowl. Chop 1 can (3 ounces) smoked oysters (with juice) and stir into the bowl. Microwave on high power until hot, 1 to 2 minutes.

To make easy crab-stuffed mushrooms, use sour cream onion dip as the base. Sauté 1/4 cup finely chopped onions, then stir in 1 can (9 ounces) sour cream onion dip, 1/3 cup chopped pimientos, 1/4 cup grated Parmesan cheese, 2 tablespoons bread crumbs, and 1 tablespoon chopped fresh parsley. Pick over 1 pound lump crab meat to remove any cartilage, then fold into the stuffing. Stuff 8 large portobello mushroom caps or 40 to 50 button mushrooms. Bake at 375°F until the mushrooms begin to lose their liquid, 20 minutes.

✳Soy Sauce

To give steamed rice a savory flavor, add 1 tablespoon soy sauce to the cooking water.

For a delicious glaze on roasted pearl onions, mix together equal parts soy sauce and molasses and toss with the onions before roasting.

To make a quick Polynesian sauce, stir together 1/3 cup soy sauce, 1/2 cup pineapple juice, 1 can (5 ounces) crushed pineapple, and 1/2 teaspoon hot-pepper sauce. Add to cooked vegetables or meat as a stir-fry sauce or serve over roasted pork, chicken, or fish.

For an Asian-style glaze, mix together 1/4 cup soy sauce or teriyaki sauce, 6 ounces Dr. Pepper, 1 teaspoon hot-pepper sauce, 1/2 teaspoon ground cloves, and 1/2 teaspoon ground ginger. Boil over high heat until reduced in volume by about half and thickened to a syrup, about 10 minutes. Brush over baked ham during the last 20 minutes of cooking.

✳Spaghetti Sauce

To flavor baked fish and keep it moist, bake fillets or whole fish in spaghetti sauce. Add a few olives, some herbs, and some citrus zest for more flavor.

For a quick sausage or steak sandwich, pan-fry your favorite sausages or thin-sliced top round sandwich steaks in a skillet. Remove the meat, then sauté sliced onions and peppers in the pan. Add your favorite spaghetti sauce and return the meat to the pan. Simmer for 5 minutes then serve on steak rolls.

To mix up a quick marinade for Southwestern-style chicken, combine 1 cup marinara sauce and 1 teaspoon pure chile powder such as ancho chile powder. Or use a blended seasoning such as chili powder. Use to marinate 1 pound chicken parts in the refrigerator for 1 to 3 hours.

For a speedy pizza, spread 3/4 cup spaghetti sauce over a prepared pizza crust (such as Boboli). Or for individual pizzas, use four pita bread rounds. Add 1 cup shredded mozzarella and 1/4 cup grated Parmesan if you like. Add any number of other toppings from anchovies to zucchini. Bake at 450°F until the cheese melts and is lightly browned, about 20 minutes.

To keep beef burritos moist and flavorful, brown 1 pound ground beef along with 1 chopped onion, 1 seeded and chopped red bell pepper, and a few chopped garlic cloves. Stir in 1 cup marinara sauce, 1 teaspoon paprika, 1 teaspoon dried oregano, 1/2 teaspoon ground cumin, and 1/2 teaspoon chili powder. Simmer on low for 15 minutes and serve with tortillas, shredded cheese, and salsa.

If you need an instant simmering liquid for clams or mussels, use jarred spaghetti sauce. Doctor up the sauce with saffron, white wine, fresh garlic, and/or chopped fresh herbs.

To make a vinaigrette for a broccoli salad, use spaghetti sauce as the base. Mix together 1/2 cup smooth marinara sauce, 2 tablespoons extra-virgin olive oil,1 tablespoon red-wine vinegar, 1 tablespoon chopped fresh parsley, 1/2 teaspoon salt, and 1/8 teaspoon freshly ground black pepper. Toss with 2 boxes (10 ounces each) thawed frozen broccoli pieces.

For a one-dish chicken meal, cook seasoned chicken parts in olive oil in a deep skillet until browned all over. Remove to a plate and keep warm, then add onions and bell peppers to the skillet and sauté until tender. Add mushrooms, thyme, red-pepper flakes, and fennel seeds and cook until the mushrooms begin to give up their liquid, about 5 minutes. Pour in jarred spaghetti sauce and bring to a simmer. Return the chicken to the pan, cover, and simmer until the juices run clear when the chicken is pierced with a fork. Serve over noodles.

To get a jump-start on the sauce for braised meats, use spaghetti sauce as the base. Most sauces include the same ingredients you would be braising with anyway, such as onions, garlic, and tomatoes.

To make gazpacho when you don't have fresh tomatoes, use spaghetti sauce. Combine the sauce in a food processor along with fresh orange juice, cucumber, bell peppers, scallions, cilantro, and a little hot-pepper sauce. Pulse until the vegetables are just chopped. Thin with a little cold water, if necessary, then refrigerate the soup for 3 hours and serve chilled.

❋Sweetened Condensed Milk

To make easy caramel sauce *(dulce de leche),* remove the label from a 14-ounce can of sweetened condensed milk. Put the unopened can in a large saucepan and cover with water by 5 inches. Bring to a boil over high heat then reduce the heat to medium and simmer for 2 hours, adding water as necessary to keep the can covered. Remove the can with tongs and cool to room temperature. Open the can and spoon the thick, sweet caramelized sauce over ice cream, brownies, pound cake, apple crisp, or your favorite desserts.

For ultra-easy strawberry sorbet, puree 1 quart strawberries with 1 can (14 ounces) sweetened condensed milk and 2 teaspoons fresh lemon juice. Freeze in a shallow metal pan, stirring occasionally. Scrape out servings with a spoon.

To roll up some chocolate truffles in no time, combine 20 ounces of bittersweet chocolate (or a mix of bittersweet and semi-sweet chocolate), 1 can (14 ounces) sweetened condensed milk, and 1/4 teaspoon ground cinnamon in a saucepan. Cook over medium-low heat until the chocolate melts and the mixture can be stirred smooth. Let cool until the mixture can be handled, then roll into 1-inch balls between your palms. Roll in powdered sugar and store in an airtight container at room temperature for up to 1 week. You can also refrigerate the truffles for up to 2 weeks, but bring them to room temperature before serving for the best flavor.

For no-fuss refrigerator fudge, combine 1 can (14 ounces) sweetened condensed milk, 3 cups semi-sweet chocolate chips, and 1 1/2 teaspoons vanilla extract in a saucepan. Cook over medium-low heat until the chocolate melts and the mixture can be stirred smooth. Scrape into a foil-lined 8-inch square baking dish. Refrigerate for 2 hours or until the fudge is firm. Grab the foil to remove the fudge from the pan, then cut into 1-inch squares.

❋Tea Bags

To flavor rice, steep a few tea bags (such as mint, orange, or jasmine) in the boiling water before adding the rice. Remove the tea bags, add the rice, and cook according to the package directions.

For a tasty topping for green beans, sauté 2 minced garlic cloves in 1 teaspoon canola oil until opaque, then add 2 cups brewed tea. Let the mixture simmer for a few minutes, then pour over a pound of steamed green beans. Garnish with sliced almonds, if you like.

To make an orange-scented sauce for pan-seared chicken or pork, remove the chicken from the pan and keep warm. Sauté 1/3 cup chopped shallots in 1 teaspoon olive oil in the same pan. Add 1 cup chicken broth, 3/4 cup fresh orange juice and 2 Earl Grey tea bags. Boil until the liquid is reduced to 3/4 cup. Remove the tea bags and whisk in 1 1/2 teaspoons honey and 1 tablespoon unsalted butter. Serve over the chicken or pork.

To make an aromatic fruit relish, brew hibiscus tea in a saucepan. (Hibiscus tea is available in supermarkets, sometimes mixed with rosehips, which works just fine.) After the tea steeps for 5 minutes, discard tea bags then add sugar and bring to a boil over high heat. Boil until the liquid reduces and becomes syrupy. Stir in finely chopped onions, pineapple, and apple and simmer over medium-low heat for 5 minutes. Serve the relish with seafood such as shrimp, scallops, or broiled fish.

For rhubarb scented with jasmine, bring 1 1/4 cups water to a boil in a large saucepan. Remove from the heat and add 3 jasmine tea bags. Cover and let the tea steep for 5 minutes. Discard tea bags, then add 2 pounds (6 cups) fresh or frozen sliced rhubarb, 1 1/4 cups sugar, and 2 tablespoons grated fresh ginger to the saucepan. Bring to a boil over medium-high heat, stirring occasionally. Reduce the heat to medium-low and simmer until the rhubarb is just tender, 8 to 10 minutes. Transfer to a large bowl and refrigerate until well-chilled, about 3 hours. Keeps in the refrigerator for about 4 days.

For a warm, energizing autumn drink, combine 4 cups apple cider, 4 cups pineapple juice, 1/2 cup water, 1 cinnamon stick, and 4 whole cloves in a saucepan. Bring to a boil over high heat, then add 1 tea bag. Let steep for 5 minutes, then reduce the heat to medium-low and simmer gently for 1 hour. Discard the cloves, cinnamon, and tea bag before serving.

To make muffins with a surprise flavor, add 1 tablespoon fine loose English breakfast or Earl Grey tea leaves to the batter of your favorite basic or blueberry
muffin recipe. Bake as directed. If you don't have loose tea leaves, open two
tea bags and add to the muffin batter.

When you want to add something different to mulled wine, toss a few lemon spice
tea bags into the simmering liquid. Remove the tea bags before serving.

✳ Tofu

To make an egg-free mayonnaise, use silken tofu as the base. In a food processor,
combine 12 ounces silken tofu, 1/3 cup olive oil, 1/4 cup fresh lemon juice,
1/2 teaspoon Dijon mustard, 1/2 teaspoon salt, and a pinch of freshly
ground black pepper. Blend in a tablespoon or two of water if the mixture is
too thick. Keeps refrigerated for up to 1 week. Be sure to buy silken tofu for
this recipe. It has a creamier texture than regular tofu. You can find it in most
grocery stores near the regular tofu.

To mix up a healthier pumpkin pie filling, add tofu to the mixture. In a blender or
food processor, combine:

12 ounces extra-firm tofu	1 egg
1 can (15 ounces) pumpkin puree	2 teaspoons vanilla extract
1/2 cup firmly packed brown sugar	2 teaspoons ground cinnamon
1/4 cup honey	1/4 teaspoon ground nutmeg
	1/4 teaspoon ground allspice

Pour into a 9-inch pie crust and bake at 350°F until set, about 5 minutes.
Cool completely before serving.

For a satisfying chocolate pudding without all the fat and calories, whip 1 box
(12 ounces) extra-firm silken tofu, 1 cup melted semi-sweet chocolate chips,
and 1 teaspoon vanilla extract in a food processor. Continue whipping the
mixture, scraping down the sides, until no white is visible. Serve immediately,
or blend in 2 tablespoons milk and refrigerate for up to 2 days (the milk
helps to keep the pudding from getting too firm when chilled). For a more
complex flavor, add a little almond, rum, or orange extract. You could also
add spices like cinnamon or allspice. For mocha flavor, dissolve 1 teaspoon of
instant coffee or espresso granules in 2 teaspoons boiling water, cool slightly,
and add along with the extract.

✳Tomato Paste

To make tomato butter, combine:

1/2 cup (1 stick) softened unsalted butter	1/2 teaspoon dried basil
1/4 cup tomato paste	1/4 teaspoon salt
1/2 teaspoon dried oregano	1/4 teaspoon freshly ground black pepper

Melt the tomato butter over broiled tomatoes, grilled steak, chicken, or vegetables.

For a super-fast and light pasta sauce, mix together 2 cans (15 ounces each) Italian-seasoned stewed tomatoes (with juice) and 1/3 cup tomato paste. Toss with hot pasta.

To stir up a quick coconut curry sauce for sautéed chicken or pork, remove the meat from the pan. Add 1/2 cup chopped onions, 3 minced garlic cloves, and 2 teaspoons chopped fresh ginger to the same pan and sauté. Stir in 2 tablespoons curry powder, 1/2 teaspoon salt, and 1/8 teaspoon cayenne pepper and cook for 1 minute. Next, stir in 3/4 cup coconut milk, and 1 1/2 tablespoons tomato paste. When the sauce is well-combined, return the meat to the pan and simmer for 5 minutes before serving.

To make tomato ice cream, combine tomato paste, orange liqueur, cream, egg yolks, and sugar. Freeze in an ice cream maker according to the manufacturer's directions.

For a delicious red salad dressing, in a small bowl, mix together:

1 garlic clove, crushed	1 1/2 teaspoons fresh lemon juice
2 anchovy fillets, finely chopped	2 teaspoons Worcestershire sauce
1 tablespoon tomato paste	2 teaspoons sugar
1 tablespoon red-wine vinegar	

Whisk in 1/2 cup olive oil in a slow and steady stream, then add 1/4 teaspoon salt and 1/4 teaspoon freshly ground black pepper.

To whip up a homemade steak sauce, combine 1/4 cup melted unsalted butter, 2 tablespoons Worcestershire sauce, 1 tablespoon brown mustard, and 1 tablespoon tomato paste.

To make moist and luscious chocolate cake, thin some tomato paste to the consistency of tomato puree and add to your regular cake batter. The sugar in the tomatoes will enhance the sweet flavor of the cake, while the acidity in the tomatoes will help to tenderize its texture.

✳Tortillas

To thicken Mexican soups, soak torn-up corn tortillas or tortilla chips in the soup's broth, then stir to break up the tortillas and thicken the soup.

For Southwestern-style baked macaroni and cheese, add a little chili powder and bacon to the cheese sauce. Top with crushed tortilla chips that have been sautéed in the bacon drippings.

To make Mexican pork stew, sauté onions, garlic, ancho chile powder, and boneless pork stew meat in oil, then add chicken broth, oregano, tomatoes, and canned hominy. Simmer on medium-low heat until the pork is fall-apart tender. Serve the stew topped with broken tortilla chips, avocado slices, and lime wedges.

✳V8 Juice

For a quick soup or stew, use V8 juice as the base. It already includes celery, onion, carrot, bell pepper, and tomato flavors, which gives you a head start on flavor.

For steamed rice with a new twist, replace half of the cooking water with V8 juice.

To make easy fish stew, sauté onions and garlic, then add V8 juice, bottled clam juice, and dried herbs. Add sliced andouille sausage or kielbasa, shrimp, clams, and halibut fillet and simmer until the fish and sausage are cooked through.

To mix up a quick sauce for baked fish fillets, stir together V8 juice and a few dashes of Worcestershire sauce.

For easy barbecue spareribs, combine 1 1/2 cups spicy V8 juice, 2/3 cup peach or apricot nectar or pineapple juice, 1/2 cup spicy barbecue sauce, and 1 teaspoon Worcestershire sauce. Mix with 3 pounds boneless country spareribs in a baking pan, cover with foil, and bake at 350°F until tender, about 2 hours.

For an instant braising liquid, use V8 juice. It's especially good with beef and pork.

To make a flavorful gravy, stir V8 juice into the drippings left in the pan after removing the roast. Boil over high heat until the liquid is reduced in volume and slightly thickened.

To doctor up jarred spaghetti sauce, simmer it in a saucepan with 1 cup V8 juice.

For an easy dressing for rice salad, use V8 juice as the base. First, bring 8 cups water to a boil in a large saucepan. Add 1 cup white rice, reduce the heat to medium, and simmer until the rice is tender, 15 to 20 minutes. Add 2 halved and sliced zucchini during the last 5 minutes of cooking. Drain in a colander. Meanwhile, in a large bowl, whisk together 1/3 cup V8 juice, 3 tablespoons fresh lemon juice, 1 tablespoon olive oil, and 1/2 teaspoon salt. Add 2 large chopped tomatoes, 1 can (15 ounces) drained chopped artichokes, 1/4 cup chopped, pitted, oil-cured black olives, 1/4 cup crumbled feta cheese, 3 tablespoons chopped fresh parsley, and the drained rice mixture. Toss to coat. To make ahead, keep the dressing and the salad mixtures separate, then combine them right before serving.

To give poached eggs a subtle tomato flavor and beautiful rosy color, use V8 juice instead of water as the poaching liquid.

For a gazpacho sauce for cooked chicken, combine 1 cup V8 juice, 2 cups leftover salad (dressed with Italian dressing), 2 tablespoons extra-virgin olive oil, 1/4 teaspoon salt, and 1/8 teaspoon freshly ground black pepper in a food processor. Pulse until the ingredients are finely chopped but not completely pureed.

❋Vinegar

To make an outrageously good sauce for grilled beef, melt a stick of butter over medium heat. When the butter foams, reduce the heat to medium-low and cook until it turns from yellow to medium brown but not black, 5 to 7 minutes. Watch the butter carefully so it doesn't burn. Pour the brown butter into a small, heat-proof bowl, leaving the sediment in the pan. Raise the heat to medium and pour balsamic vinegar into the pan, swirling it and letting it boil down to about half its volume. Remove from the heat and pour the brown butter back into the pan to combine. Drizzle over grilled steaks. A grating of fresh horseradish takes this over the top.

To make a marinade for your favorite steaks, combine 6 ounces beer, 1/4 cup tomato sauce, 2 tablespoons balsamic vinegar, and 1 tablespoon steak seasoning. Marinate in the refrigerator for 4 to 6 hours before grilling or broiling.

To rescue an egg that cracks while being hard-cooked, add a teaspoon of distilled white vinegar to the cooking water. The vinegar will cause the egg white to coagulate and stop seeping from the shell. The same principle works with poached eggs too. Add a tablespoon of vinegar to the poaching liquid to help the egg whites set up before they spread too much.

For a sweet Asian dressing, whisk together:

2 tablespoons honey	1 garlic clove, minced
2 tablespoons soy sauce	1/4 teaspoon finely chopped
2 tablespoons balsamic vinegar	fresh ginger
2 teaspoons toasted sesame oil	1/4 teaspoon hot-pepper sauce

Balsamic vinegar is sweeter than the traditional rice vinegar in Asian sauces and gives this dressing a less astringent taste.

To help a peeled and sliced cucumber stay crisp, put the cucumber slices in a colander and sprinkle them with 2 teaspoons distilled white vinegar, 1 teaspoon salt, and a pinch of sugar. Use your fingertips to rub the mixture into the slices for 1 minute. Weight down the slices with a large zip-close bag full of water and let the cucumber drain in the colander for 15 minutes. Rinse and pat dry before using for cooking or a salad.

To give shrimp cocktail just the right amount of acidity, combine 1/2 cup distilled white vinegar, 1 bottle (12 ounces) beer, 2 tablespoons crab boil seasoning, such as Old Bay, and 1/2 teaspoon hot-pepper sauce in a saucepan. Bring to a boil and add a pound of shrimp. Simmer until the shrimp are pink and cooked through, 2 to 4 minutes. Drain the shrimp and refrigerate for at least 2 hours or up to 2 days. Serve cold with cocktail sauce.

To make Brussels sprouts that everyone will love, cut the sprouts in half and cook, cut side down, in a skillet with a little olive oil until the bottoms brown, about 10 minutes. Add 2 teaspoons of best-quality balsamic vinegar, shaking the pan to distribute it evenly. Cover and simmer on medium-low until the sprouts are tender, 10 minutes. Finish with 1 to 2 tablespoons unsalted butter and season with salt and freshly ground black pepper.

❉Wine

To make an easy peach dessert, slice 2 perfectly ripe, large peaches into thin wedges. Pour 3/4 cup Chianti wine over the top and chill for 1 hour. Serve with freshly whipped cream.

To create a quick pan sauce after browning meat, remove the browned meat and add 2 tablespoons chopped shallots. Cook for 1 minute, then pour in 1 cup red wine or port, scraping the pan bottom to break up the brown bits. Boil over high heat until the liquid is reduced in volume by half. Stir in 2 tablespoons unsalted butter and 2 teaspoons chopped fresh herbs. Season with salt and freshly ground black pepper, to taste. Pour over the meat.

To give cold fruit soups a sophisticated edge, stir in a few tablespoons of white wine such as chardonnay or Chablis.

❋Worcestershire Sauce

To make better-tasting clam chowder, stir in a little Worcestershire sauce.

To give chilis and stews that *je ne sais quois*, stir in a few dashes of Worcestershire sauce. Worcestershire's blend of tart tamarind, sweet orange zest, and salty anchovies adds unmatched complexity to any meat-based stew.

For easy barbecue sauce, mix together 1/2 cup ketchup, 1 tablespoon Worcestershire sauce, 1 tablespoon apple-cider vinegar, and 1 teaspoon hot-pepper sauce. Use as a sauce for grilled chicken, ribs, or fish, or for roasts or chops.

To make a sweet tomato vinaigrette dressing, whisk together:

3 tablespoons tomato puree
1 teaspoon Worcestershire sauce
1 tablespoon honey
1 tablespoon apple-cider vinegar

1/3 cup vegetable oil
1/2 teaspoon hot-pepper sauce
1/2 teaspoon salt
1/4 teaspoon freshly ground black pepper

For a quick, creamy clam dip, soften 1 package (8 ounces) cream cheese to room temperature in a medium bowl. Stir in 1/4 cup cream or half-and-half until smooth. Stir in 1 tablespoon fresh lemon juice, 1 teaspoon Worcestershire sauce, 1 teaspoon prepared horseradish, 1 drained can (6 1/2 ounces) minced clams, 1/2 teaspoon salt, and a pinch of freshly ground black pepper. Store in the refrigerator for up to 2 days. Bring to room temperature before serving.

To enhance the flavor of gravy, stir in 2 teaspoons Worcestershire sauce per cup of gravy.

To perk up the sauce for macaroni and cheese, stir in a little Worcestershire sauce. A few dashes of the sauce does wonders for cheese soups, too.

❋Yogurt

For an instantly amazing dessert sauce, mix plain yogurt, brown sugar, and Grand Marnier, to taste. Use the sauce on flourless chocolate cake, for drizzling on dessert plates (it's a lovely color), or for a dipping sauce for fresh strawberries.

For a healthy alternative to mayonnaise, use yogurt. Or mix together 1 part mayonnaise and 1 part yogurt. This combination is excellent for egg salad and chicken salad.

For a creamy herb sauce for vegetables, sauté 2 table-spoons chopped leeks or green onions and 1/4 teaspoon minced garlic in 1 table-spoon olive oil until the leek or onion is softened. Add 3 tablespoons chopped fresh herbs and 1/2 cup broth. Cook over medium-high heat until the liquid is reduced to 1/4 cup, 8 to 10 minutes. Remove from the heat and stir in 1/2 cup plain yogurt. Serve over cauliflower, broccoli, Brussels sprouts, green beans, or other vegetables.

For a simple dip to serve with fruit kebabs, stir together 1/2 cup strawberry yogurt, 1/4 cup sour cream, and 2 tablespoons strawberry all-fruit spread. Alternately thread 2 peeled and thickly sliced kiwifruit, 8 pineapple chunks, and 8 straw-berries onto four skewers (6-inch). Serve the kebabs with the sauce for dipping.

To create softer low-fat muffins, replace half of the liquid in the batter with yogurt. The acidity of yogurt helps to enhance tenderness in the absence of fat.

To make a creamy, lemony filling for cake, drain 1 cup lemon-flavored yogurt in a cheesecloth-lined colander set over a small bowl in the refrigerator for 6 hours or overnight. Discard the liquid in the bowl and mix the yogurt "cheese" with 3 tablespoons softened cream cheese and 1/4 teaspoon grated lemon zest. Makes enough to fill a 2-layer cake.

To make a fudgy frosting for cupcakes or cakes, melt 1 tablespoon unsalted butter in a small skillet over medium heat. Continue cooking until the butter is deep amber. Pour into a medium bowl and chill until set. Return to room temperature then blend in 3 tablespoons unsweetened cocoa powder, 3 table-spoons chocolate-flavored yogurt, 2 cups confectioners' sugar, and 1 teaspoon vanilla extract. Spread over your favorite cake or cupcakes.

To make tender curried chicken, use yogurt in the marinade, which has just the right acidity to tenderize chicken meat. For example, combine in a food processor or blender:

3/4 cup plain yogurt	1 large garlic clove, sliced
1 very small onion, chopped	1 tablespoon curry powder
2 tablespoons lemon juice	1/4 teaspoon cayenne pepper

Process until smooth. Scrape into a zip-close bag and add 4 to 6 boneless, skinless chicken breast halves. Marinate in the refrigerator for 1 to 2 hours before cooking. Discard the marinade.

Index

About the Recipe Editor

David Joachim is the author of many popular cookbooks, including *The Food Substitutions Bible* (winner of the cookbook industry's top award in the food reference category); *A Man, A Can, A Plan* (more than 500,000 copies in print); and *A Man, A Can, A Grill* (a national best-seller). In addition, Joachim has collaborated on and coauthored several highly successful healthy cookbooks, such as *Lose Weight the Smart Low-Carb Way* with Bettina Newman, R.D., and *Eat Up, Slim Down* with Jane Kirby, R.D. As a cookbook editor, he has overseen such titles as the award-winning *Steven Raichlen's Healthy Latin Cooking* and *The Healthy Cook*, which has sold more than 250,000 copies.

Joachim's writing, recipes, and tips also have appeared in numerous national magazines such as *Cook's Illustrated, Cooking Light, Cooking Pleasures, Relish, Prevention, Fitness, Self, Men's Health,* and *Bicycling.* As an author and spokesperson, Joachim has made numerous national media appearances, including on ABC, Fox, the Food Network, Discovery Channel, and National Public Radio, among others. A resident of Pennsylvania, Joachim holds a master's degree in English language and literature from Binghamton University, where he taught writing classes for three years.